Major League Baseball in
Gilded Age Connecticut

Major League Baseball in Gilded Age Connecticut

The Rise and Fall of the Middletown, New Haven and Hartford Clubs

DAVID ARCIDIACONO
Foreword by William J. Ryczek

McFarland & Company, Inc., Publishers
Jefferson, North Carolina, and London

LIBRARY OF CONGRESS CATALOGUING-IN-PUBLICATION DATA

Arcidiacono, David.
    Major league baseball in Gilded Age Connecticut : the rise and fall of the Middletown, New Haven and Hartford clubs / David Arcidiacono ; foreword by William J. Ryczek.
       p.   cm.
    Includes bibliographical references and index.

    ISBN 978-0-7864-3677-4
    softcover : 50# alkaline paper ∞

    1. Baseball — Connecticut — History —19th century.
2. Baseball teams — Connecticut — History —19th century.
I. Title.
GV863.C8A73   2010
796.357'6409746 — dc22   2009042925

British Library cataloguing data are available

©2010 David Arcidiacono. All rights reserved

No part of this book may be reproduced or transmitted in any form or by any means, electronic or mechanical, including photocopying or recording, or by any information storage and retrieval system, without permission in writing from the publisher.

On the cover: The 1875 Hartford Dark Blues photographed at Isaac White's studio on April 24 (Connecticut State Library). Players identified on page 112.

Manufactured in the United States of America

McFarland & Company, Inc., Publishers
  Box 611, Jefferson, North Carolina 28640
    www.mcfarlandpub.com

*To my children,
John, Drew, Elyse and Grant*

Always keep your eye on the ball and swing for the fences

Acknowledgments

I'd like to thank the following people for their generous assistance in making this book a reality.

The Society for American Baseball Research (SABR), for helping me to rediscover my love of baseball and awakening a desire to learn about baseball's fascinating development in the nineteenth century.

William J. Ryczek, for his review of the manuscript and his valuable editorial comments. He consistently proved Mark Twain's adage, "The difference between the right word and the almost-right word is the difference between lightning and the lightning-bug."

SABR member Priscilla Astifan, who shared her passion for Rochester baseball and her expertise on Rochester's native son, John McKelvey.

Last and most important, my wife Michelle, for her support of my interest in the often obscure topic of nineteenth-century baseball. Her fervent enthusiasm for the game of baseball and the New York Yankees amazes and delights me.

Contents

Acknowledgments vi
Foreword by William J. Ryczek 1
Introduction 3

1. Center of the Base Ball Universe	7
2. The National Pastime	9
3. The Nutmeg State	14
4. Base Ball on the Brain	22
5. The Professional Mutation	31
6. The National Association	41
7. Tricks of the Trade	46
8. We Paid — We're In	55
9. Welcome to the Big Leagues	61
10. God Bless the Eckfords	69
11. Three's a Crowd	79
12. One Long Vacation	85
13. The Charter Oak City	94
14. Definitely Not Last	100
15. Captain Bob	107
16. The Elm City	114
17. A Hard Rub	119
18. Opposite Directions	124
19. An Infernal Set of Asses	131

20.	First of Idiots	136
21.	Locked Up	143
22.	The National League	147
23.	Playing Baby	153
24.	Crooked Play?	164
25.	Bulkeley's Deal	173
26.	A New Home	179
27.	Connecticut Revival?	187

Appendix A: The Players, by Team 195
Appendix B: The Curious Case of Tommy Barlow 213
Appendix C: Game Logs: 1874–1877 220
Notes 233
Bibliography 251
Index 255

Foreword
by William J. Ryczek

No one knows more about major league baseball in Connecticut than David Arcidiacono. There is something to be said for being the acknowledged expert in any field, but in this case, I am not sure what that something is; most Connecticut residents, even those who consider themselves knowledgeable baseball fans, are unaware that the state ever had a team in the major leagues, let alone three.

Winston Churchill once described Russia as "a riddle wrapped in a mystery inside an enigma." If nineteenth-century baseball is an enigma, the National Association is the mystery and Connecticut teams are the riddle. They are a niche within two broader niches. David has performed yeoman service by increasing awareness of the Middletown Mansfields, the New Haven Elm Citys and the Hartford Dark Blues, through his writing and by championing the cause of placing historic markers on the sites of their playing fields.

How did the small state of Connecticut spawn three major league clubs in a period of four years? One explanation is the limited barriers to entry in the National Association, which was the sole major league from 1871 to 1875. Any club that remitted a ten-dollar fee could join the Association, and Nutmeggers were as capable of raising ten dollars as residents of any other state. They signed up with an optimism based upon the fact that New York and Boston were centers of baseball activity, and what better way for an opposing club to make money on the way from one of those cities to the other than to stop for a lively game of baseball in Middletown, New Haven or Hartford?

As David points out so well in the following pages, optimism and a can-do attitude were not sufficient to assure either artistic or financial success for the Mansfields or the Elm Citys, which won a total of twelve games between them (while losing 59) in their single seasons in the NA. Their tribulations, however, make for a more interesting story than might have accompanied success, as the clubs scrambled for funds, bickered over schedules, and juggled rosters of marginally talented and often troubled players.

The one success among the three Connecticut nines could be found in Hartford, the capital of the state; its Dark Blues were the only club that made a concerted effort to sign players from the New York area to strengthen their team. The Hartford club finished second or third (depending on how one ranks the teams in the standings) in 1875, and was the only Connecticut club to be accepted into the National League when it was formed in 1876.

In closing, let me return to my initial question: What is to be said for being the foremost authority on major league baseball in Connecticut? Local historians and students of nineteenth-century baseball owe David a great deal of gratitude for the deepest research performed to date on the three clubs that are the subject of this volume. He exhibits a true love for the subject matter that goes beyond the minimum diligence required to write a book. Every detail of the clubs' activity is presented and discussed, interspersed with interesting anecdotes, and commentary from astute observers such as Mark Twain.

Whether you are a Connecticut historian, an aficionado of nineteenth-century baseball, or just a fan, I think you will find this book both informative and entertaining. Cherish it well, for it is unlikely that we will ever have major league baseball in Connecticut again.

William J. Ryczek is the author of Blackguards and Red Stockings, *a history of the National Association, and* When Johnny Came Sliding Home, *the story of the five-year baseball boom that followed the end of the Civil War. His recent work,* Baseball's First Inning: A History of the National Pastime Through the Civil War, *covers the history of baseball from its beginnings through 1864.*

Introduction

Major League Baseball in Connecticut?

Sandwiched between New York and Boston, Connecticut residents appear forever obliged to root for the neighboring Yankees, Red Sox, or, in a few cases, the Mets. Recent *Hartford Courant* polls show Connecticut to be split fairly evenly between Yankee and Red Sox fans. Western counties cheer the Yankees and eastern portions root for the Red Sox. The middle of the state serves as the frontline in the battle between the rival camps. In the middle of the middle sits my hometown, East Hampton. In 1977, the *Hartford Courant* dubbed East Hampton the exact midpoint — as the crow flies — between Yankee Stadium and Fenway Park.

The same geographic position that dooms Connecticut's chance of having a major league baseball club today was actually an advantage in the nineteenth century. At that time, railroads were the most efficient mode of long-distance travel, but a train ride between New York and Boston could take eight hours or more. Major league teams traveling between the two cities were eager for a layover midway between, where a good night's rest and some gate receipts could be obtained. In the 1870s, three Connecticut cities — Middletown, New Haven and Hartford — all attempted to serve this purpose. Yes, major league baseball has *already* happened in Connecticut, and in three different cities, no less![1]

For Connecticut residents accustomed to a miserable major league sports landscape, this may seem highly improbable, as the state has lost virtually every major and quasi-major league team that ever called it home. Connecticut's current major league sports scene is dismal. The National Hockey League, women's professional basketball, arena football, and indoor soccer have all come and gone in Connecticut. In 1998, it appeared that the National Football League would come to Connecticut when it was announced that the Patriots would move from Foxboro, Massachusetts, to Hartford. Two days before the final deadline, Patriots owner Bob Kraft exercised an escape clause and Hartford was spurned yet again.

Despite these recent failures, Connecticut once was at the forefront of the national pastime. Major league baseball was played in Connecticut for just four seasons, but they were four fascinating years during which baseball strained to grow from an amateur game to a professional sport. The *Middletown Penny Press* once reported that Benjamin Douglas Junior, the overlooked baseball pioneer responsible for bringing major league baseball to the state, told stories of early Connecticut baseball that were "interesting in the extreme." It is these stories — the tales of iron-fisted captain Bob Ferguson, of Tommy Barlow's tragic demise, of Hall of Famer Jim O'Rourke and the tribulations of New Haven manager Willis Arnold — which I hope to bring alive in a manner interesting to both the casual fan and serious student of the game.

Researching Connecticut's Major League History

Through the use of primary sources, I have attempted to give the reader a sense of what it was like to play and watch professional baseball in its formative years. These primary sources include contemporary newspapers, sporting periodicals, and personal correspondence. The three Hartford daily newspapers, the *Post, Times,* and *Courant,* provided a wealth of information. The *New Haven Evening Register* provided the best coverage of baseball in New Haven. The *Middletown Constitution* and *Middletown Sentinel and Witness* were weekly newspapers which provided limited coverage of the Mansfields. The *Hartford Post,* whose Middletown correspondent was the Mansfield club's president, provided the most complete coverage of the Mansfields' development from an amateur club to a major league team. The *Chicago Tribune,* especially the Sunday edition, was filled with priceless news, notes and gossip of the day concerning all major league teams. Secondary sources were also used to place baseball developments in the larger context of American society.

Having written histories of the Hartford Dark Blues and Middletown Mansfields, it seemed natural that I would someday portray the triumphs and tribulations of the final club of Connecticut's major league trio, the New Haven Elm City Club. This book has not only allowed me to do that, but also to provide a broader view of the development of baseball in Connecticut as it moved from social clubs of the late 1850s to major league teams in the early 1870s.

When I first began investigating the Middletown Mansfields in 1992, the primary research method was utilizing microfilmed copies of century-old newspapers or sometimes even the original papers. Hundreds of hours slumped at a antiquated microfilm reader were required to pick the proverbial needles from the haystack.

Today, more and more research is done through the use of digitized, searchable, historic newspaper databases. The advent of these databases saved significant time, while simultaneously allowing me to greatly expand my research into the Hartford and Middletown teams. While I certainly enjoyed the productivity-leap these databases provided, I did occasionally become nostalgic for the odor and feel of the yellowed, crumbling newspapers which had actually been held by a nineteenth-century reader. Regardless of the method, I never failed to experience great enthusiasm while researching this book. Whether it was a turn of an old newspaper page, a spin of the microfilm reel, or a click of the mouse, I always waited in great anticipation, never knowing what golden nugget about my beloved Dark Blues, Mansfields or Elm Citys might be revealed.

"[Ball playing] showed more science and skill displayed thirty years ago than is exhibited in the game as now played."
—*Middletown Sentinel and Witness*, October 5, 1867

Chapter 1

Center of the Base Ball Universe

Cantankerous catcher Doug Allison stepped into the batter's box for Hartford, his gnarled hands gripping a large hickory bat. Forty-five feet away stood Boston Red Stockings pitcher Al Spalding, one of three Boston fielders who would eventually be elected to baseball's Hall of Fame. Spalding peered in from the confines of his own box — the pitcher's box — literally a 6-foot square marked by chalk. The jeers of the partisan crowd, who recalled Spalding's preseason assessment that Hartford lacked the brains to take the pennant, rang in his ears.

Spalding drew back his arm, then, with an underhand delivery, whipped a pitch toward the plate. Allison took a mighty cut, just missing a solid connection. Still, the ball appeared to be headed safely into center field for a base hit. The enormous crowd let out a cheer, which quickly turned into a groan as Boston's speedy second baseman, Ross Barnes, made a fine running catch, especially fine considering he wore no fielder's glove.

The date was May 18, 1875, a clear, mild Tuesday afternoon. The location was the Hartford Base Ball Grounds in Hartford, Connecticut. Yes, it was "base ball," as the name of the national pastime was spelled until the 1880s. For this day at least, the eyes of the baseball world were focused squarely on Connecticut.

The Hartford Dark Blues and Boston Red Stockings had entered the game with perfect records. Hartford had 12 wins in as many tries, while Boston was even better, with 16 wins against no losses. In the 1870s, Hartford, not New York, was Boston's biggest rival for supremacy on the diamond. Similar to the recent Yankee–Red Sox rivalry, a dislike existed between the Hartford and Boston clubs, and charges of buying the pennant were alleged against each.

A holiday atmosphere prevailed in Hartford. With their club's undefeated start, Connecticut baseball enthusiasts believed that this would be the year their team would snatch the pennant from the mighty Red Stockings, champions three years running. Nearly every business in town displayed a large photo of the team, and conversations focused on the impending battle. Many local factories closed shop early to give their employees the rare opportunity to watch a game. The enthusiasm even reached the State Capitol building in Hartford, where the baseball match was discussed as much as legislation, and the House and Senate adjourned early so as not to miss the contest.

Shortly after noon, the streets of Hartford were deserted, as those who had tickets, and many who did not, headed for the ballpark. The ticket gates were mobbed, and two hours before the game, every general-admission seat had been sold. Twelve thousand spectators, reportedly the largest crowd ever in New England, overflowed the grounds, which seated about 4,000. Those too late to find seats stood in the outfield grass, corralled behind long ropes. As the throng swelled, there was no hope that the skimpy ropes would keep the crowd back, and fans spilled onto the playing field while an overmatched police squad futilely attempted to push them back. Outside the fence, scores of rowdy boys filled the limbs of adjacent trees for a free view of the game.

After Ross Barnes retired Doug Allison, Hartford failed to score. The Dark Blues then sent Arthur Cummings, all 120 pounds of him, and his wicked curveball to the pitcher's box. It appeared that the game would remain scoreless when, with two outs and two men on, Cummings induced Boston slugger Cal McVey to tap an easy groundball to shortstop Tom Carey. The Hartford crowd cheered loudly when first baseman Ev Mills caught Carey's throw, knowing the side was retired. But before the last "hurrah" had expired, Al Spalding was jawing with the umpire, claiming that Mills had not touched first base. Convinced, or perhaps just intimidated, by the famous hurler, umpire Alphonse Martin, a former pitcher known as "Old Slow Ball" in his playing days, reversed his decision and ruled McVey safe. The huge Hartford crowd loudly let Martin know what they thought of his decision. It was never good policy to give the powerful Red Stockings extra outs, and this occasion was no exception. Spalding followed with a base hit, plating two more runs to give Boston a 3–0 lead.

Another controversial call by Martin in the third inning left Hartford trailing 5–0. The protracted dispute that followed seemed to rouse the Dark Blues. Allison led off the fourth inning with a single. Several base hits and a critical Boston error by Connecticut native Jim O'Rourke, allowed the Dark Blues to narrow the deficit to 5–3. When Ev Mills redeemed himself with a base hit, driving in two teammates and knotting the score at five, the Connecticut crowd became delirious. Men tossed their hats in the air, women waved handkerchiefs, and young boys jumped about and shouted wildly. At this moment, Connecticut was the center of the baseball universe.

Chapter 2

The National Pastime

According to the once-popular legend, the birth of baseball occurred in a Cooperstown, New York, pasture in 1839. The pervasive myth named Abner Doubleday, later a Civil War general in the Union Army, as the individual responsible for inventing baseball. The tale of an American serving his country, both militarily and by inventing the game of baseball, appealed to many. In 1939, the Doubleday story was cemented in the nation's conscience when Major League Baseball marked the game's "centennial" with the opening of the National Baseball Hall of Fame in Cooperstown.

Comprehensive research by modern-day scholars has since moved the beginnings of the modern game from pastoral upstate New York to the urban center of New York City. Historical evidence shows that it wasn't until the 1840s that rules for a game that was distinctly baseball were documented. Among the true pioneers of the game was a group of men who, since 1842, had been gathering in Manhattan to play ball games. In 1845, one player, Alexander Cartwright, suggested that the loosely run group establish itself as a formal organization whose purposes would be playing ball and furthering members' social aspirations. The group accepted Cartwright's suggestion and officially adopted their rules of play and conduct. The new "Knickerbocker Club" recruited new members and secured a permanent playing field in Hoboken, New Jersey.

The Knickerbocker Club was, first and foremost, a social club, similar in concept to today's country clubs. Its forty members were an exclusive group of mostly professional men. Besides stringent social standards, members also had to meet demanding time and financial commitments. They were expected to assemble for ball games on Monday and Thursday afternoons, pay dues, and purchase uniforms. These requirements tended to insure that membership would be limited to upper-class gentlemen. The recreational ballgames played among members served as a means to the club's true pursuit of courteous socialization with men of similar social standing. Sportsmanship and camaraderie were more important than skill or victory. After games, members would often retire to lavish banquets where the merits of the club and its constituents could be properly toasted.[1]

The game the Knickerbockers played was similar, but not identical, to other games being played at the time. The Knickerbockers didn't "invent" baseball, but they were the first to codify rules for a game that was distinctly baseball. Six rules addressed administrative issues of the club, while the remaining fourteen stipulated rules of play on the diamond. The playing rules are quite recognizable to the modern fan. The game was played on a diamond-shaped field with a defined foul territory. Three strikes constituted a strike-out, and three outs were allowed per side. A batter was out if his ball was caught on a fly. Runners were out on tag plays and force plays and were forbidden to interfere with fielders. Even such details as requiring the catcher to hold the third strike and penalties for pitchers' balks were established. To be sure, there were differences between the Knickerbockers' code and today's game, but the fact remains that the Knickerbockers defined a game whose regulations still form the core of today's baseball rule book.[2]

Initially, the Knickerbockers played their games only among themselves. Occasionally, other clubs who played the "New York game" would surface. The Knickerbockers met one such club on June 19, 1846, at Elysian Field in Hoboken, New Jersey. In their first match game against a rival club, the Knickerbockers were soundly defeated by the New York Club, 23–1. Despite the impressive victory, the winning club soon faded away.

A few years later, a more enduring rival club, the Washington Club, was formed in New York. In 1851, the Washington Club began playing match games against the Knickerbockers. The next year, the Knickerbockers and the Washington club, now called the Gothams, were joined by the Eagle and Empire clubs. Two years later, representatives of the Knickerbockers, Gothams, and Eagles agreed to adopt common rules based solely on those devised by the Knickerbockers. By this time, the number of baseball clubs in New York had doubled, as four new clubs were founded in Brooklyn: the Eckfords, Atlantics, Putnams, and Excelsiors.[3]

With each passing year, baseball's popularity grew as the game moved steadily from the realm of high society to that of the common man. Working-class men in New York City enjoyed the physical aspects of the game, and soon teams of men with similar occupations were being formed. The Mutual club was composed of fire-fighters for the Mutual Hook and Ladder Company No. 1. The Manhattans were New York policemen, and the Pocahontas club represented a dairy. As the number of clubs increased, so did inter-club play, and many of New York's vacant lots were quickly being converted to ball fields. In 1856, *Porter's Spirit of the Times* observed that every available grassy lot within ten miles of the city was being used as a ball field. Brooklyn, already known as the "city of churches," was quickly becoming the "city of baseball clubs," inspiring the blessing, "God speed the churches and ball clubs of our sister city!"[4]

The increased number of clubs and games doesn't fully illustrate the strength of baseball's grip on the New York City region. Both players and spectators exhibited an intense interest bordering on obsession. Men would rise at 4:00 A.M. to practice before going to work. Even the cold winds of March and November couldn't keep enthusiastic clubs off the ball fields. Soon, complaints arose that young men were foregoing important duties "to worship at the shrine of baseball vanity — not for exercise, but for the plaudits of the crowd." In a letter to the *Brooklyn Eagle*, baseball was attacked as a "curse," which caused "strong, muscular, lazy boys, whose sole ambition is to be good ball players" to lose their jobs. It wasn't just the ballplayers who were turning their attention to baseball. Would-be spectators began using various schemes to duck out of work to watch their favorite club play.[5]

These problems became so prevalent, employers felt compelled to screen job applicants by asking if they were members of a ball team. If the answer was yes, the candidate would often lose any chance of employment. Some employers even went so far as to fire every clerk who belonged to a ballclub. The *American Chronicle* criticized such extreme measures, asserting that playing baseball was a far better habit than drinking or gambling. The paper went so far as to say that if an employee was allowed to play ball in the afternoon, he most likely would work doubly hard in the morning to ensure his work was complete. Another newspaper argued that it would cost employers less to allow clerks to play ball a few hours a week than "to drive him into the night dissipations which young men are tempted to indulge in when deprived of afternoon opportunities for relaxation."[6]

As baseball's popularity grew, ballclubs soon began to travel on "tours" to neighboring cities or even states. The Brooklyn Excelsiors made one such trip, touring upstate New York, Philadelphia, and Baltimore in 1860. Led by renowned pitcher James Creighton, one of the first hurlers to throw with speed, the Excelsiors returned home undefeated. Creighton was a legendary pitcher who, at a time when the game was strictly amateur, may have been the first to receive under-the-table payments. His career was cut tragically short however in 1862 when he suffered a severe internal injury while smashing a long hit. He was carried from the field and died a few days later at the age of 21.[7]

Aided by tours like these, baseball's popularity began to spread outward from New York City. Several clubs were organized in upstate New York. In Albany, clerks found relief from their monotonous jobs by engaging in "the healthful and pleasant game of baseball." The Buffalo Base Ball club played intra-squad games, with city alderman acting as captains. By 1857, clubs existed as far west as Cleveland, Chicago, and Detroit. Baseball games were played daily in Cleveland's Public Square despite city officials' attempts to find a law forbidding it.[8]

The eastward expansion of baseball was a bit slower, as New Englanders were reluctant to abandon their popular "Massachusetts game." This bat and ball game was played with ten to fourteen players on a side and used a smaller ball than the one used in baseball. Long stakes typically served as the four bases, and 100 runs were required to win. Proponents of the Massachusetts game thought it more exciting than baseball. It was certainly a more freewheeling game as there was no foul territory and fielders could put runners out by throwing the ball at them in a technique called "soaking" or "plugging."

It wasn't until 1857 that the newly organized Tri-Mountain Club declared their intentions to be the first Boston club to play the New York game. At first, this appeared to be a foolish move as the Tri-Mountains couldn't find any baseball-playing opponents. Finally, in 1858, the Portland Club of Maine agreed to travel to Boston to meet the Tri-Mountains in their first match game of baseball. As more games followed, New Englanders saw the merits of the New York game and came to accept it. By the close of the 1850s, baseball's popularity had spread so widely that the sport was being called "The National Game."[9]

As inter-club play increased, it soon became evident that some centralized authority was needed to lend structure to the sport. In March 1858, the presidents of the four oldest clubs called together all regularly organized ballclubs in the New York metropolitan area. Representatives of twenty-two baseball clubs met and formed themselves into an administrative organization called the National Association of Base Ball Players. The main purpose of the organization was to provide a guiding hand to the game's development as an amateur sport. It was intended to be a central authority on playing rules, club formation, player movement and conduct. To join the Association, clubs were required to have a minimum of eighteen members, none of whom could have received monetary compensation at any time, either openly or under the table. To play in match games, a man had to be a member of his club for 30 days. If a player departed one club to join another, he was required to show a clean financial slate before making the change. In addition, no player, umpire, or scorer was permitted to place bets on a game. Membership applications had to be submitted 30 days prior to the annual convention to allow ample time for an investigation of the club's character. Acceptance by two-thirds of member clubs was required for entry.[10]

Despite its name, the Association was by no means "national." Clubs from upstate New York and other sections of the country had not been invited to the initial meeting, a decision that the sporting periodical *New York Clipper* criticized, charging that a few dictators were trying to mold the group into an exclusive organization like the New York Yacht Club. The editorial urged the Association to make the game truly national by opening meetings and competition to ballplayers everywhere. In succeeding years, the Association did exactly that, a move which produced genuinely national representation.[11]

Chapter 3

The Nutmeg State

Throughout its long, rich history, the state of Connecticut has earned several nicknames. Its official designation, adopted in 1959 and still displayed on the state license plate, is "The Constitution State." In 1639, Connecticut residents ratified the first constitution written in the western tradition, creating a governmental framework in a document called *The Fundamental Orders*. Connecticut has also been dubbed "The Provisions State" for its generosity in supplying General George Washington's Continental Army with arms and "The Land of Steady Habits" for its inhabitants' consistently strict moral practices.

Connecticut's most common nickname is "The Nutmeg State," a strange label whose origin is unfamiliar even to many Connecticut residents. The brown, egg-shaped nutmeg grows on a certain evergreen tree indigenous to southeast Asia and yields two important spices, nutmeg and mace. The Dutch, who controlled the nutmeg trade for most of the seventeenth century, introduced nutmegs to Connecticut after becoming the state's first European settlers in 1614. The "Nutmeg State" designation is a compliment, albeit a back-handed one, to the ingenuity and shrewdness of the state's residents who, according to legend, would whittle "nutmegs" from wood and sell them as the genuine article to unsuspecting buyers. The term "wooden nutmeg" soon came to refer to any type of fraudulent product.[1]

Whether the story is true or not, Connecticut residents were undoubtedly blessed with great creativity. That, combined with their Yankee work ethic, quickly made the state one of the most industrialized in the nation. Several Connecticut inventors, including Eli Whitney, Charles Goodyear, and Samuel Colt, became household names in nineteenth-century America because of their life-changing innovations. Whitney, a Yale graduate, became internationally famous when he invented the cotton gin, a machine which was ten times more productive than manual labor at harvesting cotton. New Haven's Charles Goodyear gave birth to an entire industry when he developed a new compound that had the flexibility of natural rubber but didn't melt at high temperatures or become brittle in cold temperatures. "Vulcanized" rubber became the basis for the manufacture of many durable rubber products. In 1847, Hartford's Samuel Colt founded Connecticut's, and perhaps the nation's, most prominent nineteenth-century factory, the Colt's Arms Company. The Hartford factory produced several types of precision machinery and firearms, but the factory's most celebrated product was the Colt revolver, reputed at the time to be the world's most widely used modern invention.[2] The importance of the invention was attested to by a popular post–Civil War saying, "Abe Lincoln may have freed all men, but Sam Colt made them equal."

It wasn't just these three celebrated men who were creating new innovations. Many unknown "tinkerers," laboring

In 1847, Hartford's Samuel Colt founded Connecticut's, and perhaps the nation's, most prominent nineteenth century factory, the Colt's Arms Company. Upon his death in 1862, Colt's widow, Elizabeth, piloted the business to its most successful years. Elizabeth Colt leased a portion of her property to the Hartford Dark Blues, upon which the Hartford Base Ball Grounds were built (Library of Congress).

diligently in their workshops, also contributed mightily. Colt himself employed two such men. Elisha Root and William Mason earned over 100 patents for designing advanced machine tools, such as lathes, drill presses and drop hammers, which made it possible for the Colt revolver to be the first handgun produced with truly interchangeable parts. The Colt factory was crammed with a dazzling array of these machines. Renowned author, humorist and Hartford resident Mark Twain described the inner workings of the Colt factory as follows:

> On every floor is a dense wilderness of strange iron machines that stretches away into remote distances and confusing perspectives — a tangled forest of rods, bars, pulleys, wheels, and all the imaginable and unimaginable forms of mechanism. There are machines to cut all the various parts of a pistol, roughly, from the

The famous Hartford factory produced several types of precision machinery and firearms, but the factory's most celebrated product was the Colt revolver, reputed at the time to be the world's most widely used modern invention. The importance of the invention was attested to by a popular post–Civil War saying, "Abe Lincoln may have freed all men, but Sam Colt made them equal." The striking blue onion dome which founder Sam Colt had placed atop the building is visible as is the "Rampant Colt" figure above it (Library of Congress).

original steel; machines to trim them down and polish them; machines to brand and number them; machines to bore the barrels out; machines to rifle them; machines that shave them down neatly to a proper size.... It did not seem to me that in all that world of complex machinery there were two machines alike, or designed to perform the same office. It must have required more brains to invent all those things than would serve to stock fifty Senates like ours.[3]

Connecticut's innovative spirit was so pervasive it seemed everyone was patenting some new contraption. Twain himself got involved. The writer, a lover of technology who nearly went broke investing in an automatic typesetting machine called the Paige Compositor, earned three patents under his real name, Samuel Clemens. In 1871, he received his first (Patent No. 122992) for an adjustable garment strap. Perhaps due to his fame, Twain was allowed to provide less than the usual extensive documentation, declaring in his application that "the advantages of such an adjustable and detachable elastic strap are so obvious that they need no explanation." Two years later, he received his second patent (No. 140245), the only one which was commercially profitable, for a "self-pasting" scrapbook which eliminated the need for messy glue. His final patent (No. 324535) was granted in 1885 for a game which was meant to make it easier for players to remember historical dates.

Connecticut residents were so inventive that between 1790, when the federal government began issuing patents, and 1930, Connecticut led the

Mark Twain, author, humorist, baseball fan and Hartford resident, is pictured here (at center) with novelist George Alfred Townsend (left) and Twain's friend David Gray in 1871. Twain enjoyed the game of baseball and later called it "the very symbol, the outward and visible expression of the drive and push and rush and struggle of the raging, tearing, booming nineteenth century." He attended the "Grand Base Ball Match" on May 18, 1875, when the undefeated Hartford Dark Blues hosted the unbeaten Boston Red Stockings. Twain also spoke at the welcome-home banquet for the returning ballplayers that Al Spalding led on a world tour in 1888 and 1889. Hall of Fame player Adrian "Cap" Anson said of this speech, "Mark Twain may have been better than he was that night, but if so I should like some one to mention the time and place" (Library of Congress).

nation in patents per capita, with an average of about one for every 1,000 people. New Haven was the most creative Connecticut city, garnering over 3,000 patents between 1790 and 1890. Hartford was next with just over 2,000 patents during that period, followed by Bridgeport with about 1,900. The most common patent categories for Connecticut inventors were hardware, machine tools, clothing, hand tools, household goods, and firearms.[4]

In 1866, one of these Connecticut patents (No. 59313) was issued to George Hill of Deep River for his "spring bat." The device consisted of a regular baseball bat with slits cut in the upper end. When striking the ball, the slits were intended to produce a spring effect "in order that the ball may be sent a greater distance when hit." This may have been the earliest patent granted for an invention relating to the rapidly growing game of baseball.[5]

Hill's patent was just one sign of baseball's emerging popularity in Connecticut. Athletic activity in general, once frowned upon by Connecticut's Puritan culture, was now being embraced. The *Hartford Courant* reported in 1858,

> There appears to be a perfect mania at present for the physical improvement of the race. The whole world is suddenly alive to the importance of labor, of outdoor exercise, of violent amusements. Cricket clubs are numerous; match games of wicket and base ball are common; boat races are multiplying; rowing and riding and hunting and tramping generally are becoming decidedly fashionable. This is as it should be. It is all right and proper. The wise and the good will no longer frown at athletic amusements and call them "vanity."[6]

Baseball soon became the activity of choice for many, even over other bat and ball games such as cricket and its distant cousin wicket. Formally organized baseball clubs began to appear in Connecticut, first in western counties near New York, then spreading to the east and north.

New Haven had two of the earliest clubs. The Quinnipiack Base Ball Club, composed mainly of young, working-class men, was organized on May 14, 1858. Membership in the club was limited to 40 men who were required to pay annual dues of $3. Members would gather twice a week for games among themselves. During the games, the umpire was required to record the score in a book and note the names of any individuals who violated the club's by-laws.[7]

The Pine Grove Base Ball Club of the Fair Haven section of New Haven was formed in June of the following year. The club's constitution, published in a small booklet that was given to each member, stated the object of the association was "the mutual enjoyment, and physical benefit derived from the game of Base Ball."[8] Many of the newly emerging baseball clubs provided their members with these booklets, which contained the club's constitution, by-laws, and rules of baseball. Each member was expected to know and follow the team rules and conduct himself in a gentlemanly manner.

Another early ballclub was the Mazeppa Club of Stamford, which was organized in October 1858. A month after their organization, members met on Thanksgiving Day for a game of baseball, with the married men taking on the single members. The bachelors defeated the wedded by the score of 84–81.[9]

The Independent Club of Hartford was one of the first baseball clubs in the central portion of the state, initially organized at the City Hotel on May 18, 1860. Members of the club typically gathered two or three times a week to play ball among themselves. At the end of the summer, they played an interclub match with another Hartford team, the Mechanics Club, composed, naturally, of mechanics. The two teams met in Hartford's Bushnell Park, but the game ended abruptly when the Independents, who were losing 39–9, walked off the field, accusing the Mechanics of playing unfairly. Besides the Independent and Mechanics clubs, Hartford had at least two other baseball organizations, the Alligator Base Ball Club and the Rough and Ready Club of the High School. The latter two teams met for a game at Bushnell Park in 1860.[10]

Over the next few summers, the Independent Club become popular with Hartford residents, who would turn out by the hundreds to watch the club practice at Bushnell Park. The *Hartford Courant* encouraged the Independents, saying, "We hope they will follow the example of some of our sister cities and arrange for matches during the summer."[11]

In the summer of 1862, the Independent Club, under the auspices of 25-year-old Gershom Hubbell, was re-organized as the Charter Oak Base Ball Club. Hubbell, a Bridgeport native who had moved to Hartford in 1860, was a telegrapher at the American Telegraph office on Main Street. He loved all manner of sports and was well-known for being a champion billiard player. The objective of the new club was "to establish on a scientific basis the health-giving and scientific game of ball, and promote good fellowship among its members."[12] The name of the club honored one of Hartford's most enduring symbols. The legend of the famous charter oak tree began in 1662 when King Charles II granted the Connecticut colony the unique right "to have and to hold [the territory] for ever." Obtaining such a charter was an extraordinary diplomatic coup. Twenty-five years later, King James II thought better of the idea and sent an armed delegation to retrieve the document. During the ensuing debate, the charter lay on the table between the King's envoys and the colonists. Suddenly the room went dark. When light was restored, the charter was gone, supposedly hidden by one of the colonial leaders inside a huge oak tree where it remained until the King's men departed.

As the Charter Oak Club quickly learned, the middle of the Civil War was not the best time to form a ballclub. The Charter Oaks had trouble filling

The Charter Oak Base Ball Club of Hartford, circa 1866, surrounding the legendary Charter Oak tree. Organized in the summer of 1862, under the auspices of 25-year-old Gershom Hubbell, the Charter Oak Club became the premier baseball team in Connecticut and competed well against many of the best clubs in the country. Hubbell was a Bridgeport native who had moved from Bridgeport to Hartford in 1860. Starting center top and going clockwise — Gershom Hubbel, Henry Bunce, Frederick Bunce, possibly William Tate, possibly Enos Lane, unknown, possibly V. D. Perry, Ed Jewel, and Josiah (Si) Blackwell (from a private collection).

their ranks as their primary members — young, healthy men — had "answered the call of their country promptly." In 1863, the club issued a plea for new members, since so many of their ranks had left to "fight their country's battles." With America's attention drawn to more pressing concerns, the growth of baseball stalled across the country. The number of clubs in the National Association dropped significantly from pre-war levels, and although the New Haven Quinnipiaks had become the first Connecticut club in the Association in 1860, no Connecticut clubs were members during the Civil War years.[13]

After four brutal years of conflict between the north and the south, the spring of 1865 brought with it the surrender of Robert E. Lee's Army of Northern Virginia and the effective conclusion of the war. The joy of peace was short-lived, however, as five days later, on April 14, John Wilkes Booth fatally shot Abraham Lincoln. Once the grief of this tragedy subsided, America was ready for more enjoyable pursuits, and baseball was poised to become the country's foremost pastime.

Chapter 4

Base Ball on the Brain

With the restoration of peace in 1865, the nation's interest in baseball exploded. Record attendance and a tenfold increase in clubs made the 1866 season the most successful ever. It was claimed that for one game between the Brooklyn Atlantics and Philadelphia Athletics, 20,000 people rushed out to see the game, using any available vantage point including windows, housetops, and trees. Unfortunately, the crowd also surged onto the field, forcing the game to be postponed.[1]

Eighteen sixty-seven marked the first tour of an eastern club to the central and western portions of the country. The Washington Nationals, a team consisting mostly of government employees, boarded a train in Washington, D.C., on July 11 and arrived in Columbus, Ohio, two days later. There they beat the Capitol Club, 90–10. After destroying seven opponents in four states, the Nationals arrived in Chicago. Expecting similar results, the Nationals met the Forest City Club of Rockford, Illinois. The Rockford club, led by a 16-year-old pitcher named Al Spalding, shocked the Nationals, handing them their only loss of the trip by a score of 29–23. The victory touched off a week-long celebration in Rockford. The Nationals' well-publicized tour proved to be a huge success and helped to further bolster baseball's popularity.[2]

In 1868, an estimated 200,000 people watched the leading games, with matches in the largest cities drawing up to 10,000 spectators. Charles Peverelly explained the growing phenomenon in his 1866 *Book of American Pastimes*, "The game of Base Ball has now become beyond question the leading feature of the out-door sports of the United States, and to account for its present truly proud position, there are many and sufficient reasons. It is a game which is peculiarly suited to the American temperament and disposition.... From the moment the first striker takes his position, and poises his bat, it has an excitement and *vim* about it, until the last hand is put out in the ninth innings.... In short, the pastime suits the people and the people suit the pastime."[3]

During this period, all classes of Connecticut residents were drawn to the game, both as players and spectators. "Base ball is fast becoming popular both with the old and young. Staid old gentlemen are induced to join in match games ... while Young America does scarcely nothing but play ball and talk ball from sunrise to sunset," observed the *Courant* in 1867. It was true. Connecticut residents were playing baseball and forming clubs at a rapid rate. Factory workers, men's clubs, neighborhoods, and virtually any common association of men or boys formed ballclubs. There were games between the gun factories, railroad shops, boot blacks, and printers. In Hartford, the State Street clerks challenged the Asylum Street clerks, while the junior and senior classes of the high school also met. It seemed that everyone in Connecticut had baseball on the brain.[4]

Even those less privileged at the time, such as African Americans and females, were drawn to the national game. In 1866, African Americans in New London formed a club, but only after securing a 25-cent loan to buy a bat and ball. The next year, a "colored nine" and "white nine" met in Bushnell Park in what the *Hartford Courant* believed was probably the first interracial game in the state. The African American club was leading by several runs when the teams were chased off the grounds by other players. "Superior intelligence in the 'national game' is an immense thing," noted the *Courant*.[5]

By 1868, Hartford had at least two organized African American clubs, the Oceanus Club and the Young Pacifics. Middletown's Hero Club was so well organized that it played match games at Douglas Park with other African American clubs in front of *paying* crowds. One such game was played at the end of July against the Hartford Oceanus Club, with the winner earning a silver pitcher. The Oceanus Club had been reluctant to travel to Middletown, but agreed once the Heroes offered to pay a portion of the transportation costs. A 25-cent admission fee was charged. The Oceanus Club took home the game ball and the silver pitcher.[6]

Some bold Connecticut females were also drawn to the "manly" game of baseball. In 1867, the female students at Miss Porter's School for Girls in Farmington approached head mistress Sarah Porter about forming a baseball club. Eager to encourage physical activity, Miss Porter agreed — with one stipulation. Aware that many would find the idea of girls engaging in such physical activity offensive, Miss Porter required the students to play where they could not be seen by people passing by. The girls agreed, and the Tunxis baseball club, named in honor of a local Indian tribe that once inhabited the area, was formed. Former student Kate Stevens remembered that the club "played, or tried to play, a few games," but after receiving a challenge from the boys at Trinity College, the girls' parents sent "rather peremptory letters" that put a stop to the ballplaying.[7]

Just as New York had witnessed a decade earlier, Connecticut cities found vacant lots rapidly converted to makeshift ball fields. In New Haven, several lots throughout the city were used for baseball. There was the small "Elm Street lot" near the New Haven Green and the larger "Hospital lot" just south of New Haven Hospital. Local player Clarence Deming, later captain and center fielder for the Yale University nine, class of 1872, recalled, "The Hospital lot itself, fairly level, hard-soiled, zigzagged by footpaths, larger in area than New Haven Green, was a vast unbroken square expanse owning its half-dozen rough diamonds, where almost as many matches might be in progress at once."[8]

New Haven boys also used parcels of land on Congress and Ashmun Streets for their games, the latter being big enough for two games at once, but as Deming remembered, it "was hardly an ideal ball field by the modern standard; its surface was wavy and humpy, disconcerting to fielders; its backstop was a broken board fence shutting off some low tenements among which high fouls dropped persistently and many a ball got lost, strayed or stolen; and to the right, across Ashmun Street, was the [Grove Street] cemetery into which other foul balls dropped, bounding erratically among the tombs and entailing hard and cooperative climbs of the high stone wall."[9]

Alert Connecticut businesses took notice of the game's immense popularity and began to stock baseball equipment. In the spring of 1866, Hartford's Geer and Pond Store announced, "We have just received a fresh lot of REGULATION BASE BALLS and BATS from the best manufacturers." The next year, Arnold's store in Middletown advertised that they were carrying a large supply of bats featuring "kim, basswood, rosewood, maple, and English willow bats." In 1866, some enterprising Hartford residents even started a small newspaper devoted to the national game. *The Bat and Ball* was issued twice a month at five cents a copy or by subscription, eight copies for 30 cents.[10]

Eager to satisfy baseball-hungry fans, regular Connecticut newspapers began extensive reporting on local ballclubs, often in excruciating detail. Even pick-up games played by "muffins," as novice players were labeled, were covered. One Middletown newspaper provided the following humorous first-person account of a muffin catching a simple pop-up: "A ball was hit, it rose in the air and unfortunately near us — a terrible camanche [sic] yell rose too — we held out our hands, the ball struck — and lodged between our fingers — the yelling increased, we became confused, whirled around like a horse with the blind staggers, and before becoming unconscious made a frantic effort to get rid of the ball and hurled it at the first person at hand...."[11]

Not everyone was pleased with the increasing popularity of the sport. Middletown residents living near the West Green on Washington Street filed a petition with the city against ball playing "owing to the danger to life, destruction to property, and the profanity and vulgarity used by certain persons." The city sided with the residents and ordered the sheriff to keep the park clear of ball players.[12]

The ballplaying of young boys also raised the ire of many Hartford residents. The fact that "two lads can hardly meet on any street without going at it — tossing a ball, and often in close proximity to the heads of people passing," led Hartford's chief of police to issue the following warning:

> The playing of ball in public streets is by ordinance classed as a nuisance, and it is found to be so by many citizens, who have made complaint to me. I therefore issue this warning to the boys of the city, who are in the habit of playing the game in streets, and tossing balls on sidewalks, that a violation of the ordinance in the future will subject the offenders to arrest and punishment. Grounds are allotted on the Park for the game, and there are many vacant lots which may be resorted to, without infringing upon thoroughfares.[13]

The baseball mania also led some to break Connecticut's "blue laws," which prohibited many Sunday activities, including ball playing. The *Hartford Courant* reported one story in amusing fashion, saying that two New Haven teams had just begun playing on the Sabbath, when police arrived. "Fifteen of the Sabbath-breakers made 'home-runs,' while the other three unlucky players were 'scored' for the police and lodged in the lock-up."[14]

In the fall of 1866, the *Bat and Ball* reported there were astounding 232 baseball clubs in Connecticut. New Haven and Hartford led the way with 42 and 41 clubs, respectively. Norwich boasted 15, Bridgeport 14, Waterbury 13, and New Britain 9.[15]

Although not among the cities with the most clubs, Middletown saw several baseball nines surface after the war, the first being the Agallian Club of Wesleyan University. Founded in the autumn of 1864 by Stephen Olin (class of 1866), the club took its name from Agalles, the supposed inventor of the game of ball in Greece.[4] Olin, who would later become president of Wesleyan, was an avid devotee of the game. In a letter home to his mother, he wrote, "You can't imagine the excitement and pleasure of a hard-fought game of ball."[16]

The Agallians met Yale in the first intercollegiate game in the state on September 30, 1865. Several Yale students had organized an informal club in 1864, but the following year the University established a formal team selected from the entire student population. In this historic meeting, Yale defeated the Agallians, 39–13. In 1923, nearly 60 years after starting the Agallian club, Stephen Olin's efforts were recognized when Wesleyan awarded him a varsity letter, something which was not a part of college athletic systems in 1865. The Agallians played for about six seasons before being displaced by the "University Nine," which became Wesleyan's inter-collegiate baseball team.[17]

Several Middletown businesses, such as the Russell Manufacturing Company and the State Hospital for the Insane, now called Connecticut Valley Hospital, also formed baseball clubs. Two other organizations, the Forest City and Mansfield clubs, retained the services of the town's most skilled ball-tossers.

The Forest City club, organized in June 1866, was the first team composed solely of Middletown residents. Although lasting only two years, the club managed to generate some excitement before folding. In November of its first year, they faced the second nine of the Hartford Charter Oaks and trounced the Hartford club's back-ups by the eye-popping score of 100 to 40! Even at a time when high-scoring games were prevalent, news of the triple-digit score created quite a stir in Middletown.[18]

Shortly after the Forest City club was formed, the Douglas Pump Company organized a competitor. The Douglas Company was a prosperous factory that had been producing hydraulic pumps in Middletown for 40 years. The factory was headed by wealthy industrialist Benjamin Douglas, Sr., an influential man who once held several political offices, including mayor of Middletown and lieutenant governor of Connecticut. Douglas had four sons. Sixteen-year-old, Ben, Junior, was a great lover of baseball and it was said he "would go ten miles on foot, over any obstacles, rather than miss seeing a good game." Finding the game more interesting than factory work, Ben organized the Douglas factory's ballclub.[19]

Douglas originally designated the baseball nine the "Douglas Club," but quickly changed the name to "Mansfields" in honor of General Joseph Mansfield, a Middletown native and Civil War veteran who was killed at the Battle of Antietam. Mansfield was a graduate of West Point, long-time Army engineer, highly decorated Mexican-American War veteran, and one-time inspector general of the Army.[20] Although General Mansfield certainly deserved the honor, probably the most important factor in naming the team was that he was young Ben's great-uncle.

After limited practice, the naive Mansfields boldly challenged the Lincoln Club of New Britain. Unfortunately, the Lincolns accepted. Upon arriving in New Britain, the Mansfields proceeded to exhibit a keen lack of skill as they were humiliated by the score of 50–1. Despite the magnitude of the loss, the Mansfields agreed to a return match in Middletown. With three additional weeks of practice, the Mansfields somehow managed an incredible reversal of fortunes, beating New Britain 44–31 in front of 200 spectators. A third match to decide the series was reportedly to be played in Hartford but never was.[21] The pair of games represented the extent of the Mansfields' 1866 matches.

In 1867, Middletown's enthusiasm for baseball continued to blossom.

Ben Douglas, Jr., founder of the Middletown Mansfields and Hartford Dark Blues, standing in the doorway with his father and unidentified Douglas Pump Factory employees in Middletown. Ben found baseball much more interesting than factory work, so as a 16-year-old he organized the Douglas factory's ballclub, which he later named the Mansfields, in honor of General Joseph Mansfield, a Civil War hero and his great-uncle. Ben Douglas was a true lover of the national pastime. He was once described as someone who "would go ten miles on foot, over any obstacles, rather than miss seeing a good game." As he once told Boston's Harry Wright, "You know Harry that my whole soul is in base ball." Of the six New England cities which have had major league baseball teams, Ben Douglas founded three of them (courtesy of Middlesex County Historical Society).

Even the city's more prominent citizens were starting to pay attention. One of these residents was Julius Hotchkiss, a politician who was the Democratic nominee for state representative. Early in the year, Hotchkiss provided the Forest City Club with a parcel of land next to his south-end home for their use as a ball field.[22]

This seemingly generous gesture drew heavy fire in the conservative *Hartford Evening Post*. In a letter to the editor, one Middletown resident dismissed Hotchkiss' gift as a transparent attempt to gain political favor. The writer claimed that at the end of 1866, the Forest City Club approached Hotchkiss about using some of his property for a baseball field. Hotchkiss said he would only grant the club use of his land if they paid a rental fee of $100. In addition, he made it clear that the ballclub would bear full responsibility for the expense of grading the field, making the total cost nearly $200. This price was far too steep, so the Forest City Club continued their search elsewhere.[23]

Several months later, after being nominated for state senate, Hotchkiss suddenly had a change of heart. He informed the Forest Citys that he would now grade the field himself and allow the club to use it for free. Based on the suspicious timing of his about-face, it seemed apparent to the letter writer that Hotchkiss was trying to capitalize on the popularity of baseball and win political points with his gift.[24]

Of all the Connecticut clubs in existence at that time, probably the best known was the Charter Oak Club of Hartford. Clarence Deming fondly remembered the first Hartford team: "On its list were carried names hardly second, in state fame at least, to those of the baseball *colossi* of the Atlantics and Eckfords.... Seen now through the baseball mist, the old Charter Oaks earned their renown fairly by good discipline, steady work and the germs of team play when that baseball trait was almost unknown."[25]

After the Civil War, the club's games, as well as its victories, became more numerous. The Charter Oaks, who had played only two games in 1864, played ten in 1865. Their most noteworthy match of that season took place on July 31, as part of the "College Day" celebration in Worcester, Massachusetts. Hartford's opponent on this day was the mighty Harvard nine, which defeated them 35–13. The next day, John Belden, a Hartford resident and avid baseball enthusiast, presented the Charter Oaks with a miniature bat made from the wood of the original Charter Oak. On one end was a silver plate with an engraved picture of the famous tree and the words "Emblem of the Championship of Connecticut." The bat came in a rosewood case and was accompanied by the following letter from Belden:

> As a lover of the manly game of base ball, I take great pleasure in presenting a miniature bat, made of the wood of that famous old oak so rich in historical associations, name of which you have adopted as your own. The bat, which is intended as the emblem of the championship of the State of Connecticut, you are to retain until challenged for and won according to the rules of base ball play by any club in the state. Any challenge must be responded by actual play, within *[blank]* weeks of the date of the challenge, under the penalty of the forfeiture of the bat to the challenging party.

"May the best play win," is my motto; but I trust it will be pardonable if I express the hope that the Charter Oak boys *will* make the best play.[26]

This was a meaningful gift as the fabled Charter Oak Tree, although felled by a storm in 1856, was still revered in Hartford. Countless stores and businesses were called the Charter Oak such and such, and it seemed that every home in Hartford had a chip from the old tree, or at least claimed to. The ubiquitous adoration of the late tree became tiresome to Mark Twain, who, on one early visit to Hartford, was ushered about by a friend to view all manner of articles fabricated from the cherished tree's wood. "He took me around and showed me Charter Oak enough to build a plank road from here to Great Salt Lake City. It is a shame to confess it, but I did begin to get a little weary of Charter Oak...."[27]

In 1866 and 1867, the Charter Oaks played several of the most famous baseball nines in the country. When a well-known team such as the Atlantics of Brooklyn or the Unions of Morrisania (Bronx) arrived in Hartford, the Charter Oaks greeted them at the rail station and gave the visitors a grand tour of the city. Following the game, entertainment was provided at the Allyn House or the United States Hotel. Occasionally, the hosts would even bestow an insurance policy from the Travelers Insurance Company on the visiting club, literally insuring their safe return home.[28]

As public interest in the game grew, so did National Association membership. In 1866, the first full year of peace, membership jumped from 91 to 202 clubs. Previously, Association clubs had been primarily limited to those in close proximity to New York City, but now the Association boasted clubs from 17 states and the District of Columbia. New York topped the representation with 73 clubs, Pennsylvania was next with 48, and New Jersey followed with 26. The number of clubs represented at the Association's annual convention continued to grow through the end of the decade, reaching nearly 350 in 1868.[29]

After a five-year hiatus during the Civil War, Connecticut's clubs followed suit and began to join the National Association. In 1866, five Connecticut clubs—the Charter Oaks of Hartford, the Waterbury Club, the Chester and Uncas Clubs, both from Norwich, and Yale—joined. For the 1867 season, Connecticut membership jumped to 22 clubs, representing all sections of Connecticut. The member clubs were the Charter Oak, Howard, and Alert Clubs of Hartford; the Quinnipiack, Pine Grove and Yale Clubs of New Haven; the Agallian, Forest City and Ecliptic Clubs of Middletown; the Alert and Liberty Clubs of Norwalk; the Chester and Uncas Clubs of Norwich; the Monitor and Waterbury Clubs of Waterbury; the Pequots of New London, Bridgeport Club, Hockanum Club of North Manchester, Marvin

Club of Norwichtown, Monitor Club of Westport, New Britain Club, and the Oceanic Club of Mystic.

The incredible increase in club representatives at the annual convention led the National Association to change the requirements. Individual clubs would now need to be part of a state association to be considered for membership. Representatives of the state association would then attend the convention.[30]

In March of that year, representatives of 16 Connecticut clubs met in Hartford and formed the Association of Connecticut Base Ball Players. A constitution and by-laws were adopted, and the Charter Oaks were unanimously voted the reigning state champions.[31] Connecticut's love affair with baseball was now official.

Chapter 5

The Professional Mutation

During the period of its rapid growth after the Civil War, the nature of baseball changed markedly from the earlier gentlemanly era. No longer were spectators content to watch their favorite team; they now wanted to watch their favorite team *win*. Fierce rivalries between neighboring towns became commonplace. This new emphasis on victory extended to the ballclubs as well. Originally, membership of many clubs was restricted to local, upper-class gentlemen. With the influx of new clubs from the working class and the new importance of victories, many of these clubs began bending or breaking their once-strict membership rules. Now, any skilled player, regardless of his residency or pedigree, was welcomed, the only stipulation being that he help the home team win. With players able to join any team, the ultimate free-agent system existed, and it wasn't long before clubs began offering payment to attract the most talented players. Although strictly forbidden by the Association, the practice spread quickly as clubs were fearful of being left behind. Clubs initially compensated players under the table in the form of gifts or jobs that paid several times the going wage. Many local businessmen, eager to be associated with a winning ball team, were happy to provide cushy positions for skilled athletes. It didn't matter if the player knew anything about the business for which he was employed; his real job was playing ball.

This type of bidding for players led to a problem that would plague baseball for several years — revolving. This term referred to the practice of contract-jumping by players. After agreeing to play with a club, and even accepting some payment, a player would jump to another club that made a more attractive offer. A more subtle form of revolving involved bringing in "ringers" for important games. The Association's requirement that a player be a club member for thirty days before taking the field was a direct attempt to combat this practice.

As the public's passion for the game grew, Brooklyn's William Cammeyer recognized the commercial opportunity and leapt at it. In 1862, Cammeyer invested considerable capital to prepare a ball field at the Union Grounds in Brooklyn and surround it with a fence. The fence was the critical feature. Its presence allowed Cammeyer to get a return on his investment by charging a 10-cent admission fee to those who wanted to enter the grounds to view the game. When other entrepreneurs saw the simple brilliance of the fence, enclosed fields began to proliferate. When the famous Brooklyn Atlantic club began playing on the newly enclosed Union Grounds, the crowds and gate receipts swelled. Despite some complaints from patrons about having to pay to see a game, many spectators felt that an enclosed field provided an improved view of the game and more orderly crowds.[1]

During this period, the practice of gambling on baseball flourished, and spectators often attended games as much for the opportunity to bet as to cheer. The primary danger of wagering on games is that it can easily evolve into fixing games. Regrettably, this progression held true for baseball as well. No longer satisfied to *risk* their money, some bettors would arrange the outcome of games in advance by bribing players. Sometimes this practice would take a more subtle form called "hippodroming," in which opposing teams would agree to take turns losing to one another so as to appear evenly matched. The payoff would come when larger crowds would shell-out cash to see the two clubs square off in a final deciding match.[2]

Baseball's meteoric growth in popularity and the resulting influx of player payment, betting, and game-fixing overwhelmed the loosely run National Association. Its eligibility rules and regulations against betting and paying players were increasingly ignored. Even when violations were called to its attention, the Association was largely ineffective in enforcing its own regulations, only hastening baseball's march toward professionalism.

For several years, the National Association failed to take a firm stand on either side of the issue, mouthing the language of amateurism, yet allowing the trappings of professionalism to flourish. This fostered a great dispute among the baseball fraternity about the merits of the professional game. Some clubs, like the Albany Knickerbockers, stood firmly on the side of amateurism. They condemned the growing trend toward play for pay, arguing that baseball's reputation as a pure sport would be destroyed and that if professionalism went unchecked, unfriendly rivalries between clubs would result.

The old Knickerbocker Club was also against paying players. The club initially maintained its honorable code and refused to play in games for which admission was collected. It eventually softened this position and allowed itself to play in these games, but refused to take any share of the money for themselves. Even this moderate stance failed to satisfy one of the club's oldest members, James Whyte Davis, who had been with the club for 24 years. In his letter of resignation, Davis stated that by playing in games where admission was charged, the club had "desecrated its time honored principles of playing Base Ball for health and recreation merely."[3]

Not all agreed that professionalism was an abomination. Some viewed it as simply the next logical step in the development of the game. The *New England Base Ballist* favored recognizing professionals, observing that many skilled ballplayers were so attached to the game that they were unfit for everyday occupations. If professionalism was legal, ballplayers wishing to pursue the sport for payment could do so openly without fear of reprisal. It was also reasoned that open professionalism would improve the caliber of play as the paid professional would have the time and incentive to hone his skills.[4]

New York's opening game of 1868 was viewed by many as a barometer of public support for the professional game, since the majority of players taking part were known professionals. The fact that 1,000 spectators paid 25 cents to see this game spoke volumes about the status of professional baseball. As a result, the National Association was forced to admit the obvious. At its annual meeting that year, President Sands conceded that professional baseball had been "gradually gaining strength and influence" and was not going away. The Association then concluded that ballplayers should be divided into "two distinct classes of players," amateur and professional.[5]

On the heels of the official recognition of the professional baseball player came the first openly professional, all-salaried team. Surprisingly, it was not in New York, where baseball roots ran the deepest, but in Cincinnati. The Red Stocking club of that city was founded in 1866 by a group of local attorneys, including 24-year-old Aaron Champion. Harry Wright, born in England to renowned cricket player Sam Wright, joined the baseball club shortly thereafter.

In 1869, the Red Stocking club was deeply in debt. With no viable local competition, team president Champion believed the best way to retire the debt was to organize a first-class nine and travel east to play the best clubs in the nation, with the promise of return engagements in Cincinnati. Instructed by Champion to assemble the best team in the land, Harry Wright signed ten players, many of whom originated from the east coast, to salaries ranging from $600 to $1400.[6]

Led by Harry and his younger brother George, a talented shortstop, the Red Stockings won at an astounding rate. The new juggernaut toured the country in 1869, winning 57 times with only a single tie game blemishing its record. As they overwhelmed opponents throughout the west and east, well over 100,000 spectators saw first-hand the superiority of a professional team. The following year, the Red Stockings won their first 27 games before finally succumbing 8–7 to the Brooklyn Atlantics in a thrilling eleven-inning contest. News of the stunning end to Cincinnati's unprecedented string of victories was quickly telegraphed throughout the country.

The 1869 Cincinnati Red Stockings were the first all-salaried baseball team. Led by Harry Wright and his younger brother George, the 1869 Red Stockings won 57 times with only a single tie game blemishing their record. Starting from upper left and moving counterclockwise this lithograph shows Fred Waterman, Cal McVey, George Wright, Doug Allison (who would catch for Hartford in 1875–1877), Harry Wright, Charlie Gould (who would play and manage the 1875 New Haven club), Andy Leonard, Charlie Sweasy, and Asa Brainard (Library of Congress).

5. The Professional Mutation

Connecticut clubs now faced a choice. Should they follow the path of the professionals or cling to the idyllic amateur ways? It might have seemed that the Charter Oaks would have been in the best position to move on to professionalism, but the 1867 season proved to be that club's pinnacle of success. That summer, the champion Charter Oaks met the New London Pequots in a best-of-three series. After splitting the first two games, the deciding match was played on July 4th at New Haven's Hamilton Park. With the possibility of the Connecticut championship changing hands, baseball fever swept the state. Extra trains from Hartford and New London accommodated the flood of spectators. Supporters of the Charter Oaks offered special prizes to inspire their club's best efforts — $30 to the man who made the most total bases, $20 to he who put out the most opponents, and a gold Charter Oak pin to the best overall player. After five innings, the game was tied at 18. Then the Pequots took charge, and despite Hartford's ten-run ninth inning, New London prevailed, 44–34.[7]

Over the next several years, the Charter Oaks faded into obscurity. The club was never able to adequately replace pitcher Josiah Blackwell after he graduated from Trinity in 1866 and left the Charter Oaks. The Charter Oaks suffered another devastating blow with the loss of Gersh Hubbell in 1867. Early in the season, Hubbell severely injured his knee. He re-injured it during the third game against New London, forcing him to leave the game. Hubbell never played again. Once the state championship and Hubbell were lost, the Charter Oaks' status diminished rapidly. In 1868, the club was practically non-existent. Although they still received challenges from top teams, such as the Washington Nationals and Brooklyn Atlantics, the Charter Oaks were forced to decline. In one of the few games they played that year, Hubbell was reduced to umpiring as the Charter Oaks were embarrassed by a club from Lowell, Massachusetts, 61–12.[8]

Surprisingly, Middletown led Connecticut's march toward professional baseball. Despite its strategic location on the Connecticut River, late-nineteenth-century Middletown was not a major American city. In fact, with only 11,000 residents in 1870, Middletown was only Connecticut's seventh largest city. For years, its downtown area was more rural than urban, with so many large trees crowding the business district that Middletown was dubbed the "Forest City." But as the new decade of the 1870s approached, Middletown was riding a wave of economic growth which transformed its residential Main Street into a more commercial zone.

One factor in Middletown's development was its transition from river port to minor railroad center. As trains proved more efficient at moving people and goods throughout the country, the United States' rail system had grown at a fantastic rate. In 1830, the entire nation had only 23 miles of track.

By 1860, this number had jumped to 30,000 miles, and by 1870 it had nearly doubled to 60,000 miles. In 1871 alone, 8,000 miles of track were laid across the nation. In Middletown, the Valley Railroad, which ran from the Connecticut shore northward through Middletown, was opened in 1871. More importantly, the first leg of the Air Line Railroad was opened from New Haven to Middletown in 1870. Designed to be the shortest route between New York and Boston, the Air Line was viewed as the key to Middletown's continued growth and prosperity. Funding for the Air Line remained stalled in the Connecticut legislature for over 20 years as Hartford politicians fought to ensure that all rail traffic between New York and Boston would pass through Hartford. Due largely to the efforts of Middletown businessman Owen Vincent (O.V.) Coffin, the state finally approved the funds. Coffin would later become mayor of Middletown in 1872 and governor of Connecticut in 1895.[9]

The Mansfield Base Ball club had been progressing just as Middletown was. After steady improvement in the preceding seasons, the Mansfields took three distinct steps toward professionalism in 1870. The first was obtaining an enclosed ball field in which to play their home games. This move was forced on the Mansfields after city officials, at the request of neighboring residents, banned the Mansfield and Wesleyan clubs from playing baseball in Washington Park.[6] In need of a suitable field, the two teams searched in vain well into spring. Finally, in early May, O.V. Coffin graciously offered some of his land for use as a ballground. The donated lot was located at the corner of Washington and Berlin Streets, not far from the Washington Park field.[10]

When the lot was graded and developed into a baseball field, the Mansfields invited the Hartford Charter Oaks to play in the grand opening. The barely existent Hartford club was forced to decline, so instead of a great unveiling, the Coffin field was opened quietly on May 18 with an intra-squad game among the Mansfields. Midway through the season, the Mansfields improved the grounds in hopes of luring larger crowds. Seats for 1,500 people were added and a variety of refreshments were made available to spectators. The dominant feature of the field was a thorny hedge which lined the western side of the diamond.[11]

Although locals felt the new ballyard was one of the best in the state, others disagreed. After a visit to Middletown, the Brooklyn Stars complained about the field's poor condition, saying, "Now this thriving place, lacking the spirit of emulation which incites other towns to improve their abiding places by adding a first rate ball ground to their local attractions, obliges the baseball fraternity to content themselves with a common rough field, half plowed over, the result is that any display of skillful fielding, except in the way of catching high balls, is out of the question and the local clubs are the sufferers."[12]

Despite the complaints, the Mansfields' enclosed field allowed them to charge for admission to their games. Single-game tickets could be purchased for 25 cents apiece, and season tickets were also available. Although New Yorkers had been doing it for over a decade, the idea of paying to see a ballgame was new in Middletown. The *Wesleyan Argus* wasn't keen on the idea and stated emphatically that the Wesleyan ballclub would not follow suit, saying, "We think it comes under the heading of extortion, almost, to charge twenty-five cents to see a game of Base Ball where the score runs as high as it did in the late contest with the Trinity club. Though the Mansfield may have set us the example, we are, by no means, obliged to follow it. A game is rendered much more interesting by having a large number of spectators present, and it seems a little rough to keep people away by the admittance fee, when thanks are due them for climbing the hill (from Main Street) to witness such playing as is usually done there."[13]

Now that they could charge admission, the Mansfields were able to entice better opponents to Middletown. The Mansfields offered a 50–50 split of the gate money, a generous proposal, as home teams customarily offered only one-third of the net receipts to visiting clubs.[14]

The Mansfields' second move toward professionalism was cemented at a June business meeting when the club voted to make a "professional trip" to Boston. This excursion would be the Mansfields' first outside of Connecticut and the first requiring overnight lodging. On August 1, the club boarded the train to Boston.[15] They spent nearly a week playing Boston-area clubs. Although the Mansfields went winless in five games, the road trip could still be considered a success as the club gained valuable experience both on the field and in the business of baseball. Upon returning from the Bay State, the confident Mansfields declared themselves champions of Connecticut and challenged all other state clubs, offering a silver ball worth $25 to any club that could beat them two out of three games. In addition to issuing their challenge, the Mansfields reorganized their club, naming pitcher Clytus "Cy" Bentley captain of the nine. Bentley was a hard-throwing 18-year-old whose deliveries, according to the *Middletown Press* were "swift but a *little wild*" [original italics].[15]

The third advance surfaced in the form of a telegram from Philadelphia saying the Athletic Club would be coming to Middletown in September to play the Mansfields. This was a significant development, since it would mark the first time a professional club ever played in Middletown. News of the Athletics' impending arrival spread quickly, setting Middletown abuzz with excitement. With a large crowd expected to ante-up the 25-cent admission fee, it was decided that under no circumstances would anyone be allowed into the game free. A strong police presence would be on hand to maintain order and ensure that no one snuck into the game without paying.[16]

The day before the game, the Athletics, "a fine, gentlemanly group," arrived in Middletown and checked into the McDonough House. That evening, the cocky A's offered to bet $100 to $5 that they would not only beat the Mansfields the next day, but would also hold them scoreless. There is no word on whether the Mansfields dared to accept this bold wager.[17]

The day of the game featured fine, late-summer weather, and 2000 people crowded the field for a look at the professionals. Even ladies, who often avoided baseball games because of the sometimes rough nature of the players and spectators, were well represented. The Mansfields arrived at the field smartly attired in their new uniforms, which had been "selected for beauty as well as for service." The uniform consisted of blue checked woolen shirts and caps, white corduroy pants, and the Mansfields' signature dark blue stockings. Red piping trimmed the entire outfit.[18]

The Mansfields, who admitted they didn't anticipate winning or even scoring many runs, fulfilled their expectations beautifully. Philadelphia dominated the game from the start and nearly backed up their pre-game boasting, holding Middletown scoreless over the first six innings on the way to a 32–5 victory. Philadelphia's first baseman Wes Fisler, known as "the Icicle" for his ability to remain cool in hot weather and in a tight spot, led the way, banging out seven hits and scoring seven runs.[19]

Another of the nation's premier professional clubs, the famous New York Mutuals, arrived in Middletown at the end of September. The Mutuals had been declared national champions in 1868 and would also proclaim themselves champions after the 1870 season. In addition to their obvious talent, they sported a shady reputation. The club's president was notorious political operator William (Boss) Tweed. Through the 1860s, Tweed provided jobs for many of his players at the New York City coroner's office. A total of $30,000 of city money was reportedly paid to Mutual players during Tweed's term as president. The Mutuals were also constantly suspected of associating with gamblers. Not coincidentally, they were involved in the first baseball fixing scandal in 1865.[20]

Fully aware that they were no match for the powerful Mutuals, the Mansfields invited them anyway with the expectation of immense gate receipts from Middletown residents eager to see the famous team. About 1,500 locals took advantage of this opportunity, but when they arrived at the field it was evident that the Mutuals weren't at full strength as catcher Charlie Mills and pitcher Rynie Wolters were both missing. Wolters, a native of Holland, would later gain a reputation for being absent as he disappeared several times in 1871 and 1872, forcing his team to play with only eight players.[21]

Despite the seemingly crippling disadvantage, the powerful Mutuals were intent on playing with just seven players. While their defensive capabilities may have been diminished, the Mutuals' batting certainly didn't suffer. The New Yorkers pounded Cy Bentley's deliveries throughout the contest, on their way to a 50–20 victory. In a wonderful public relations spin, it was reported that Bentley's fast pitching "seemed to bother the batters a good deal and consequently the score was kept down."[22]

With its move toward professionalism, Middletown also witnessed some of the more unpleasant sides of baseball. While arranging a game with the Aetna Club of New Britain, it became apparent to Ben Douglas, Jr., that New Britain was surprisingly confident of victory. On game day, many New Britain residents traveled to Middletown with the Aetnas, bringing with them handfuls of cash "which they shook in the faces of the people assembled" at the game. They didn't have to wait long for takers as Middletown bettors were equally sure of a Mansfield victory.[23]

At first, the visitors' boasting seemed prophetic, as the Aetnas scored six runs in the first inning. After this initial outburst, though, it was all Middletown, as the Mansfields scored at will on their way to a 48–17 victory. This result sent New Britain fans home about $2,000 poorer. During the game, a fight involving players and spectators broke out. It's unclear what precipitated the brawl, but soon punches were being thrown by Middletown's first baseman Tom Furniss and his father, who was a spectator. Events escalated to the point that clubs were raised and pistols drawn. Cooler heads finally prevailed before anyone was severely injured or worse.[24]

A few days later, the Mansfields' escalating rivalry with the clubs from

William (Boss) Tweed was a notorious political operator and also the president of the New York Mutuals. Through the 1860s, Tweed provided jobs for many of his players at the New York City coroner's office. A total of $30,000 of city money was reportedly paid to Mutual players during Tweed's term as president. Convicted of misusing hundreds of thousands of dollars of New York taxpayers' money, Tweed was sentenced to jail in 1873. He escaped in 1875, fleeing to Cuba, then Spain, where he was re-arrested. Tweed died in New York City's federal prison on April 12, 1878 (Library of Congress).

Meriden erupted into a full-scale battle. It all started when the Mansfields traveled to Meriden, where they were soundly defeated by the home club, 28–16. In the *Hartford Post*, Augustus Putnam, the Middletown correspondent to that paper, who also happened to be the Mansfields' president, excused Middletown's loss for a variety of reasons. First of all, the Mansfields were tired from playing a game earlier in the day and they were was missing two men, both of whom had to be replaced with players from the Mansfields' second nine, the Junior Mansfields.[25]

Putnam continued his laundry list of excuses, saying that besides these initial handicaps, two more Mansfields were injured during the game, as Cy Bentley split open his hand and Tom Noble sprained an ankle. Despite all this, the Mansfields still would have won, opined Putnam, had it not been for the Meriden crowd which "hooted at them, crowded about the bases, and interfered with the game in an indecent and obnoxious manner." The harassment didn't end after nine innings. As the Mansfields walked off the field, the crowd shouted more insults and began hurling rocks at them. One rock, "as big as a man's fist," found its mark on the back of Gus Smith's neck. The Mansfields, who quickly retreated without further injury, were furious that neither Meriden city officials nor the ballclub put a stop to the rowdy crowd's antics. After all, Putnam explained, the Mansfields "are not roughs or fighting men, nor have they any desire to be."[26]

At the close of the 1870 season, the Mansfields' record stood at 21 wins and 13 losses. The club officially closed its season by sending William Rackliff and Ben Douglas, Jr., to the Connecticut Baseball Association's season-ending convention in Hartford. At the meeting, the Mansfields were voted the amateur champions of Connecticut, but only after it was decided that college clubs weren't eligible for the state championship. This meant that Yale's victories over the Mansfields wouldn't prevent Middletown from being voted champs.[27]

The season of 1870 was truly a coming-of-age year for the Mansfields. They played well enough on the diamond to be recognized as the best team in the state, but their progress off the field was even more impressive. Securing an enclosed field was undoubtedly the most important move, but, as would be proven over the next two years, the extended road trip was also extremely valuable. The tour of Massachusetts spread the Mansfield name throughout that baseball-rich state, and as a result, the Mansfields would be able to upgrade their roster by luring players from that area.

Chapter 6

The National Association

Seeing the overwhelming success of the Red Stockings, other clubs organized themselves in the same fashion, and by the end of 1870 at least five teams paid regular salaries to their players. Despite the National Association's recognition of the distinct classes of ballplayers, the continuing spread of professionalism still irked the amateurs. The issue finally came to a head at the Association convention in the fall of 1870. Concerned that the rapid growth of professionalism was ruining baseball, amateur clubs demanded its abolition. The passionate debate that followed included a stand against professionalism by the Charter Oaks' Gersh Hubbell. With no resolution in sight, the amateurs, who far outnumbered the professionals, walked out in protest. This proved to be a tactical error as the professional clubs were now left with the ideal opportunity to chart their own course, an opportunity they quickly seized.[1]

On March 17, 1871, representatives of ten professional clubs gathered at Collier's Rooms, a saloon located at the corner of Broadway and 13th Street in New York City. Initial expectations for the meeting were limited. Nick Young, secretary of the Washington Olympics, had suggested the gathering to formalize a playing schedule for 1871. J.M. Thatcher, secretary of the Chicago club, felt that a code of rules and criteria for selecting umpires should also be discussed. That was it. Influential sportswriter Henry Chadwick, a prolific journalist whose baseball writing appeared in a wide variety of newspapers, instructional manuals, guidebooks and sporting periodicals, envisioned a more substantial outcome. Chadwick saw the meeting as a formal parting of the ways between professionals and amateurs. "If the convention fails to organize a regular [professional] association on Friday night," he declared in the *Clipper*, "their meeting will have been ... a failure."[2]

When the delegates convened at 7:30 P.M., James Kerns of the Philadelphia Athletics was elected chairman. Kerns began his chairmanship with the obligatory statement that the professionals had been forced to take action by the hostility of the amateurs. His point was not mere hyperbole. The professionals truly had been backed into a corner. The amateur clubs appeared intent on holding their own convention and establishing a separate organization which prohibited professionals.

The delegates at Collier's authorized J.W. Schofield of the Troy club, Alex Davidson of the New York Mutuals, and Harry Wright to draft plans for a response. After adjourning to a separate room, the trio returned with the recommendation that the clubs form the National Association of Professional Base Ball Players, or more simply, the National Association. The proposed league's name was identical to that of the old Association except for the addition of the word "Professional." The delegates accepted the recommendation and adopted the playing rules and constitution of the old Association.[3]

The formation of the new Association marked the beginning of a new era in which the professionals would conduct their own game. For better or worse, the old National Association had governed baseball for thirteen, often tumultuous, years, but lack of institutional control proved to be its fatal flaw. The time had now come to forge ahead to the new era of professional baseball.

A scant six weeks after the initial meeting at Collier's, the new National Association began its inaugural season with nine teams competing for the professional championship. The Athletics of Philadelphia, Olympics of Washington, Mutuals of New York, Haymakers of Troy, Red Stockings of Boston, Forest City Club of Rockford, Illinois, Forest City Club of Cleveland, White Stockings of Chicago, and the Kekionga Club of Fort Wayne, Indiana, all were in the race.

Baseball in the first professional league was different from today's major leagues. A good example is the battle between the pitcher and batter. The pitcher did not pitch from a mound 60 feet 6 inches away from home plate as he does today. Instead he stood in a six-foot square box whose closest side was 45 feet from home. The pitcher delivered the ball from a level surface, as the development of the pitcher's mound was still many years in the future.

Hurlers were obliged to use an underhand delivery to pitch, not throw, the ball. The distinction between the two being that a pitch was dispensed with a straight arm, swinging perpendicularly to the side of the body, while a throw consisted of the same swinging motion, but with the addition of a wrist snap, like that used in fast-pitch softball. The required underhand motion was meant to resemble pitching horseshoes. Most hurlers ignored the prohibition on bending the elbow or snapping the wrist in order to generate more speed or an occasional curve ball. Unrestricted overhand deliveries were not legalized until 1884.[4]

With the curveball not yet in common use, successful pitchers relied on keeping the batter off balance by changing speeds. The pitcher's ability to use sheer speed was limited by the capacity of their catchers, who wore limited protection, to handle the pitches. In the 1870s, the catcher's gear consisted of a rubber mouthpiece to protect the teeth and possibly a pair of primitive gloves to help cushion the impact of the pitch a bit. These thin, fingerless gloves in no way resembled today's thickly padded catcher's mitts. The face mask was not introduced until 1877, and the chest protector and shin guards even later. With no runners on base, the catcher stood far behind the plate and caught the pitch on a bounce. With runners on base, the catcher moved closer to the plate in order to prevent a stolen base. In this position, wild pitches and foul tips exacted a heavy toll on the catcher's body.

Control and pitch location were essential to a successful pitcher. Batters had the right to call for a high or low pitch when they stepped to the plate. A high pitch had to be delivered between the waist and the shoulders, a low pitch below the waist and above the shin. Foul balls were not counted as strikes, and a batter hit by a ball was not awarded first base.

Stamina was also an important quality as teams typically employed just two pitchers. The primary pitcher started most games and was expected to pitch the entire nine innings. The "change" only made spot starts and perhaps relieved in a few games. As a result, pitchers would often accumulate 500 to 600 innings pitched in a season. Even accounting for the reduced stress of the underhand delivery, this was a heavy load.

The dominant feature of the new league's brand of baseball was offense. A typical game would feature a total of about 20 runs. Thirty runs or more were not unheard of though, and in a game between the Philadelphia Athletics and Troy Haymakers on June 28, 1871, a total of 82 runs were scored. Philadelphia won 49–33 as both teams scored in every inning. The restricted pitching wasn't the only reason for the heavy offense. Lack of fielding gloves, which didn't become prevalent until the 1880s, also contributed heavily. Instead of settling into the pocket of a nicely padded glove, line drives and sharply hit grounders would often smash the would-be fielder's fingers and bounce away. The fair-foul rule was also in effect, which meant a ball that touched fair territory before rolling into foul ground was a fair ball, giving the batter a much wider area in which to hit. By today's rules, the ball must *pass* third or first base in fair territory in order to be ruled fair. One of the few concessions to the defense was that foul balls caught on one bounce were outs. Despite all the scoring, games were played quickly, most being completed in two hours or less.

Professional players were typically from the middle class. The majority hailed from cities, with many born or raised in New York City. All, except

Cuban-born Steve Bellan of the Troy Haymakers, were white. The players were young, averaging about 24 years of age, and small by today's standards. Adrian Anson, at 6 feet 3 inches and 200 pounds, was gigantic for the times. Even players considered power hitters, like Cal McVey and Lipman Pike, weighed no more than 170 pounds. Some of the top stars in the league, like shortstops Davy Force (5'4", 130 pounds) and Dickey Pearce (5'4", 161 pounds) and pitcher Arthur Cummings (120 pounds), were downright tiny.[5]

A typical contract for a National Association player ran for six months and stipulated expected conduct and the salary to be paid in return. A portion of the first professional contract for Adrian "Cap" Anson, who went on to a prolific 27-year career in which he would become the first player to collect 3,000 hits, is shown below. His contract paid him a total of $400 for the season, in six monthly installments, for which he was expected to abide by the following conditions (rendered in original form):

> To use his best efforts to advance the interests of said Club, by cheerfull, prompt and respectfull obedience of the Directions and requirements of the Directors thereof, or of any person by said Directors placed in authority over him, as well as the by laws of said Club;
>
> To abstain from the use of Alcoholic Liquors: unless medically prescribed, and to conduct himself, both off and on the Ball Ground, in all things like a gentleman;
>
> To report promptly for duty at the grounds of the Club for all games, and for practice at the hours designated there for by the officers of the Club, and upon the grounds, to abstain from profane language, scuffling and light conduct, and to discourage the same in others.
>
> To practise at least two and a half hours per day. On each and every practice day of the Club, and at all times both in games and at practice, to use his best endeavours to perfect himself in play. Always bearing in mind that the Object in view in every game is to win.
>
> And in further consideration of the premises said party of the second part promises and agrees that he will not make, or procure to be made for him, or in any [way] be concerned or interested in, any bet or wager upon the result of any game, or upon the playing of any member of the club, or upon anything connected with any game, in which said Forest City Club, may engage during the time of his engagement hereunder.[6]

The first professional pennant race was a close one. Early in the year, the New York Mutuals and Chicago White Stockings battled for first, but the Mutuals faded in July. Boston and Philadelphia climbed into the race with Chicago and fought for the lead until the end of the season. In a signal of things to come for the National Association, controversy arose when the time came to determine the league champion. Philadelphia challenged the results of two early season losses to the Rockford Forest City club on the basis that Rockford had used Scott Hastings, who Philadelphia believed was ineligible to play with Rockford. The league agreed and awarded Philadelphia two forfeit victories. Those two wins gave Philadelphia the championship pennant. Many blamed Philadelphia's undue influence in the league office for this favorable ruling.[7]

Another interesting twist to the 1871 season occurred in October when the Great Chicago Fire destroyed a large portion of that city. Nearly 300 people died and 90,000 were left homeless. Thousands of buildings were destroyed, including the White Stockings' Lake Front Park and all but two of the White Stockings players' homes. Despite these hardships, the team decided to finish the season, accepting free rail passes and playing with borrowed uniforms of assorted colors. The ballground had been insured for only $4,000, or just 10 percent of the total value, so there was little hope of rebuilding. When the season ended, the club had only $2,000 in its treasury, yet owed $4,800 in back salaries.[8]

With the completion of a generally successful first season, the professionals had made their break, and there was no turning back. Open professionalism led to improved play, as players quickly learned to specialize in one or two positions. Strategic innovations were quickly developed, as each team searched for a competitive advantage. Many strategies that we take for granted today emerged at this time. These techniques included the first baseman playing off the bag when no runner occupied the base and holding the runner on when the base was occupied. Outfielders learned to shift their locations to best position themselves for certain hitters. The practice of fielders backing-up one another was also instituted.[9] In very little time, the professional game, which featured most of the best ballplayers in the country, outshone the amateur game and commanded most fans' interest.

Chapter 7

Tricks of the Trade

Despite the establishment of the new professional league, the Mansfields continued as amateurs for 1871. However, when the Mansfields' roster was announced, it was immediately evident that the previous year's "professional tour" of Massachusetts had paid great dividends, as the Mansfields had signed two players from opponents they had met on that trip. William Kelly, formerly of the Springfield Mutuals, joined the Mansfields and was named captain of the nine. Frank Allen, a "fine catcher and one of best batters in New England," signed on after playing for the Fairmount Club of Marlboro.[1]

In addition to their two Bay State acquisitions, the Mansfields added Benson Marks and Frank McCarton; both were culled from the roster of the Warren Club of New York City whom the Mansfields had played the previous September. McCarton played center field while Marks manned first base for Middletown. Willis Arnold, who had been with the club since its inception, was back, as was Jim Tipper, a "first class outfielder, who stands A1 as a sure fly catcher."[2] Pitcher Cy Bentley returned for his third season with the Mansfields, and shortstop George Fields, a Waterbury native, returned for his second.

With the Mansfields' steady progression toward a more professional organization, the administrative duties required to run the ballclub demanded increasing amounts of Ben Douglas' attention. In the days before pre-determined schedules and telephones, coordinating playing dates with other teams was an extremely time-consuming chore. Numerous hand-written letters or sometimes telegraph messages, exchanged over the course of weeks, were often required before reaching agreement on a playing date and monetary arrangements. This duty, plus arranging travel plans and handling the club's finances, fell to Douglas. As a result, Ben, who played only sparingly in 1870, was listed as a substitute for 1871 and never again saw meaningful action on the ball field.

The Mansfields began preseason practice on the Coffin grounds, knowing they couldn't stay there long. Coffin had decided to subdivide the ball field into building lots, forcing the Mansfields to search for a new home for a second consecutive year. Given Middletown's growing industrial workforce and the resulting surge in housing starts, Coffin couldn't resist the opportunity to cash in on this large, level tract of land in a prime location. In early April, the Middletown Common Council agreed to open Lincoln Street and Park Place through the old ballgrounds.[3]

The Mansfields' search for a new field continued for several weeks. In mid–May, it was reported that they would probably play on the Spring Street circus grounds, but in reality the issue hadn't been settled. Although they didn't know where they would be playing, the Mansfields knew they would look good as their new uniforms arrived in early May. The outfits consisted of a white shirt and knee breeches trimmed in blue, blue stockings, a white flannel hat with a blue band and blue belt.[4]

As the season rapidly approached, Dewitt Clinton Sage, owner of a Middletown brick factory, made a generous gesture, presenting the Mansfields with a portion of his property "near the shirt factory, five minutes' walk from the McDonough House, for their free use as a base ball ground for five years." This lot, located south of downtown near the Connecticut River, was an especially convenient location as the Valley Railroad ran adjacent to the field.[5]

Although thankful for the gift, the Mansfields now faced the daunting task of transforming the bare hillside previously used for grazing cows into a baseball field. The plan was to grade the land and fence the lot with a 450 by 350 foot enclosure made of eight-foot boards. This proved so time-consuming that the Mansfields decided to forego any games until the task was finished. The goal was to have the field ready for a May 31 game against Adrian Anson's Rockford Forest City Club. Unfortunately, the Mansfields weren't up to the task, and the Rockford game had to be cancelled.[6]

The field's grand opening was re-scheduled for June 9 against the Brooklyn Atlantics. The Atlantics were once a great amateur club who for many seasons during the 1850s and 1860s were considered the best club in the country. With a diligent effort, the Mansfield players completed the park a few days before the re-scheduled opener. Fans were encouraged to attend so that the Mansfields could recoup some of the money they had spent preparing the grounds. Tickets for all games were 25 cents and could be purchased at Rackliff's tobacco store, C.E. Putnam's stationery store, or from any officer or member of the Mansfields. Season tickets were also available for $3.[7]

On the day of the inaugural game, a festive atmosphere prevailed as 650 enthusiastic spectators gathered for a first-hand look at the new ballgrounds. When they arrived, they were greeted by the sight of a fine ball field with seats for 800 people. The field's elevated location afforded a fantastic view of both the city and the river to the north. Frale's Excelsior Band and the Amy Stone Dramatic Troupe were on hand to provide additional enjoyment for the fans. Unfortunately, the entertainment in the stands was superior to what the Mansfields provided on the diamond.[8]

After winning the toss, Middletown sent the Atlantics to bat first. Undoubtedly a bit nervous on this big day, the Mansfields fielded terribly in the first inning and quickly found themselves in an 8–0 hole. Brooklyn plated nine more runs in the third inning. At this point, it became obvious, at least to the Mansfields, that the umpire didn't fully understand his duties and needed to be replaced. The Atlantics agreed, and John Kenney of the Brooklyn club was chosen to take over. Over the next few innings, the Mansfields play improved, but their lack of practice due to working on the field was evident. The final score stood 30–14, Atlantics.[9]

After a week-long break, the Mansfields faced their first National Association club, the Troy Haymakers. The Haymakers were a talented team run by "Big John" Morrissey, a shamefully corrupt New York politician who was once a champion boxer. Morrissey later opened several gambling houses in New York and held a controlling interest in the race track in Saratoga. In 1869, the Haymakers had given Cincinnati its only blemish of the season, tying the mighty Red Stockings in a game that by most accounts was fixed. At Morrissey's instruction, Cincinnati pitcher Asa Brainard was reportedly paid $500 to throw the game. After allowing 13 runs in the first two innings, Brainard appeared to have earned his money. But when the Red Stockings fought back to tie the score, Morrissey began to get nervous about losing the reported $60,000 he and his cronies had laid on the Haymakers. When a dispute arose over a foul tip, Morrissey saw his chance to escape unscathed and ordered his team off the field. The Troy club also featured Cuban-born infielder Esteban "Steve" Bellan, the only Hispanic player to appear in the National Association. On this day in Middletown, Bellan and his mates far outclassed the Mansfields to the tune of 23–1.[10]

The next big game came on July 4th against the amateur Brooklyn Stars. The Stars were making their second straight Independence Day appearance in Middletown. The year before, they had whipped the Mansfields 44–9, even without the services of their best pitcher Arthur Cummings, who was on his honeymoon. Although this year's match with the Stars looked to be even more of a mismatch since Cummings would be in the pitcher's box, the game remained tight as both teams fielded exceptionally well. The Mansfields committed just four errors while Brooklyn made only one. While these error totals may seem unremarkable by today's standards, they were exceptional at a time when fielders wore no gloves and playing fields were often quite rough. Middletown could only muster three hits off of Cummings, two by Benson

Marks. The Stars meanwhile banged out nine hits on their way to a 5–3 victory. The scarcity of runs reportedly made this the lowest scoring game between two amateur teams and the third-lowest scoring game ever.[11]

Three weeks later, the Mansfields packed their bags for another "professional" road trip. Hoping for better fortune than their winless 1870 tour, the Mansfields avoided Boston and traveled to western Massachusetts and New York instead. After easily defeating the Old Elm club of Pittsfield, Massachusetts, the Mansfields played a rematch with the Haymakers in Troy. After the 23–1 debacle in Middletown, betting heavily favored Troy scoring more runs in one inning than the Mansfields would the entire game. This started to look like a sure bet when Bentley, who began the game in the box, was hit by a line drive in the fourth inning and had to be replaced. Despite losing their best pitcher, the Mansfields played better than anyone expected and proved those who bet against them wrong, resulting in over $1500 changing hands. In fact, the Mansfields played so well in the 19–11 loss to the professionals that the Troy Putnams, who were on hand for the game, decided to cancel their next day's game with Middletown. The Mansfields completed their tour with an 11–7 victory over Utica and a tough 16–15 loss to the Atlantics in Brooklyn.[12]

Upon their return home, the Mansfields had no time to rest, as the powerful Boston Red Stockings, one of the strongest National Association clubs, would be in town the next day. The Boston entry was led by former Cincinnati manager Harry Wright. Wright had moved to Boston after his famous Cincinnati Red Stockings disbanded when spoiled fans lost interest in the club after its first loss to Brooklyn and a few more setbacks later in the season. Wright brought along several Cincinnati teammates, including his talented brother George, first baseman Charlie Gould, and hard-hitting Cal McVey. Besides the Cincinnati contingent, Wright also convinced pitcher Al Spalding and second baseman Ross Barnes to leave Rockford for Boston. Both were critical acquisitions.

The diminutive Barnes was an excellent batsman who would become a two-time league batting champion. His signature stroke was the fair-foul hit, a difficult maneuver, successfully executed by only a small number of clever batsmen. As was his prerogative, Barnes would request a low pitch, which was much easier to chop down into fair ground. If performed properly, the ball would spin off into foul territory, far from the fielders' stations. Aided by the fact that foul balls were not yet counted as strikes, Barnes could pursue a successful fair-foul hit while not being assessed a strike for any failed attempts.[13]

While Barnes bolstered Boston's offense, Albert Goodwill Spalding handled the pitching. Spalding was an intelligent, calculating hurler who would become the all-time victory leader in the National Association. Spalding was born to an affluent family in Byron, Illinois, in 1850, and his father passed away when Albert was just eight years old. His mother moved the family to Rockford, where young Al joined the Forest City baseball club. He first received national acclaim in 1867 when he gave the Washington Nationals their only loss on their famous western tour. In 1870, Spalding pitched Rockford to a win over the Cincinnati Red Stockings, catching the eye of Harry Wright in the process. His decision to go to Boston may have been motivated as much by the business possibilities in that city. Spalding had such desire to succeed that he later abandoned pitching when presented with the opportunity to enter the infant sporting goods industry. In 1876, he and his brother Walter opened the Spalding Sporting Goods Store in Chicago. After the 1877 season, Al left baseball completely to run the firm. Within ten years, he was the millionaire head of a vast sporting goods company that bears his name to this day.[14]

Ben Douglas, Jr., had written to Harry Wright and invited the Red Stockings to Middletown a few weeks earlier. Wright responded by first congratulating Douglas on the Mansfields' excellent showing against the Brooklyn Stars, saying the results were very good for a "country club." This phrase was often used to describe the Mansfields because they were from a rural area, while the best clubs were generally based in larger cities. After dispensing with the pleasantries, Wright got down to business, stating that Boston would only travel to Middletown if $150 plus expenses were guaranteed.[15]

When Boston arrived at Mansfield Park, both teams entertained themselves and the crowd with some fancy "ball-tossing" prior to the game. Shortstop George Wright was especially impressive at showing-off his fielding and throwing skills. The Boston players continued to show their talent when the real game began, jumping out to an 8–0 lead and cruising to a 23–9 victory. The *Hartford Post* was critical of the Mansfields, saying that even though Boston "took it easy" throughout the game, substituting liberally and using many players out of position, the Mansfields were still outplayed.[16]

Mansfield president Augustus Putnam, who obviously didn't cover the game for the paper himself, took offense at the *Post*'s coverage, saying the criticism was unwarranted. He defended the Mansfields, saying that although they weren't as good as the pro clubs, they had still fared reasonably well against them in the past. Putnam explained that the main reason the Mansfields played the professional clubs was to give Middletown residents a chance to see the best clubs in the country. In addition, Putnam quite candidly admitted that these games gave the Mansfields "some good practice, and what is more important to them, considerable gate money."[17]

After losing to the Red Stockings, the Mansfields made some significant roster changes, adding two talented newcomers to the nine. Eddie Booth, "a fine, sure thrower and catcher, and an average batsman,"[18] was added to shore up Middletown's infield. He had played with several of the best amateur clubs in Brooklyn, including, not coincidentally, the Brooklyn Unions whom the Mansfields played twice in 1870.

Timothy Murnane also joined the Mansfields, after playing with the Savannah, Georgia, club. Murnane was a Connecticut native, born in Naugatuck. He began his baseball career with the Liberty Club of Norwalk in 1869, then caught for the Stratford Osceolas in 1870. Later that year, he traveled to Savannah, where he made the local team. Murnane recalled that while traveling north with the Savannah team he was in contact with Ben Douglas, who offered him a job in a sewing machine shop in Middletown and a position on the Mansfields. In his first appearance with the Mansfields, Murnane dropped an easy fly ball which cost the Mansfields the game. That evening, the board of directors met to discuss the new player. Only after teammate Tom Furniss pleaded his case was Murnane allowed to remain with the team.[19] With their

A native of Naugatuck, Connecticut, Tim Murnane joined the Middletown Mansfields in 1871 after Ben Douglas offered him a job in a sewing machine shop in Middletown and a position on the Mansfields. After his playing career, Murnane became a well-respected sports editor for the *Boston Globe*. In 1978, Murnane was honored by the Baseball Hall of Fame as recipient of the J. G. Taylor Spink Award for excellence in baseball journalism. He is pictured here on a 1909 tobacco card when he was president of the New England League (Library of Congress).

improved nine, the Mansfields played well in two losses to National Association teams, falling to the Rockford Forest City club, 17–9, and to the Brooklyn Eckfords, 11–10.

Even while playing on the national stage, the Mansfields were still playing some very interesting local contests. Early in the year, the Stratford Osceolas had come to Middletown with their talented battery of pitcher Frank Buttery and catcher Jim O'Rourke and were soundly defeated, 40–22. The Mansfields' victory was highlighted by Ham Allen's blast over the left field fence, the first home run hit completely out of the new Mansfield Park.[20]

The rematch was played in front of a large crowd at Bridgeport's

Cameron Trotting Park. As had become the norm, the clubs couldn't start the game without an argument. This time, the fuss started when the Mansfields insisted on using their own umpire, an idea the distrustful Osceolas quickly rejected. After a long dispute, the two clubs finally agreed on an ump, and the Mansfields took up the bat.[21]

The game was tight throughout as both teams fielded well despite the rough grounds. After six innings, the Mansfields led 9–8, and the gamblers in the crowd loved their chances of victory, setting the odds in Middletown's favor at 2–1. The game quickly turned however, as Stratford out-scored Middletown 7–0 over the final two innings to take the contest, 15–9. The game was stopped after eight innings so the Mansfields could catch the five o'clock train back home.[22]

As if the bickering before the game wasn't enough, a huge controversy erupted afterward when the Osceolas refused to give any gate money to the visiting Mansfields. The Osceolas said they were keeping all proceeds because they didn't get any money from the first game in Middletown. Middletown's managers admitted that was true, but argued it was justified because the Osceolas didn't have an enclosed field for a return match. The Mansfields reasoned that since this second game was played on neutral grounds, both clubs were entitled to a portion of the receipts. After a long, loud debate, the Osceolas finally relented, agreeing to send Middletown home with the grand total of four dollars. The Mansfields were furious, since this paltry sum was not nearly enough to cover the forty dollar cost of their round-trip to Bridgeport.[23]

The rubber game of the series was played a week later at New Haven's Hamilton Park. Expecting an exciting contest, many Middletown supporters traveled to New Haven and upon arriving at the field started offering large odds in favor of their club. The Middletowners' bold display didn't scare the Stratford faithful, as they eagerly laid down large sums of money on the Osceolas.[24]

On the field, the Mansfields had built a comfortable 10–0 lead when their catcher David Lenz was injured and had to leave the game. The game quickly deteriorated, and the Mansfields shoddy defense allowed Stratford to take a 12–10 lead into the ninth inning. Thoroughly demoralized, Middletown went down weakly in their final at bat in the top of the ninth. When the last Mansfield was retired, the crowd erupted with wild cheering, and one Stratford player threw the ball into the crowd in celebration.[25]

By today's rules, of course, this game was over, since the home team led after eight and a half innings. For much of the nineteenth century, however, a game wasn't complete until the full nine innings were played, regardless of the score. This custom was a remnant from the gentlemanly roots of baseball when the game was a social event and ending it early, just because of the score, would have been considered poor manners. Middletown attempted to twist this rule to their advantage. When the game ball couldn't be found after being tossed into the crowd, the Mansfields refused to take the field for the bottom of the ninth. They claimed that the ball used to finish the game must be the same as the one used to start the game. Since the ball couldn't be found, the Mansfields reasoned that the game could not be completed, thus preventing them from losing.[26]

As can be imagined, Middletown's nonsensical logic infuriated the victorious Osceolas. This was trivial, however, to the bombshell that was about to be dropped on them. As the Mansfields prepared to depart, the Osceolas suddenly realized that they weren't going to receive any gate money. After much discussion, it was revealed that the Mansfields, intent on revenge against the Osceolas, had instructed a third party to rent the New Haven ballgrounds and then take the gate money after the game. This technicality allowed the Mansfields to argue that neither club made arrangements with the owner of the field, thus neither club had any right to the proceeds. After returning to Middletown, the Mansfields' hired gun would then, of course, present them with the cash.[27]

The Osceolas, on the other hand, argued that each visiting club should split the remaining money after the expenses (in this case, 33 percent of the "gate" and $4 for two gate-tenders) were paid. The Mansfields ever so sweetly offered to instruct the third party to send the Osceolas four dollars, the same amount the Mansfields received after the game in Bridgeport.[28]

This dubious behavior led many in neighboring Bridgeport to agree that the Mansfields' "high-handed appropriation, not to say robbery of both clubs' share of the gate money, should be sufficient to expel them from the association they have disgraced." When a rumor circulated a few days later that the Mansfields had challenged the Osceolas to a new championship series, the Osceolas responded that they wanted nothing more to do with the Mansfields, who "have shown themselves unworthy of recognition by all fair dealing clubs."[29]

Besides all the other problems surrounding their match series, Stratford protested the last two games, charging the Mansfields with using two illegal players, Murnane and Booth, neither of whom had been with the Mansfields for the required 60 days. Mansfield managers acknowledged the charge, but countered with the argument that both players lived in Middletown, were currently employed there, and had replaced members who had been discharged from the club.[30]

Then, figuring the best defense is a good offense, the Middletown managers accused the Osceolas of importing players themselves. In fact, it was claimed that only three or four of the Osceolas were from Stratford, the rest living in Bridgeport, New Haven, and even New York.[31]

The *New Haven Palladium* got the final word in the argument when it reported the receipt of an apologetic note from one Mansfield player. The letter was written under the heading "Please publish and oblige the players of the club." In it, the unnamed player tried to disassociate himself and his teammates from the Mansfields' officers, saying they were in no way responsible for the business management of the club. The *Palladium* acknowledged this, saying, "This is true, as the players themselves are, with perhaps a few exceptions, the creatures of the management, owing their 'fat' places in the Middletown shops to these men. We will say that the players themselves, although given perhaps a little too much to the 'tricks of the trade,' are in the main as gentlemanly and fair a set as the generality of professional nines. We don't wonder they are ashamed of their officers."[32]

The Mansfields completed the 1871 campaign with a mediocre record of 19 wins and 19 losses. Although rather poor compared to their 21–13 record in 1870, they had significantly upgraded their schedule, playing seven professional clubs in 1871, while only playing two the previous year. Against some of the best collections of ballplayers in the country, the Mansfields had shown some promise. Mixed in among a couple of blowouts were one run losses to the Brooklyn Atlantics and the Eckfords. The Mansfields also made respectable showings against the Troy Haymakers and the Rockford Forest City club.

Possibly as a result of their games against National Association clubs, the *Wesleyan Argus* reported at the conclusion of the season that "the Mansfields are going to swing out as a professional nine next year." The report was based on a rumor that the Mansfields were offering $3000 of stock to start out as a pro team, and two or three excellent players had already been engaged for the next year. Augustus Putnam denied that the Mansfields had taken such action, saying it was doubtful that they would want to become a professional club.[33]

Chapter 8

We Paid — We're In

Late in February 1872, Ben Douglas, Jr., called together several prominent Mansfield supporters to begin preparations for the upcoming season. The group assembled at the ballclub's Main Street office, located on the second floor above Brewer's Dry Goods. Tastefully decorated with the many souvenir balls that the club had won, this rented room served as a general meeting place for the ballplayers and site of the Mansfields' weekly business meetings.[1]

At this initial meeting, Augustus Putnam was re-elected president for 1872, and Douglas was returned to his position as the club's corresponding secretary. The newly elected officers immediately decreed that the Mansfields would operate according to the rules of temperance, meaning no liquor could be sold at the ballgrounds and each Middletown player would be required to sign a pledge swearing off liquor, "it having been found by experience that no man can play his game if in the habit of taking strong drink."[2] This may have been due to the influence of Ben Douglas's father, Ben, Sr., who was president of the local Temperance Society.

In addition to proclaiming the Mansfields a "dry" club, the officers announced that the team would remain an amateur one, temporarily laying to rest the persistent rumors of impending professionalism. The club's amateur intentions were further solidified in mid–March when Ben Douglas, Jr., and William Rackliff represented the Mansfields at the national convention of amateur baseball clubs in New York City. While there, Rackliff accepted election as an officer of the amateur association.[3]

Influential sportswriter Henry Chadwick was enthusiastic about the Mansfields' prospects for the season, praising their board of officers and predicting a strong bid for the amateur championship. Chadwick added, "They are well situated in one of the best ball towns in Connecticut, having a fine enclosed park, and guarantee professionals one-half net gate," instead of the more customary one-third.[4]

As the season approached, everything appeared to be in place for the Mansfields' continued operation as amateurs. Their preseason preparation was uneventful, until a team practice in late March. As the Mansfields worked out on the South Green, a female passenger in a carriage entering Middletown passed by the public park just as one of the scatter-armed Mansfields uncorked a wild throw. The wayward sphere flew into Main Street, striking the unsuspecting woman squarely in the chest and severely injuring her. This unfortunate incident led to another loud outcry for a less public place for playing ball.[5]

When not worrying about one of his players killing someone, Ben Douglas was busy with his annual chore of arranging playing dates for the upcoming season. He contacted Harry Wright in Boston in hopes of enticing the popular Red Stockings back to Middletown. Wright curtly advised Douglas that the Red Stockings would only return if the receipts were better than the previous year, when the gate money "did not come up to the expectations we were led to indulge in." Having been burned once, Wright didn't trust Douglas's rosy promises of large crowds and insisted that Douglas guarantee an amount that would more than cover Boston's expenses for the trip.[6]

Stung by the harsh reply, Douglas attempted to play hardball with the experienced veteran, brazenly informing Wright that if the Mansfields must guarantee a minimum take, then Boston must do likewise. Wright simply laughed at this idea, declaring that if a game between the two clubs "depends upon a mutual guarantee," then "there is not much likelihood of any being played."[7] With the most celebrated nine in the country, Wright was inundated with invitations from clubs across the country and didn't need to comply with any conditions Douglas might try to impose.

Wright concluded his message with the fateful suggestion that would eventually put Middletown on the baseball map. He advised Douglas that if the Mansfields were truly interested in playing professional clubs then they should pay the $10 entry fee and join the National Association of Professional Base Ball Players. If the Mansfields were admitted to the league, the professional clubs would have no choice but to play them.[8] Inspired by Wright's novel idea, Douglas wasted no time gathering the Mansfields together for a team meeting. Douglas laid out his proposal to join the professional ranks and concluded his presentation by asking for a vote on the matter.

Now the Mansfields were certainly a good amateur team, but joining the professional league was a huge leap. While they had occasionally acquitted themselves well against some pro teams, the sad fact was that they had failed to defeat a single one. Given this, it was hard to imagine that they could consistently compete with the best ballplayers in America.

Besides the very real concerns about their talent, Douglas was undoubtedly aware that Middletown's small population didn't guarantee the club sufficient attendance to remain solvent. With only 11,135 residents, Middletown's population paled in comparison to other National Association cities. Boston, Philadelphia, Baltimore, New York, and Brooklyn all boasted more than a quarter of a million people while Washington and Cleveland were each home to about 100,000. The smallest city in the league was Troy, which was still more than four times larger than Middletown. A typical club might expect to ring up about $8000 worth of expenses with the vast majority going to travel and salaries.[9] Finding enough paying customers to cover these costs would be extremely difficult.

Despite the rather daunting obstacles, the Mansfields boldly voted to defy the odds and send the $10 entry fee into Alex Davidson at the League Championship Committee. Once Douglas had carried out this duty, everyone sat back and held their breath.[10]

Unfortunately, the Championship Committee didn't move as quickly as the Mansfields. After receiving Middletown's entry fee, the committee sat on it, leaving the Mansfields to wonder if their daring proposition would be accepted. After a week with no news, a nervous Douglas contacted Harry Wright, asking about Middletown's chances. Wright couldn't offer much hope, saying, "In regard to your club being accepted as a contestant for the championship, it is all in the hands of the Championship Committee." Wright added that the Mansfields' chances looked bleak, since at their last meeting many committee members had voiced opposition to Middletown's entry.[11]

Henry Chadwick, who just a few weeks earlier praised the Mansfields, was beside himself when he heard of their professional intentions. Dead set against allowing Middletown into the league, Chadwick wrote, "The Mansfields state that they have sent on $10 entry fee to Mr. Davidson. Inasmuch as the Mansfields have hitherto claimed to be an amateur club, and not in any way professional, it is not thought that the Professional Championship Committee can allow them to enter, as they were not members of the Association in 1871, nor were they represented in Cleveland (at the professional convention). We state this for the information of the Connecticut club, in order that they may understand how the case stands."[12]

Three days before the start of the season, it still wasn't completely clear if the Mansfields were accepted by the National Association or not. The *New Haven Palladium* reported that Middletown wouldn't be allowed to play professionally because the league had decided it already had enough clubs. Augustus Putnam used his position at the *Hartford Post* to smugly reassure everyone that the Mansfields were indeed members of the pro league and would soon play their first game.[13] Putnam was secure in the knowledge that by tendering the $10 fee, Middletown had fulfilled the National Association's sole requirement for entry. Bound by their own rules, the Championship Committee was powerless to exclude the Mansfields. As improbable as it was, Middletown was now a major league city!

Once the immediate excitement of being allowed to play with the big boys subsided, Douglas had to face the harsh reality that his club desperately needed to upgrade its roster. By the end of the 1871 season, the Mansfields had built a reasonably talented nucleus. The outfield of Frank McCarton, Willis Arnold, and Jim Tipper was solid, while the infield sported Ham Allen, George Fields, and Tim Murnane, with Cy Bentley in the box. This was fine when Middletown was playing local amateur clubs, but much more talent was required to have any hope of beating the pros.

In these formative years of professional baseball, ballclubs had no standard process for signing players. Without today's rigorous scouting system, clubs often relied on the ballplayer to initiate contact. A young man who desired a position on a ballclub simply wrote to the team, described his past experience, and requested a tryout. One such letter was written by John Clapp to Boston's Harry Wright prior to the 1872 season. Clapp had been catching for the amateur Clipper club of Ilion, New York, and was seeking to make the jump to the professional league. In his reply, Wright complimented Clapp's obvious confidence, but he wasn't yet convinced of the catcher's value. He grilled the young prospect for more information. What caliber and speed of pitching had Clapp caught the previous year? Was Clapp sure he could "catch a swift pitcher" like Al Spalding "up to or close behind" the batter? Could he substitute at any infield position in the event of injury? Could he successfully bat against swift pitching, and was he prepared to go to Boston at his own expense and display the level of his baseball skills? Wright added that he was assuming, of course, that Clapp was "gentlemanly and temperate at all times."[14]

With 194 pounds packed on his 5'7" frame, the twenty-year-old Clapp was a natural backstop who could hit. Fortunately for Middletown, Wright chose to pass on Clapp since he had Cal McVey, the National Association's leading hitter in 1871, returning as catcher. The Mansfields quickly signed Clapp, who the *Sporting Life* described as a "cool, easy-going fellow, not easily 'rattled' ... As a player he ranks high."[15]

Middletown was also able to lure pitcher Frank Buttery and catcher Jim O'Rourke away from the Stratford Osceolas. These two men had formed an impressive battery for the Stratford club and had always given the Mansfields trouble. In addition to being an effective pitcher, the twenty-year-old Buttery was also an upstanding citizen. He was frequently called "Deacon," a nickname commonly hung on gentlemen who didn't pursue the pastimes of drinking and gambling preferred by many ballplayers of the time. It was a

Bridgeport native Jim O'Rourke began his prolific major league career with the Middletown Mansfields in 1872. During his career, O'Rourke was a player, manager, umpire, and minor league president. Whether it was a big game in the pennant race or the latest controversy involving players' rights, O'Rourke was always in the middle of things. On September 22, 1904, he became the oldest player to play a full nine innings, catching the entire game for the New York Giants and recording the final base hit of his major league career. O'Rourke amassed over 2,300 hits and was elected to the Hall of Fame in 1945 (Library of Congress).

fitting designation since Buttery was the only Mansfield to sign a temperance pledge upon joining the club.[16]

O'Rourke was a handsome nineteen-year-old with curly black hair, who would soon sport the large handlebar moustache that was so common with ballplayers of the day. He possessed only average speed and a mediocre arm, but he was an accomplished batter. His first experience with an organized club came with the Bridgeport Unions. At sixteen, Jim joined the Stratford Osceola club. He never knew when a game would be played until shortly before the first pitch, when one of Stratford's wealthy young men would drive his carriage to the O'Rourke farm and deliver Jim to the ball field.[17]

Jim's father had passed away in 1868, leaving him and his brother John to help their mother with all the farm work. Both boys loved baseball and would take turns playing with the local club while the other stayed home to finish the chores. On the days when he was left at home working, young Jim often dreamt of playing ball in front of a big crowd while being dressed in a real baseball player's uniform. Ben Douglas and the Mansfields were prepared to make this dream come true, but first Douglas had to promise to pay Jim enough money so that his mother could hire a man to help with the farm work.[18] O'Rourke would also fulfill the Mansfield's temperance requirement as he never took liquor or tobacco. Instead, he was a great milk drinker. Tim Murnane recalled, "As a ball player he was noted for the amount of milk that he drank. Often before starting for a game he would dispose of two or three glasses...."

With the additions of Clapp, O'Rourke, and Buttery, the Mansfields had certainly improved themselves. Although it was reported that every man playing for the Mansfields was "an old and experienced player,"[19] in reality they were about to become the youngest club in the National Association. The youngest player was Frank McCarton, still a baby at the age of seventeen, while the average age of the Mansfield players was just over twenty. In fact, their *oldest* player, Jim Tipper, who hadn't yet turned 23, was younger than the average league player, who was about 24 years of age. Despite this disturbing fact, the frightfully inexperienced Mansfields were about to leap headlong into professional baseball.

Chapter 9

Welcome to the Big Leagues

In their first professional season, Middletown battled ten other teams for the championship flag. Six of the clubs — Philadelphia, Boston, Troy, the Washington Olympics, New York Mutuals, and the Forest City Club of Cleveland — were holdovers from the 1871 National Association campaign. The Brooklyn Eckfords, unofficial entrants the previous year, officially joined the league in 1872, along with four new teams: the Lord Baltimores, Brooklyn Atlantics, Washington Nationals, and the Mansfields.

The Mansfields would be a cooperative, or co-op, club, which meant they would rely solely on gate receipts to sustain the team. Players for co-op clubs were not paid regular salaries but instead received a share of the gate receipts. The Eckfords, Atlantics, Olympics, and Nationals were also co-ops.[1] The other six National Association clubs were the more financially stable stock-funded teams. A stock-funded team raised its initial operating capital through the sale of common stock at the beginning of the season. This start-up capital, plus the revenues produced during the season, covered operating expenses such as travel costs and player salaries, which ranged anywhere from $500 to $2,500 per player. This higher figure was a king's ransom compared to the average Mansfield player, who, as Tim Murnane later recalled, could hope to receive at most $80 per month.[2]

When the re-configured Mansfields assembled for their first practice, John Clapp appeared at the field neatly dressed in a uniform which included a red belt with white letters spelling the word "CAPTAIN." In those days, the captain of the team was selected by the players, but, as Tim Murnane quipped, since "Mr. Clapp could not play without wearing that belt, and he could not very well wear that belt without being captain," the only thing the Mansfields could do was grant him that position.[3]

Each day, the players gathered on the field for an hour, honing their fielding and batting skills. Since the ballpark was located close to the banks of the Connecticut River, many balls were lost during practice after they bounded over the backstop and rolled into the water. After their workout, the team would run three miles over Middletown roads and then return to their accommodations at the Mansion House on Main Street for a refreshing bath and a hearty meal. The owner of the Mansion House took excellent care of the players since he was an ardent supporter of the team. He made sure that the players' hearty appetites were satisfied by serving large meals with seconds on dessert. All of this was made available to team members for the low price of $6 per week.[4]

After several intra-squad practices, the Mansfields attempted to arrange a practice game with the Rose Hill Club of Waterbury. Unfortunately, the Rose Hills had to decline since they didn't have the proper baseball attire. It seems that after the club raised $125 for uniforms at a benefit dance in February, their unscrupulous secretary skipped town with the money, leaving the club penniless and without uniforms.[5] Instead, the Mansfields warmed up with a game against the Junior Mansfields. Although the junior club included Mike Dorgan, who later had a very successful ten-year major league career, it didn't provide much competition in the Mansfields' 26–2 victory. After a few more practices, it was time for the real show. On April 24, the Mansfields boarded a train bound for Troy, where each Middletown player would make his professional debut.[6]

The Troy Haymakers looked like a formidable Opening Day opponent for the inexperienced Mansfields. Although they only finished sixth in the National Association in 1871, the Haymakers had strengthened themselves considerably in the off-season. Five players were added from the disbanded Chicago White Stockings, the most important being pitcher George "The Charmer" Zettlein. Zettlein was a real character who derived his nickname from a dancer in Hooley's Minstrels. The Charmer relied almost exclusively on pure speed, caring little for pitch location or changing speeds. This brute-force style had brought him success, as he led the league in ERA in 1871 while compiling an 18–9 record for the pennant-contending White Stockings.[7]

A crowd of about 800 Troy fans turned out to see the revamped Haymakers take on the upstart Mansfields.[8] Middletown took the field with the following lineup:

> Clapp C
> Buttery 3B
> Bentley P
> Murnane 1B
> Booth 2B
> Tipper LF
> O'Rourke SS
> McCarton CF
> Arnold RF

Middletown native Mike Dorgan played with the Junior Mansfields in 1872 as a 17-year-old. He gained national recognition in 1876 by batting .406 as a catcher for the Syracuse Stars, a strong independent club. He later joined the New York Giants National League baseball club. Never a statistical leader, Dorgan earned a reputation as an excellent all-around player. His most productive offensive season was 1885, when his .326 batting average ranked third in the league. In 1887, Dorgan injured his knee going over the fence to make a game-saving catch. This serious injury effectively ended his playing career. He retired with a career batting average of .272 over ten seasons. In 1909, he underwent surgery to repair his damaged knee but died from complications of the surgery. Dorgan is shown here on an 1887 tobacco card (Library of Congress).

The acquisition of Zettlein paid immediate dividends for the home team, as his swift deliveries kept the Mansfields off balance all afternoon. Cy Bentley also pitched surprisingly well, keeping Troy scoreless through the first three innings. Over the next three frames, however, the Haymakers found the measure of his offerings and plated eight runs. Meanwhile, Zettlein was completely dominant. He rendered the Troy outfielders virtually unnecessary, rarely allowing Middletown batters to hit the ball out of the infield, while whitewashing Middletown, 10–0. The young Mansfields' ineptitude with the bat made history, as it was reportedly the first time a team failed to score a single run in a nine-inning game played in Troy.[9]

The other noteworthy event of the day, according to the *Troy Daily Times*, was that both teams remained so well mannered that "the game proved that men who play baseball for a living can behave themselves in public."[10] The game was "entirely devoid of those petty bickerings and wranglings, and outside contaminations, which in so many instances heretofore, cast odium upon these contests. The players on both sides, while they strove earnestly for victory, maintained throughout the game a becoming demeanor, and their gentlemanly conduct to each other caused nothing to occur to mar the festivities of the occasion."[11]

These observations were necessary because, as the common man replaced the gentleman as the game's main participant, ballplayers had begun to acquire a somewhat unsavory reputation. Their frequent association with gambling and gamblers was well known. Drinking and fighting were all-too-common habits. One Connecticut newspaper summed up the situation as follows: "It is a well established fact that to be a professional base ball man is the sure way to bring on disease and shorten life."[12]

In its account of the game, the *Clipper* saw fit to mention, once again, that the Mansfields had sent delegates to the amateur convention, not the professional one.[13] Meanwhile, Middletown's loss was gleefully reported in the *Bridgeport Post*, which said that the Mansfields, "reorganized this year to whip the Osceolas and all the rest of creation" had lost to Troy.[14]

After a good night's rest, the Mansfields got a chance to redeem themselves the next day in a re-match against the Haymakers. Without much of a bench, Middletown made only one lineup change, replacing right fielder Willis Arnold, who had been a non-factor the day before, with Ham Allen.

Whether it was the lineup change or just conquering Opening Day jitters, Middletown played much better. After ten fruitless innings over the course of two games, the Mansfields finally pushed across their first runs as a professional club, scoring twice in the second inning. With a six-run eruption in the fifth inning, the Mansfields knotted the score at nine. From that point on, Troy outscored Middletown 18–1 on their way to a 27–10 victory. For the second day in a row, Bentley's fastballs weren't fast enough, and each Haymaker managed at least one base hit.[15]

After the pair of losses in Troy, the Mansfields completed their New York swing with a game against the Mutuals in Brooklyn. Like Troy, the Mutuals were veterans of the 1871 National Association. They finished fourth with a 16–17 record but, having added star pitcher Candy Cummings, looked to be much improved. Cummings had come to the Mutuals after a lengthy contractual battle which involved several teams. Although it was announced in November 1871 that Cummings would not leave the Brooklyn Stars and turn pro, he had actually signed contracts with both Troy and Philadelphia. This led to a protracted debate over who actually owned him. Philadelphia dropped out of the race, seemingly leaving Troy in control. However, Cummings' wife let it be known that she had no desire to go to Troy. This re-opened the issue, and the Mutuals eventually signed Cummings. The *Clipper* felt that this move had both pros and cons, as Cummings certainly was a great talent, but he had been a prima donna with the semipro Stars and would need to be retrained to become a team player.[16]

Despite good weather, the Mansfield-Mutual game was not well attended. Incredibly, New Yorkers thought the game was just an exhibition, since they were still unaware that the Mansfields were members of the professional league. Unfortunately, Middletown's play did little to convince those in attendance otherwise. Pitching his third consecutive game, Bentley fared well, blanking the Mutuals in five of the nine innings.[17] This was not good enough, as Cummings was simply masterful. The diminutive right-hander completely dominated the over-matched Mansfields, holding them to four hits over nine innings. Finding it nearly impossible to make solid contact, the Mansfields continually popped the ball up, and all but six of their outs were recorded on weak fly balls. In seven of the nine innings, Cummings set the Mansfields down in order, and not once did a Middletown runner advance past second base.[18]

Besides lacking offense, Middletown fumbled its way to eighteen errors, six by Cy Bentley alone. Even when they managed to field the ball cleanly, the Mansfields often didn't know where to throw it, and when they did, the throw was usually wild. The game ended 12–0 in favor of New York, giving Cummings one of his league-leading three shutouts for the year.[19] Despite the lopsided loss, the *New York Times* saw some cause for optimism, reporting that with more practice the Mansfields "may yet take a respectable position" among league teams.[20]

With the three losses in New York, including two rare shutouts, the wave of optimism that had surrounded Middletown's prospects at the start of the season quickly began to fade. Excuses started to surface, especially from Augustus Putnam in the *Hartford Post*. Putnam tried to rationalize the losses by saying that the club began the season without any practice games and several of the new players had never played with the Mansfields before. On the brighter side, the Mansfields returned home from their winless road trip, "all in good health and spirits."[21]

After their rude initiation to the big leagues, the Mansfields took a few days to recover and prepare for their professional debut in front of the hometown fans. The opponent for this game would be the Brooklyn Atlantics, who, like the Mansfields, were playing their first season in the National Association. Eager to snap their three-game losing streak, Middletown could draw some solace from the fact that they had nearly beaten the Atlantics the year before. Unfortunately, the fates appeared to be conspiring against the Mansfields, as both Cy Bentley and Jim O'Rourke would be absent. Bentley had returned home due to the death of his mother, and O'Rourke was sick. In addition, the morning of the home opener brought rain which, coupled with the absence of the two Middletown starters, kept attendance down.[22] This was not how Douglas wanted to start the season, as the home opener had been expected to draw a sizable crowd.

The loss of their starting pitcher and shortstop forced the Mansfields to juggle their lineup considerably. Frank Buttery, who didn't throw as hard as Bentley, but was just as effective, would get his first opportunity to pitch.[23] George Fields logged his first playing time of the year, subbing for O'Rourke at shortstop.

The Atlantics also sported a new look, as a youngster by the name of Jim Britt would be handling the pitching chores. Britt, who celebrated his sixteenth birthday just two months earlier, was making his professional debut. Even with their inexperienced pitcher, the Atlantics were made huge favorites by New York gamblers. To keep bettors in New York apprised of game developments, results of each inning were telegraphed from Middletown.[24]

When the game started, the Mansfields took early advantage of the rookie pitcher, scoring five runs over the first three innings. On the other side, Buttery was sailing along, holding the Atlantics scoreless for six straight innings after allowing a single run in the second. In the ninth, the Atlantics added another meaningless run, a run which rightfully shouldn't have scored. For this final tally the Atlantics could thank a group of young boys who had gathered near home plate and prevented John Clapp from catching a foul bound off the bat of Jack McDonald. Given a second life, McDonald singled and eventually scored. For the game, Buttery allowed just six hits and starred at the bat as he and Booth each stroked three hits in Middletown's 8–2 win. This impressive victory re-ignited Middletown's waning enthusiasm for the Mansfields.[25]

After their success against Brooklyn, the Mansfields taught the Wesleyan freshmen a harsh lesson, crushing them 32–2 in six innings. The Mansfields returned to more serious matches, squaring off against Yale in a highly anticipated meeting. Most of Connecticut had been anxious to see how the new professionals would fare against Yale, which was traditionally a very strong club. Ben Douglas was especially eager for this match, since Yale had little trouble whipping the Mansfields in the past, and it was his fondest wish to finally defeat them.[26]

A large crowd turned out at Mansfield Park for the 3 P.M. match. Despite an early four-run deficit, the college boys played smartly and led 10–5 after five innings. Sensing the game was getting away from them, the Mansfields called on Frank Buttery to relieve Cy Bentley. This move proved quite effective, as the Deacon continued his form from the Brooklyn game, yielding only three hits and, more importantly, no runs over the final four innings. Meanwhile, Middletown's bats warmed to the task, and after eight and a half innings, the Mansfields led, 13–10. They batted in the last of the ninth anyway, tacking on another eleven runs to make the 24–10 final score deceivingly lopsided.[27]

This loss was reportedly Yale's first ever to a Connecticut team, and it ignited great rejoicing throughout Middletown. A generous supporter even provided each Mansfield player with free tickets to the theater. The *New Haven Register* tried to take some of the luster off the victory, saying that the Yale nine was disorganized and forced to use substitutes. Ben Douglas quickly refuted this charge in a letter to the *Hartford Courant*, saying that Middletown had indeed defeated Yale's regular nine.[28]

The star of the game was John Clapp, who took a beating behind the plate. He was hit on the side with a bat, struck on the head with a foul tip, and had one of his fingers "knocked out." Despite the injuries, Clapp showed he was the "pluckiest ever," as he continued to play with scarcely an error.[29] Although the catcher most often stood several feet behind the batter, when runners were on base he moved closer in order to throw out would-be base stealers. As Clapp could attest, these occasions left the catcher especially vulnerable to injury, especially during this era when catchers wore very limited protective gear.

After a 26–11 defeat of Wesleyan's regular nine, Middletown met the Troy Haymakers for a third time. On a blustery day, a good crowd of 800 spectators gathered at Mansfield Park for the game. The stiff wind, coupled with the rough condition of the field, resulted in erratic fielding by both sides. After six innings, Middletown's surprisingly lively bats had produced a 10–5 lead. Shocked to find themselves in such a hole, Troy batters became much more deliberate, purposely taking twice as long for each at-bat. This strategy paid dividends, as the Haymakers rallied in the seventh inning, scoring nine runs with the help of many Middletown throwing errors. Once they had recaptured the lead, Troy brought in the Charmer to close out the game, and he did exactly that. Again the Mansfields could do nothing with Zettlein's offerings and were blanked the rest of the way, leaving the final score 18–10, Haymakers.[30]

The Mansfields then played a re-match with Yale, this time at New Haven's Hamilton Park. New Haven residents were anxious to see Yale exact revenge on the Mansfields, and 500 partisan Yale students came out for the game. The Yale boys would not have a decided home field advantage, however, as the Mansfields brought 500 of their own fans with them. During the train ride to New Haven, the raucous Mansfield supporters were spurred on by a musical band which played for the passengers' pleasure.[31]

Initially, the contest failed to justify the pre-game hype, as both pitchers worked very deliberately. After seven innings, Middletown held a commanding 16–3 lead, keyed by a surprising home run by Tim Murnane. When Murnane, who rarely hit for power, stepped to the plate on this occasion, Yale's captain and center fielder, Clarence Deming, ordered his outfielders to play shallow. Taking note, a determined Murnane drove the next pitch directly over Deming's head. As the stunned outfielder chased the ball to the farthest reaches of the field, Murnane made an electrifying run around the bases while the Middletown contingent howled with delight.[32] The game ended 16–9 in favor of Middletown.

A few days later, Middletown resumed its professional schedule with a game against the Forest City Club of Cleveland. Cleveland came to Middletown as part of their much ballyhooed eastern tour. During the winter, the club had spent considerable money to retain their players, and they came east with high expectations.[33] Unfortunately, their performance on the trip was disappointing.

The game started as soon as Cleveland stepped off the train from New York. The Mansfields had no trouble hitting the submarine deliveries of pitcher Rynie Wolters, so Cleveland brought in hard-throwing Al Pratt. The visitors led 5–4 in the sixth inning, but Middletown scored the game's final six runs to win 10–5. Cleveland's pitching wasn't the real problem, as none of Middletown's runs were earned. The porous Cleveland defense was truly to blame, as they committed an astounding 27 errors! The Mansfield's victory over Cleveland marked the first time all season that a co-op team had beaten a regular professional stock club.[34]

The *Cleveland Daily Herald* was appalled with the result, declaring that the club's general performance on the trip was bad enough, but a loss to the Mansfields, "located in a little town in Connecticut, and made up of players who were found 'lying around loose' and gathered up after all the other clubs had completed their organizations" was inexcusable.[35]

The Cleveland club's management agreed, and immediately after learning the result of the game, the officers telegraphed team captain Scott Hastings and ordered him to skip the scheduled games with the Mutuals and Eckfords and proceed home directly after playing Troy. Upon returning to Cleveland, the team was cross-examined about the results of its disastrous eastern swing. The club had come east with such high expectations that it was suspected that the players might be selling out. With shoddy defensive performances such as the one in Middletown, it's no wonder some questioned the players' integrity.[36]

After this stirring victory, the Mansfields boarded the Air Line train to start their second road trip of the season. As they pulled away from the station, the Middletown boys had good reason to be optimistic. Although their league record stood at two wins and four losses, they had played well of late, winning two of three games and giving Troy a tough time in the one loss.

Chapter 10

God Bless the Eckfords

The first stop on the Mansfields' excursion was Baltimore, where they met the Lord Baltimores on May 24. New to the National Association, the Baltimore club had so far proven themselves to be a very strong nine. Their roster was composed of experienced players, each of whom had been a regular with another National Association team the previous year.[1] The Lord Baltimores, or Canaries as they were often called because of their bright yellow uniform tops, were led by the veteran battery of Bobby Mathews and Bill Craver.

Despite being only 5'5" and 145 pounds, Mathews excelled in the pitcher's box, relying on a good curveball and perhaps one of the first spitballs. Umpire Hank O'Day recalled that Mathews "used to cover the palm of his left hand with saliva and rub his hand in it." His 132 career victories in the National Association would place him third behind only Al Spalding and Dick McBride.[2]

Catcher Bill Craver was well-known for his toughness behind the plate, but he also had a shady reputation, dating back to 1870, when he was suspected of throwing games in Chicago. Suspicions seemed to be confirmed in 1876, when during a pregame warm-up, Craver was mercilessly beaten by a gambler, apparently the punishment for double-crossing the bettor.[3]

When the Mansfields arrived at Baltimore's Newington Grounds, they were greeted by a crowd of about 1,000 people. Losing the toss, Middletown took up the bat first and promptly grabbed the lead when Clapp walked and came around to score on right fielder Dick Higham's misplay of a base hit. Unfortunately, Bentley didn't hold the slim lead long, as Baltimore scored six runs in their half of the first inning. Despite several excellent scoring opportunities, the Mansfields trailed the entire game, which ended 13–6 in favor of Baltimore. The *Baltimore Sun* wasn't impressed with the quality of Middletown's play, but remarked that John Clapp was the best catcher seen in Baltimore all season.[4]

The following day, things looked brighter as Middletown faced the winless Washington Nationals. The Nationals were an extremely weak team, composed mostly of local amateurs. In less than a month, they would drop out of the professional league with no wins in eleven tries. In this game, the Mansfields chose to use a lively ball instead of the more customary "dead" ball which couldn't be batted as hard or as far. This was Middletown's prerogative as the rules allowed the visiting team to pick the game ball. The choice was necessary since the National Association had not prescribed a standard ball, instead specifying only basic size standards. While the size of the balls may have been the same, there were often differences in the type of rubber. For instance, two of the most frequently used balls differed significantly, as the Van Horn ball was much more lively than the Ryan ball. The Mansfields' choice of the lively ball led to a slugfest in which Middletown narrowly prevailed, 28–23.[5]

The road trip was scheduled to continue two days later against Washington's other club, the Olympics, who had managed only two victories all season, both against the hapless Nationals. The game was never played, however, as the financially strapped Olympics had folded just days earlier due. The Mansfields returned to Baltimore where they lost to the amateur Olympic Club, 15–13.[6]

After this embarrassing loss to an amateur club, the Mansfields had to face the powerful Athletic Club in Philadelphia. The A's, who had won the National Association championship in 1871, were led by a number of veteran ballplayers, many of whom had played together for several years. Hard-throwing pitcher Dick McBride had played for Philadelphia for nearly a decade, while the team's best hitter, 6'1" "Long Levi" Meyerle, had played with the club since at least 1869.[7] In addition, the A's had signed rising star Adrian "Cap" Anson, formerly of the Rockford Forest City Club, to play third base.

On the day of the game, the weather was beautiful and the crowd of 1,000 spectators was large, "considering the known superiority of the Athletics over their opponents." That superiority showed as the Mansfields played an extremely sloppy game, allowing runs in every inning but the eighth, giving up seventeen unearned runs, having two men thrown out at the plate, and hitting into two double plays in a 27–11 loss. To add insult to injury, the Mansfields still weren't allowed to shake their amateur reputation, being called "amateur aspirants for championship honors" by the *Philadelphia Press*. The newspaper noted that the Mansfields had individual talent but simply didn't work together as a team. The Mansfields attributed their poor play to the fact that they had traveled from Baltimore during the morning and this was their first match against the mighty A's, so naturally they were nervous.[8]

Middletown's next game was against the amateur Elizabeth Resolutes in

New Jersey on May 31. The Resolute Club was at a crossroads in its existence. The club had been reorganized during the winter with the full understanding that if it played poorly, any idea of having a first-class team in Elizabeth would be abandoned forever.[9] The Resolutes appeared to be passing the test, as they had already defeated two professional clubs, the Eckfords and Atlantics. In fact, the Resolutes continued to play well enough in 1872 to justify entering the National Association in 1873, but their attempt at professionalism failed as the out-manned Resolutes finished the 1873 season with a 2–21 record.

The Mansfields joined the Resolutes on the train to the Waverly Fairgrounds, where the latter team played their most important games. A large crowd, including many of Elizabeth's leading citizens and city officials, had assembled there. The New Jersey club looked dazzling, and perhaps a bit gaudy, in their white uniforms with the word "Resolute" splashed across their chest in red, bright red stockings, and purple belts.[10]

The Mansfields took control of the game from the start and led 8–4 entering the bottom of the ninth. A Resolutes' rally was cut short by an erroneous decision by the umpire. After the game, both the umpire and Mansfields admitted there had been an error, but Middletown's 8–5 victory stood nonetheless. Clapp, who had moved out from his usual spot behind the plate to shortstop, led Middletown with three hits and two runs scored.[11]

The Mansfields traveled to Brooklyn for an appointment with the Atlantics. For the second time on the trip, a scheduled game was not played, as the Atlantics failed to show.[12] These types of scheduling problems were a constant headache for National Association clubs. Instead of setting playing dates for all clubs prior to the season, the league let teams fend for themselves. The only requirement was that they play one another five times during the season. This left teams jockeying to play only on the most advantageous days and often resulted in teams being stood up at the last moment when their opponents found a more attractive game for the day.

The Mansfields remained in Brooklyn to play the Mutuals. Only 500 spectators were on hand since the Mutuals were expected to breeze past Middletown. To everyone's surprise, Cy Bentley matched Cummings pitch for pitch. When the Mansfields took a 4–3 lead in the fourth inning, the Mutuals realized they had better get to work. Try as they might, they couldn't touch Bentley, who whitewashed them for the next four innings.[13]

After seven innings, Middletown was still clinging to a one-run edge, but as was fast becoming their habit, they couldn't hold the lead. Becoming "nervous" in the last two innings, the Mansfields made two critical errors which allowed the Mutuals to score two runs in the eighth and one in the ninth, resulting in a 6–4 victory. The next day, the Mansfields missed out on another game in New York, as their encounter with the Eckfords was rained out.[14]

The Mansfields returned home licking their wounds after this rather dismal road trip. They lost three of four games against pro clubs and even dropped one to an amateur team. In addition, three scheduled games weren't played, which was a direct hit to the players' pockets on a co-op club. At least the Mansfields could comfort themselves that they had the best record of any co-op team in the league. There was a great disparity between the records of the co-ops and regular stock clubs, so great, in fact, that the *Clipper* reported their standings separately, and the *New York Times* chose not to publish the standings of the co-ops at all. After the Mansfields' June 3 loss to the Mutuals, the complete league standings, by total number of victories, read as follows[15]:

	Wins	Losses
Lord Baltimores	12	5
Troy Haymakers	11	5
Boston Red Stockings	9	1
New York Mutuals	9	4
Philadelphia Athletics	7	2
Cleveland Forest Citys	4	7
Middletown Mansfields (co-op)	3	7
Washington Olympics (co-op)	2	7
Brooklyn Eckfords (co-op)	0	4
Brooklyn Atlantics (co-op)	0	5
Washington Nationals (co-op)	0	10

For the Mansfields' return, Augustus Putnam urged Middletown citizens to welcome them home, saying the club was returning from their trip "flushed with success." Middletown residents heeded the advice and presented the returning Mansfields with a pennant bearing the club's name. In addition, the club received two white foul marker flags with the letter "M" stenciled on them in blue. In total, the three gifts were valued at about $40.[16]

The Mansfields were eager to put the failed road trip behind them and get back on the winning track in a game against first-place Baltimore. Unfortunately, the Canaries had other ideas. Instead of traveling to Middletown on the agreed-upon date, they decided to remain in Boston and make up the previous day's rainout. Baltimore figured it would pay better to play Boston, since they had given the Red Stockings a good game earlier in the year and a large crowd was expected. Upon learning of this decision, Ben Douglas was livid, since he had already spent money to advertise the game. The umpire awarded the game to the Mansfields, but later in the year Douglas officially notified Baltimore that Middletown would not claim a forfeit victory.[17]

10. God Bless the Eckfords

Forced to cool their heels for two more days, the Mansfields anxiously awaited the arrival of the Trinity College nine. The college boys were in trouble from the moment they stepped off the train, as the Mansfields vented their frustration on the overmatched collegians, pasting them 48–6.[18] After this blowout, the Mansfields had to wait nearly another week before playing again, not taking the field until Philadelphia came to town. The game was arranged for 2 P.M., the earlier start allowing the Mansfields to catch the 6 P.M. train to Boston for the next day's game against the Red Stockings.[19]

Under gloomy skies, Middletown won the toss and sent the Athletics to bat first. The A's went down without a run, and the Mansfields responded in kind in the bottom of the first. In their second at-bat, the A's scored twice and were poised to score more when Tim Murnane squelched their rally with a beautiful one-handed leaping grab of a high throw that looked to be uncatchable. It all started when the A's swift left fielder Ned Cuthbert hit a grounder to Tipper at third. Tipper unleashed a wild throw to first, but Murnane leaped high in the air and managed to snatch the ball with one hand. When Cuthbert saw the high-flying Murnane snare the ball, he stopped short of first and exclaimed loudly, "Where have you been?!" The catch so impressed Hicks Hayhurst, the Athletics business secretary, he ran across the field and handed Murnane several cigars, vigorously pumping his hand while proclaiming he had never seen such a play in his life.[20]

There was more to the circus catch than just Murnane's leaping ability. After playing for Middletown for parts of two seasons, Murnane had seen many wild throws from the erratic arms of his fellow infielders. Figuring he could use all the help he could get, Murnane took action. At the time, bases were crude, handmade bags, so Murnane decided to make his own first base bag, but with a secret modification. He stuffed two stiff steel springs into the base, packed it hard with damp sawdust, and sewed it tight. Now the contraption was more than just a base; it was a springboard which increased Murnane's ability to reach high throws by nearly a foot. On Tipper's throw to first, Murnane caught the spring perfectly and propelled himself surprisingly high into the air.[21]

Murnane's great play excited the crowd and lit a fire under the Mansfields. In the bottom of the inning, after their first two batters went out quietly, the Mansfields strung together several hits, and by the time the third out was recorded, Middletown had scored five times. This offensive outburst left Middletown with a surprising 5–2 lead over the vastly superior Athletics. The lead quickly vanished, as the A's evened the score with three runs in the top of the third. Then, with the Mansfields batting in the third inning, the storm clouds which had been threatening all game finally let loose, scattering the crowd and forcing the stoppage of play. As they ran for cover, the disappointed Mansfields and their fans could only ponder what might have been had the game continued.²²

After the rain-shortened affair, the Mansfields hopped the train for Boston for a game the following day which would kick-off that city's Jubilee Celebration. Two weeks earlier, Harry Wright had encouraged Douglas to bring the Mansfields to town on that day, promising it would be the best payday of the season. Since large crowds were expected in Boston the entire week, Wright suggested that the Mansfields stay for a few days and play several games against Boston-area teams. He even advised the Mansfields to convince some New York teams to meet them in Boston for games that week.²³

Ben Douglas either couldn't or wouldn't take Wright's advice, informing Wright that the Mansfields would only play one game in Boston. When the holiday morning dawned sunny and mild, it seemed that Wright's prediction of a big payday would materialize. Unfortunately, the Mansfields

Above and opposite: Scorecard from the Middletown Mansfields' 24–3 loss to the Red Stockings on June 15, 1872, in Boston. Pre-printed scorecards like this were sold at the games in Boston. The front of the scorecard shows a humorous baseball scene. The reverse shows the Middletown and Boston lineups and scoring. To date, this is the only known piece of memorabilia from the Mansfields' lone major league season. It is known that a photo of the Middletown club was taken, as it was reported that Ben Douglas had hung the portrait in the Hartford Dark Blues' headquarters in 1874. So far, a copy of this team portrait has yet to surface (courtesy of Middlesex County Historical Society).

10. God Bless the Eckfords

BOSTON Base Ball Club.

PLAYERS.	Pos.	1	2	3	4	5	6	7	8	9	0	R.	B.
1. G. Wright	S S	0	1		1	1		0		# 1			
2. Barnes,	2d	0	1		1	1		0		0			
3. Leonard,	L F	0	0		10	1		0					
4. McVey,	C	0	0		10	#		0					
5. Spaulding,	P		1	1	10			#					
6. Gould,	1st	1	#	1	1	0		# 2					
7. Schafer,	3d	1	0	1	1	#		0					
8. Rogers,	R F	1	0	0	F	0			0				
9. H. Wright,	C F	0	1	11	0	#		0					
Totals.		0	6	1	11	6	0	0	0	0			

Scorer, _____ Umpire, _____

MANSFIELD Base Ball Club.

PLAYERS.	Pos.	1	2	3	4	5	6	7	8	9	0	R.	B.
1. Clapp,	C	0		0	0		#		# 3	0			
2. Buttey,	R F	0	0	0	0		0		5	0			
3. Bentley,	P	0		0	0		0		8	0			
4. Muman,	1st	0	1	0	1			2	2				
5. Booth,	2d	0	1	#	0			2	1				
6. Tipper,	3d	#	0	0	#			2					
7. O'Rourke,	S S	#	#		0			1					
8. McCarton,	C F	0	0		0	0		4					
9. Fields,	L F		0	0	#		0	3					
Totals.		0	0	0	2	0	0	0	1	0			3

Scorer, _____ Time of Game, __ Hrs. __ Min.

PRINTING of every description executed with Neatness and Dispatch, at **THE RICE, GODDARD & CO.**, Printing Establishment, No. 41 Milk Street, Boston.

weren't enough to bring out the crowds, as only 400 Bostonians paid to witness their professional debut in Boston. By abstaining, fans demonstrated a keen knowledge of baseball, as the match proved to be a tremendous rout.

With the powerful talent that had been amassed in 1871 back for a second season, the Boston nine far outclassed Middletown at virtually every position. This was especially true in the pitcher's box, where Bentley would face baseball's premier pitcher, Al Spalding. Boston won the toss and took the field first. Confident of victory, the Red Stockings started the game with two players playing out of their regular positions, as Dave Birdsall caught and Cal McVey played right field.[24] Spalding set the Mansfields down in order in the top of the first. Then, to the surprise of everyone, Bentley returned the favor in the bottom of the inning.

In the second inning, Boston's bats came to life while Middletown's fielding died. Clapp's three passed balls and Tipper's pair of errors at third base were only the most glaring lowlights as each Mansfield took a turn at muffing. The end result was six runs for Boston, only one of which was earned.[25]

Meanwhile, Spalding held the Mansfields scoreless until the fourth inning when Murnane started a two-run rally with a base hit. Tipper followed with a double, and then Jim O'Rourke banged out another base hit. Boston quickly laid to rest any ideas of an upset however, exploding for eleven runs in the fourth inning, highlighted by George Wright's home run over the left-field fence.[26]

With the lead safe in hand, Spalding handed off the pitching duties to Harry Wright, who hurled the final five innings as Boston cruised to a 24–3 victory. Middletown played so poorly that the small crowd felt they had not gotten their money's worth, since the Mansfields' play was "not up to the average of amateur nines in the vicinity." Some Boston journalists weren't quite so harsh, agreeing with the earlier observation of the Philadelphia press that the Mansfields had good individual players but didn't play well as a team. They failed to do the little things, like backing each other up, which made the Red Stockings so tough to beat. This was shown at a critical point in the game when Harry "Silk Stockings" Schafer was caught in a rundown but made it back to third base safely because none of the Mansfields' infielders covered the bag. A similar instance occurred when Charlie Gould occupied the Mansfields' attention by getting in a rundown while two Red Stockings crossed the plate. After all that, Gould *still* landed safely at first base.[27]

After suffering their own version of the Boston massacre, the Mansfields returned to Connecticut and resumed their league schedule against Baltimore. Prior to the game, William Rackliff, one of the Mansfields' directors, paraded across the field sporting a fine white high hat. This sight prompted a loud yell of "Shoot the hat!" from the crowd, and Baltimore's Cherokee Fisher gladly obliged. Firing the ball from a long distance, Fisher plugged the hat dead on, sending it rolling along the ground to the delight of the spectators. Before leaving town that night, Fisher made arrangements to settle with Mr. Rackliff for the hat.[28]

When the real game started, Middletown jumped out to a 1–0 lead, but Baltimore tied it in the third and then broke the game open with seven runs in the fourth. Baltimore hit Bentley so hard, and O'Rourke played so poorly at first base, that the Mansfields were forced to make several changes in the fifth inning. Buttery came in to pitch, O'Rourke became the catcher, and Clapp moved from catcher to first. This was a definite improvement, and the Mansfields managed to stay close with the help of three double plays. Unfortunately, Middletown's bats remained quiet, and they could never quite catch the Canaries. Power-hitting Lipman Pike capped Baltimore's scoring with a home run in the ninth, making the final score 11–5.[29]

The Mansfields then caught a break, playing consecutive games with the lowly Brooklyn Eckfords, who, two months into the season, had yet to post a victory. The first meeting took place in Hartford at the Trotting Park on Albany Avenue. For over a month, the Mansfields had been investigating the possibility of playing in Hartford to draw larger crowds. After some negotiations, they finally struck a deal with the owners of the park. The ball field at the Trotting Park was rough and uneven, with no level place for the catcher to stand, nor any dirt paths between the bases, just grass.[30] Despite this, Douglas was eager for more gate money, and if more paying customers came out in Hartford, the Mansfields would play there, regardless of the field conditions.

The Eckfords arrived in Connecticut by boat, stopping in Middletown to pick up the Mansfields before continuing up the Connecticut River to Hartford. Upon arriving at the Hartford docks, both clubs were met by horse-drawn carriages which took them to the field. Despite the heat, a good crowd of 1,000 spectators attended the game, a definite improvement over most crowds in Middletown.[31]

The game began at 3 P.M. with the Eckfords at bat, and it wasn't long before the scene devolved into chaos. One of the first batters hit a ball down the third-base line which rolled into the midst of several carriages. The carriages were parked too close to the diamond because the ill-prepared Hartford Park failed to install a rope to keep the crowd back. Next, the Hartford crowd quickly became restless when the umpire failed to call balls on the Eckford pitcher, who was finding it impossible to get the ball over the plate. The umpire's casual attitude brought a shower of jeers and catcalls from the stands.

The third inning brought even more excitement when Brooklyn's Jim Snyder tried to reach second base but got tangled up with Eddie Booth, who severely spiked Snyder in the leg, drawing blood. In the bottom of the third, all eyes turned from the playing field to the grandstand where two thugs had started a skirmish. A policeman rushed in to break up the fight, but the two combatants turned on the officer and began assaulting him. At this point, the ballplayers had seen enough of the crowd's antics and began yelling insults at the rowdy fans.[32]

Back on the field, there was far less excitement. After trailing 3–2, the Mansfields broke the game open in the fourth inning, paced by Clapp's three-run homer to left field. From then on, the game was long and boring. In the ninth inning, Murnane made what was reportedly his first error in 35 games. The game, which ended with Middletown winning 26–6, was deemed by the Hartford press as the most "tedious and uninteresting game" ever played in Hartford.[33]

The following day, the Mansfields and Eckfords met again, this time in Middletown. The Eckfords started well, scoring five first-inning runs, albeit mostly due to Middletown errors which the Mansfields blamed on the wet grass. Despite their early success, the Eckfords were whitewashed for the next seven innings. Meanwhile, the Mansfields scored no less than three runs in each of the first seven innings. Lasting nearly three hours and featuring 32 Brooklyn errors, this game proved to be even less interesting than the one in Hartford. The 36–6 final score completed a three-day shellacking of the pitiful Eckfords. Before losing consecutive games to the Mansfields, the Eckfords were in Boston getting blasted by the Red Stockings 24–4. This left the Eckfords' three-game total at 16 runs, while their opponents piled up 86.

The two wins against the feeble Eckfords gave the Mansfields their first winning streak of the season. No one suspected the sad truth: the Mansfields had won their last professional game.

Chapter 11

Three's a Crowd

As May slipped into June, the shrewd business mind of Harry Wright began pondering the big payday that an Independence Day game could deliver. Spurred by the Worcester (Massachusetts) Park Association's request for two professional clubs to play there on July 4th, Wright formulated a grand holiday scheme. He liked the idea of playing in Worcester, believing the financial return would be substantial, but a single holiday game wasn't enough for him. In order to maximize profits, Wright envisioned playing in Worcester in the morning before returning to Boston for an afternoon game in front of the home fans. He immediately contacted Ben Douglas to see if the Mansfields were interested in playing either of these games.[1] Douglas declined, since the Mansfields had already arranged a game for the Fourth with the Baltimore Olympics. Two weeks passed, and with no takers for his doubleheader, Wright's grandiose plan was in shambles. He reluctantly informed Worcester that the Red Stockings wouldn't be playing there, since most professional clubs were already engaged for the holiday.[2]

While Wright scrambled to organize his schedule, the Mansfields were forced to rearrange their own holiday plans after the Baltimore game fell through. They quickly moved to fill the void by inviting the amateur Resolutes of Elizabeth, New Jersey. Hesitant about spending the money to travel to Middletown, the Resolutes were urged to make the trip by the local press. The *Elizabeth Daily Journal* felt that if the Resolutes went to Middletown "there is no doubt but that they will have one of the most pleasant times they have ever enjoyed." With this encouragement ringing in their ears, the Resolutes decided to make the journey.[3]

Meanwhile, Harry Wright was beginning to panic. With less than a week before the big holiday, Wright and Boston still didn't have even one July 4th opponent, let alone two. Missing out on the considerable cash that large holiday crowds would provide was unthinkable to Wright. In a last ditch effort to find an opponent, he contacted Douglas once again about playing in

Worcester and/or Boston. Wright's desperation was apparent as he tried to pressure the financially insecure Mansfields into accepting his proposition, saying, "If you want to do well in gate receipts this is the best opportunity that you will have this season and I trust you will accept it." As an added incentive, Wright promised to play return games in both Hartford and Middletown if Douglas agreed.[4]

This was truly unfamiliar territory for Wright. As manager of the premier team in the country, he was accustomed to dictating where, when, and, most important, for how much money the mighty Red Stockings would play. In the days before a formalized schedule existed, Wright worked tirelessly to ensure that his team played the most desirable opponent on the most advantageous date to secure the most profitable return.

Douglas, on the other hand, found himself in the driver's seat for a change. With a holiday game already booked and Wright out in the cold, he wasn't about to waste his opportunity to call the shots.

After giving it some thought, Douglas figured that if the Red Stockings were in such dire straits, maybe they should be coming to Middletown on the Fourth, instead of the Mansfields traveling to Boston. Enamored with this possibility, Douglas quickly forgot his prior arrangements with the Resolutes. For the financially strapped Mansfields, meeting the most famous team in the country at home on a big holiday was infinitely more attractive than playing the amateur club from New Jersey. With this in mind, Douglas suggested to Wright that Boston should come to Connecticut for a game on the Fourth.

This certainly wasn't what Wright had in mind. After all, games in Boston would draw larger crowds, and the Red Stockings could keep two-thirds of the net receipts. By playing in Connecticut, Boston would be forced to play before smaller crowds and take home only one-half of the net, not to mention spend money for travel and lodging. Unfortunately for him, Wright was in no position to argue and agreed to be in Connecticut for successive games on July 3 and 4.

While Douglas and Wright haggled over their schedules, the Elizabeth Resolutes and their fans went merrily about the business of preparing for their excursion to Middletown. Wanting to get an early start to Connecticut, many Resolute faithful boarded the 11 P.M. boat on July 3. Others chose to wait until the next morning and traveled on the 6 A.M. boat with the Resolutes.[5]

Back in Connecticut, Hartford's Trotting Park was preparing to host the first match between the Red Stockings and Mansfields. This time, the facility was better prepared than it was for Middletown's first game there. Ropes were placed around the playing field to keep the crowd from interfering with play, and the scorekeepers and reporters were provided with a covered table and chairs to keep them from baking in the hot sun.[6]

Although the park was ready to receive a large crowd, only 600 showed up for the contest. The disappointing attendance was due in large part to the sweltering heat that had been baking the northeast for a week. Besides, many people decided to wait a day and see the same two clubs play in Middletown, where Independence Day festivities could also be enjoyed. Those who did attend the game were more interested in getting a first-hand look at the best team in the country than seeing the Mansfields. The Red Stockings entered the game having won 28 of 29 games, and, despite the fact that first baseman Charlie Gould was out with rheumatism, the crowd fully expected a Boston victory.

The first pitch was slated for 2:30, but it wasn't until nearly 3:30 that John Clapp finally stepped to the plate. The delay didn't affect the Middletown catcher, as he quickly rapped a solid single off Al Spalding. Frank Buttery then was put out at first on an infield grounder. On the throw to first, Clapp raced to second and aggressively rounded the base. Unfortunately, he was a bit too daring and got himself caught in a rundown. At 5' 7" and nearly 200 pounds, Clapp wasn't exactly built for speed, but he decided to make a mad dash for third anyway. Pumping his arms and legs so hard that the *Hartford Post* declared that even "if old cloven hoof had been at his heels with a fire brand" he couldn't have gone any faster, Clapp beat the throw to the base. As he reached his destination, his spikes caught on the bag, and the big catcher crumpled to the ground, where he was tagged out.[7]

Even worse than the rally-killing play was the fact that Clapp had severely sprained his left knee and was forced to the bench for the rest of the game. Without him, the Mansfields had to quickly shuffle their lineup. Ham Allen filled in at shortstop while O'Rourke took Clapp's spot at catcher. The loss of their valuable captain dampened the Mansfields' spirits considerably as they took their positions in the bottom of the first inning.[8]

On the merits of his superb relief performance against Boston three weeks earlier, Buttery was in the box for the Mansfields. It quickly became apparent that this game would be much different, as Boston pounded Buttery's first-inning deliveries and sent home five men. The Mansfields tried to climb back into the game but only became more dejected as each ball off their bats found its way into the sure hands of Boston's splendid fielders. After four innings, Middletown still hadn't scored, and Boston led 9–0.[9]

In the seventh inning, Middletown finally pushed across a pair of runs on consecutive two-out hits by Murnane, Booth, and Tipper. When Murnane crossed the plate with the first run, a loud cheer erupted from the stands and wads of cash changed hands, as many in the crowd had bet that Middletown wouldn't score the entire game. In the ninth inning, with the lead safe in hand, Boston's defense got careless, allowing the Mansfields four meaningless runs which left the final score 16–6.[10]

The following day's weather provided no relief from the week-long heat wave, and the mercury in Middletown soared to a stifling 98 degrees. Despite the "hot, dusty, and exceedingly uncomfortable" conditions,[11] the city wasn't about to call off its grand July 4th celebration. In previous years, the holiday had been celebrated very quietly in Middletown, but this year would be different. Determined to prove itself a first-class city, Middletown was prepared to host festivities that would draw people from all corners of Connecticut. City merchants were anticipating a windfall from the train-loads of visitors who were expected from Hartford, New Haven, and towns along the shoreline.[12]

The storekeepers weren't disappointed, as people flocked to Middletown to partake in the gigantic celebration. Among the events planned for the day were a military and dress parade, fireworks, a regatta, and the ballgame. The first event was the military parade, whose line of march was reduced because the soldiers appeared to be wilting in the oppressive heat.[13] After the parade, 3,000 people made the walk out to Mansfield Park for the ballgame. Attendance would have been even larger except that many people cut short their celebration because of the storm clouds that were gathering in the western sky. As it was, this was by far the Mansfields' largest home crowd of the year. This, coupled with the fact that admission was 50 cents a head instead of the usual 25 cents, meant a financial bonanza for the club and its players.[14]

Besides the relative fortune being collected at the gate, the day proved memorable in another way. To everyone's surprise, the long-forgotten Resolutes appeared at Mansfield Park ready to reap their own holiday riches. Upon their arrival, the Resolutes were shocked to see that the Mansfields, with what the *Elizabeth Daily Journal* labeled "a meanness unparalleled in the annals of ball playing," were already entertaining the Red Stockings. The New Jersey club rightfully charged Douglas with making arrangements with Boston long after Elizabeth had accepted his invitation. Furthermore, the Resolutes weren't informed of the new arrangements until they arrived at Middletown. Douglas was guilty of the first charge but denied the second, claiming he had sent word to New Jersey telling the Resolutes to stay home.[15]

The Mansfields were accustomed to being stood up by teams, but never before had a pair of clubs appeared to play them at the same time. Despite the Resolutes' protests, the Mansfields quickly, and not surprisingly, chose to continue with their plans to play Boston. Realizing they were about to lose out on a good chunk of money, the Resolutes tried to cut a deal with Douglas, offering to stay in town overnight and play the next day, provided their extra expenses were paid for by the Mansfields. Ben Douglas refused.[16]

Finally resigning themselves to the fact that they weren't going to be playing any game in Middletown, the Resolutes angrily stormed off the field.

11. Three's a Crowd 83

Incredibly, only one Middletown paper found this whole commotion worthy of mention. The *Middletown Constitution* quickly dismissed it as an "unfortunate misunderstanding."[17] The "misunderstanding" wasn't taken so lightly in Elizabeth, as the Resolutes' mistreatment was angrily described in the *Elizabeth Daily Journal* under the headline "CHAMPION CONNECTICUT CHEATS."[18]

Once the Resolutes were cleared from the scene, the Mansfields and Red Stockings took the field. The condition of the diamond was very poor, as the grass at Mansfield Park was high and weeds were plentiful. Groundskeepers were a luxury for the Mansfields, who limited the cutting of the grass to once a year. Since this annual ritual was still nearly a month away, the thick grass provided a distraction for shortstop George Wright, who amused himself between pitches by pulling up the weeds which flourished around his position.[19]

For the second day in a row, Buttery received the dubious honor of trying to quiet Boston's big bats. Despite playing without Clapp, who was on crutches, the Mansfields greeted Al Spalding with four runs over the first two innings, while Buttery was throwing zeroes at the Red Stockings. In the top of the third, Boston managed a single run, but the Mansfields responded with five of their own. Incredibly, the Mansfields had built a 9–1 lead over the stunned Boston club.[20]

As each of the first three innings passed, the Mansfields' confidence grew, and they even began to imagine that victory was possible. Most of the Middletown faithful were ecstatic, but the older fans in the crowd were skeptical and weren't afraid to tell anyone who would listen that it was only a matter of time before the mighty Boston bats were heard from.[21]

While the Mansfields built their lead, the western sky was growing ominously darker with threatening rain clouds. Faced with the large deficit and a potential quick ending to the game, the Red Stockings realized they were in a tight spot and needed to produce in a hurry.[22] As a result, when Boston stepped to the plate in the fourth inning, base hits began to pile up at an alarming rate. With each additional Boston safety, the Mansfields' confidence was deflated, and even catchable balls turned into Middletown errors. By the time the onslaught was over, eleven runs had crossed the plate, and the Red Stockings had made up their daunting deficit, plus three.[23]

Once the offensive assault ended, the shaken Mansfields could only scratch back with a single run, leaving Boston with a 12–10 edge after four innings. Even though the Mansfields trailed by just two, the crowd felt that the deficit would only widen, the question was by how much. Sure enough, Boston continued to pull away, and the lead ballooned to 25–13 after eight innings. As the final inning was getting underway, the heavy rain that had been threatening finally came down, sending the crowd and players running for home. The storm continued unabated through the evening, cancelling the city's $300 fireworks display, the regatta, battalion drill, and dress parade.[24] Despite the disappointing come-from-ahead loss, the Mansfields could take some comfort that they had scored more runs against Boston than any other team that season. Previously Philadelphia had generated the most offense against Boston, scoring ten times while handing the Red Stockings their first loss. Only Troy, who would score 17 against the Red Stockings later in the season, was able to better the Mansfields' mark.[25]

Harry Wright would finally get his coveted doubleheader, the first in major league history, the following July 4th in Boston. On that day, in front of a large holiday crowd, the Red Stockings split a pair of games with, ironically, the Elizabeth Resolutes.

Chapter 12

One Long Vacation

With the two losses to Boston, Middletown's record stood at 5 wins and 11 defeats. While unimpressive, this was still the best record of any co-op team. During the next three weeks, the Mansfields took a break from league games. The numerous open dates left the players with ample time to partake in the many picnics and fishing trips which were so popular in Middletown. It was in lighter moments like these that Tim Murnane exercised his bountiful sense of humor. Always a prankster, Murnane enjoyed making teammates the butt of his practical jokes. In one such instance, Murnane persuaded George Fields to dress up as a girl and then convinced one of the young pitchers, probably from the Junior Mansfields, to throw to the "peach." Of course, Murnane made sure to alert his teammates so that all could witness the event. As the "young lady" swatted pitch after pitch into the field, the pitcher's embarrassment grew, pleasing the giddy spectators all the more.[1]

The Mansfields maintained their playing trim with a light schedule against local clubs, easily winning four games. First, Middletown met the Waterbury Mutuals in Middletown. John Clapp was still on crutches, and Frank Buttery did not play. Despite this, the Mansfields thrashed the Mutuals 30–3 in a long, dull game witnessed by very few spectators. The next two games saw the Mansfields beat up on their junior club. In the first game, the Seniors whitewashed the Juniors, 24–0. Frank Barrows, who had played with the Boston Red Stockings in 1871, manned right field for the Mansfields. This may have been a tryout for Barrows, who had been spotted with the club for several weeks, or perhaps he was just a last minute replacement for Buttery, who was home visiting family. The second game between the two clubs resulted in a 23–3 victory for the professionals, who then whitewashed the Wallingford Quinnipiacs, 17–0.[2]

During this time, Cy Bentley's personal life was turned upside down. On July 15, Bentley's wife, Maggie, gave birth to the couple's first child. Unfortunately, the joy surrounding the birth of their baby boy quickly faded, as only a week later, Clytus Bentley, Jr., passed away. This was the second tragedy that Bentley faced during the season, as just three months earlier his mother had died.

After their three-week hiatus from professional matches, the Mansfields traveled north to Springfield, Massachusetts, to take on their old nemesis, the Troy Haymakers. By playing in Springfield, both clubs were trying to take advantage of the crowds there for the college regatta on the Connecticut River. The ballgame was scheduled for 10 A.M. at Hampden Park. Middletown residents were encouraged to attend the game, being reassured that it would not interfere with the boat races, which wouldn't begin until 3 P.M.[3]

Middletown's prospects for the game seemed poor, as Troy was coming off an impressive 17–10 victory over Boston. In addition, John Clapp was still unavailable for duty. Despite these factors, a large crowd of about 1,200 spectators was in attendance. The crowd was a rather tame collegiate assembly, as school ribbons were prevalent and there was very little betting action.[4]

George Zettlein was in the box for Troy, and the Charmer continued his mastery over Middletown, rarely allowing the Mansfields to bat the ball out of the infield. Bentley also pitched well, and the game remained scoreless until Troy pushed across four runs in the fourth with the help of several wild throws. The game ended 7–0 in favor of Troy, giving the Haymakers their fourth victory of the season against the Mansfields. The high points of the game were Zettlein's two strikeouts at the bat, both of which elicited laughter from the crowd.[5]

This proved to be Troy's final game of the season, as shortly thereafter the insolvent Haymakers disbanded. Their departure from the league meant they ended their season exactly as they had started it, with a shutout of the Mansfields. Several of the Troy nine, including Doug Allison, Al Gedney, and George Zettlein, joined the Brooklyn Eckfords for the balance of the season.

The decision to play in Springfield paid off for Middletown, as their share of the gate came to $400. Even with $100 of expenses, this was an excellent take for the Mansfields. People hadn't exactly been flocking to see them play in Middletown, and the club was struggling financially. Improving gate receipts by moving some games to larger cities like Hartford and Springfield was helping, but it still wasn't enough. As a result, $2,500 worth of stock was offered to the public in hopes of stabilizing the club's fiscal health. It was reported that one half of the stock had been sold by the end of July.[6]

Besides trying to improve themselves off the field, the Mansfields were looking to better themselves between the lines. When famous pitcher Asa Brainard become available after the Washington Olympics disbanded, the Mansfields, along with Cleveland, immediately showed interest in obtaining the "Count," as he was called. Brainard, who first gained fame as the star hurler for the 1869 Cincinnati Red Stockings, was a clever pitcher who baffled hitters by changing speeds. Although his skill was obviously waning, he was only a few years removed from being a dominant pitcher.

While eager to bolster his woeful pitching staff, Douglas was well aware that Brainard often marched to the beat of a different drummer. This march often included late-night drinking binges and missed practices. As a result, Douglas felt it would be prudent to first check with Harry Wright, Brainard's old manager in Cincinnati, before signing Brainard.

Wright confirmed Brainard's poor reputation, but added that with the proper prodding he would be a good addition. Yes, said Wright, Brainard would occasionally "shirk practice" and get "notions in his head, but a little plain talk, play or no pay," was usually effective. Wright warned that any agreements with him should all be "on paper, and properly signed and witnessed," but Brainard's "experience for the last two seasons, and his being a married man" made him "a good investment for this year and the next also." Wright encouraged Douglas to pursue Brainard, saying, "You can get him, for he wants to play with you.... He is a hard worker in games, especially first class ones, and plays a good uphill game, and would give your men confidence and steadiness." Based on this recommendation, Brainard was a member of the Mansfields by the end of July. Asa may have also had some family in the vicinity. Brainard is a common surname in the Middletown area, and Asa's father, Leonard, was born in Connecticut, while his mother died in Stamford, Connecticut, in 1896.[7]

In their next game, Middletown hosted the New York Mutuals on a Saturday afternoon. The night before, the Mutuals had telegraphed Douglas and informed him that they wouldn't play unless Richard Higham of the Baltimore club umpired. This was the same Mutual club which had a well-deserved reputation for dishonest play. Their insistence on using Higham was even more alarming, since he also had a checkered past. The *New York Clipper* frequently took him to task for his "erratic" and "uneven" play, implying that his inconsistency was related to gambling.[8] Higham also had close ties with the Mutuals, having played with them in 1871.

Despite his concern about the Mutuals and Higham, Douglas was in a tough spot, as the game had already been extensively advertised around Middletown. Rather than disappoint the public and lose a good payday, Douglas reluctantly agreed to let Higham umpire.[9]

When the game began, Douglas's worst fears were confirmed, as nearly all of Higham's calls went against Middletown. Mansfield supporters were convinced that Higham had been paid to rule in favor of the Mutuals. It wasn't long before they were jeering his every call and screaming all manner of vulgarities at him. The acrimony didn't deter Higham in the least, and his bogus calls helped the Mutuals defeat Middletown by the score of 26–9.[10]

At the conclusion of the game, the enraged crowd wasn't about to leave until they got their hands on Higham. Chaos reigned as they pushed and shoved each other in an attempt to reach him and repay him for his bad calls. Only a great effort by the Middletown police force and Mansfield club managers preserved Higham's safety. After escaping the field, Higham returned to the relative safety of the McDonough House, a hotel on Main Street, where he boasted of his shameful umpiring. The rest of the Mutuals admitted they had received unfair treatment, but were quick to point out that they were not bound to give back their victory. Higham continued his antics in front of the hotel, staggering about pretending to be drunk. His actions led many to call for his arrest.[11]

Umpiring was a persistent problem for the entire league, not just Middletown. The root cause of the problem was that the arbiters were not paid professionals, but volunteers, mutually agreed to by the two teams. The home team picked the umpire from a list of five names submitted by the visiting team. The umpire was often a player from another club, but it was not uncommon for a substitute from one of the participating teams to be chosen. This practice, along with the need to seriously consider threats from the home crowd, often led to biased decisions. Even completely honest umpires often ruled incorrectly due to their lack of knowledge of the oft-changing rule book. With only one umpire making calls over the entire field from his position in foul ground, one can understand the difficulty. The problem was so pervasive that umpires were sometimes replaced in mid-game, and on more than one occasion a game was called off because the two teams could not agree on an umpire. It wasn't until 1889 that the National League appointed a permanent umpiring staff.

After the farce with the Mutuals, the Mansfields vowed that Higham "has done his first and last umpiring for the Mansfield club, who have up hill work enough to do, to play their games with an honest umpire." This was a wise decision, as a decade later Higham became the first and only umpire banned from baseball for reportedly betting on games and making decisions favoring the team upon which he had wagered.[12]

The Mansfields then embarked on their third pro tour—first stop, Baltimore. With John Clapp back in the lineup after missing three games, all Middletown losses, the Mansfields were hoping to return to the winning side. Adding to their optimism was the fact that Asa Brainard would make his debut in a Middletown uniform. Brainard was immediately handed the pitching duties for the pitching-poor Mansfields.

At the start, it looked like Middletown might be onto something, as Clapp doubled and scored, and Brainard made a nice fair-foul hit. Over the next three innings, Middletown couldn't muster any more offense, while Baltimore plated a total of six runs. With his team leading 6–1, Baltimore's Lipman Pike stepped to the plate in the fourth and promptly swatted a Brainard pitch for a long home run. It was one of the longest hits ever made in Baltimore and sent the crowd into a frenzy. Pike's clout made the score 8–2. The Mansfields pulled closer in the fifth when Clapp and Fields both scored on Bentley's base hit.[13]

As the sixth inning began, the sky became overcast, and the wind whipped a blinding dust across the field. With the Mansfields at bat and two men away, a hard rain let loose, scattering everyone. The deluge wouldn't let up, and the game was called with Baltimore the victors, 8–4. Brainard pitched well in his first appearance, but the Count was not supported by his teammates, who made six errors at critical junctures.[14]

The same two teams met the next day with the Mansfields intent on redeeming themselves. Their resolve quickly faded when Baltimore immediately scored six runs with the help of three errors by Tim Murnane. Middletown could only respond with one run aided by an error by their old friend Higham in right field.

When the Mansfields took the field for the second inning, they made wholesale defensive changes. The battery of Brainard and Clapp was replaced by Bentley and O'Rourke, respectively. Clapp moved to center field and Brainard to right field. The changes didn't help much, as Baltimore put the game away with ten runs over the last three innings, and the final score stood 19–9.[15]

The Mansfields then moved on to Philadelphia, where they met the Athletics at the 25th and Jefferson Street grounds in front of about 1,000 spectators. Clapp was out of action again due to an injury he apparently sustained in the last Baltimore game. The A's started the scoring with two runs in the second and would have had more except Tipper made an excellent running catch in left field. Offensively, the Mansfields were dead, as they went down in order in each of the first three innings.[16]

Both teams put up a pair of runs in the fourth, with Middletown's two runs coming on hits by Booth, Bentley, and Murnane. During this inning, the already shorthanded Mansfields faced a scary moment. Allen was at bat when one of Dick McBride's swift deliveries sailed in on him. Unable to dodge the fastball, Allen absorbed a direct hit squarely on top of his head. The collision sent him directly to the ground while the ball rebounded straight up, forty feet into the air. Allen remained down for some time, but after clearing his head, pronounced himself fit and remained in the game.[17]

In the fifth inning, another player had a violent meeting with the ball. This time, Philadelphia catcher Michael McGeary was nearly knocked unconscious after being hit in the face with a foul ball. At first, he appeared to be seriously injured, but after drinking some water and gathering his wits, McGeary returned to his position to the loud cheers of the crowd.[18]

After five innings, the A's held a surprisingly slim 5–3 lead, but broke the game open over the last four innings, outscoring the Mansfields twelve to one. Only Tipper's great defense in left field kept the A's from scoring even more. He made one fine catch after another, impressing everyone in the crowd. The final score stood 17–4 in favor of the Athletics.[19]

After the game, the Mansfields traveled to New York for a rematch with the Mutuals. When they arrived in the city, they were met by several supporters from Middletown. Prior to the contest, betting in the stands was brisk, and the Mutuals, who had been playing well, were heavy favorites. Pools sold at $50 to $18 that the Mutuals would better Middletown's run total for the entire game in two innings, and $25 to $4 that they would do so in just one. These odds were surprising, since the Mutuals had only beaten the Mansfields 6–4 in their last meeting in New York. This time, however, the Mansfields were without John Clapp, and some probably recalled the one-sided affair in Middletown that Higham presided over.[20]

After yielding three runs in the first two innings, the Mansfields drew even in the second with the help of a throwing error by the Mutuals' notoriously bad-fielding third baseman William Boyd. Sadly, this proved to be the extent of the Mansfields' offense, as they became helpless at the bat. Over the last seven innings, Middletown batters only managed to reach first base three times. Despite this, the game remained close, and going to the final frame the score was only 7–3 in favor of the Mutuals.[21]

Unfortunately, the Mansfield's fielding fell apart, and they allowed seven runs in the last inning, making winners of all who had laid money on the Mutuals. Middletown fans went home disappointed, as their club lost for the fourth time in as many tries against the Mutuals. Henry Chadwick declared that the Mansfields exhibited "a lack of discipline and careful training, which, it is to be hoped, will soon show a marked improvement now that Asa Brainard is to be captain of the nine."[22]

The following day, the Mansfields met the Atlantics in front of a disappointing crowd of only 500 people at the Capitoline Grounds in Brooklyn. A brief rain shower shortly before game-time prevented a larger turnout. With a healthy knee again, John Clapp was back behind the plate, so a close game was expected. Middletown got off to a rocky start, allowing five Brooklyn runs in the first. To their credit, the Mansfields showed some heart and stormed back to grab an 8–5 lead after five innings.[23]

At this point, Atlantics' captain Bob Ferguson loudly instructed his boys to bear down harder and step up their play. The pep talk did the job, as the Atlantics immediately responded with five runs. The Mansfields couldn't muster any more offense, and the final score stood 15–8. Jim O'Rourke played an excellent third base while Eddie Booth, with five hits, performed the best with the bat. The *Hartford Post* reported that the Mansfields had "their usual luck" as their losing streak against league clubs stretched to nine games.[24]

Upon their return to Connecticut, the Mansfields met the Atlantics in the second game of a doubleheader played at Hartford's Trotting Park. The first game of the twin-bill featured two amateur clubs, the Grant Club of Collinsville and the Red Clouds of Southington. The professionals squared off immediately following that match. In order to accommodate the fans, extra trains were run in accordance with the scheduled times of the games, and a new park entrance was opened right at the train stop. The crowd of about 600 people appreciated these efforts.[25]

The game was closely played, and after seven innings the score was knotted at six. Brooklyn then put up four runs in the eighth on a combination of good batting and "nervousness" by the Mansfields, "who have shown a great tendency to lose their coolness in a tight place." Bentley was the prime culprit, as he pitched wildly, and for good measure dropped an easy pop-up which sustained the rally. Brooklyn added one more run in the ninth while the Mansfields put together a mini-comeback but could only muster a pair of runs, leaving the final score 11–8, Brooklyn.[26]

During the game, some of umpire Charlie Mills's decisions were called into question. The *Hartford Post* reported that Mills had a good reputation within baseball circles and the Mansfields' loss was not due to his decisions, but simply their own poor play.[27] It seems likely that this was another example of a New York team bringing their own umpire and forcing the Mansfields to accept him. Mills was the catcher for the Mutuals, who had previously brought Higham along to umpire unfairly in Middletown. The New York clubs may have believed that the Mansfields were so desperate to play and make some money that they would accept any umpire.

The next day, the Mansfields were scheduled to meet the Atlantics again, this time in Middletown. Not surprisingly, Brooklyn again insisted on using Mills as the umpire. This time, the Mansfields refused, since they felt he had been unfair the previous day in Hartford. The Atlantics remained adamant about their choice, and when Middletown continued to resist, they stormed off the field. The *Hartford Post* supported the Mansfields' decision to stick to their guns, saying, "'Country clubs' won't stand everything."[28] When the Mansfields walked off the field that day, little did they know that they had made their last appearance as a professional club.

Over the course of the next three days, the Mansfield managers apparently realized that the club could not survive financially. On August 13, the Mansfields suddenly ceased operations and disbanded as a professional team.

At first, the *Hartford Post* reported that "the Mansfields are having a vacation." The next day, the paper acknowledged the sad truth that the Mansfields, "finding the national game unremunerative, have disbanded."[29] No mention was made of the public stock offering which had commenced earlier in the summer.

For the season, Middletown batted .288, tied for fifth overall with Cleveland. The offense was well balanced, as several players led the team in various batting statistics. Clapp led the team in extra-base hits and slugging percentage, swatting six doubles and the only Mansfield home run of the year. Murnane led in batting average, hitting a lofty .359. Jim Tipper paced the club with 15 RBIs, while Murnane was second with 13.

While Middletown's offensive production was respectable, their pitching and defense were terrible. The pitching staff had an earned run average of 5.67, which left them in eighth place in this category. Frank Buttery was the pitching "star" of the team, managing three victories against two losses. He pitched more frequently in the middle of the season when it was obvious that Cy Bentley wasn't getting the job done. Once Asa Brainard joined the club, however, Buttery didn't play in another game. With his winning record, it's surprising that he didn't pitch more.

Middletown also allowed nearly nine unearned runs per game, a statistic that implicates the Mansfields' defense as much as the pitching staff. Defense was a key ingredient to winning games in the high-scoring National Association. Any team that could catch and throw the ball well gave themselves a chance to be in every game.

The Mansfield club failed because it couldn't draw enough paying customers. While unable to increase its small fan base, the club certainly could have better capitalized on the growing relationship between newspapers and baseball. At this time, newspaper coverage of sports was growing rapidly, to the mutual benefit of both. Granted, Middletown newspapers were only weekly until July of 1872 when the *Middletown Constitution* became a daily, but still, baseball coverage was poor. Reporting was limited to games involving the Mansfields or other Middletown teams. General baseball stories — for instance, results of other professional games or league standings — were almost never mentioned. Coverage of these aspects of the game may have stimulated further interest in attending a Mansfield game.

When the Mansfields finally succumbed to these obstacles, no one blamed Ben Douglas, Jr., The *Middletown Sentinel & Witness* opined that if all club members were as dedicated as Douglas, the team would have been one of the best in the country. When Wesleyan students returned from summer vacation, the campus newspaper lamented the silencing of the Mansfields' bats. The paper asserted that the club would be sorely missed by the student body and that, with more practice, the Mansfields could have been as good as any team in the country. On the positive side, it was noted that students' grades would probably now improve since they could concentrate on their studies instead of baseball.[30]

Almost immediately after the Mansfields collapsed, a call arose for another Middletown club to be organized "on a new and better basis." By mid–September, a new team was indeed formed. The "Middletown Nine" consisted of several ex–Mansfields, including Tim Murnane, Jim Tipper, Cy Bentley, Frank McCarton, and Willis Arnold. The remainder of the roster was filled with local players. In its first game, the reconfigured team thrashed the Junior Mansfields 36–3 in front of a non-paying crowd. It was reported that the new club would continue playing every day during the upcoming week. This was just wishful thinking though, and the only game played was another one against the Junior Mansfields.[31]

Chapter 13

The Charter Oak City

The Mansfields' abrupt demise made them the fourth of five clubs to withdraw from the National Association in 1872. The Olympics, Nationals, and Haymakers all preceded them. Cleveland, which broke up on August 20, outlasted Middletown by a week. With teams collapsing at such an alarming rate, the Association's Judiciary Committee voted to increase the required number of matches between teams from five to nine. The remainder of the 1872 season saw Boston capture the pennant, with Baltimore finishing second and the New York Mutuals taking third place. The final 1872 standings are shown below.

	W	L	Pct
Boston Red Stockings	39	8	.830
Lord Baltimores	35	19	.648
New York Mutuals	34	20	.630
Philadelphia Athletics	30	14	.682
Troy Haymakers	15	10	.600
Brooklyn Atlantics	9	28	.243
Cleveland Forest Cities	6	16	.273
Middletown Mansfields	5	19	.208
Brooklyn Eckfords	3	26	.103
Washington Olympics	2	7	.222
Washington Nationals	0	11	.000

Notice that a team's rank is not based on winning percentage, but total wins, as National Association rules dictated. This edict left the Philadelphia Athletics in fourth place, despite having the second-best winning percentage. Also note that the league was split into two distinct classes. The top five teams played .600 ball or better, while the bottom six all had winning percentages under .300. Middletown's five wins and nineteen losses earned them eighth place. All five victories came against the worst teams in the league, who somehow managed to combine for an abysmal record of eighteen wins and eighty-

13. The Charter Oak City

one losses. The Mansfields had considerably less luck against the top five teams in the league, going winless in seventeen tries.

In 1873, Harry Wright led his band of talented ball-tossers to a second consecutive championship, outdistancing the Philadelphia Athletics by seven victories. During the winter, the *Hartford Courant*, illustrating that charges of teams buying the pennant are not new, attacked the state of professional baseball, saying,

> Instead of the best youths of the land striving in honest rivalry with parents and friends as witnesses of their skill, hired hands of trained players scour the country, followed by crowds of gamblers and pick pockets.... What do the highest baseball honors now signify? Simply that Boston last year was willing to pay professionals more than other cities.... Middletown had some aspirations that way, and it only needs some enthusiastic citizen of means to go $5,000 or so better than Boston to float the whip pennant on the banks of the Connecticut.... We are waiting for a great American novel, for an American opera, and a drama worthy of the name. We must also wait for our national game.[1]

But Middletown was a failed experiment, and major league baseball was simply not coming back there. In fact, most people felt major league baseball would never be played again anywhere in the state. Gersh Hubbell himself told the *New York Clipper* that he believed there would never be a professional club in Connecticut again. Sentiments like these failed to deter the strong-willed Ben Douglas, Jr. Douglas knew that the National Association still wanted a club located between New York and Boston. With an Association club so positioned, other teams could layover midway between the two cities, securing gate money and a night's rest. Painfully aware that a larger market than Middletown was required, Douglas became convinced that Hartford was the answer.

Hartford was indeed much larger and more developed than Middletown. With 37,000 residents in 1870, Hartford was the thirty-fourth largest city in America and, in terms of per capita income, the most affluent in the entire nation. "The best built and handsomest town I have ever seen ... the Center of Connecticut wealth," was Mark Twain's description of Hartford in 1868. Bolstered by an educated work force and abundant water power from the Connecticut River, Hartford and the surrounding Connecticut Valley became America's first high-tech industrial corridor. Everything from firearms and sewing machines to bicycles, machine tools, and typewriters was produced there. In addition to its manufacturing capabilities, Hartford's five railroads and its distinction as the Connecticut River's northernmost navigable point by deep-draft sea vessels made the city a natural hub for the distribution of goods throughout western New England.[2]

Book publishing was also an important industry in Hartford, so much so that popular writer Mark Twain was drawn to the city to be near his publisher. Twain settled in the close-knit literary community of Nook Farm, where his next-door neighbor was renowned writer Harriet Beecher Stowe, author of the anti-slavery novel *Uncle Tom's Cabin*. Twain and his family moved into a rambling nineteen-room home that was as colorful as its owner. Its combination of different colored bricks and mortar, Gothic turrets, and riverboat deck led the *Hartford Times* to call it "one of the oddest looking buildings in the State ever designed for a dwelling, if not in the whole country."[3] While residing in Hartford, Twain penned some of his most popular works, including *The Adventures of Tom Sawyer*, and *A Connecticut Yankee in King Arthur's Court*.

Despite these other industries, the business of Hartford undoubtedly was, and is, insurance. Spawned by the common desire of businessmen to share the high risk of losing their wooden factories to fire, the Hartford Fire Insurance Group was formed in 1810. Over the ensuing decades, dozens of other nationally recognized insurance companies, including Aetna, Travelers, and Phoenix, were established in the city. The city's reputation as a reliable insurer was cemented during the disastrous New York City fires of 1835 and 1845 when Hartford insurers fulfilled their payment obligations while many others did not. Hartford's insurance companies even survived their darkest day, paying out $10 million in claims arising from the Great Chicago Fire in 1871.[4]

In his inimitable way, Twain summarized the business of Hartford: "[Its] fame as an insurance center has extended to all lands and given us the name of being a quadruple band of brothers working sweetly hand in hand — the Colt's Arms Company making the destruction of our race easy and convenient, our life insurance citizens paying for the victims when they pass away, Mr. Batterson perpetuating their memory with his stately monuments, and our fire insurance companies taking care of their hereafter."[5]

Early in 1874, Ben Douglas and his old Mansfield teammate Tom Furniss gathered together many of Hartford's prominent businessmen to sell them on the benefits of professional baseball. The meeting got off to a rocky start when Douglas had to apologize for the absence of well-known outfielder George Hall. It had been advertised that Hall would appear at the meeting, serving as an example of the fine ballplayers Hartford would sign, but, Douglas explained, Hall had missed his train. Douglas then launched into his sales pitch, making clear that professional baseball was not only good for the host city but could also prove profitable to investors. Douglas put his money where his mouth was, investing $600 of his own funds in the fledgling enterprise. By the end of the night, Douglas had succeeded in garnering a total of $5,000 in pledges for a new Connecticut team. Gershom Hubbell, the old Charter Oak player, was elected president of the new club, and Douglas was named corresponding secretary. The name "Hartford Base Ball Club" was chosen after "Charter Oak" and "Connecticut" had been considered.[6]

Although the club started out with $5,000 subscribed capital, the *New York Clipper* said, "The question is do they have a good ground, if not they had better save the money."[7] The selection of a convenient ballpark site, located within easy walking distance of the downtown or on a main travel route, was critical to the financial success of any ballclub in this era. Although some spectators arrived at the field in their own carriages, parking them in foul territory or deep in the outfield, the majority of patrons relied on walking or public transportation. Hubbell and Douglas were considering three sites. The Charter Oak Trotting Park, located about a mile north of downtown, had served as "home" field for a few Mansfields games during their abbreviated 1872 season. There were also two properties south of downtown, one on Wethersfield Avenue and one at the corner of Wyllys Street and Hendricxsen Avenue. The latter parcel was owned by Elizabeth Colt, the widow of famed gun-maker Sam Colt. The most prominent feature of this plot was its close proximity to the Church of the Good Shepherd, a magnificent brownstone structure built by Mrs. Colt as a memorial to her deceased husband and children.

The Trotting Park was removed from consideration, since its proprietors wanted to keep one-third of the revenue collected at the games, although they did offer to grade the grounds and furnish seats. The other two sites could "be favorably leased." Despite being south of downtown and not directly on the main transportation routes, the Colt lot was selected by the Hartford managers, who believed it could be easily adapted to a ball field and that special trains for spectators could be run on game days.[8]

The 600 by 400 foot grounds were graded and surrounded by an eight-foot fence. The rectangular shape of the enclosure made for a very deep center field and somewhat short foul lines. A 500-seat pavilion was erected behind home plate, abutting Wyllys Street, which would provide covered seating for stockholders and season-ticketholders. Tiered, general-admission bleachers stretched down the foul lines, with accommodations for more than 2,000 spectators. The bleachers down the third-base line were reserved exclusively for ladies and the gentlemen accompanying them. There was also plenty of room for carriages in the outfield. No liquor would be sold in the park, nor any pool-selling allowed for gamblers.[9]

After procuring the field, it was "virtually decided" that the club's uniforms would be gray with magenta trim. The front of the shirt would be adorned with a Roman-style letter "H." Magenta belts, white canvas shoes, and white and magenta striped stockings were to round out the ensemble. Two weeks later, new uniforms were ordered — gray flannel with *dark blue* trim as previously described.[10] Thus, thankfully, were born the Hartford Dark Blues, not the Hartford Magentas.

In early March, club officers called in the first 25 percent installment of stock subscriptions, which Hubbell took to Philadelphia, Baltimore, and Washington to sign players. His job was particularly difficult because, due to the Hartford club's late organization, most of the best players had already signed with other teams. Hubbell returned a week later, having contracted several experienced, if unspectacular, players for salaries ranging from $800 to $2,000.[11]

Pitcher Bill "Cherokee" Fisher would make Hartford his fourth club in as many years. In his three previous seasons, he had amassed a mediocre record of 17–21, but this included a promising 1872 season in which he earned ten wins against only a single loss. Fisher was regarded as one of the fastest pitchers in the country. Unfortunately, he wasn't always sober enough to get the ball over the plate, probably accounting for his bouncing from team to team. One example of his erratic behavior occurred in 1872 when he pitched for Baltimore and had recklessly plugged the top hat of Mansfield officer William Rackliff prior to a game.[12]

Hard-throwing right-hander Bill Stearns would be the "change pitcher." Stearns started his major league career with a 2–0 record for the Washington Olympics in 1871, but he had been simply awful since, going 0–11 in 1872, and 7–25 in 1873.

Catching for these two journeymen hurlers would be Scott Hastings, "a very quiet, gentlemanly fellow" who played "a square, manly game on all occasions." Hastings had caught Fisher when they were teammates in Rockford, Illinois, and knew how to handle his rapid delivery. Hastings also had some experience in pennant races, although probably not the type desired by Hartford. In 1871, Hastings's participation in four Rockford victories was ruled illegal since he had not abided by the National Association rule requiring players to wait 60 days after leaving one club before joining another. Hastings started the year with the Lone Star Club of New Orleans, but left them after an April 16 game. He appeared in a Rockford game three weeks later, a clear violation of the rules. When the Association's Judiciary Committee, in one of its rare displays of discipline, overturned the four Rockford victories in which Hastings played, the Philadelphia Athletics were awarded two additional victories, just enough to give them the first National Association pennant over Boston.[13]

Manning the bases would be Everett Mills at first, veteran Bob "The Magnet" Addy at second, and 21-year-old Bill Boyd at third. Mills was coming off a sterling year in Baltimore, for whom he batted .331, leading the league in triples and finishing second in doubles. Addy was "one of the best of the lot, a good, hard, hustling ballplayer ... honest as the day is long...."[14] Boyd was solid at the bat, but unreliable in the field.

Completing the infield would be shortstop Tommy Barlow, a promising youngster whose quickness and agility allowed him to move from catcher, where he had played the last two years for the Atlantics. Barlow was one of the first practitioners of the bunt, using a very short bat to block the ball into the unmanned area between the catcher, pitcher, and third baseman. In the early days of baseball, this novel tactic was often ridiculed as unworthy of a professional player.[15]

Barlow employed two methods of executing his bunts. For the first, he "stood at the plate, with the bat outstretched directly in front of him, like a musket at present arms. Thus holding the bat he let the ball hit it squarely.... Immediately the ball dropped, jumped in front of the home plate," and Barlow would scamper to first base before the pitcher could field the ball. In the second method, instead of holding his bat straight out, Barlow "tossed it at the ball just before it was over the plate. That swerved the ball so that it rolled rather slowly towards third base." Although he was probably not the first to have used this tactic, Barlow became so adept that the bunt became known as "Barlow's dodo."[16]

The outfield would consist of former Mansfield player Jim Tipper, an excellent fielder who was considered "death on fly balls." Bill Barnie, the son of a wealthy New York builder, would make his professional debut in right field. Completing the outfield and captaining the nine would be Lipman Pike, a well-known veteran player who had begun his career in Brooklyn. In 1866, he joined the Philadelphia Athletics and in one game that year swatted six home runs. The *New York Clipper* said Pike was "a very hard hitter ... a sure catch, a remarkably fast runner, and singularly graceful in all his movements." Of Dutch-Jewish descent, Pike is generally regarded as the first Jewish player in the major leagues.[17]

Six of the club's ten men — Fisher, Hastings, Mills, Addy, Pike, and Stearns — were married, which, the *Hartford Courant* thought, is "in their favor or ought to be." The *New York Times* said this collection of players "is a very hard team to beat and if managed properly will not be last in the race."[18] Well, the *Times* would prove to be half right.

Chapter 14

Definitely Not Last

Upon reporting to Hartford in early April, Hubbell's collection of journeymen got directly to work, practicing four hours a day, outside on pleasant days and in the Trinity College gym otherwise. After a few weeks of practice, the Dark Blues met the Yale University nine in a preseason tune-up. Things got off to an inauspicious start for the new professional club when, prior to the game, a portion of the right field stands collapsed. The seats had been built near a brook, which, with the abnormally wet spring, had overflowed and formed a large pond of standing water under the stands. The soft ground allowed the supporting posts to shift, and three of the upper rows of stands collapsed, spilling nearly 100 people to the swampy ground below. Although it was first thought certain that many were gravely injured, only one boy was hurt seriously, when a heavy timber struck him above the right eye. Many spectators received bruises, and a nearby drugstore did a brisk business in liniment and court plaster after the game.[1]

Many boys found safer and less expensive vantage points in the trees that grew adjacent to the field. Later in the season, the presence of the youngsters would prove to be an annoyance, as the boys typically shouted a constant barrage of insults at opposing players. Inevitably, nearby spectators would complain to team officers, who would order the boys to quiet down.

Once the game with Yale began, Cherokee Fisher justified his fireballing reputation, striking out ten overmatched college boys who simply couldn't catch up to his "rippers." Despite being limited to a sidearm delivery, Fisher generated blinding speed. Standing to the right side of the box, Fisher would sling his rising fastball so that it would slice across the outside corner of the plate.[2]

Batters weren't the only ones troubled by Fisher's deliveries. Catchers often had to be rotated to save their tender hands, which were barely protected by primitive fingerless gloves. The *Clipper* reported that in this game, catcher Scott Hastings "faced the music well for a few innings, and then gave Tommy Barlow a chance. Tom put on his gloves and took them in quite naturally."³

When the professional season started, Hartford's competition would be much tougher than young college boys. Seven teams would battle the Dark Blues for the championship pennant. The Boston Red Stockings, New York Mutuals, Philadelphia Athletics, Philadelphia White Stockings, Brooklyn Atlantics, and Baltimore Lord Baltimores were all returning members of the National Association. In addition, the Chicago White Stockings were re-entering the league after a two-year absence caused mainly by the Great Chicago Fire.

While Hartford eagerly awaited the start of the regular season, Mother Nature had other plans. Despite a harsh spring, the Philadelphia Whites traveled to Boston, hoping to kick-off the season on Saturday, April 25. While the

By 1889, a pair of fingerless gloves was being worn by the majority of defensive players. The evolution to a single, full-fingered, more generously padded, fielding glove was also beginning at this time. As noted in the August 29, 1888, *Sporting Life*, catcher Al Bushong "wore no glove on his right hand while he was here. He was very anxious to catch the Browns' base-runners, and he kept them hugging the bases." "Irwin's" gloves mentioned in the advertisement refer to gloves made by Arthur Irwin, who, while playing shortstop for the Providence Grays in 1885, wore a padded glove to protect a broken finger. The glove proved so popular that Irwin began making gloves and selling them through a mail order business from his home. Spalding Sporting Goods then purchased the rights to the Irwin glove.

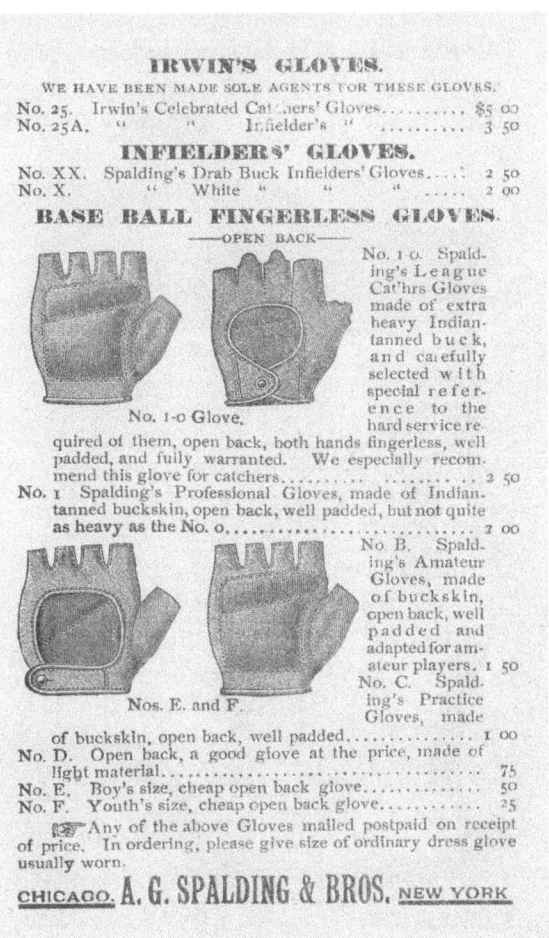

Whites prepared to depart their hotel for the field, it began to snow heavily. Although the Red Stockings and a large crowd were waiting at the field, the Philadelphia players changed out of their uniforms and proceeded to catch a train to Hartford, hoping for a game on Monday. Two club officials remained in Boston to arrange a Tuesday game with the Red Stockings. When Sunday morning dawned with six inches of snow covering the Hartford field, it was obvious no game would be played the next day. The Whites, "being baseballers not snowballers," headed back to Philadelphia, foregoing a return to Boston and vowing to stay out of New England until winter was over.[4]

A few days later, Boston and Hartford made another futile attempt at starting the season. The Dark Blues planned to leave at 6 A.M. on April 30 for a game that afternoon in Boston. Just as they were about to depart, more snow began to fall. Not wanting to risk a fruitless journey to Boston, Hubbell cancelled the trip, thoroughly annoying Boston's Harry Wright in the process. Wright chastised Hubbell for making him spend advertising money for nothing. "We were very much disappointed in your not coming on after agreeing to do so," he wrote, "as notice and advertisements of the game were in all the morning papers.... There was a high wind but there has been neither snow or rain. A number of people visited the grounds in the afternoon."[5]

Finally, on May 1, the Dark Blues made their major

Albert "Doc" Bushong, wearing a pair of catcher gloves in 1888. During the 1870s, use of gloves by catchers, who had occasionally experimented with them in the 1860s, became more frequent. The gloves, typically with the fingers cut off, were worn in pairs and offered only a small degree of protection. Hartford's Tommy Barlow wore a similar pair of gloves in 1874 when catching the rapid deliveries of Cherokee Fisher, who was considered the fastest pitcher in the country (Library of Congress).

league debut against the New York Mutuals. Although the Mutuals had a dubious reputation, on this day their numerous errors couldn't be blamed on any illicit influences, as both teams fielded poorly on a field still soggy from the recent snow. The Dark Blues scored six runs in the third inning on the way to a 10–7 victory. Following the contest, Lip Pike, who had the most hits in the game, was presented with a wooden nutmeg made from the famous Charter Oak. The opening day attendance of 3,000, three times what the Mansfields had drawn in their first game two years earlier, surely pleased Ben Douglas. In addition to the victory, another equally important accomplishment was achieved: "The seats, which have been rebuilt and extended, although filled to their capacity, showed no signs of giving way."[6]

Hartford followed their initial win with another against the Philadelphia Athletics. Another large crowd, this one numbering 2,500, was on hand. After six innings, the Athletics led 6–5, but Hartford regained the advantage after eight innings, 8–7. In the top of the ninth, Scott Hastings led off with a double, and Lip Pike knocked him in with a long triple, scoring himself when the throw to the infield was wild. Pike's gargantuan hit and mad dash around the bases sent the crowd into a frenzy. The Athletics made it interesting with two runs in the last of the ninth, but Hartford prevailed, 10–9.[7]

Two more wins, both against Baltimore, left the surprising Blues with an unblemished record of 4–0. Cherokee Fisher continued to pitch well and live up to his advance billing as the fastest pitcher in baseball. In the third inning of the second Baltimore game, he struck out the side, a feat which was considered without precedent in professional ball. The next inning, he fanned two more and finished the game with seven strikeouts, an excellent total for the time, when a pitcher could lead the league by averaging about one strikeout per game.[8]

A Hartford resident who lived in the city at this time later recalled that the club's fast start took many in Hartford by surprise. Many had thought the ball team was just another fad, like the recently built skating rink, designed to hoodwink city residents into opening their purses. Others dismissed the team as nothing more than a gambling institution. But these early victories changed their mind, at least temporarily, as they discovered that the club's managers "were not such big fools after all, and that we really had one of the strongest nines in the country."[9]

Unfortunately, the Dark Blues were about to get a cold dose of reality from the Boston Red Stockings, winners of two consecutive National Association pennants. The Massachusetts team was loaded with four future Hall of Famers. Al Spalding and Harry and George Wright had remained with the team since moving there in 1871. The fourth star, Jim O'Rourke, had joined the Red Stockings after his one season with the Mansfields. Boston complimented this brilliant nucleus with solid veterans at every other position.

Although both Boston and Hartford were undefeated, few of the 3,000 Bostonians in attendance expected a close game. The Dark Blues were missing Bob Addy, who was injured in the Athletics' game. Captain Lip Pike moved himself from his usual outfield position to Addy's spot at second base. This was Pike's first mistake of the day, as he would commit seven glaring errors at his new position. Matters weren't helped when Cherokee Fisher was forced to leave the game after five innings with a sore arm. After Boston completed the 25–3 embarrassment, Pike shouldered much of the blame, saying, "Never in my life did I begin to play so poorly."[10]

The next day, the two teams met again, this time in Hartford. A huge crowd of 4,500 enthusiastic spectators, from all walks of life, came out to see the contest. With Addy back in the lineup and Fisher pitching the complete game, Hartford put up a more respectable effort, losing 8–1. When Scott Hastings scored Hartford's lone run in the eighth inning, on a groundout, loud cheers erupted from the Hartford supporters, who had been silenced all day. Many older spectators believed that Boston had sympathetically allowed Hastings to score as a gift to the Hartford crowd.[11]

Despite the two losses to Boston, Hartford still sported a respectable 4–2 record as they departed on their first road trip. The road was not kind, however. The Dark Blues dropped their first three games of the tour, forcing Gershom Hubbell to encourage the home fans to remain faithful. "We trust our many warm friends will not get discouraged, for we mean business, and will send good news home yet."[12] Alas, there would be precious little good news, as the Dark Blues lost three of the final four games and returned home with a 5–8 record.

Despite their fast start, the first week of July found Hartford, at 6–14, battling Baltimore, at 5–19, to stay out of cellar. Both teams were light-years behind first-place Boston, which sported a 26–7 record. Not only had the Dark Blues played poorly on the diamond, their lack of restraint off the field had many in Hartford criticizing the club's lack of discipline. Management attempted to remedy the situation by suspending and fining Bill Boyd and Cherokee Fisher, who, the *Hartford Post* said, was rapidly proving "that he could pitch whiskey down his throat much easier than he could pitch a base ball." The message failed to register, however, and three weeks later Fisher was expelled for a second time. Some thought the second suspension would have a positive effect on the club's other hard-drinking players, who "cling to their love for strong drink, for a round of pleasure at the hours when they should be abed." Perhaps the suspension would have had the desired effect had it lasted longer. But with an eye on shaky backup pitcher Bill Stearns, the team allowed Fisher to return to the club after one day, with the promise "to reform and attend strictly to business."[13]

While Hartford was struggling to simply maintain order, Harry Wright was preparing an ambitious journey to Great Britain by the champion Red Stockings and their perennial rivals, the Athletics. Wright was confident that England's eagerness to see the new game would make the trip a financial success. On July 16, the steamship *Ohio* embarked from Philadelphia with 23 ballplayers and 40 others, including stockholders, reporters, and supporters on board. The expected English crowds never materialized, and the two teams lost a combined $2,500 on the venture. The international ambassadors returned to Philadelphia's Christian Street Wharf on September 9.[14]

With the Red Stockings in Europe, the Hartfords and Philadelphia Whites quickly moved to fill the void in Boston. Anticipating a huge turnout by the presumably baseball-starved Bostonians, who hadn't seen a pro game in a month, the two teams scheduled a pair of games, but only 500 hearty souls watched the first contest. "This number was more than sufficient for the occasion," though, as Hartford made numerous errors, many of a nature that would embarrass an amateur team. Boston newspapers searched for something positive to say, but the best they could muster was, "One thing, however, may be said in favor of both clubs ... there was little or no loud talk indulged in ... they were on hand at the appointed time..."[15] Mercifully for Boston fans, the second game was rained out.

With the Dark Blues struggling to avoid last place and the crowds for regular match games dwindling, club managers scrambled to draw paying customers in any way they could. They arranged a foot race between renowned speedster Lip Pike and Stephen Brady, a player with the Hartford amateur team who had signed with the Dark Blues in mid-season. Pike had run in several challenges while with Baltimore in 1873, including one against a racehorse named Clarence. A surprisingly large crowd of 300 people paid to watch Pike easily beat Brady. The team also found time to practice cricket and even considered scheduling matches with other cricket clubs. They played a game against the Josh Hart Comedy Troupe, which was performing at Hartford's Opera House for the week.[16]

In early August, things went from bad to worse for the Dark Blues. First, Bill Boyd abandoned Hartford for the Brooklyn Fire Department, taking his team-leading .350 batting average with him. Boyd had also hit with power, attested to by his .487 slugging percentage, which led the league at the time he left. Boyd later claimed that he was forced off the Hartford team for failing to go to Baltimore when his wife was very sick.[17]

On the heels of Boyd's departure, the Dark Blues lost the services of shortstop Tommy Barlow. Barlow returned to the team for several games in September, but he played poorly and missed the final six weeks of the season. The reason for Barlow's absence is unclear. It may have been due to a severe illness or injury and subsequent addiction to the prescribed painkiller, morphine.[18] (See Appendix B for more details on Barlow's absence and the strangely sudden end to his career.)

The final month of the season saw Hartford's losses continue to mount, highlighted by a nine-game losing streak. The Blues broke this skein with consecutive victories over the Athletics and then the Philadelphia Whites in the season's last home game. "The agony is over," was the *Hartford Post's* blunt summation of the just-completed home schedule.[19] Hartford closed the books on its season by running its surprising winning streak to three games with a 17–11 win over the Red Stockings in Worcester. This loss hardly prevented Boston from capturing its third consecutive National Association pennant. The Mutuals had tried to make a race of it by thrashing the lesser teams of the league while the Red Stockings and Athletics were overseas. As late as October 9, the two teams were tied with 39 victories each, but the Red Stockings played 17 games in the final three weeks, winning thirteen to take the pennant easily. The final standings for 1874 were

Team	W	L
Boston Red Stockings	52	18
New York Mutuals	42	23
Philadelphia Athletics	33	22
Philadelphia Whites	29	29
Chicago White Stockings	28	31
Brooklyn Atlantics	22	33
Hartford Dark Blues	16	37
Baltimore Lord Baltimores	9	38

The Dark Blues' first season was a disappointment in many ways. With their four victories to start the season and three to close it, they won nearly as many games in those three weeks as they did in the intervening 25. The four-game winning streak at the start of the season was their longest undefeated stretch of the year. They were much more successful at maintaining losing streaks, including ones of 4, 5, 6, 7, and 9 games. In their season summary, the *Hartford Post* reported good news and bad news. The good news was that no players had been charged with selling games. The bad news was that the team was virtually incapable of winning games to begin with, thus never earning the opportunity to throw games.[20]

Many attributed the Dark Blues' poor performance to the indifferent leadership of Lip Pike. Although he led Hartford in nearly all offensive categories, and led the league in doubles and slugging, Pike was unwilling or unable to instill discipline in his team. He convened few practices during the season and allowed the boys to maintain an active nightlife. A dramatic change was about to occur. Old Fergy was coming to town.

Chapter 15

Captain Bob

An early February stockholders meeting kicked off the Dark Blues' second season. When Gersh Hubbell turned down re-election as president, respected businessman Morgan Bulkeley was unanimously elected to succeed him. Bulkeley was a rising star in Hartford. Son of Eliphalet Bulkeley, founder of the Aetna Life Insurance Company, Morgan started as a floor sweeper for the company at age 14. He then apprenticed at an uncle's dry goods firm in Brooklyn, where his astute business sense led him to a partnership in the firm in just seven years. Upon his father's death in 1872, Bulkeley returned to Hartford to help run Aetna, earning a reputation for strong leadership and dedication to both public service and private profit.[1]

Morgan Bulkeley, president of the Hartford Dark Blues, 1875–1877. Bulkeley moved the Dark Blues to Brooklyn after the 1876 season, ending Connecticut's status as a major league baseball state. He was also the first president of the National League. As a result of this largely figurehead position, he was elected to the Baseball Hall of Fame in 1937. After leaving baseball following the 1877 season, Bulkeley embarked on a stellar business and political career. He became president of Aetna in 1879, mayor of Hartford in 1880, governor of Connecticut in 1888, and United States senator in 1905. He is shown here in a 1917 portrait (courtesy of Connecticut State Library).

In addition to the front office shuffle, the club's on-field leadership also changed. Intent on remedying the previous year's "poor discipline and loose personal habits," the club turned to the most authoritarian captain in the game, veteran third baseman Bob Ferguson.[2]

Born in 1845, Ferguson first played with the Frontier Club of New York. He joined the Brooklyn Atlantics in 1866, rotating among the infield positions and excelling at them all. Ferguson's defensive prowess is often credited with garnering him one of the all-time best nicknames: "Death to Flying Things." Attributing this nickname to Ferguson appears to be incorrect. If Ferguson had any nickname, it seems to have been "Old Fergy." The confusion may stem from the fact that "Death to Flying Things" was the nickname of Ferguson's old friend and Atlantics teammate Jack Chapman, who was an accomplished outfielder.

Besides being an excellent fielder and solid hitter, Ferguson was an upstanding citizen. At a time when not many ballplayers could say the same, Ferguson was a teetotaler and a scrupulously honest player who abhorred gambling. On several occasions, he loudly rebuked the gamblers assembled near the ball field, charging them with destroying the honor of the game and threatening to personally punish them if they did not leave.[3]

Despite his many positive qualities, Ferguson was the antithesis of Boston's Harry Wright, to whom he was often compared. While Wright, fondly referred to as "Uncle Harry," possessed an unassuming manner, Ferguson was often testy and quick-tempered. One of the most shocking displays of Ferguson's temper came in 1873 while he was umpiring a game between New York and Baltimore. When the Mutuals' casual defensive play in the last inning turned victory into defeat, Ferguson questioned the integrity of Mutuals catcher Nat Hicks. Hicks vehemently denied the charge and called Ferguson a "damned liar." Ferguson then grabbed a bat and ended the argument with a full swing. Hicks missed the remainder of the season with a fractured arm.[4]

Wright was also a master handler of his men, mixing encouragement and support with toughness when required. He always seemed to know which players needed a pat on the back and which needed a kick in the pants. When he needed to chastise an undisciplined player, he was eminently fair and honest. As a result, every man on his nine could be counted on to give his all for the team. Ferguson, on the other hand, knew only one way. As Al Spalding recalled, "He was no master of the arts of finesse. He had no tact. He knew nothing of the subtle science of handling men by strategy rather than by force."[5]

Harry Wright's teams were also known for teamwork, a quality Ferguson's teams could never be accused of possessing. He was responsible for what

Harry Wright managed the Boston Red Stockings from 1871 to 1881, leading the team to six championships. During this time, Wright was viewed by most as the model manager in the country. His unassuming manner, impeccable integrity, and encyclopedic knowledge of the rules of the game made him one of the most respected men in baseball. In the 1870s, a manager's tasks fell into two domains, on-field strategy and handling of the men, and the business management of the club. Wright excelled at both. Wright's impact on the game was so great that he was often called the "Father of Professional Baseball," an honor Wright humbly deflected, saying, "You make me feel awful old when you say I am looked upon as the 'father of the game.' You must look farther and I am certain you will fare better." He is shown here on an 1888 tobacco card (Library of Congress).

became called the "Boston plan," which emphasized training, temperance, and discipline. Wright also pioneered many on-field strategies related to teamwork. He was the first to have his team backing up one another in the field, executing the hit and run, and hitting behind the runner. During Ferguson's tenure with the Atlantics, the powerful team was known for its lack of unity and constant arguing among its players. When Ferguson was named captain in 1870, the club's reputation grew worse. Until then, Ferguson had been "a quiet, hard working member of the nine." After the promotion, Ferguson began "lord[ing] it over his men in an insultingly demonstrative and domineering way," seemingly unable to perform "unless he heard his own sweet voice in full play."[6]

Tasked with whipping the Hartford team into shape, the demanding Ferguson started by bringing with him Atlantics teammate Tommy Bond, a hard-throwing teenager from Ireland. In 1874, Ferguson had ignored the objections of his critics and groomed Bond as a pitcher. Under Ferguson's tutelage, Bond responded with 22 victories and a near no-hitter against the Mutuals, throwing eight and two-thirds hitless innings before Joe Start knocked a double to left field.[7]

The Dark Blues also signed a second top-shelf pitcher, Arthur Cummings. After starring as an amateur pitcher for the Brooklyn Stars, Cummings had continued his winning ways in the National Association, amassing 89 victories between 1872 and 1874, fourth best in the league over that period. He played with the Philadelphia Whites in 1874, and when their fans heard of his signing with Hartford, he was roundly abused for failing to stay. The club pressured him to remain by offering to increase his salary, but Cummings kept his word to Hartford.[8]

Although just 5'9" and 120 pounds, Cummings was one of the nation's best pitchers, thanks to his deceptive curveball, a pitch he is commonly credited with inventing. Although the curveball's exact origin is unclear, Cummings's claim has generally been sanctioned. Al Spalding said Cummings was the first pitcher he ever saw throw a curveball, with Bobby Mathews following soon after. "Both men were very light small fellows," Spalding recalled, "with long, sinewy wrists, and having a peculiar wrist-joint motion with a certain way of holding the ball near the fingers' ends that enabled them to impart a rotary motion to the ball, followed by a noticeable outward curve."[9]

In a 1908 article titled "How I Pitched The First Curve," Cummings told how in 1863 he and his friends watched the clam shells they were throwing curve gracefully through the air. It occurred to Cummings that perhaps he could make a baseball curve too, and he began practicing every chance he could. In 1867, Cummings's Brooklyn Excelsior club traveled to Boston for a series of games. Cummings said, "It was during the Harvard game that I became fully convinced that I had succeeded in doing what all these years I had been striving to do. The batters were missing a lot of balls; I began to watch the flight of the ball through the air and distinctly saw it curve. A surge of joy flooded over me that I shall never forget. I felt like shouting out that I had made a ball curve; I wanted to tell everybody; it was too good to keep to myself. But I said not a word and saw many a batter at that game throw down his stick in disgust. Every time I was successful, I could scarcely keep from dancing from pure joy. The secret was mine."[10]

When originally signed, both Bond and Cummings had been told that each would be considered "regular pitchers" and either could be called on to pitch at any time. This strategy was a departure from the typical management of a pitching "staff" in the 1870s. Usually a team had one superior pitcher who handled the majority of games and a less talented "change" pitcher who filled in occasionally.

The reconstruction of the Hartford nine continued with the importation of the Mutuals' entire middle defense. The double-play combination would be slick-fielding second baseman Jack Burdock, whom Henry Chadwick called the "model fielder in the country," and shortstop Tom Carey. Center field would be patrolled by Jack Remsen, an excellent outfielder who had severed his connection with the Mutuals because of their indifferent play.[11]

Veteran catcher Doug Allison, a tough-as-nails backstop who first made his name with the famous 1869 Cincinnati Red Stockings, rounded out the middle of the diamond. At a time when the custom was to play farther back, Allison was one of the first catchers to stand close to home plate. Years later, he recalled first moving close while playing with the Mechanics Club of Philadelphia:

> I began to believe it possible to get clean up to the bat, so as to catch the ball, and thereby prevent so many runners from stealing second and third bases. I put my theory in motion, and that was way back in 1866 I first tried it, going in up on the side in order to allow the pitcher to throw them wide, but gradually worked over behind the batter, so as to fool him as well as the base-runner. My success in this style of play was remarkable, and naturally the talk of the place, until our games began to draw crowds simply because "Alison was behind the bat." This is not egotism, but the fact, and my method soon had lots of imitators in and around Philadelphia, but, strange to say, few made success of it.[12]

Unfortunately, Allison's toughness often manifested itself in arguing and moodiness on the diamond. Former manager Harry Wright later recalled that Allison "had to be treated very gingerly at times."[13] A contributing factor may have been Allison's hearing problem, which had supposedly developed as a result of his service during the Civil War. In 1876, the *Boston Globe* reported:

> It has been noticed that Allison is somewhat deaf, which infirmity has led to some unfortunate mistakes by the veteran in base running, when balls have been declared foul. On one occasion in particular last year, in a game with the Bostons, Doug started from first base and got nearly to third before Ferguson could stop him, and the ball being foul, of course he was out before he could get back. Allison was a gunner in Fort Sumpter [sic] during the late war, and is the only survivor of three batches of gunners of six men in each batch. His service during the war accounts for his impaired hearing.[14]

Subsequent research by Peter Morris, a member of the Society for American Baseball research (SABR), has cast doubt on whether Allison's regiment actually saw combat duty.

Thomas Jefferson York, whose "affable and courteous demeanor has won him a popularity surpassed by no other of the professional fraternity," was signed to play left field.[15] Everett Mills was the only player from the disastrous 1874 season to return for 1875, retaining his spot at first base.

As a successful businessman, president Bulkeley was accustomed to running a tight ship, and he was determined to erase the embarrassment of the previous year. As soon as his team reported to Hartford, Bulkeley gathered the men together and lectured them on "the necessity of honest and harmo-

The 1875 Dark Blues photographed in Hartford at Isaac White's studio on April 24. The club finished second to Al Spalding's Boston Red Stockings in the final season of the National Association. Top row, left to right: Doug Allison, Tom York, Candy Cummings, Tommy Bond and utility man Bill Harbidge. Bottom row, left to right: Jack Burdock, Everett Mills, Captain Bob Ferguson, Jack Remsen and Tom Carey. This club finished second in the final National Association season (courtesy of Connecticut State Library).

nious work." He further warned that "any trickery or dishonesty on the part of a player would be visited with immediate expulsion ... even if it resulted in the disbanding of the club." He then introduced Ferguson as their captain.[16]

While expecting excellence from his men, Bulkeley reciprocated by increasing the benefits associated with playing for the Dark Blues. He authorized the rental of a suite of rooms on Main Street for the players' use. A billiard table was placed in one room, and the other, filled with all the latest sporting periodicals, was used as a reading and meeting room and could also be used to entertain visiting teams.

Bulkeley remade the club's baseball grounds in state-of-the-art fashion, commissioning acclaimed architect John Mead for the project. The old pavilion behind home plate was replaced by a larger one, 100 by 40 feet, with tiered seating for 800 spectators. It housed twelve rows of numbered seats separated by three aisles extending from front to rear. This covered seating area was reserved for season-ticket holders, who were entitled to the seat whose number was shown on their ticket. The seats were reached by way of a broad staircase leading from the main entrance on Wyllys Street directly into the pavilion. Only two of the eight roof supports were placed close to the field so as not to obstruct the spectators' view. On top of the grandstand was a domed tower where scorers, a telegraph operator, and one reporter from each city newspaper could sit. Capping the tower was a flagpole from which the national colors proudly flew. Underneath the pavilion were two large club rooms for use by the Dark Blues and the visiting club.[17] The third-base side had a single bleacher area holding 1,500 people. The first-base side had a pair of sections, each capable of seating 1,000 spectators. The total seating capacity of the revamped grounds was about 4,300.

Other improvements to the grounds included an enlargement of the left-center field portion of the enclosure to include "the triangular piece of ground included in their lease, but which was not fenced in, and this new ground will be allotted to carriages." In addition, Bulkeley ordered wood to be installed over the troublesome brook into which the seats collapsed in 1874. The wood was then covered with good soil and grass to make a solid right field. Beautifully tiled washrooms, featuring running water and a service attendant, were erected behind the first-base bleachers.[18]

In 1923, veteran baseball umpire and Hartford resident Charley Daniels, one of the original National Association and National League umpires, remembered the grounds this way: "The Hartford baseball field at Colt's Meadow was then the finest in America — as fine as will be found in the present days. The playing field was a great diamond as smooth as a billiard table. At the time it was the largest ball field in the country. The field was so spacious ground rules were unnecessary.... Harry Wright said to me once that if the field was in Boston, he'd be willing to pay $200,000 for it."[19]

With all the positive changes in Hartford, optimism abounded. Ferguson was so giddy with the retooled roster he promised that Hartford would beat Harry Wright's Red Stockings in at least half their games. Vice President Corbin thought the team could make a successful run at the pennant and offered to be one of ten men to give $50 each to the players if they won the championship. Even the Red Stockings had taken notice of the revitalized Dark Blues. The *Clipper* said, "If Hartford doesn't win the pennant in 1875 it won't be the fault of the managers for not getting the best players. Harry Wright has been looking pale since he heard of the new team."[20]

Chapter 16

The Elm City

Hartford wasn't the only Connecticut city planning for the 1875 National Association season. Preparations were also under way in New Haven, where 24-year-old Willis Arnold, who had played sparingly with the Middletown Mansfields in 1872, was in town trying to spark interest in an "Elm City Nine." New Haven was a natural choice for a professional club, better suited than either Middletown or Hartford. With 51,000 residents, New Haven was Connecticut's largest city and the twenty-fifth largest in the country. Like Middletown and Hartford, New Haven experienced tremendous economic growth during the later half of the nineteenth century. Located on the coast of Long Island Sound, the city possessed natural harbors that made it an excellent transportation center and allowed many local shops to blossom into larger factories. From 1850 to 1900, the number of factories in the city more than quadrupled. New Haven's establishment as an industrial center led to a tenfold increase in population from 10,000 residents in 1830 to 108,000 in 1900.[1] New Haven was also a progressive city, instituting a public tree-planting program which eventually produced a canopy of mature vegetation, including many large elms which led to the nickname "The Elm City."

Arnold proposed to raise $3,100 to organize a first-class professional nine. The *New Haven Register* was cool to the idea, saying, "It remains to be seen what support our citizens will give to the project." That question was at least partially answered when an initial informational meeting was lightly attended. Despite the disappointing turnout, Arnold remained optimistic, and the *Register* now confidently encouraged businessmen to invest, saying, "$3,100 is all that is required to make the project a sure thing, and once under way it cannot fail to prove a profitable investment."[2]

A subsequent meeting in February, at the Tontine Hotel, proved more productive. Arnold provided a thorough explanation of the project and reported on the various players with whom he was in contact. Club officers were elected, and Carlos Smith, who would later become a Connecticut state senator, was chosen president. Julius Tyler, a partner in the well-known Tyler and Frost grocery store on State Street, was elected vice president along with H. L. Bradley. William Ward, who in 1865 helped found the West Haven Horse Rail Road Company, a horse-drawn trolley that ran between West Haven and New Haven, was voted treasurer. Arnold was named manager and corresponding secretary.[3]

Potential sites for the ball grounds were also discussed at this meeting. The main location of interest was a vacant parcel of land on the western side of the city's harbor-front. The Howard Avenue lot was bordered by Spring Street, Cedar Street, and the track of the New York, New Haven and Hartford Railroad. It also had the advantage of being adjacent to the track of the West Haven Horse Railroad. The property owner lived in Philadelphia but traveled to New Haven to negotiate terms and sign the lease.[4]

The first step in assembling the team was to identify a captain. Veteran Jack Chapman, who had gained fame with the renowned Brooklyn Atlantics in the 1860s, was first offered the captaincy, but declined since he had already signed with St. Louis.[5] The club then focused its attention on 27-year-old Charlie Gould. A member of the 1869 Cincinnati Red Stockings, Gould was a lanky first baseman, tall for the era at 6 feet, and nicknamed "Bushel Basket" for his prowess at catching anything thrown his way. He was honored as follows in the Cincinnati Base Ball Club Song of 1869:

> In many a game we have played,
> We've needed a first base,
> But now our opponents will find
> The "basket" in its place.
> And if you think he "muffs" the balls,
> Sent into him red hot,
> You'll soon be fooled by "Charlie Gould,"
> And find he muffs them not.[6]

Gould followed Harry Wright from Cincinnati to Boston in 1871 and had most recently played with Baltimore. He was quiet and workmanlike and sported a prominent goatee. After being contacted by Arnold, Gould replied with a letter stating his terms for accepting the captaincy. Believing the conditions reasonable, the stockholders voted to make Gould an offer, which Charlie accepted a week later. Upon arriving in New Haven with his wife and young daughter, Gould received a congratulatory letter from his old manager Harry Wright, who expressed his hope "that you will succeed in making base ball a permanent institution in New Haven, professionally."[7]

Signing additional ballplayers to complete the team proved much more difficult. With 13 teams preparing to play in the upcoming season, players were in short supply. New Haven's late organization didn't help, as most of the best players were already committed. Several reports in the New Haven press told of various men being signed, only to be denied by the players. Some players were signed on a probationary basis, but were released before the start of the season.[8]

Willis Arnold's biggest headache with engaging players came in the form of Tommy Barlow, the former Hartford shortstop. After missing most of the last two months of the 1874 season, Barlow was attempting a return to baseball, claiming he was in excellent health and never in better condition. In November 1874, Barlow received $75 advance money to return to his hometown Atlantics. Three months later, however, he signed a second contract to play with New Haven. Upon learning that Barlow had first signed with the Atlantics, Arnold visited Brooklyn to question him. Barlow's defense was flimsy and inconsistent, initially stating that his agreement with the Atlantics stipulated that if a more financially stable stock-funded team offered a job, he could accept it. Later, Barlow claimed that the Brooklyn contract was simply a fake intended to prevent him from playing with New Haven. Since the Atlantics contract appeared valid, Arnold cancelled his agreement and stopped payment on the $200 advance check he had given Barlow. Believing the matter could be settled amicably, Arnold did not bring up the case with the National Association's Judiciary Committee, and Barlow started the season with the Atlantics.[9]

By late February, Arnold was finally making headway on assembling a team. The battery would be catcher John "Stud" Bancker and pitcher Fred "Tricky" Nichols. The 24-year-old Nichols, a Bridgeport native, was a happy-go-lucky sort who had found success pitching for his hometown club, The Bridgeport Friendly United Social Base Ball Club, informally known as "The Big Fuss" or "TBs" for short. Nichols did not have a great fastball, but instead relied on "tricking" the batter, reportedly using five different styles of deliveries.[10] Very little is known about Bancker, an amateur player who would be making his major league debut with New Haven. His date and place of birth are unknown.

In addition to Charlie Gould at first base, the infield would consist of Billy Geer, a 25-year-old utility player from New York who could play either outfield or infield. The extent of his major league experience consisted of two games with the Mutuals at the end of the 1874 season.

John "Mac" McKelvey of Rochester, New York, was signed after Arnold received a letter of recommendation from his team, the amateur Rochester Alerts. Mac was a veteran player, only a few days younger than Gould. He had made a name for himself with the Alerts with several spectacular defensive plays against the famous 1869 Cincinnati club.[11]

Anchoring the infield at shortstop was Sammy Wright, the 26-year-old,

Harry and George's younger brother. Harry believed Sammy had an abundance of talent, saying, "When boys, Sam's fielding always pleased me better than George's. He was more earnest and persevering, and time and again I have seen him take balls that George would shirk." The *New York Clipper* agreed, saying he would "undoubtedly become as famous as his two brothers."[12]

The outfield included speedy Jim Tipper, playing for his third Connecticut team, and two Philadelphia natives, 18-year-old Henry Luff, a solidly built player at 5'11" and 175 pounds, and 21-year-old Johnny Ryan, who had played with Baltimore the previous year. Ryan was a good fielder, having set the league record for outfield putouts in a game with 12, but was a weak hitter, batting only .192 for Baltimore.[13]

Once players were signed, the next chore was actually getting them to New Haven. Arnold instructed all players to report by March 22, but a week after that deadline only six were on hand. Finally, exactly nine players, no substitutes, arrived in town. Their preseason workouts, held in the recently opened New Haven gymnasium, consisted of "each man run[ning] a quarter of a mile, then gentle exercise upon the horizontal bar is taken, after which a trial at vaulting on the vaulting horse is indulged, then a series of Indian Club swinging, followed by the whole team pulling about one mile on the rowing apparatus. After all this, the club retires to a bowling alley where they pass and strike balls."[14]

Preparation of the Howard Avenue grounds wasn't going much better. Despite reports in February of the imminent awarding of contracts for refreshments, construction of the grandstand, and advertising rights for the fence boards on Howard Avenue, none had been signed by mid–March. New Haven's sale of advertising rights for the fence may have been a first in baseball, although it is unclear if the ads were meant to appear on the inside of the fence facing the playing field or on the outside facing Howard Avenue. This was one of several ways by which New Haven club officers hoped to diversify revenue streams. They were also investigating renting the grounds for activities other than baseball and considering putting a quarter-mile track around the outside of the diamond to be used for horse races.[15]

The bases for the diamond were laid out and the grounds enclosed. The entire enclosure measured 549' on Howard Avenue, 530' on Spring Street, 305' on Cedar Street, and 597' along the tracks of the New York, New Haven and Hartford Railroad. The main entrance was on Spring Street, while the exit gate was on Howard Avenue. Western Union built a telegraph station on the grounds to send inning-by-inning scores to businesses in New Haven and other cities. Despite this progress, with little more than a week before the season, the playing field was still uneven and rough and in need of immediate attention. Unfortunately, all of the club's funds had reportedly been exhausted.[16]

At the same time, the development of the Elm City Nine hit another snag when Willis Arnold suddenly announced his resignation. The trouble may have been inadvertently precipitated by Harry Wright's earlier congratulatory letter to Charlie Gould. In addition to sending his best wishes, Wright also suggested that Gould bring the New Havens to Boston early in the season.[17]

It appears that when Gould offered this idea, Willis Arnold rejected it, having already announced that New Haven would start the season with three games against the Philadelphia clubs, prior to meeting Hartford on May 3. Arnold wanted the inexperienced New Haven club to start off against easier competition. He believed that playing Boston and other strong clubs would only result in embarrassing defeats. These lopsided losses would then hamper future gate receipts, since New Haven residents would not want to be associated with a losing concern. The club officers disagreed and backed Gould. Arnold then resigned, surrendering his $1,200 salary, and returned to Middletown to play ball with an amateur club. Gould was named his successor as the club's business manager.[18]

Arnold denied that he had resigned due to these scheduling issues, but didn't specify why he had. "My reason for resigning," he said in a letter to the *New Haven Register*, "was because the best interests of the club could be served by my doing so.... The feeling between the officers and myself is the pleasantest, and they are fully competent to perform all duties devolving upon them."[19]

The evidence suggests otherwise, as three weeks later New Haven was opening the season with a home-and-home series with the Red Stockings. Perhaps worried that New Haven would back out, Wright advised Gould, "You are advertised here for the 19th and you must not fail to come. It is a holiday and we are certain of a very large crowd."[20]

The organization of the New Havens had not gone as smoothly as planned. Their founder and business manager was gone, they only had signed the bare minimum of nine players, and their home field was in no condition to host games. The *Register* delicately assessed the prospects for the upcoming season, saying, "New Haven has her nine, but it is yet in its infancy and we have to see what it will do ere we pass further criticism. One could hardly hope that the pennant should be with us next year...." Hartford captain Bob Ferguson wasn't so cautious though, quickly dismissing any pennant aspirations the New Haven club might entertain, saying, "The stockholders will probably have the pleasure of seeing the name of their club at the foot of the list, at the close of the season.... Pleasant prospect for 'em, isn't it?"[21]

Chapter 17

A Hard Rub

With their new schedule, New Haven had the honor of kicking off the 1875 National Association campaign, playing in Boston two days before any other National Association team took the field. New Haven was one of six new entries in the thirteen-team Association. There were two new teams in St. Louis, the Red Stockings and Brown Stockings, a third team in Philadelphia, the Centennials, the Washington Nationals, and the Westerns of Keokuk, Iowa.

The opening game was played on "Centennial Day" in Boston, a date commemorating the 100th anniversary of the initial battles of the Revolutionary War at Lexington and Concord. Today, these events are honored with a Massachusetts state holiday called "Patriot's Day." Since the early 1900s, the Patriot's Day celebration has included a morning home game for the Red Sox and the running of the Boston marathon.[1]

Since the Elm City club still consisted of the minimum nine players, they were obliged to bring along Lester Dole, the instructor in the gymnasium where the New Havens had been training, as a substitute.[2]

Prior to the game, the Red Stockings raised the 1875 championship pennant. Once the festivities were complete, New Haven took the field in their white flannel uniforms with "New Haven" stitched in blue on the chest and white and blue checked socks.[3] The starting lineup was

    Geer 2B
    Wright SS
    Luff RF
    Bancker C
    McKelvey 3B
    Gould 1B
    Ryan LF
    Tipper CF
    Nichols P

Tricky Nichols and Al Spalding squared off in the box, trading blanks in the first inning. In the second inning, Boston plated four runs with the help of a critical wild pitch by Nichols. Despite this mistake, Nichols pitched well, and with the help of excellent defense by Jim Tipper in center field, the game remained close. Boston added single runs in the third and fifth innings while New Haven could do nothing with the bat. The final score was a surprisingly close 6–0. The *New Haven Register* was pleased with the result and made certain to mention that the previous year Hartford had traveled to Boston early in the season and was crushed, 25–3.[4]

Two days later, the teams played a return match in New Haven. Boston arrived in New Haven on the 1:45 train and went directly to lunch at the Tontine Hotel. They wolfed down their meal and rushed to Hamilton Park for the 3 P.M. game. The teams were forced to play at Hamilton Park because, as Harry Wright had feared, the Howard Avenue Grounds were still not ready. Earlier in April, while attempting to arrange the opening games with New Haven, Wright voiced concerned about the lack of progress on New Haven's field, asking, "Will it not pay you to hurry up the preparation of your grounds?"[5] Despite these concerns, Hamilton Park was a reasonable substitute. For many years, Yale played its biggest games there. The forty-acre facility featured picnic areas, provisions for exhibits, ice skating in season, and a race track encircling two large baseball fields. The ball fields stood in the shadows of the steep rocky ledges known as West Rock.

Perhaps due to their late arrival, Boston started slowly, spotting New Haven two runs in the first inning on Henry Luff's double. Boston failed to score in the first two innings, but once warmed up, they rolled to a 14–3 victory.[6]

Three days later, the Howard Avenue Grounds hosted their first game, as New Haven defeated Yale, 15–5. The playing field was in shape, but neither the 1,000-seat grandstand nor the bleachers had been built. Fortunately, the fence was solid and high enough to thwart the attempts of several young boys who tried to climb over to get into the game for free. Seeing there was no chance of going over the fence, a number of the enterprising youths tried to burrow *under* the fence until they were stopped by police. Others watched the game for free from the trees that grew on the eastern boundary of the field along Cedar Street. Spectators also crowded the balconies on the residences on the opposite side of Spring Street to the north.[7]

A few days later, New Haven played its first National Association game at the Howard Avenue Grounds against the Brooklyn Atlantics. Prior to the game, the Atlantics insisted that Charley Daniels of Hartford serve as umpire. Daniels was an experienced arbiter who would later become one of the original National League umpires, commencing a long, distinguished career.

17. A Hard Rub   121

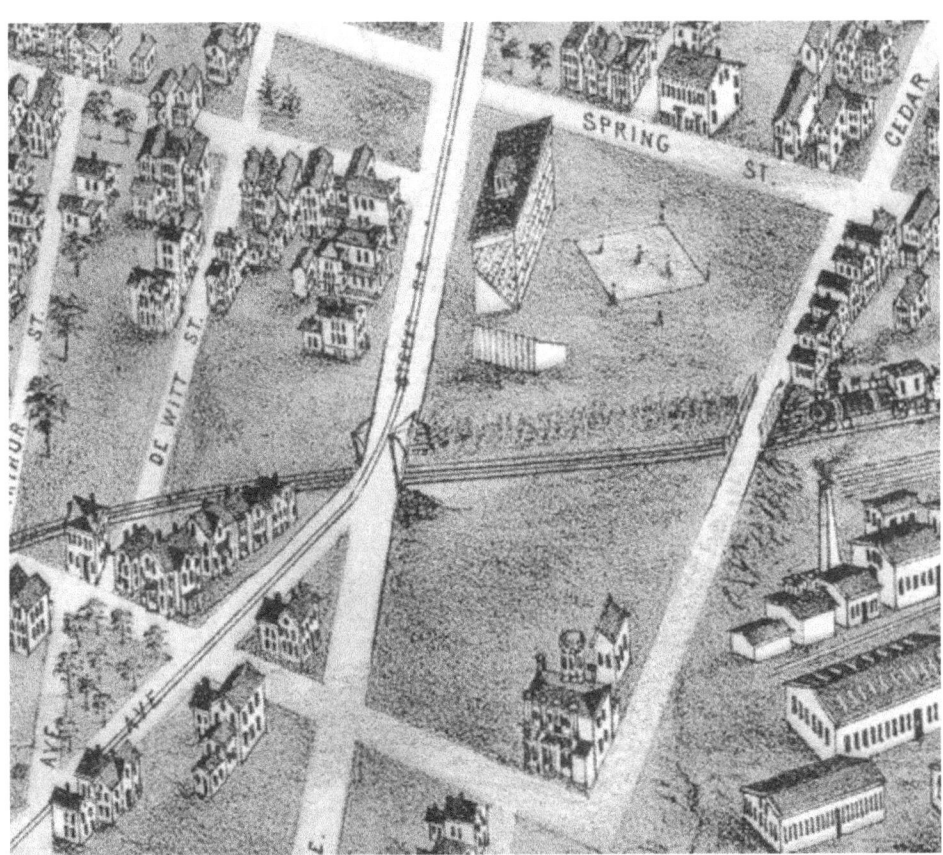

New Haven's Howard Avenue Grounds shown in bird's-eye view drawing, 1879. The New Haven Elm City club may have been one of the first to sell advertising rights for the baseball field's fence, although it is unclear if the ads were meant to appear on the inside of the fence facing the playing field or on the outside facing Howard Avenue. This was one of several ways by which New Haven club officers hoped to diversify revenue streams. They were also investigating renting the grounds for activities other than baseball and considering putting a quarter-mile track around the outside of the diamond to be used for horse races (Library of Congress).

Despite his obvious qualifications, New Haven was reluctant to let a Hartford man officiate their game. They finally relented, however, and the game began with five scoreless innings. The two teams entered the ninth inning tied at two. Two questionable fair-foul calls by Daniels gave the Atlantics the deciding run in their 3–2 victory and enraged the New Haven crowd. Apparently unaware of how horrendous the Atlantics would eventually prove to be (they would win only two games all year, both against New Haven, and lose their final 31 games of the season), the *Register* felt New Haven's performance showed they could compete for the championship.[8]

Meanwhile, in Hartford, the most pressing task facing Captain Ferguson was choosing a starting pitcher from his two aces. He chose to make the veteran 27-year-old Cummings his regular pitcher and play young Tommy Bond in right field. In their first game, Hartford's revamped nine met Ferguson's previous club, the Brooklyn Atlantics. Hartford scored three times in the first inning, but the Atlantics responded with three runs of their own, helped by former Dark Blue Bill Boyd's double. Trailing 5–3, Hartford fought back with three runs in the eighth, the final two scoring on Ev Mills' base hit. The crowd, who had thought the game lost, became ecstatic. Cummings set the Atlantics down in order in the ninth to complete the 6–5 victory.[9]

Next came the game that all of Connecticut had been waiting for, the first match between two major league teams from the state. Hartford was 3–0, with easy wins against the Atlantics and Centennials after their opening-day victory. The victory over the Centennials was later marred by complaints that Hartford had ignored the rule requiring round bats and "played a trick ... by using bats which had been made flat on one side and they were painted black to hide the change."[10] In contrast to Hartford's unblemished start, New Haven was winless in four tries.

The excitement of the first meeting of major league clubs from Connecticut was heightened by a lingering resentment between the two cities. The bitterness stemmed from their recent battle to become Connecticut's sole capital city. Since the 1660s, Hartford and New Haven had alternated as the capital, with the General Assembly sitting in each city every second year. By the mid-nineteenth century, the cumbersome logistics of such an arrangement precipitated a decision to name one city as the permanent capital. The matter was complicated when neither city wanted to relinquish the honor. In 1873, Connecticut voters declared Hartford the winner with 37,000 votes to 31,000 for a disappointed New Haven.

Hartford residents often needled New Haveners that the capital now resided in Hartford. New Haven's earlier reluctance to allow Charley Daniels to umpire their game gave the *Hartford Post* an opportunity to tweak New Haven, saying, "Queer town that New Haven, having lost the semi-capital, it don't even want a Hartford umpire at her base ball matches."[11]

Nearly 5,000 spectators, including many ladies, came to the Hartford Base Ball Grounds, believing their Blues would have an easy time of it. Hartford won the coin toss and sent New Haven to bat first. Despite a base hit by John McKelvey, New Haven did not score. Nichols kept the partisan Hartford crowd quiet by blanking Hartford in the first two innings. In the third inning, Hartford scored three runs on hits by Tom Carey and Ev Mills.

17. A Hard Rub

Trailing 3–0, New Haven bounced back in the sixth inning. Nichols and McKelvey singled, and then Billy Geer lofted a short fly ball to center field. Either one of the two Jacks, Remsen or Burdock, could have made the catch, but poor communication allowed the ball to drop safely to the ground. Remsen retrieved the ball and fired it to Candy Cummings, but Ferguson told the pitcher to let it go. Hartford wasn't able to retrieve the ball until Geer had circled the bases and tied the score at three. New Haven kept the momentum in the bottom of the sixth, holding Hartford scoreless with the aid of the game's only double play. The Elm City club was done scoring for the day, however, and loose fielding in the last two innings allowed Hartford to score three runs and escape with a 6–3 victory. Connecticut baseball fans could not stop talking about the surprisingly "hard rub" that New Haven had given Hartford.[12]

Chapter 18

Opposite Directions

After their first meeting, Hartford and New Haven continued to go in opposite directions. New Haven lost two straight to the Philadelphia White Stockings, 3–2 and 13–0, followed by a tough 2–1 loss to the Mutuals in eleven innings. The hapless Washington Nationals then came to town for a pair of games. New Haven citizens expected their club to register its first victory against the Nationals, who were simply awful. Washington had lost its first eleven games, allowing an astounding 20 runs or more in six of them. Washington was so bad that it was rumored they would disband after their games in New Haven.[1]

The New Haven crowd became boisterous when the home team scored twice in the first inning, but the local fans were quickly silenced when Washington responded with five runs of their own on the way to a surprising 8–4 victory. Two days later, New Haven's sloppy play gave Washington its second victory, 10–7.[2]

With only nine players on the roster, New Haven had no flexibility to accommodate the injuries that were so common at this time. Tim Murnane once recalled that in the days before fielding gloves, injuries were so common that arnica, a liniment rub meant to soothe aching muscles and reduce swelling, was the ballplayer's best friend. As a result of their lack of manpower, any serious injury forced New Haven to seek a replacement player. They often turned to Tricky Nichols's former club, the Bridgeport TBs, for assistance. The TBs were a strong amateur club that defeated the Washington Nationals after the Nationals had defeated the professional Elm City club.[3]

The need for a replacement player first arose in the fourth game of the season against the Philadelphia Centennials. With Sammy Wright out, New Haven turned to a player named Booth to play shortstop. Two weeks later, New Haven was obliged to use another substitute, as a man named Sullivan, from Bristol, Rhode Island, played the outfield in the first two games against the Nationals. Sullivan made the most of his only two career games, producing three hits in eight at-bats. In the second Washington game, New Haven also used 17-year-old catcher Jim Keenan, a New Haven native, who would play five games for New Haven in 1875. Keenan would later play ten years in the major leagues.

The next short-term substitute to don a New Haven uniform was Rit Harrison, who played his only major league game on May 20 against the Athletics. The next day found another new player on the field, a man named John Smith, who filled in at second base. A week later, Lester Dole, the gym instructor, made his only major league appearance, stroking two hits in four at bats against Bobby Mathews and the Mutuals. A few days later, a player named Evans duplicated the feat, going two for four in his only career game. Most of the replacements played well in limited action and probably should have been given more of a chance.

New Haven native Jim Keenan served as a replacement player in five games for the New Haven Elm City club in 1875. He batted a measly .077 that year, but later played several seasons for Cincinnati in the American Association (Library of Congress).

Desperate for a permanent extra player, New Haven turned to Tommy Barlow, who wasn't meeting the Atlantics' expectations in Brooklyn. It had been thought that he would be the Atlantics' starting catcher, but by May he hadn't appeared in any games and was reduced to umpiring, while weak-hitting Jake Knowdell caught. The catching-poor Atlantics used six different receivers during the year, none of them Barlow. This, coupled with the *Brooklyn Eagle's* mid-season report that his "physique had been materially weakened by his Winter's illness," indicates Barlow was continuing to have health problems. Barlow didn't meet expectations in New Haven either, as he played just one game at shortstop before returning to the Atlantics, for whom he played a single game at the end of July. Sadly, this was Barlow's last major league appearance.[4]

While New Haven was struggling to field a team, Hartford kept winning, easily taking their first dozen games. Most of the credit for Hartford's fast start was assigned to Bob Ferguson. His oft-repeated admonition, "Have a care boys!" was being heeded by his men. The *Courant* said, "Captain Ferguson is a master at coaching the team and to him and his headwork much credit is due." The *Clipper* chimed in, "The strict discipline observed on the field will win games and may bring the pennant to Hartford." Local citizens were fully behind the team and its leader. One novelty item being sold about town was a new brand of cigars called the "Captain Bob," with a picture of Ferguson on the cigar box label.[5]

With their club's undefeated start, Hartford enthusiasts were stricken with baseball fever and eagerly awaited their first battle with the Red Stockings. This is what the team had been built for, to finally snatch the pennant from the mighty Red Stockings, champions three years running. The day before the highly anticipated meeting, fans gathered around the bulletin boards outside the city newspaper offices for word on the Boston and Hartford scores. When Boston's easy 12–0 victory over the Athletics was announced, a hush fell over the crowd. The silence quickly turned to loud cheers when Hartford's 5–0 shutout of the Atlantics was posted.[6] The stage was now set for the May 18 heavyweight match between the 12–0 Dark Blues and the 16–0 Red Stockings.

The meeting between the two undefeated opponents would take place in Hartford, thanks to Ben Douglas. Since the National Association had never instituted a pre-determined league schedule, the date and location of the game was open to negotiation. Harry Wright wanted to play in Boston. Douglas felt the game should be in Hartford, since the clubs' first match in 1874 was played in Boston. When Douglas informed the venerable Wright of his position, he received a stinging reply:

> As the champion club we consider ourselves entitled to the first game of the series on our grounds. This has been conceded by all the clubs without dispute.... In arranging with you we were willing, as friends and neighbors, to comply could we mutually agree on dates, but we did not expect that it would be compulsory for us to accept dates named by you under the plea that they were "the only ones left." If that is the case they must certainly be of great value to you, particularly so when they "are being rapidly taken up." We would be sorry to deprive you of the "last of the lot" to replete our stock, nor will we be compelled to accept remnants.[7]

Douglas held firm, and when the big day arrived, fans from all over New England and New York arrived in Hartford, not Boston. A holiday atmosphere prevailed in the city. Nearly every business in the city displayed a team photo of Ferguson's men, and conversation focused on the impending battle.

Many local factories, including Colt's, closed shop early to give their employees the rare opportunity to watch a game. The enthusiasm even reached the state capitol, where the match was discussed as much as legislation, and the House and Senate adjourned early so as not to miss the contest.[8]

Shortly after noon, the streets of Hartford were deserted, as those who had tickets, and many who did not, headed for the ballpark. By 2 P.M., every general admission seat was occupied. Those too late to find seats stood in the outfield and squeezed into foul territory between the bleacher sections and the grandstand. The standing crowd was corralled behind long lengths of rope, but as the mass of humanity increased, there was no hope that the skimpy ropes would keep the crowd back. Scores of fans spilled onto the playing field while an overmatched police squad futilely attempted to push them back. The officers enlisted the help of the men guarding the fence to make sure no one sneaked into the game. This was a mistake. As soon as the guards deserted their posts, scores of boys immediately scrambled over the untended barrier, making the crush of spectators even worse. The sea of 12,000 rooters was reportedly the largest crowd ever in New England. They weren't all supporters of the Dark Blues, as over 200 men had made the trip from Boston to see their club defend the championship.[9]

Polite applause greeted the ballplayers when they began arriving on the field. The last to enter was Captain Ferguson, and the Hartford crowd welcomed him with a tremendous roar. The throng was especially partisan this day, knowing that Spalding had earlier belittled their hometown club. In a preseason newspaper interview regarding the upcoming pennant race, Spalding acknowledged that Hartford had an excellent collection of talent, yet the pitcher dismissed their chances of taking the pennant from his Boston team, saying, "They are an unruly set of fellows. They want more of the qualities which carry us on to glory every year. I mean brains...."[10]

The team captains met for the coin toss, which Boston called correctly, sending Hartford's leadoff hitter Doug Allison to bat. Allison selected one of Spalding's offerings and looped what looked to be a sure base hit over second base. Ross Barnes had other ideas, however, and to the chagrin of the huge crowd, Boston's speedy second basemen made a fine running catch. Jack Burdock aroused the crowd with a clean single to center, but the joy was short-lived, as he was immediately cut down attempting to steal second. Tom Carey followed with another base hit, but he was quickly retired after failing to return promptly to his base after a foul ball. In 1876, a foul ball became live again when it was returned to the pitcher's hands. If a runner had not returned to his base by that time, he could be put out.[11]

Hartford then sent Cummings and his "terrible parabolic curves" to the box. George Wright found one not so terrible and stroked a single. Barnes then launched a long drive to right field, and the assembly held its collective breath. An audible sigh of relief followed when Bond hauled in the well-struck ball. Connecticut's own Jim O'Rourke followed with a single. Cummings then retired Andy Leonard on a comebacker to the box. It appeared the game would remain scoreless when Cal McVey tapped an easy grounder to Carey. The smooth-fielding shortstop gathered the ball in cleanly and fired straight and true across the diamond to Ev Mills. The crowd cheered when the first baseman caught the ball, knowing the side was retired. But before the last "hurrah" had expired, Spalding was on the diamond, claiming that Mills had not touched first base. "Helping" the umpire was nothing new for the Boston club. Their champion status and Harry Wright's extensive knowledge of the rules often allowed them to intimidate an unsure umpire. Sure enough, umpire Alphonse Martin, a former pitcher known as "Old Slow Ball" in his playing days, reversed his decision and ruled McVey safe. The huge Hartford crowd loudly let Martin know what they thought of his decision. It was never good policy to give the powerful Red Stockings extra outs, and this occasion was no exception. Spalding followed with a base hit, plating two more runs and giving Boston a 3–0 lead.[12]

Two innings later, Hartford fans had more reason to harass "Old Slow Ball." Andy Leonard made an infield hit which scored Ross Barnes and advanced Jim O'Rourke to third. During the play, Martin quietly called time out and then just as quietly called time back in. Unfortunately, no one, including O'Rourke, heard him. Martin ruled O'Rourke out for failing to retouch second after time had been called. Spalding immediately reappeared on the field. Martin seemed to welcome his assistance, and the two men spent fifteen torturous minutes thumbing through the rulebook while the impatient Hartford crowd shouted, "Read it out loud!" and "Pass it around and let us all read it!" In the end, Martin let O'Rourke re-occupy second base as if nothing had happened. The mood in the stands turned ugly, especially when Cal McVey singled to center, scoring O'Rourke and giving the champs a 5–0 lead.[13]

The protracted dispute seemed to rouse the "never say die" Dark Blues. Doug Allison led off the fourth inning with a single. Burdock then sent a slow grounder to third. Jim O'Rourke fielded it cleanly, but his throw to second flew wildly into right field. This miscue left runners on second and third with nobody out and the crowd thirsty for blood. Carey popped out, but Cummings broke the shutout by scoring Allison with a long flyball. Although two were now out, Hartford was far from done. Tom York singled in Burdock and took second on a passed ball. Bob Ferguson scored York with a base hit, and Remsen reached on another Boston error. Ev Mills then made up for his earlier miscue with a single over George Wright's head, driving in his two mates and knotting the score at five. As Remsen crossed the plate with the tying run, the crowd was delirious, as men tossed their hats in the air, women waved handkerchiefs, and young boys jumped about and shouted wildly.[14]

The score remained tied until Boston added a pair of runs in the seventh inning. Spalding had no trouble holding the lead, and when Hartford was retired in the top of the ninth, the vast crowd streamed onto the field despite the best efforts of the police. Once the field was cleared, Boston added three superfluous runs to make the final result 10–5.[15]

Although many in Hartford wanted to blame the loss on the umpire, the *Hartford Courant* said the Blues lacked the coolness which had heretofore marked their play. Ev Mills, who luckily was "especially jolly under trying circumstances," came in for some sharp criticism. "Mills ... lost the game, giving the Bostons their three runs in the first inning, by his stupidity, rather than carelessness.... He is the weak spot in the nine, and should try and improve his play...."[16]

Two days later, one of the game's spectators placed the following advertisement in the *Hartford Courant*:

> TWO HUNDRED AND FIVE DOLLARS REWARD — At the great base ball match on Tuesday, while I engaged in hurrahing, a small boy walked off with an English-made brown silk UMBRELLA belonging to me and forgot to bring it back. I will pay $5 for the return of the umbrella in good condition to my house on Farmington Avenue. I do not want the boy (in an active state) but will pay two hundred dollars for his remains. SAMUEL L. CLEMENS[17]

Clemens, also known as Mark Twain, enjoyed the game of baseball and later called it "the very symbol, the outward and visible expression of the drive and push and rush and struggle of the raging, tearing, booming nineteenth century."[18] He was accompanied to the game by his close friend Reverend Joseph Twichell, pastor of the Asylum Hill Congregational Church. "Preachers are always pleasant company when they are off duty," wrote Twain. It may have seemed a bit odd that Twain carried an umbrella to the ballpark on a clear, mild day. But Twain never trusted New England weather. "Yes, one of the brightest gems in the New England weather is the dazzling uncertainty of it. There is only one certain thing about it. You are certain there is going to be plenty of it — a perfect grand review. But you can never tell which end of the procession is going to move first. You fix up for the drought, you leave your umbrella in the house and sally out, and two to one you get drowned."[19]

Twain's humorous ad reportedly backfired on him when a local medical student had some fun at his expense. The imaginative student left one of his case studies — the corpse of a boy — on Twain's porch, along with a note claiming the reward money. A nervous Twain was concerned that he'd be suspected of murder, until the janitor of the medical college came to claim the subject and clear the author's name. The *Hartford Courant* dismissed these reports as absurd (also see additional source for note 20 in the notes).[20]

That evening, the Dark Blues and Red Stockings boarded the same train bound for Boston and a rematch the next day. One can only imagine the feelings of the beaten Hartford players as they watched the scene unfold. After news of the Red Stockings' victory reached Boston, the team's headquarters was besieged by fans who were "nearly frantic with delight." On the train, the ballplayers got wind of the impending celebration and remained alert for the first signs of a welcome. Around 10 P.M., about 400 revelers, including a 20-piece German band, marched to the train station to greet their conquering heroes. The Red Stockings disembarked to loud cheers while the band serenaded them with "Hail to the Chief." The crowd escorted the team back to its headquarters. Leading the way was the band, followed by 50 men carrying brooms as if they were rifles, with hundreds more bringing up the rear. The two teams remained at the club rooms, recounting the game, then went to Grieves' Hotel, where a large banquet was served. Complimentary toasts were given by each team to the other before the men adjourned for the night.[21]

The Blues had their chance to exact swift revenge against the Red Stockings the very next day. Six thousand Bostonians crowded the field, eager to see first-hand a repeat of the previous day's result. So many were present that the start of the game was delayed to allow the overflow crowd to purchase tickets and enter the grounds. The game was tight for five innings, and the score stood 3–2 in favor of Boston. The last four innings were a completely different story. Hartford batters couldn't touch Spalding, while Boston scored ten times against Cummings, to win going away, 13–2.[22] The demoralized Dark Blues returned home — their season in disarray. Two short days earlier, they were a confident, undefeated bunch. Now, the Red Stockings had abruptly laid bare their weaknesses and, at least for the moment, doused their championship aspirations.

Chapter 19

An Infernal Set of Asses

With losses in their first dozen games, the New Havens appeared determined to prove Bob Ferguson's prediction of a last-place finish correct. The club took to the road in search of its first victory. The quest was made more difficult due to the absence of Tricky Nichols, who had broken a finger in the last game before the trip, and Sammy Wright, who was also injured. As a result, New Haven was forced to travel with four replacement players — Jim Keenan, Tommy Barlow, Lester Dole, and a new pitcher named Perroy — plus the seven healthy regulars.[1]

The first stop was New York, where they would meet the Atlantics, whose only win had come against New Haven. Charlie Gould chose to use Henry Luff in the box instead of the new man Perroy. This proved to be a bad choice, as the Atlantics' woeful offense scored twice as many runs as it would in any other game all season, in a 14–4 victory. In the next game, an 8–5 loss to the Mutuals, Johnny Ryan pitched. Perroy would never get a chance to play in the major leagues, as Luff and Ryan shared the pitching duties on the trip.

While on the road, the New Havens took the opportunity to add several players to their roster. On May 24, the new Philadelphia Centennials, finding it impossible to sustain themselves in a city with three major league teams, became the first of four National Association teams to disband. New Haven signed two of the former Centennials, 22-year-old rookie second baseman Ed Somerville and rookie catcher Tim McGinley. Neither was much of a hitter, both having batted about .230 for Philadelphia. This was better than the players they would be replacing, though, as Sammy Wright finished the year at .189, while Stud Bancker hit a minuscule .153.[2]

New Haven also signed stocky first baseman George "Jumbo" Latham, who had just been released by Boston. Latham was a 22-year-old rookie from Utica, New York, who also answered to "Juice," a nickname hung on him for his lack of speed on the basepaths. Prior to the season, Latham had boldly written to Harry Wright looking for a job with the Red Stockings. Wright admitted he was interested but cautioned Latham, saying, "You must remember you are unknown to the club either personally or by reputation, and that when I saw last you were not able to run, although in all other respects I was favorably impressed with your playing." After some negotiation, Latham signed a three-year deal worth $560 for 1875 and $800 for each of the next two seasons. At a time when contracts were typically for one year, Boston pioneered the three-year deal. These were not like the guaranteed contracts today's players receive, but instead were renewed on an annual basis at the discretion of the club. Still unsure about Latham, Wright made the first year of the contract contingent upon a three-month probationary period during which Latham needed to demonstrate "continued good play, condition and conduct."[3]

Latham later recalled that when he arrived in Boston, he was cocky. "I thought I knew the game. After I had been training with Spalding for awhile I found there was a little more to it than I thought." Although he had been a second baseman in Utica, Latham began the season as Boston's first baseman. Unfortunately, his playing time decreased after his batting and fielding proved mediocre at best. As the probationary period drew to a close, Boston terminated Latham's contract, allowing him to sign with New Haven, a move which Latham recalled left him "plumb tickled."[4]

New Haven then played three straight games with the Nationals, who still hadn't beaten a league team other than the Elm City club. In the first game, New Haven trailed 11–10 in the bottom of the ninth when Charlie Gould suddenly began to complain that Bill Parks's pitching was illegal. The umpire disagreed, saying his pitching was no different than in the earlier innings. Gould refused to play if Parks continued to pitch. When the umpire failed to relent, Gould took his players off the field, and the umpire awarded a 9–0 forfeit victory to Washington.[5]

Finally, after 15 straight losses, New Haven recorded its first victory of the season, beating Washington 9–2 on the final day of May. The next day, New Haven nearly made it two victories in a row, but narrowly lost to the Nationals, 8–7.

Hoping to build on this bit of momentum, New Haven traveled to Philadelphia for three games. Unfortunately, there was no carry-over effect, and they were crushed in all three games by an average margin of 12 runs. After the final loss, the *Brooklyn Eagle* commented, "The New Haven nine is not well managed apparently. Thus far it has been a more experimental team, and hence its losses."[6]

Another sportswriter wasn't so kind. After the Philadelphia Centennials had disbanded, this journalist declared, "There will be a shout of joy among the base-ball reporters, if in no other quarter, when the Atlantic, the New

Haven, and the Washington nines follow the example just set them by the Centennials. The general public have long since ceased going to witness a game in which either of these clubs participate, but the unfortunate base-ball reporter must go to their games so that he can tell the public the next morning what an infernal set of asses they are."[7]

The disgruntled reporter continued, "In all probability you of the west will not be tortured by the presence of any of this small fry this season, for none of them will ever get money enough together to pay their car fare ... however I understand there is a movement on foot in this section to raise sufficient money by subscription to pay the Atlantics' passage out west," those donating certain that once out west the Atlantics would never be able to get back and they'd be rid of "an unmitigated nuisance."[8]

Upon returning from the trip with one win in eight tries, New Haven met Hartford for three games. Hartford wasn't playing quite as well as they had at the start of the year, losing nearly half their games since winning their first dozen, leaving their record at 19–5. Despite winning nearly 80 percent of the time, the Dark Blues were quickly gaining a well-deserved reputation for bickering and complaining, or "growling," in the nineteenth-century vernacular. Bob Ferguson had surely improved discipline, but his overbearing ways were becoming divisive. As the losses mounted, he found it increasingly difficult to keep his temper in check. Should someone on the nine dare to make an error, "Fergu-

Burdock joined the Hartford Dark Blues for the 1875 season. Henry Chadwick called him the "model fielder in the country." He led all second basemen in putouts for five consecutive seasons from 1876 to 1880. Later in his career, Burdock suffered injuries and began drinking, earning himself the nickname "Black Jack." Despite his difficulties with alcohol, Burdock had a long, productive career. Only three players from the first National League season, Cap Anson, Jim O'Rourke, and Paul Hines, had longer careers. He is shown here on an 1887 tobacco card when he played for the Boston Nationals (Library of Congress).

son [would] swear until everything looks blue." He was particularly rough on Jack Burdock. On one occasion "he yelled out at Burdock that if he [Burdock] did not shut his mouth he [Ferguson] would mash it for him. Another time he was going to ram his fist down Burdock's throat, and so expressed himself before several thousand people."[9]

Some players were afraid to resist the captain's heavy-handed approach, but Tom Carey, Jack Remsen, Jack Burdock, and Arthur Cummings refused to comply. Whenever they found themselves the subject of their captain's bullying, Carey and Remsen would not hesitate to yell back. Burdock and Cummings, on the other hand, would get mad and sulk. Sometimes they would retaliate by feigning sickness and playing half-heartedly or not at all.[10]

The growling in Hartford was so bad that the supporters of the Dark Blues joined in, even when their club was 14–2. The fans' constant complaining infuriated John Belden, the sports editor of the *Hartford Times*. This was the same John Belden who had given the Charter Oaks the championship bat a decade earlier. Belden wrote that the club's 14–2 record "ought to satisfy any reasonable being, and we presume that it does. But the two lost games give the handful of 'croakers' an opportunity to talk, and the way they croak and caw would put a crow convention to shame. These unreasonable fellows ought to drop baseball and join a croakquet club." Belden accused the croakers of demoralizing the club with their criticism and by spreading false rumors, like Ferguson was going to resign, or Bond was angry because he wasn't called upon to pitch, or Cummings was mad because he had to pitch. "Give the boys a fair show," Belden concluded, "and they will give a good account of themselves. *Stop Croaking!*"[11]

Against this backdrop, the Hartfords traveled to New Haven, where 1,500 spectators, the largest crowd yet in New Haven, gathered to witness the match. Despite their club's poor record, many New Haven residents were optimistic about their chances because of the "hot fight" they had given Hartford in their first meeting and New Haven's new players.[12]

Although it had been hoped that Tricky Nichols would be ready to pitch against Hartford, his finger still wasn't completely healed, so New Haven was obliged to continue using Luff. Luff's new curveball wasn't fooling anyone this day, as the Dark Blues batted the ball all over the lot. New Haven managed only five hits, two by the recently acquired Ed Somerville, as they went down weakly 12–0. The ease of the victory and New Haven's utter lack of offense exasperated the city's residents.[13]

The next day, the two teams met again, this time in Providence, Rhode Island, at the newly opened grounds on Adelaide Avenue. Johnny Ryan took to the box in place of Luff, and the move paid off as Ryan held Hartford to just two hits. New Haven led 3–2 after four innings, and held on despite serious scoring threats by Hartford in the eighth and ninth innings. The final result shocked not only the Dark Blues and the Providence crowd, but the New Haven players themselves.[6] The victory was a "*god send!*" said the *New Haven Register*. "It has raised the hopes of one and all. Those opposed to base ball heretofore will now enter into all the customary proceedings with a vim and will doubtless support the nine as they deserve hereafter ... the nine did nobly and we hope for a repetition of it today."[14]

Those hopes were quickly dashed. Despite pleasant weather, only a small crowd of 400 was present, as Hartford residents dismissed the results in Providence as a mere aberration and not a true sign of the relative strengths of the teams. After his success in Providence, Ryan was in the box again, but Hartford quickly extinguished any thoughts of a repeat performance, cruising to a 10–0 win. The enthusiasm of the large crowd that had gathered in New Haven to get the telegraphed results by innings quickly expired as the zeroes piled up on the bulletin board.[15]

New Haven was scheduled to return to Hartford the next day, but when Nichols was still unavailable, New Haven chose to forego the trip, considering it better to forfeit the game "than to suffer a disastrous defeat through the want of a good pitcher."[16] After the disappointing losses to Hartford, New Haven made further changes. Jumbo Latham was appointed captain in place of Charlie Gould, who remained with the club as a player and the business manager. In addition, the club voted to increase its capital to $5,000, and, as had been predicted by that ornery New York sportswriter, the proposed western trip was postponed.[17]

Under the new captain, things went from bad to worse, as New Haven dropped a game to Yale, 6–4.[18] Even the return of Nichols didn't help. In his first two games back, a rusty Nichols was shellacked by Philadelphia to the tune of 18–2 and 12–1. There was little indication of what was to come next.

Chapter 20

First of Idiots

After the New Haven series, Ferguson led the Hartfords into Boston for a third meeting with the Red Stockings. Boston had continued its blistering pace, remaining unbeaten through the month of May. Finally, on June 5, after 26 consecutive victories, the Red Stockings lost to pitcher George "Grin" Bradley and the St. Louis Brown Stockings. Ferguson's decision to send Cummings to the box in the first two Boston games, both losses, had drawn criticism from the *New York Clipper,* since Bond had beaten Boston four times the previous year. Ferguson was well aware of Bond's ability, but he believed he had a superior strategy. Wanting Bond to add the curveball to his pitching repertoire, Ferguson kept Tommy in the outfield early in the season, while he learned the curve from Cummings. By midseason, the pupil had so completely mastered the pitch, many viewed his curve as superior to his teacher's. At the same time, Bond modified his delivery so that his hand would sweep down within six or eight inches of the ground, making his new curveball even more difficult to hit.[1]

Bond's curves were so effective that not only did they fool batters, they baffled spectators and umpires as well. Jimmy Clinton, a part-time player for the Atlantics, remembered seeing the curveball for the first time while umpiring a game in which Bond pitched in St. Louis. Clinton recalled that on this day in 1875 the large crowd wasn't very pleased with his calls.

> From the first Hartford took a decided lead, and the ill success of the home pets was visited on the umpire, especially as batter after batter of the St. Louis was seen by the audience to jump back from the plate for balls on which I called strikes. The people could not understand it, and hooted and yelled and threatened, and I was beginning to feel rather shaky when I called Pierce [Dickey Pearce] and two or three others of the St. Louis to witness that the balls on which I called strikes cut the plate in two, although they seemed until nearing the plate to be going right for the batter. Pierce confirmed this to the crowd and told them, "I-hope-I-may-die if it ain't so," but they wouldn't have it that way. I thanked my lucky stars for a whole hide when the game was over and took the

first train to Louisville, without waiting to umpire the other two games for which I had been engaged.[2]

After using Cummings in the box for the first 27 games, Ferguson felt the time was right to unleash the new and improved Bond on the Red Stockings, a decision the *Clipper* praised as "good captainship." Bond proved his captain's confidence to be well founded, holding Boston scoreless through five innings. His teammates, however, offered no support with the bat, going down in order in seven of the nine innings. Bond finished with a neat four-hitter, but came out on the short end of a 4–0 Boston victory.[3]

After the game, Hartford embarked on a western excursion—first stop, Chicago. The White Stockings were led by young outfielder Paul Hines, a budding star who would become the first Triple Crown winner in 1878 when he batted .358, with 4 home runs and 50 runs batted in. The Dark Blues and White Stockings put on a fantastic display of pitching and defense. Cummings surprised the Chicago crowd by sustaining his fine performance throughout the game, despite his slight build, which had them convinced he would falter. In an unprecedented development, the game remained scoreless through ten innings.

Scott Hastings opened the Chicago eleventh with a single. Hard-hitting Jim Devlin then grounded to Bob Ferguson at third base. Fergy threw to second baseman Jack Burdock for the force out, but when Burdock attempted to turn the double play, he threw wildly into the stands, allowing Devlin to go all the way to third base. Paul Hines then stepped to the plate, and Cummings later recalled, "I was trying my best to have him hit to center field. Instead the ball was hit to left and right away I knew it was all over. I ran behind the catcher to back him up, but knew it was useless, for the man in left field [Tom York], while he could throw home, invariably sent the ball far over the catcher's head." York caught the ball, and Devlin broke from third. Just as Cummings had anticipated, the ball sailed over the catcher's head where Cummings gathered it in as the game ended. The *Chicago Tribune* reported, "When at last Devlin galloped from third base across the homeplate every pair of lungs exerted themselves to the utmost, and stamping and clapping of hands were added to the vocal uproar." Henry Chadwick happily reported that this was the third 1–0 game ever, the first to require extra innings. "Had that run been shut off," said Cummings, "there is no telling how long that game would have lasted."[4]

For years, baseball games had been dominated by the offense, but now low-scoring games were becoming increasingly common. Henry Chadwick was a great proponent of the "scientific game" over the power-hitting approach and cherished contests in which "batsmen are forced to depend on brain-work, instead of mere muscle in handling the ash." The 1875 season must have pleased Chadwick greatly, as batting and slugging averages plummeted. In its first four years, the composite National Association batting average was generally in the .280s. In 1875, it plunged to barely .250. With no major rule changes to account for the precipitous drop, it appears that the league's expansion from eight teams in 1874 to thirteen in 1875 was responsible. This is the reverse effect of what usually occurs in today's major leagues, where expansion is generally accompanied by a jump in offense due to the teams' inability to find enough major-league caliber pitchers. In 1875, however, a team needed only two qualified pitchers, at the most. Thus the problem wasn't finding enough pitchers, but finding another ten or so skilled batsmen who could hit, especially ones who could handle the increasingly popular curveball.[5]

The Elm City club hosted Boston on July 2 in front of a large crowd. Their recent play, including the loss to Yale and a near-loss to the Bridgeport TBs, gave no indication of anything unusual about to happen. Boston entered the game with an amazing record of 37 wins and just 3 losses. Jim O'Rourke later remembered that great Boston team, which would win 71 of 79 games and not lose at home all year, saying, "I remember how easy the games were for us that year...."[6]

In the bottom of the first inning, hard-hitting Cal McVey gave Boston a 1–0 lead with a home run over the left field fence. Surprisingly, New Haven responded with three runs in the second inning and two more in the third to take a 5–1 lead. Boston looked to be making its inevitable comeback when they cut the deficit to 5–4 with three runs in the third inning. But to the crowd's surprise, New Haven stretched the advantage and led 10–5 going to the bottom of the ninth inning.

The crowd was tense as Boston took the bat, because, as the *New Haven Register* noted, "it is proverbial that the Bostons often rally at the last scratch." The inning started ominously as Ed Somerville muffed Al Spalding's grounder. Jim White hit a foul pop which catcher Tim McGinley snared on the bounce for the first out. Jim O'Rourke hit a foul ball, and New Haven managed to catch Spalding before he returned to first base. O'Rourke then hit a foul pop out to end the game. When the last out was made, jubilant New Haven supporters rushed the diamond where they lifted the victorious players on their shoulders and paraded them about the field. "What man in New Haven would have ventured a bet in favor of New Haven yesterday?" asked the *New Haven Register*. "If any man had dared to make such a wager, ball-players would have rated him as the first of idiots."[7]

After the stunning loss to New Haven, Boston met Hartford for two games. These games were critical to the Dark Blues' pennant aspirations since they trailed the Red Stockings by five victories. For these two important games, Ferguson again deployed Bond. The first contest was played in Boston in front of 3,000 fans. Bond yielded just six hits, but once more he was not supported by his teammates, either offensively or defensively. With the bat, the Dark Blues managed a paltry pair of hits off Spalding. In the field, Jack Burdock's muff of an easy popup led to two unearned runs, giving Boston a 3–1 victory.[8]

Two days later, the teams clashed in Hartford. Expecting another huge turnout like the one for their first meeting in May, Morgan Bulkeley ordered an extra 2,000 seats to be erected at the field's south end and employed several additional policemen. Bulkeley's work did not go unnoticed, even by the visiting Red Stockings, who pronounced the grounds to be the finest in the country. The crowds didn't disappoint, as 8,000 fans watched Bond perform well again, allowing only six hits and two earned runs.[9] It wasn't good enough, though, as Boston rolled to an easy 7–0 win.

Disheartened by the two losses to the league leaders, Hartford dropped a pair of games to the Mutuals. In the first match, Cummings surrendered nine runs in four innings, forcing Ferguson to bring in Bond, who blanked the Mutuals the rest of the way. Bond's two good outings against Boston and effective mop-up work against New York convinced Ferguson to make him the team's number-one pitcher. The use of Bond didn't prevent a second loss to the Mutuals, though, this time 6–2.[10]

As the Dark Blues fell further off the blistering pace set by the league-leading Red Stockings, the growling in Hartford only got louder. Things got so bad that the *Courant*, which had lavishly praised him earlier in the year, turned on Ferguson. "Captain Ferguson is complained of justly by his own men and by spectators for too much talking on the field. There is an impression that the club would work in better harmony if he were less disposed to shout at players. Moreover, his own playing is not up to the standards of the others in the nine...."[11]

While Hartford was struggling, the New Havens were jelling as a team and playing better baseball. After their shocking victory over Boston, the club traveled to upstate New York, where they won eight games against amateur teams such as the KuKlux Club of Oneida and the Active Club of Wappinger Falls.[12] About this time, Charlie Gould left the club completely, going to Cincinnati to be player-manager for the newly organized amateur club there.

The club's improved play continued at home as New Haven defeated the Chicago White Stockings and St. Louis Brown Stockings. New Haven also played well in several close losses, including three by one run. New Haven's three victories in July were more than they had managed in the first three months of the season. The improvement could be credited to the pitching and defense. They were still scoring the same number of runs per game, but with the return of Tricky Nichols and new players on defense, they were allowing only five runs per game, instead of ten. The *Hartford Courant* noticed the change, saying, "The New Haven nine was never in so good condition as now."[13]

About this time, stunning news made the rounds in the baseball fraternity. The Red Stockings, who had retained the same core players for four dominant years, would be dismantled at the close of the season. Al Spalding, Ross Barnes, Cal McVey, and Jim "Deacon" White were leaving Boston to play for Chicago. The White Stockings' fearless secretary William Hulbert had initiated this bold move. In coaxing Spalding to Chicago, Hulbert appealed to his Midwestern roots, saying, "If you'll come to Chicago, I'll accept the Presidency of this Club, and we'll give those fellows a fight for their lives."[14] After signing with Chicago, Spalding recruited his three teammates. As if these players weren't enough, Hulbert supplemented his Boston trophies with star players Adrian Anson and Ezra Sutton from Philadelphia.

All participants attempted to keep these developments under wraps, due to the National Association's rule against signing players from rival teams before the season ended. Blockbuster news like this couldn't be kept a

James "Deacon" White was one of the true pioneers of the game. He played for four decades, starting with the amateur Cleveland Forest City Club in 1868 and finishing with the Buffalo club of the Players League in 1890. He was a star player for the Boston Red Stockings in the 1870s and was one of the "Big Four" Red Stockings who jumped to the Chicago White Stockings for the 1876 season. He was a talented and well-respected player who many feel has been unjustly denied admission to the Baseball Hall of Fame. He is shown here on an 1887 tobacco card when he played for the New York Giants (Library of Congress).

secret long though, and two weeks later a Chicago newspaper broke the story. Boston managers first got word of it while dining prior to a game in Taunton, Massachusetts. Cal McVey casually remarked that he wasn't going to play ball in Boston next year. Believing it to be a joke, Harry Wright was initially unconcerned, but after supper he nearly regurgitated his meal when Deacon White confirmed that the heart of the team was indeed headed west.[15]

All of Boston was shocked by the news of the imminent breakup of a team that had met with unequaled success. "Secession!" screamed the *Boston Advertiser's* headline. "The time is out of joint. Tweed is escaping from the penalty of his crimes, there are bad crops in Europe, the Democratic party is marching rapidly under its soft-money flag, the Monarchista are gaining victories in the French Assembly,—and now the famous Boston nine has been assaulted and captured by Chicago. There is probably no paragraph of news this week that has caused so much real vexation out of doors in Boston as this last." The *Worcester Spy* commiserated with Boston on the loss of Spalding, "for whom there is no substitute in the country," and opined that if the players had not left the Hub, all four "might have had their portraits in Faneuil Hall or their statues in the Public Garden."[16]

Ezra Sutton, Boston Red Stockings, 1887. Sutton played third base for the Philadelphia Athletics and Boston Red Stocking for many seasons. He was an excellent fielder and a power hitter who swatted the first two home runs in the National Association in 1871. Along with Boston's Big Four, Sutton signed to play with William Hulbert's Chicago White Stockings for 1876, but had a change of heart and remained in Philadelphia (Library of Congress).

Spalding remembered that after the story broke, the "Big Four," as they were called, were "caricatured, ridiculed, and even accused of treason. Boys would follow us on the streets, shouting 'Oh, you seceders; your White Stockings will get soiled,' and would hurl all kinds of facetious remarks at us."[17]

The New Havens played the first game in Boston after this astounding news became public. The bitter Boston crowd cheered the visitors, while good plays by the home team were met with silence. When Spalding muffed a pop fly, allowing Ryan to score, "the error was greeted with a storm of derisive hoots and yells, mingled with cheers for the visitors."[18]

Fully aware that they had been treated well in Boston, Spalding and the others began having second thoughts. But it was too late. "We had gone too far," he said. "We had signed contracts with President Hulbert to go to Chicago the following year. Because of this he had accepted the Presidency of the Chicago Club and assumed financial obligations based upon our assurance that we would be with him in 1876. Our inclinations drew us back towards Boston, but our duty surely called us to Chicago."[19]

Chapter 21

Locked Up

While their play on the field had improved, the New Havens' financial condition had not. Attendance had been poor, and players were owed several hundred dollars in back-salary. Things were so bad that Jim Tipper couldn't pay his rent, and after the season the outfielder was arrested for failing to pay his boarding fee for ten weeks.[16] The lack of fans was bad enough, but the financial situation was made worse by lax gate tenders who allowed many people to enter without a ticket, claiming they had forgotten them at home.[1]

With financial disaster staring them in the face, New Haven again decided to forego a trip to play the western National Association teams and traveled instead through upstate New York and Canada. The club fared well on the trip, except for a strange incident in Syracuse in which, according to the *Syracuse Courier*, the team showed itself to be a "set of loafers." During the game, New Haven players acted strangely, "jeering and singing in the field, and making themselves obnoxious to both spectators and players."[2] On the final leg of their trip, New Haven returned to National Association games with a 13–6 victory over the Atlantics.

The club's triumphant return home was spoiled when scandalous news was reported in New Haven. While touring Canada, the team lodged at the Tecumseh House in London, Ontario. At checkout, the hotel proprietors and several teammates noted that Billy Geer and Henry Luff had considerably more luggage than when they arrived. After the team departed, the suspicious owners investigated and learned that an expensive coat was missing from the room adjacent to Geer's and Luff's. The owners wired the news to the New Haven directors, who alerted the New Haven chief of police. Officers Brewer and Reilly located the two players in a Chapel Street bar and placed them under arrest. The room they shared in a local boarding house was searched, and several expensive garments, including the missing coat from Ontario, were found. The two men were "locked up and denied all communication with counsel and friends" and immediately released from the team.

In court, their case was heard and continued and both men were released on bail.³

Luff proclaimed his innocence, saying his only mistake was rooming with a player who was caught with stolen goods. Geer also asserted his innocence in a letter to a friend. The evidence continued to mount, however, as New Haven police received a letter from a Scranton, Pennsylvania, hotel saying that several items, including clothes, a revolver and ammunition, were missing from there as well. Some of these objects were found in Geer's room.⁴

The *Chicago Tribune* commented that "housebreaking is a new accomplishment for ball-players, but Connecticut gets up many new ideas.... The New Havens claim to have re-engaged McGinley, Somerville, Nichols, and Geer, but at last accounts some Canadian police authorities had an engagement with one or more of the nine which was likely to last several years." Despite these predictions, both Geer and Luff played major league ball again. In fact, Geer even umpired a game between the Atlantics and Mutuals on September 25.⁵

Already shorthanded due to the dismissal of Geer and Luff, New Haven also lost George Latham, who left to play with the London (Ontario) Tecumsehs, one of the teams New Haven had played on their trip. The departure of three starters forced the club to sign new players. George Trenwith, formerly of the disbanded Centennials, was signed, as was veteran Charlie Pabor and young John Cassidy from the Brooklyn Atlantics. Pabor, who had been captain of the Atlantics, was named captain of New Haven. The new trio's first game was a lopsided 16–1 loss to Boston.⁶

The New Haven club's lone bright spot for the remainder of the season came at the end of September, in the second game of a two-game set against the Mutuals in Brooklyn. After pitching well in the first game, a 4–2 loss, Tricky Nichols came up with a sore arm. Charlie Pabor elected to give George Knight, a Yale student and pitcher for the university's baseball club, the chance to pitch in the major leagues. Knight had umpired many games for Hartford and New Haven during the last two seasons and probably had made the trip with New Haven to serve in that capacity. This game looked to be a mismatch, as Knight was making his major league debut against accomplished veteran Bobby Mathews. Knight was up to the task, however, as he pitched New Haven to an 8–6 victory.⁷ This would prove to be Knight's only major league appearance, making him the only National Association player to achieve a complete-game victory in his only appearance.

Meanwhile in Hartford, hopes had soared with the belief that the Red Stockings would collapse under the knowledge that their team was being torn asunder. The rejuvenated Blues quickly broke their four-game losing streak and won 17 of their next 20 games. Leading the resurgence was Tommy Bond.

21. Locked Up

Now the team's undisputed number-one pitcher, Bond was pitching phenomenally. Three games during this stretch were certifiable gems. First, in mid–August against the Mutuals, Bond pitched what was reportedly the first one-hitter ever. The Mutuals' lone hit was a hard groundball by Jim Holdsworth that Jack Burdock initially stopped, but was unable to recover quickly enough to throw Holdsworth out.[8]

Two days later, Bond limited the Mutuals to just one run over nine innings, but Hartford failed to score going to the bottom of the ninth. With a steady rain falling and the Mutuals clinging to a 1–0 lead, veteran pitcher Bobby Mathews resorted to a variety of stalling tactics, hoping the game would be called and the victory given to the Mutuals. He held the ball interminably, and when he finally did pitch, it was well out of the batter's reach. With two outs, Tom York finally got a pitch to hit and tripled to center field. Bob Ferguson, generally regarded as baseball's first switch hitter, stepped to the plate left-handed. As a switch hitter, Ferguson would change sides of the plate depending on where he wanted to place the ball. He did not adhere to today's convention of batting from the opposite side of the pitcher's delivery. After fouling off several pitches, Ferguson turned around and batted right-handed, rapping a double past third base to tie the score. Mathews now insisted that the game be stopped. The umpire agreed and declared the game a draw. A week later, Bond was at it again, pitching his second one-hit game in ten days. Old friend Bill Boyd got the Atlantics' only hit in Hartford's 2–0 victory.[9]

Unfortunately, while Hartford was on its tear, the anticipated collapse of Boston never materialized. The Red Stockings finished the season with an astounding record of 71 wins and 8 losses, including a perfect 37–0 record at home. Hartford fell far short of their captain's boast that the club would win half or more of their matches with Boston. In fact, in ten tries, the club took only a single game from Boston, and that in their last meeting of the season. The victory was far too late to help in the pennant race, but it did allow the Dark Blues to edge the Athletics for second place, despite the Athletics' higher winning percentage. The final standings for 1875 were

Team	W	L
Boston Red Stockings	71	8
Hartford Dark Blues	54	28
Philadelphia Athletics	53	20
St. Louis Brown Stockings	39	29
Philadelphia White Stockings	37	31
Chicago White Stockings	30	37
New York Mutuals	30	38
St. Louis Red Stockings	4	15

Team	W	L
New Haven Elm Citys	7	40
Washington Nationals	5	23
Philadelphia Centennials	2	12
Brooklyn Atlantics	2	42
Keokuk Westerns	1	12

For the year, excellent fielding and pitching, but poor hitting, marked the Dark Blues' play. Hartford's pair of aces, Bond and Cummings, combined to lead the league with 13 shutouts. Cummings had a career year, going 35–12, while Bond finished 19–16 after becoming the regular pitcher in July. Despite a record just three games over .500, Bond had pitched spectacularly. His 1.56 ERA was lower than Cummings's and good enough for second best in the league.

Although the pitching and defense were strong, not one Hartford player hit over .300. Tom York led the team with a .296 batting average, followed by Jack Burdock at .294. No other player managed to top .270. The Red Stockings had six players bat .300, including the league's best three in average, Deacon White at .366, Ross Barnes at .361, and Cal McVey at .352. Unfortunately for Boston, all three of these players' stockings would soon be white, not red.

At the conclusion of the season, Chicago and Boston played an exhibition pitting the 1876 Chicago team with Spalding, White, McVey, and Barnes against the 1876 Boston club. Reluctant to face his former Boston mates, Spalding sent Cal McVey to pitch. The White Stockings won decisively, 14–0, conclusively demonstrating that the balance of power had shifted from east to west.[10]

Chapter 22

The National League

Chicago's hard-driving William Hulbert orchestrated the White Stockings' stunning acquisition of Boston's Big Four. Born in upstate New York, Hulbert moved to the Windy City at an early age, became successful in the coal industry, and was a member of the city's Board of Trade. Hulbert was a bombastic, uncompromising man whose drive to succeed was surpassed only by his love of Chicago. He once proclaimed proudly, "I would rather be a lamp-post in Chicago than a millionaire in another city."[1] When he purchased stock in the White Stockings club in 1870, Hulbert, never having played baseball, was mostly interested in the economic possibilities of the game. He advanced quickly into increasingly more powerful positions with the club, becoming a director in 1872, secretary in 1874, and president in 1875.

Hulbert saw the Gilded Age success of captains of industry such as John D. Rockefeller in oil and Andrew Carnegie in steel and was intent on applying the same corporate principles to baseball. As a result, he developed a plan to reform, or better, replace, the loosely run National Association with a new, financially stable league that would simultaneously return integrity to the national game. Believing the former was not possible without the latter, Hulbert envisioned a two-pronged approach. On the business side, his prime focus was addressing the fly-by-night nature of the co-op clubs, who, Hulbert believed, were like "vampires thriving upon the blood of solid organizations." Stock-funded clubs had typically been reluctant to invest travel expenses to play these often distant clubs, knowing that recouping their expenditures was unlikely. Hulbert theorized that restricting league membership to a single stock club in the nation's largest cities would be more financially beneficial to member clubs than the National Association "structure" which allowed clubs to self-declare membership by simply paying the league entry fee.[2]

On the integrity issue, Hulbert envisioned strict sanctions to address the National Association's persistent problems with gambling or suspected gambling. The *Hartford Times* felt that gambling had become so pervasive in baseball that it was "dragging it down towards the level of the dog and cock pit.... Gamblers congregated, and by their vile practices, at first, ladies were driven from the ball field, and with the restraining influence removed, the betting men took partial or full control, and at last edged into the official management of some clubs, until unseemly rows and bitter accusations of fraud were fast driving away the reputable portion of the sterner sex."[3]

Hulbert probably had another motive for starting the new league. He was undoubtedly concerned about disregarding the National Association's rule against signing opposing players before the season was over. Possible retribution could have included returning "The Big Four" to Boston and, in the worst case scenario, Chicago being banned from the National Association. A punishment of that extent was probably unlikely, as many teams were guilty of the same offense in past seasons, although none had involved so many high-profile players.

William Hulbert, president of the Chicago White Stockings and founder of the National League. It was Chicago's hard-driving William Hulbert who orchestrated the White Stockings' stunning acquisition of Boston's Big Four in 1875. Born in upstate New York, Hulbert moved to the Windy City at an early age, became successful in the coal industry, and was a member of the city's Board of Trade. Hulbert was a bombastic, uncompromising man whose drive to succeed was surpassed only by his love of Chicago. He once proclaimed proudly, "I would rather be a lamp-post in Chicago than a millionaire in another city" (Library of Congress).

In December 1875, Hulbert hosted a secret meeting in Louisville with representatives of four Western teams — Chicago, St. Louis, Louisville, and Cincinnati. The meeting culminated with general agreement that a new league should be formed. Hulbert and Charles Fowle of the St. Louis club were commissioned to go to New York and present to four eastern clubs what amounted to an ultimatum — join the new league or be left behind.

The two men sent the following invitation to the Boston, Hartford, New York Mutual, and Philadelphia Athletic clubs:

St. Louis, Jan. 23 — The undersigned have been appointed by the Chicago, Cincinnati, Louisville, and St. Louis clubs a committee to confer with you on matters of interest to the game at large, with special reference to the reformation of existing abuses, and the formation of a new association, and we are clothed with full authority in writing from the above named clubs to bind them in any arrangement we may make with you. We therefore invite your club to send a representative clothed with like authority, to meet us at the Grand Central Hotel, in the city of New York, on Wednesday, the second day of February next, at 12 o'clock pm. After careful consideration of the needs of the professional clubs, the organizations we represent are of the firm belief that existing circumstances demand prompt and vigorous action by those who are the natural sponsors of the game. It is the earnest recommendation of our constituents that all past troubles and differences be forgotten, and that the conference we propose shall be a calm, friendly and deliberate discussion, looking solely to the general good of the clubs who are calculated to give character and permanency to the game. We are confident that the proposition we have to submit will meet with your approval and support, and we shall be pleased to meet you at the time and place above mentioned.[4]

On February 2, Hulbert unveiled his plan for the new National League of Professional Baseball Clubs, laying out drafts of constitutions and bylaws. He proposed limiting membership to the eight stock clubs represented at the gathering and enforcing stringent entrance requirements to keep out marginal cities. A threshold requirement of 75,000 residents was proposed for a city to have a National League team, unless member clubs gave unanimous approval. This requirement would be waived for Hartford and its 40,000 residents. Hulbert undoubtedly liked the fact that the Hartford club was competitive, finishing second in 1875, had shown the ability to draw considerable crowds, and was headed by well-respected businessman Morgan Bulkeley. Each team would be granted exclusive territorial rights to its own geographic area.[5] It was further proposed that the eight clubs play ten games against each other team, three games per week. Expulsion from the league would be the price paid for failure to do so. Hulbert also proposed strict bans on gambling, liquor sales, and Sunday games.

Although they would be forced to surrender some autonomy and submit to a central authority, the assembled representatives offered little resistance to Hulbert's plan. Bulkeley said, "It was agreed to overlook the shortcomings of the past, both in clubs and players, and to start afresh, believing that the rules which we adopted would give us such control over both that dishonest practices in play would meet with so swift and sure a punishment that the professional arena would soon be rid of all inclined to persist in the course which has brought so much discredit on the game in some of our cities."[6]

At the conclusion of the meeting, a league president was chosen.

Accounts vary on the method of selection, some sources say by lottery, others say by Hulbert's appointment. Whatever the process, Morgan Bulkeley's appointment as president was at least symbolic of the National League's intent to restore integrity to the game. As the *Hartford Times* observed, "The fact that such a gentleman is at the head of the base ball interests of the nation should elevate the sport in the estimation of the people of the whole country."[7] Despite Bulkeley's title, Hulbert maintained nearly complete control over the league.

While the chosen eight clubs offered scant resistance to Hulbert, many others did. Foremost among the opposition were former National Association clubs like New Haven, which had been excluded from the new professional league. There had been rumors at the end of the 1875 season that a "new clique" of clubs, not including the Elm City club, would be formed for 1876. Most people doubted that such a league could be formed, though, since the concept of an exclusive closed-circuit organization, determining its own membership, was a new idea. Both the old and new National Associations had been self-determining leagues; that is, individual clubs could decide if they wanted to join and, provided they paid their dues, all were admitted.[8]

The news reports of Hulbert's New York meeting left New Haven club directors fuming. They had spent $1,600 on advanced salary payments and even more on field improvements with the belief that it would be recovered by playing against the top professional clubs in the nation. Always suspicious of Hartford, many in New Haven believed that new National League president Bulkeley was responsible for their city's exclusion. The *New Haven Evening Register* said, "The Hartford managers have undertaken to clear the state of a rival nine which threatened to deprive them of a position in the contest for the championship, and of gate money. They are determined that every dollar spent by those in this state interested in the game shall pass into their hands. And by misrepresentation and sharp play they have succeeded in excluding the New Havens."[9]

The spurned New Havens had two options. They could work to make the emasculated National Association as strong as possible, or they could attempt to join the new league. It first appeared that New Haven and the Philadelphia White Stockings, who had also been jettisoned, would choose the former course. When New Haven suddenly reversed course and made a written request to become the ninth National League team, they were sharply criticized in the City of Brotherly Love. The *Philadelphia Press* said, "The New Haven club has come to the conclusion that toadying to the great I AMS is the way to open the season, and, against the wishes of their friends, they have been cringing and supplicating for admission to the 'charmed circle,' for the past week...."[10]

New Haven's formal letter of application to the National League contained a long list of reasons why they should be admitted. First, it was explained that the club was not now, nor ever had been, a co-op club. Furthermore, the club's stock subscription had been increased to $10,000. In addition, New Haven's directors claimed that not a single club lost money when visiting New Haven in 1875, as was being alleged. The directors boldly asked Hulbert himself to help their cause by opening Chicago's books to show that games in New Haven paid as well as games in Hartford. "It's true they do that," admitted Hulbert in a letter to Charles Chase, "but when away from home they don't begin to draw as the Hartfords do." Believing that the previous season's problem with stolen goods was keeping them out, New Haven's application also emphasized their improved character, saying the nine was now completely honest, as all but two of their players from 1875 had been replaced. The *Boston Globe* mockingly summarized New Haven's position, saying, "The New Haven base-ballists say they want to come in. They won't steal any more clothes or watches and they say it's a mean, nasty shame that Hartford should be let in and New Haven left out in the cold."[11]

The Elm City club went so far as to offer the National League a bond to insure the league that New Haven would fulfill all player contracts in 1876. The *Philadelphia City Item* ridiculed this move, saying New Haven had "given up all dignity and manliness, by offering to give a bond for their good behavior and financial status. Could a club fall lower than this?"[12]

Despite the uncertain situation, preparations for the upcoming season continued in New Haven. The club had managed to put together a much stronger nine than the 1875 Association entry. Although he had been offered the captaincy of the National League Louisville club, Charlie Pabor remained in New Haven to captain the Elm City nine. John Cassidy, Sammy Wright, and Tricky Nichols also returned, and several experienced players, such as Frank Fleet and Charles Waitt, were added. Unlike the previous year, players reported early, with seven of nine in the city by the end of February. In addition to the roster upgrades, the Howard Avenue Grounds were being improved with new seating, and new gray uniforms were purchased.[13]

The National League attempted to use New Haven's desire to join as an opportunity to eliminate competition from any National Association that might remain for the 1876 season. National League clubs agreed to play New Haven, even if they weren't admitted to league, so long as they severed all ties with the National Association. At the end of February, New Haven accepted this offer and formally withdrew from the National Association.[14]

In his role as National League president, Morgan Bulkeley supplied copies of New Haven's application to the eight member clubs. Lacking the minimum required population of 75,000, New Haven needed unanimous approval. To increase their chances of acceptance by clubs who might be inclined to deny their request, New Haven supplemented the paperwork with a personal visit from their secretary. Despite early favorable indications, when Bulkeley counted the votes, two clubs had voted no. There were differing reports about the identity of the two clubs, but the one constant, as expected, was Hulbert's Chicago club.[15] The official reason for New Haven's exclusion was that the city did not have the required population, despite the fact that the 1870 census showed New Haven, with its 50,840 residents, to be substantially larger than Hartford, which had only 37,180 citizens.

After being officially rejected by the National League, officers of the New Haven club began to believe they were better off as an independent club. Given that National League clubs had agreed to play them, New Haven would reap the benefit of playing league teams without being bound by its rules. For instance, New Haven would not be obligated to travel west as they would have had to if they were members of the league. They could make the trip, though, if they believed it would be profitable. Furthermore, the directors thought the club would benefit at the gate due to the extensive publicity garnered from the national discussion concerning their application. The officers claimed that even if the National League now reversed course and allowed New Haven to join, they would decline the offer.[16]

There was one final issue left to decide — the fate of the National Association. Although exhibiting only a faint pulse, the National Association was still not quite dead. Their annual meeting was scheduled for March 1 in, of all places, New Haven. Of course, the eight clubs that had just formed the National League would not attend, nor would the New Haven club, but it was thought that the remaining National Association clubs, plus the best semi-pro clubs, could combine to form a strong league. When representatives from only eleven weak nines arrived at the convention, this hope was extinguished, and the National Association was allowed to pass quietly away to make way for the brave new world of Hulbert's National League.[17]

Chapter 23

Playing Baby

Despite the disappointment of not wresting the pennant from Boston's clutches in 1875, expectations for the Dark Blues' upcoming season remained high. Their nine was largely unchanged, except for the addition of outfielder/catcher Richard Higham, who was signed to address the club's urgent need for hitting. Higham was indeed a strong batter, but many felt Bulkeley was making a colossal mistake by signing another player with a considerable reputation for growling, and worse. Henry Chadwick described Higham as "rather careless in his habits, impulsive in temper, and in some respects not a model player." Although Chadwick concluded that Higham could "be relied upon for honest service," there were myriad accusations of Higham associating with gamblers and throwing games.[1]

In 1875, Higham had been relieved of his Chicago White Stockings captaincy and was forced to the bench, as management thought him more interested in selling, than winning, games. The *Chicago Tribune* reported:

[H]e is one of the best players in the country when he wants to be.... It may be Higham's fault, or his misfortune, that he is suspected of purposely losing games, but in either case he is better out of this nine until he can regain confidence as an honest player.... The principal cause of suspicion attaching to Higham is the character of the men he is uniformly found with. It is not always safe to judge a man by the company he keeps, but it is no credit to any man to be seen continually, and almost exclusively, with thieves and bunko ropers.[2]

Despite these allegations, Chicago management lacked hard evidence against Higham and returned him to the lineup five days after his benching. In mid–August, the club released him from his contract. The *Chicago Tribune* moralized, "His fate should serve as a warning, and convince base-ball players that selling out games is a practice that cannot easily be concealed, and that eventually it is certain to be discovered."[3] In a pre-season letter to the *Hartford Times*, Higham denied all charges, claiming his discharge was voluntary and honorable. His problems, he said, were the fault of an unforgiving Chicago press.

I failed to win the love of the Chicago reporters: consequently I received no very flattering notices. On the contrary they gave the public to understand that I was responsible for all games the club lost. I finally applied to Mr. Hulbert for my discharge — an honorable one, if he thought me entitled to it: if not, the reason or reasons why I should not have it. The result was he gave me an honorable discharge, and, in addition, $500, which amount was not my due, nor would it have been until the close of the season. The discharge I have in my possession and shall be pleased to show it to any person who may have an interest in seeing it. In conclusion, I have only to say that I shall strive in the future, as in the past, to play for the best interest of my club, and to secure a record that I can feel proud to show to my friends and the patrons of the ball field.[4]

While it's probably disingenuous to blame all of Higham's troubles on the Chicago press, there is no doubt that Windy City writers could be ruthless. When the White Stockings were winning, praise flowed freely. When the team was losing, it was cursed, often in sarcastic and overly dramatic terms. As early as 1867, when most papers still wrote quite gently about their local teams, Chicago newspapers, driven by a nearly fanatical civic boosterism, demanded a winner. This type of journalism marked a change from the early days of baseball, when newspaper coverage of the sport was "as tame as a clergyman describing a prize fight." When a professional team was formed in 1870 at great expense, the Chicago press became even more hard-hitting.[5]

Despite Higham's past problems, Bulkeley undoubtedly signed him on Bob Ferguson's advice. Ferguson, who was impeccably clean when it came to gambling, must have trusted his former teammate, since he presumably would not have suffered the presence of a dishonest man on his nine.

The westward move of the Big Four made Chicago the favorite to take the championship, with Hartford expected to provide the most competition. Al Spalding handicapped the upcoming pennant race, saying the Hartford nine would "no doubt share some of the laurels, and it would really astonish some Chicagoans could they hear the manner in which this club is extolled in Hartford.... It is my impression that they form one of the best fielding nines in the country, but their weakness seems to be chiefly in their batting. The fact that the Hartfords have the best base ball grounds in the country is something that should not be lost sight of. The support given the Club by the people of Hartford is of the most liberal character considering the size of the city, and is from the very best class of people."[6]

At least one reporter agreed with Spalding, saying Hartford would be much improved since, with virtually the same nine returning, they had a year's experience playing together. Perhaps more importantly "they have not that fearful red-legged Boston nine to unnerve them, as was the case last season...." Despite their breakup, the specter of the Red Stockings still haunted the Dark Blues. Jack Burdock cautioned those who were ready to dismiss Boston, saying,

The 1876 Hartford Dark Blues. The club finished second to Al Spalding's Chicago White Stockings in the inaugural season of the National League. Back row, left to right: Tommy Bond, Candy Cummings. Middle row, sitting, left to right: Tom Carey, Everett Mills, Bob Ferguson, Bill Harbidge, Tom York. Front row, left to right: Dick Higham, Jack Burdock, Jack Remsen, Doug Allison. This club finished second in the inaugural season of the National League (courtesy of Connecticut State Library).

> Now don't forget that they've got a nine up in Boston, and these clubs that are counting on a walk-over up there will be mightily mistaken if they think they've got a lot of kids to buck against. I tell you Harry Wright ain't a fool, and somebody may get a thundering big surprise party when they get hold of the Reds; they may be little fellows, but they'll play ball with the Wrights back of 'em, sure![7]

Regardless of the preseason hype, Chicago was having trouble getting all its new acquisitions to report. Although the Big Four were determined to honor their promise, the two Philadelphia signees weren't so committed. Unable to resist the temptation of the higher salary offered by the Athletics, Ezra Sutton simply ignored the contract he signed with Chicago. Adrian Anson was also having second thoughts and persistently petitioned Hulbert to release him. When Hulbert ignored the requests, Anson felt duty-bound to report. He arrived at Chicago's first practice, albeit reluctantly, appearing in dress clothes instead of a uniform. After observing for a few moments, Anson could resist no longer and instructed Al Spalding to toss him a ball. Spalding obliged, while simultaneously instructing Anson to be at the field the next day — in uniform. Anson followed Spalding's order and remained in Chicago for the next 22 years.[8]

The National League season opened for Hartford on April 27 against the New York Mutuals. As he had done for the latter half of the 1875 season, Ferguson called upon Tommy Bond to pitch. Through four innings, the Dark Blues played like the championship contender they were supposed to be, as Bond limited the Mutuals to one hit and Hartford led 3–0. Things went awry in the fifth, however, as Hartford's usually impeccable defense committed four consecutive errors, including one by Higham, the former Mutual, who lazily watched a high flyball to right field land at his feet. The Mutuals followed these giveaways with three solid base hits, resulting in six runs on their way to an 8–3 victory.[9]

The next game was Hartford's first test against the depleted Red Stockings. Harry Wright had brought in several new faces to replace his departed quartet. Former Mansfield first baseman Tim Murnane replaced Cal McVey, Lew Brown took the place of Deacon White at catcher, and "Honest John" Morrill played second in place of Ross Barnes. Joe Borden would replace Spalding in the pitcher's box. Borden first appeared on the baseball scene in 1875 with the Philadelphia Whites, joining the team in July when Cherokee Fisher

Boston native John Morrill began his career with the Red Stockings in 1876. He replaced George Wright as captain of Boston in 1879 and succeeded Harry Wright as manager of the Red Stockings in 1882. Later, he earned the nickname "Honest John" for his truthful assessments of his teams. Morrill is shown here on an 1887 tobacco card (Library of Congress).

was released for drunkenness and insubordination. To prevent his well-to-do father from learning of his ballplaying, the 21-year-old Borden asked to be listed as Joe Josephs. In his second appearance, "Josephs" no-hit the Chicago White Stockings, the first such accomplishment in professional baseball history, earning the nickname "The Phenomenal One."[10] He played the remainder of the 1875 season under his assumed name, but by 1876 felt it safe to use his family name.

Boston opened the scoring with two runs in the fourth inning, but the Dark Blues tied it in the seventh, and the game proceeded to extra innings. In the bottom of the tenth inning, Tom York stroked a double and moved to third when Ev Mills went out on a comebacker to Borden. Borden then uncorked a wild pitch which allowed York to scamper home with the winning run. With this victory, Hartford accomplished a feat which had proven impossible in 1875, beating the Red Stockings in Boston. Unaccustomed to seeing their team lose, the Boston crowd swarmed the umpire at the end of the game, but the players prevented the unruly fans from harming him.[11]

After a travel day, the two teams met again in Hartford. Prior to the game, while speaking with Morgan Bulkeley, Harry Wright learned that he was supposed to be dead. His death from consumption had been erroneously reported in the April 28 *Cincinnati Enquirer*. Wright ensured everyone that he was quite alive, although he may have wished otherwise after the Dark Blues disposed of the former champs by the shockingly one-sided score of 15–3. Despite Burdock's preseason warning, Boston wasn't the same without the Big Four, especially in the pitcher's box. Borden had no hope of adequately replacing Spalding, and before the end of the season Boston was offering to buy-out his three-year contract for $1,000. To Harry Wright's dismay, Borden was a persistent soul, and he remained in Boston, practicing his pitching. Despite the Boston club's attempts to work Borden so hard that he would voluntarily leave, Borden cheerfully performed all tasks, even when he was relegated to groundkeeping duties. The *Hartford Times* summed up the new condition of things this way: "The proverbial power of those red stockings to scare the life out of the blues is no more. It is a new order of things and the Dark Blues possess the superiority over the Reds henceforth."[12]

Next were two games with the New Haven club. As they had hoped, New Haven had benefited from all the publicity surrounding their attempt to join the National League. Harry Wright agreed to open the season with several games against New Haven at various venues in Massachusetts and Connecticut. Boston won all the matches, but the games were mostly well-attended, including an excellent crowd of 2,500 people in New Haven.[13]

The first game between Hartford and New Haven was played in Hartford in front of 1,000 spectators. Thinking his team would have an easy time of it, Ferguson rested Tommy Bond and had Arthur Cummings pitch. For five innings, things went according to plan, as Hartford led 4–0, but New Haven tied the game in the sixth inning and won it in the ninth when two runs scored on Frank Fleet's base hit.[14]

The Elm City club's victory in Hartford brought out a large, enthusiastic crowd the next day in New Haven. Once again, Cummings and Hartford led early, this time 5–2 after five innings. New Haven tied it with three in the sixth, and the game went to the tenth inning still tied at five. New Haven scored two in the top of tenth while Hartford could only manage one.[15] Despite these early losses, Hartford would beat New Haven several times later in the season, although the games were typically close.

A week after the New Haven games, Hartford fans witnessed a National League first. In the fifth inning of a game on May 13, the Dark Blues were thumping the Mutuals to the tune of 18–0. At that point, the Mutuals banished starting pitcher Bobby Mathews to right field and brought in Eddie Booth, the former Mansfield player. This was Booth's first, and thankfully last, appearance in the pitcher's box, as he stood nervously in the box, timidly tossing the ball to the batters, as if he was pitching to a young child. Hartford immediately scored three runs and loaded the bases, still with no outs. Dick Higham stepped to the plate and stroked a hard line drive. Second baseman Bill Craver snared the ball and threw to first baseman Joe Start to catch Remsen. Start returned the ball to Craver, who put out Burdock for the first triple play in the young National League's history. The beautifully executed 4–3–4 triple play received a loud and long ovation from the Hartford crowd.[16]

Later in May, the White Stockings arrived in Hartford for a three-game showdown with the Dark Blues. The Chicago club was a confident bunch that, according to the *Hartford Times*, carried "the same dignified, pompous, conceited air which characterized the Boston Reds last season." Thanks to Al Spalding and his recently launched sporting goods empire, each member of the team wore different colored caps, making them look like "a Dutch bed of tulips."[17]

In the first game, Chicago scored single runs in the first and third innings. In the fourth, they teed off on Tommy Bond, scoring four earned runs, much to the disgust of the partisan Hartford crowd. Hartford reached Spalding for a pair of runs in the fourth and another deuce in the fifth, but they couldn't complete the comeback, losing 6–4.[18]

The rematch two days later proved much more satisfying to the home crowd. Hartford led 3–1 in the sixth inning, thanks to several Chicago errors which had Spalding giving dirty looks to his infielders. In the seventh inning, things really got interesting. Just as Ev Mills crossed home plate with Hartford's fourth run, the chimes at the neighboring Church of the Good Shepherd rang out the old hymn "We're Homeward Bound," bringing gales of laughter from the crowd. Chicago tried to rally in the bottom of the inning. With Adrian Anson on second and Cal McVey on first, Spalding grounded to shortstop Tom Carey. After forcing McVey at second, Carey employed an old trick that Hartford had successfully executed several times in the season. Instead of returning the ball to Bond, Carey held it while casually sauntering over to third base, pretending to speak with Bob Ferguson, while discretely slipping the captain the ball. Carey returned to his position and Bond prepared to pitch. When Anson led off third base, Ferguson promptly tagged him out. Initially, Anson didn't comprehend what had happened and was shocked when Ferguson coolly revealed the ball. The trickery elicited more laughter from the Hartford crowd. No more runs were scored, and the final score was 4–1, Hartford.[19]

In the rubber game of the series, Chicago sent first baseman Cal McVey to pitch against the Hartfords. Born in rural Iowa, McVey was a versatile athlete who could play any position on the field. He threw much harder than Spalding, who relied on deception and pitch location for his success. While the Hartfords were initially glad to avoid Spalding, they were helpless against McVey's rapid deliveries, and Chicago

Adrian "Cap" Anson (here in 1888) was, literally, the nineteenth century's biggest baseball star. At 6 feet 3 inches and 200 pounds, Anson was gigantic for the times. During his prolific 27-year career, he become the first player to collect 3,000 hits. He was elected to the Hall of Fame in 1939. In an important 1876 game in Hartford, Dark Blues fans were delighted to see Anson fooled by the hidden ball trick, executed by Tom Carey and Bob Ferguson (Library of

took an easy 8–1 victory. With this win, Chicago maintained first place with 12 wins, Hartford was second with 10, and St. Louis and Boston were tied for third with 9 victories apiece.[20]

Despite their success on the diamond, the Hartford club was struggling financially, as were most National League teams. After expanding for the better part of the last three decades, the nation's economy was in the midst of a depression that would not end until 1879. The downturn was touched off when the powerful banking firm of Jay Cooke & Company realized it had overextended itself with railroad investments and declared bankruptcy on September 18, 1873. This move ignited a major economic panic across the nation. The so-called "Panic of 1873" saw the stock market drop so precipitously that trading was suspended for ten days. Thousands of businesses failed over the next two years, and unemployment rose to a frightening 14 percent.[21]

Attendance in Hartford was lagging far behind the previous year, forcing Morgan Bulkeley to search for any way to increase revenue. This mission led him into a fierce battle with the city's newspaper and telegraph operators. During home games, inning-by-inning scores were posted outside the newspaper and telegraph offices. Believing this practice was keeping paying customers away from the ballpark, Bulkeley ordered it to stop. The *Hartford Courant* argued that removing this cheap form of advertisement, which actually increased interest in the team, would be shortsighted.[22]

The *Chicago Tribune* concurred, saying,

> One of the stupidest ideas that ever entered into the head of base-ball managers is the new arrangement on the Hartford grounds, by which they refuse to permit the transmission of any report of the game by innings. As the "*Courant*" well says, those who have been visitors to the bulletins are those who have an interest in the game, which is kept alive by their opportunity of watching the board, and the increased interest they have had has made them visitors to the games when a game of special interest has been played, or when they could get away from their business to attend. Not to continue the score by innings is to remove a very excellent and cheap feature of advertising, and, in a money way, to cause a loss to the ball manager.[23]

Bulkeley persisted, however, and banned Western Union from their typical perch on the ballpark's pavilion roof. Gershom Hubbell, now manager of Western Union, wasn't going to be stopped so easily. Hubbell sent a messenger inside the park to relay scores to a telegraph operator set up outside. Club officers stopped the first messenger, so the company had another employee purchase a ticket and sit in the stands. He would write the result of each inning on a paper and toss it over the fence to the operator outside. Officials made the spectator change his seat, but he just moved to where he could signal the score to the operator with his fingers.

The next day, Bulkeley himself refused to sell a ticket to an employee of the telegraph company, but the man purchased his ticket elsewhere and went about his business. When he threw down his first report, Bulkeley commanded the young boy acting as the runner to disregard it. Ignoring the order, the boy snatched the report and took off on a dead run. Bulkeley demanded that the police seize the impudent lad. When the rascal eluded the slow-acting officers, the frustrated team president loudly chastised the policemen for their incompetence. Public opinion was so firmly against Bulkeley's actions, however, that he didn't try to intervene again. If he didn't have enough trouble with urchins and telegraphers, Bulkeley also had to contend with some enterprising men who were pulling carriages up to the fence on Wyllys Street and charging people ten cents to climb up and watch the game. Bulkeley ended this annoyance by constructing a high addition to the fence in this area.[24]

Back between the lines, Hartford hosted three games with the hapless Cincinnati Red Stockings, the club Charlie Gould had left New Haven to manage in 1875. Although they had the same name as the famous 1869 club and two of the original players in Gould and Charlie Sweasy, the 1876 version was a poor imitation. By the conclusion of the season, the Red Stockings would compile a woeful record of 9 wins and 56 losses. They came into Hartford as losers of ten straight.

Ferguson decided to take this opportunity to rest Tommy Bond and give Arthur Cummings, who had only appeared in five non-league games against New Haven, some work. In his National League debut, Cummings stifled Cincinnati on a three-hitter as Hartford won, 6–0. This masterful performance prompted Bob Ferguson to proclaim, "God never gave him any size, but he is the Candy."[25] The nickname "Candy," which meant "best" in nineteenth-century slang, stuck for the rest of Arthur's life.

Once again, pitching and defense were carrying the Dark Blues. The year before, Chicago manager Jimmy Wood called Hartford the best fielding team in the country, and this year was no different. Ferguson was a master tactician who deserved much of the credit. His years of experience had allowed him to study batters' tendencies, and he would shift his fielders accordingly. For right-handed pull-hitters, such as Louisville's Jim Devlin, Ferguson employed an extreme shift which left right field virtually unguarded. He would order his second baseman to join the shortstop and third baseman on the left side of the infield, while simultaneously pulling his right fielder in so shallow that he could throw out the batter at first base.[26]

Ferguson also had definite ideas on the proper way for his men to field the ball.

> Some players will shin the ball, that is, they will stop it with their shins with the intention of picking it up quickly, but in doing this the ball is apt to bound away from them. Again, some players will "crowd" a ball by dropping on it with their hands and knees, but unless they are very quick they are not able to recover themselves in time. Then I have seen players "draw" the ball, as it is called, by standing in front of it with legs close together and let the ball run up to their hands. This is the worst of the lot, for if the ground is in any way rough the ball

is sure to bound away to one side. The perfect plan is the one which I always used, and that is to scoop the ball as it comes to you. This I do by holding the hands close together and give the arms full play. As the ball comes up let the hands go back between the legs slightly, and when the ball is about a foot from you, suddenly bring the hands forward and run the fingers under the ball. It is easy and sure.[27]

Despite their captain's advanced strategies, Ferguson's men chafed under his iron-fisted rule. The captain's quick temper continued to get the better of his judgment, leading him to holler frequently and loudly during the course of the game. The sensitive players on the team couldn't bear to be publicly rebuked, and their play suffered. Harry Wright had heard that the growling was so bad that there were hardly two men on the Hartford club who were on speaking terms with all the others.[28]

The *Hartford Times* marveled at the steady play of the nine despite Ferguson's tactics, saying, "We can't see how the men work as well as they do, if this is the kind of treatment they receive." Although the team was playing well, dissension still simmered just below the surface, waiting for something to ignite it. The spark came in the form of an 8–2 loss to lowly Cincinnati in the second game of the series. Losing to a team that hadn't won in a month, and wouldn't win again for another five weeks, was so implausible that some believed Cummings had thrown the game. The blame more correctly belonged to Hartford's usually superb defense, though, as none of Cincinnati's runs were earned.[29] This humiliating loss outraged Hartford fans and prompted John Belden at the *Hartford Times* to harshly denounce the team and their captain.

> There is something rotten in the Hartford club.... He [Ferguson] is Captain of the nine, and it is *his business* to see that the team work harmoniously together and always does its level best; if powerless to do this, resign.... These players are paid big salaries and they have no business to let petty jealousies and bickerings interfere with their play. If one of them gets his "nose out of joint" over some real or imaginary grievance, he shows his spite by mugging on the ball field. One complains because Captain Ferguson talks too much and refuses to play his game; another declares he won't back up Cummings; and somebody else, likely enough, is miffed because the hands of the South Church clock are not clapped every time he makes a passable catch. The men are hired to play ball — *not to play baby*....[30]

Hartford managed to momentarily get past their squabbling and take the third game from the Reds, in front of a miserable gathering of 200 spectators. Despite the embarrassing loss to Cincinnati, the Dark Blues were by no means out of the pennant race. They were still tied for second with the St. Louis Brown Stockings, who would be in town for three pivotal games. The

Browns were led by pitcher George Bradley, who was on his way to compiling a fantastic 45–9 record with sixteen shutouts. On paper, it looked to be a tough series for the weak-hitting Dark Blues, but the Hartford club showed considerable grit by tagging Bradley for a total of 33 hits and 20 runs, sweeping the series and taking sole possession of second place.[31]

The Dark Blues continued their winning ways with three victories against Louisville, thanks mostly to the superb pitching of Tommy Bond. In the three games, Bond limited Louisville to a grand total of one run. In two of the games, he allowed only a single hit. Realizing his immense value, Hartford quickly dropped the idea of obtaining Bobby Mathews and signed Bond for the 1877 season. When word of Bond's engagement hit the streets, the joy in Hartford was palpable. One probably apocryphal story making the rounds was that of a Hartford merchant hastening down the street while another merchant anxiously tried to catch his attention. Figuring there was something urgent afoot, the first man nervously awaited the important news. His friend overtook him and all out of breath, his face beaming, exclaimed, "I'm glad to see you; I've some good news. *Bond has signed to the Hartfords for next year!*"[32]

As Hartford headed off for a long western swing, the Cincinnati debacle was a distant memory. Winners of seven straight, the club now trailed the White Stockings by only two victories, with three games scheduled for Chicago. The *Brooklyn Eagle* credited John Belden's tirade for the tightening of the pennant race, saying, "Since the hot pitching into Father Belden gave the Hartfords after their defeat by Cincinnati, the nine have been doing yeomen service. It seems to have had the effect of rousing up the team to the importance of doing something to really earn their salaries...."[33]

Chapter 24

Crooked Play?

The Dark Blues made their way west by train, the typical mode of transportation between National League cities. Train travel was generally hot and uncomfortable, although the Pullman sleeping cars that came into wide use after their introduction in 1865 had greatly improved conditions. After stops in Louisville and Cincinnati, the Dark Blues steamed into Chicago, three victories behind the White Stockings. A Windy City sweep would give the Connecticut club a share of first place.

The first game between the two pennant contenders was on Independence Day, which in 1876 was celebrated with extra fervor, since it marked the nation's centennial. A carnival atmosphere prevailed at the ball field as a raucous crowd, 12,000 strong, filled the grounds two hours before game time. Tickets were in such demand that grandstand seats were being scalped at a 200 percent premium. The White Stockings' arrival was greeted with loud cheers, but some rowdy fans went overboard, igniting firecrackers and even shooting pistols.

The action between the lines featured no offensive fireworks and remained scoreless through six innings. Finally in the seventh, Hartford pushed across the game's only runs, scoring three times off Spalding with the help of two critical Chicago errors. When the White Stockings failed to score in the top of the ninth, the unruly crowd, knowing their club had lost, streamed onto the grounds. When the police just stood by and watched the invasion, the umpire was forced to call the game before the Dark Blues got their final turn at bat.[1]

Back in Hartford, 1,000 people had gathered at the Dark Blues' headquarters awaiting word from Chicago. The scores were received three innings at a time. The first two bulletins, covering six innings, showed all zeros. The posting of the final dispatch sparked a great celebration punctuated by loud cheering, hat throwing, and hand-shaking. After sending a congratulatory note to Bob Ferguson, a giddy Bulkeley, who later declared that winning this game was the proudest event of his life up to that time, provided a sumptuous spread in the clubrooms and sent for a shipment of fireworks. Later in the evening, the Dark Blues' victory and the nation's 100th birthday were joyously celebrated with a grand display of pyrotechnics launched from club headquarters with responding fireworks from the *Hartford Times* office.[2]

Two days later, with an even bigger crowd of 2,000 supporters assembled outside the Dark Blues' headquarters, the notoriously weak-hitting Jack Remsen led off the second game in Chicago. Remsen had a peculiar swing that was preceded by an elaborate wind-up. His histrionics didn't prevent him from driving one of Spalding's pitches over the fence, giving Hartford a lead they would never relinquish. Not only was this Remsen's only home run of the year, it was the first lead-off home run in National League history. Tommy Bond's curves were especially effective on this day, fooling even the umpire, who called many of them strikes, even when they broke well out of the strike zone. The fans directly behind home plate gave the arbiter an earful each time this happened. The final score was 6–2 in favor of Hartford.[3]

The Dark Blues were now just a single victory from sweeping the mighty White Stockings. The Connecticut press was bold and confident. The *Hartford Post* struck back at those who had denigrated Hartford's headwork, posing the sarcastic question, "Wonder if Chicago had *all* the brains in the games of Tuesday and Thursday?"[4] The *Courant* predicted unequivocally that the Blues would be in first place when they returned home.

Chicago's captain Al Spalding was in a quandary. His competitive nature told him that he should pitch the third game against Hartford, but his results against the Dark Blues suggested otherwise. The best pitcher in baseball had started four games against Hartford and had lost all but one. Gallantly putting his team before his ego, Spalding sent change pitcher Cal McVey back to the box to stop Ferguson's surging nine. McVey, who had beaten Hartford earlier in the year, came through again. His rapid deliveries blanked Hartford for the first seven innings. Meanwhile, Chicago built a 7–0 lead on their way to an easy 9–3 victory. The two clubs had now split their six games, each winning two in the other team's park. When Hartford departed Chicago, the standings were as follows[5]:

Team	W	L
Chicago	26	7
Hartford	24	6
St. Louis	20	12
Boston	17	16
Louisville	14	18
New York	10	20
Philadelphia	10	22
Cincinnati	6	26

Despite the loss, the Dark Blues remained upbeat as they traveled to St. Louis, poised to continue their success. Backed by the flow of gambling money, rumors were rampant that the Browns would lie down for Hartford and allow them to take all three games. The purported reason was that George Bradley would rather see Hartford take the pennant over Chicago.[6] This proved to be far from the truth.

Things got off to a rocky start for the Hartfords, even before the first game was played. Upon arriving in St. Louis, the team boarded at the LaClede Hotel, which had given the club a special rate of $2 per day, per player. Prior to leaving for the field for the first game against the Brown Stockings, some unspecified dispute arose between Bob Ferguson and the hotel management. As a result, Ferguson became intent on finding other lodgings. He demanded the bill and was shocked to see it was for the regular rate of $3 per day. Ferguson refused to pay and led his team over to the Planters Hotel. Unfortunately, Ferguson had forgotten that the Laclede still held the team's trunk, which carried their extra uniforms. Despite Ferguson's demands, the hotel refused to give it back, leaving Ferguson pondering legal action against the hotel.[7]

Later that day at the Grand Avenue ballpark, the Dark Blues' troubles continued. Hartford had punished George Bradley's pitches earlier in the year, but "Grin" was about to exact revenge — in spades. A heavy shower delayed the start of the game before Jack Remsen stepped to the plate. In Hartford's previous game, Remsen had homered to lead off the game, but this time he struck out, to a round of cheers.

St. Louis scored two runs in their half of the first inning on Joe Battin's double. From that point, there was no further scoring, as the wet grass made the ball as dead as a wet rag, and, according to one St. Louis newspaper, it became "impossible to drive the wet and unshapely ball out of the infield." Bob Ferguson's frequent demands for a new ball were ignored. The 2–0 loss was Hartford's first shutout of the season. Two days later, Bradley made it two whitewashes for Hartford, with the eighth of what would be his league-leading 16 shutouts, this time winning 3–0.[8]

Stunned by the sudden turn of events, Hartford needed to salvage the third game to remain close behind Chicago. The game started well for Hartford, as Tommy Bond retired Ned Cuthbert on strikes. Former Mansfield catcher John Clapp, now the backstop for St. Louis, then lined a base hit to left-center field. A wild pickoff throw by Bond allowed Clapp to scamper all the way to third base, and he scored on Mike McGeary's fly ball. Hartford failed to score in their first turn at bat, despite Jack Burdock reaching on an error and advancing to third. He was stranded there, as Ferguson flew out to end the inning.

The second inning saw St. Louis score another unearned run when Ev Mills' error on an easy grounder allowed Joe Blong to score. Meanwhile, George Bradley was in a groove. He retired Hartford in order in the next four innings and limited Hartford to just two more base runners over the first eight innings. Jack Remsen reached base on an error in the sixth, and Tom York walked in the eighth.

In the ninth inning, Hartford was determined to break Bradley's string of 26 straight goose eggs. Remsen grounded out to start the inning. Jack Burdock then reached on an inexcusable error by third baseman Joe Battin. Next, Dick Higham took the bat and smashed Bradley's delivery down the third base line. Battin redeemed himself splendidly with a fantastic stop of the hot ball which started a double play and ended the game. The stunned Dark Blues departed the field as St. Louis players and fans celebrated. Unaware that Bradley had just held Hartford hitless, the celebration's focus was the three consecutive whitewashes. Bradley's amazing feat put the Dark Blues on the wrong end of the National League's first no-hitter and the league's first triple play suffered earlier in the season.[9]

Years later, when retired in Philadelphia, Bradley was asked about his accomplishment. He replied, "Didn't know anything about it at the time.... You go out there interested in winning. You didn't remember anything except to pitch to the batter's weakness and not let him connect." Bradley said that one key to the victory was a trick he and his catcher used. "It was the quick return," explained Bradley. "I would stand all ready on the slab and when the batter got into the box I would swing it to him. Then Clappie [John Clapp] or Miller [Tom Miller] would snap it back, and because of the peculiar wrist delivery that Tommy Bond and I got — peculiar at that time — I could snap the ball back before the batter got set. The result was that he would be all at sea and keep swinging all the time and hitting nothing usually."

During the interview, Bradley mistakenly recalled his no-hitter against Hartford as being a perfect game against Boston. He was confusing his win against Boston in 1875, after the Red Stockings had won their first 26 games, with the Hartford no-hitter. Bradley did remember the three shutouts against Hartford, but then said Boston came to town and he held them scoreless, "and now that you mention it, I remember distinctly that not a man got to first."[10]

What Bradley failed to mention was the choice of balls St. Louis used for home games. As was their prerogative, they chose the dead ball instead of the more lively version, which contained more rubber at the core. For some reason, the ball in St. Louis was so dead that the *Chicago Tribune* called it a "putty ball" and said that "instead of responding with a click when hit, it simply gave a dull thud like a chuck of mud. The hardest pounding could not drive the sphere anywhere in particular." In later years, rumors surfaced that St. Louis may have benefited from the "double ball racket" in the Hartford games. In this scheme, a team would use a dead ball when pitching, then switch in a lively ball when batting.[11]

The three losses to St. Louis were devastating. All the benefit from the hard-earned victories in Chicago had been undone, and the Dark Blues now trailed the White Stockings by five victories. When they returned home, Hartford wasn't in first place as the *Courant* predicted; in fact, they weren't even alone in second, as St. Louis had drawn even. The excitement that had enveloped the city three weeks earlier had evaporated. In a startling display of apathy, only 200 people bothered to attend the Dark Blues' first home game in nearly five weeks.[12]

Meanwhile, things were looking brighter in New Haven. By July, the New Havens had defeated St. Louis twice and Boston and the Athletics once each. The *Chicago Tribune* voiced what many in the National League believed: "The New Haven Club would have evidently made a better showing in the race than the Cincinnatis."[13]

After their ninth win over a National League team, a 9–2 victory over the Mutuals, the *New York Sunday Mercury* praised the New Haven club, saying that all National League teams should thank them, since visiting teams get paid better in New Haven than in Hartford. With a bigger population, plus 900 Yale students, who were avid supporters of the game, the *Mercury* felt that New Haven was a better baseball city than Hartford. As a result, the newspaper was expecting New Haven to be admitted to the National League for the 1877 season. The rumor that New Haven would be admitted to the League in 1877 became so strong that Al Spalding felt the need to say he would fight against the club's admittance.[14]

Unfortunately, New Haven's success on the field did not translate into paying customers at the gate. The *Register* noted about the Mutual game, "As has become too common ... but few people were present." The club's financial status was so desperate that, despite the persistent demands of the players, salaries hadn't been paid in two months. The club had started the season with many outstanding debts from 1875, including $800 owed in back-salaries. Upon returning from their road trip, the team was forced to pay several outstanding bills, leaving them $7,000 in debt.[15]

Things were so bad that the New Haven club was sued by the estate of Philos Tyler, who had died earlier in the year. It appears that Tyler was the property owner from whom the club leased the Howard Avenue lot. His estate was suing the club for $700 for use of the land. The fence, grandstand, and both sections of seats were being called for.[16]

Faced with such deep debt, team directors declared bankruptcy and decided to operate the club on a co-operative basis, under which players would receive no salary, just a portion of the gate receipts. As the situation deteriorated in New Haven, the vultures started circling, and players were getting offers from other teams. Most chose to remain with New Haven, at least temporarily. However, as the situation worsened, players signed with other teams, and the season came to a close by the end of September. Charlie Pabor did not desert the team. He remained in the city to run a cigar store, with the promise that if a nine was organized for 1877, he would run it.[17]

Trouble was also brewing in Hartford, as the Dark Blues struggled to maintain second place, let alone advance on Chicago. In a 13–4 loss to Boston, Tommy Bond was ineffective, while Bob Ferguson committed several errors at third base. Afterwards, the young pitcher publicly accused his manager of "crooked work."[18]

Any charge of throwing games was serious business, especially when leveled against Ferguson, who had a spotless reputation when it came to gambling. Al Spalding said of him, "Robert Ferguson was ... a man of sterling integrity and splendid courage. He knew all about the iniquitous practices which had become attached to the game as barnacles to a ship, and he was sincerely desirous of eradicating them. But he lacked the essential qualifications of a reformer. Could it have been possible to eliminate gambling by physical demonstrations, Robert Ferguson would have cleared the Base Ball atmosphere of one of its most unsanitary conditions at that time...."[19]

Ferguson had demonstrated exactly that in 1873, when he boldly confronted a group of gamblers after an Atlantics game. Ferguson approached the gamblers who had operated openly next to the field, yelling,

> I've marked you, you infernal (we draw the adjective mild, for fear of offending polite ears) thieves and robbers. I'll bust you yet, and drive you out of here, you contemptible scoundrels, thieves and blackguards. I'll teach you to buy up my men, you low-lifed loafers-every one of you. There ain't one of you who wouldn't steal a penny from your dead mother's eyes, and kick the corpse because it wasn't a quarter. Come out here, if you want to, any one of you who don't like it, or whom the coat fits, and I'll warm the ground with your miserable carcass till you won't want to buy up my men again."

Even though the pool sellers far outnumbered Ferguson, his challenge went unanswered because the gamblers knew Ferguson was a dangerous man to tackle when he was angry.[20]

Bond's surprising accusation may have resulted from prior problems between Bond and Ferguson. Their relationship had reportedly become so strained that earlier in the season Bond had fled to New York, refusing to return unless Ferguson apologized for some misdeed. Ferguson, however, denied any previous trouble with his star pitcher.[12] His response to Bond's unseemly charges appeared in the *Hartford Times*.

> To the Editor of the Times: In your issue of Wednesday is published an article in which my name figures to a considerable extent, charging me with selling games. It has been my good or bad luck, as the case may be, to often see my name in print, but, from whatever source, cause, or inspiration, I have heretofore passed all insinuations by in silence. The article published on Wednesday evening is so astounding in its charges that they call for an immediate denial. That they were made with a malicious purpose I have no doubt, but I can do no more at this time than pronounce them each and every one false in every particular. By giving this to the public, before whom I have always borne a good character, you will greatly oblige, yours respectfully, Robert Ferguson, Manager Hartford Base-Ball Club.[21]

A day later, the *Post* published Bond's reply to a letter of inquiry from Bulkeley.

> In reply to your letter in regard to Captain Ferguson's play in recent games, I desire to say that whatever charges of crooked play or willfully losing games were made by me, were entirely unfounded, and made in a moment of excitement, and I cheerfully acknowledge the wrong I have done both to the club and it manager, and make this the only reparation in my power.[22]

Despite Bond's casual retraction, the ill will between the men lingered, destroying "what little of harmony existed before." Finally, Bond informed Bulkeley that he wouldn't play with Hartford as long as Ferguson remained on the team. Forced to decide between the two adversaries, Bulkeley stood by his manager. He annulled the remaining portion of Bond's 1876 contract and released him from his 1877 commitment. Incredibly, less than three weeks after the initial charge, all connection between the Hartfords and their star pitcher was severed. Bond played the remainder of the year for New Haven, who harbored dreams of signing him for the following season.[23]

On the field, Ferguson quickly deployed Candy Cummings in the pitcher's box. Despite languishing on the bench since the embarrassing loss to Cincinnati in early June, Cummings responded heartily, beating Boston 10–4. He continued to pitch well, winning five of the next six games, including a history-making two games on September 9. On that Saturday, Hartford played Cincinnati in a regularly scheduled game and then in a make-up of the previous day's rain-out. Normally, the make-up game would have been played on Monday, since Sunday games were prohibited. Delaying the game until Monday would have caused Cincinnati's room and board expenses to double to $88, likely exceeding their share of receipts. In order to allow Cincinnati to leave Saturday, the decision was made to play both games that day. In the morning, Cummings beat Cincinnati, 14–4. He completed his doubleheader sweep that afternoon, pitching Hartford to an 8–4 victory. Unfortunately, barely anyone witnessed Cummings' iron-man feat, as the combined attendance for the two games was a meager 500 fans.[24]

Next was a two-game set with the White Stockings. Hartford desperately needed both games to maintain their faint pennant hopes. In the first game, they trailed 5–0, but once again Al Spalding couldn't put them away. Led by Richard Higham, who went 5 for 5 against his old team, Hartford showed amazing tenacity, storming back to take the game, 8–7. Having learned his lesson yet again, Spalding sent Cal McVey to the box the next day. Most of the excitement took place before the game, when the teams' center fielders, Jack Remsen and Paul Hines, squared off in a foot race. Both players strained themselves so badly that Hines had to sit out the game entirely, while Remsen retired in the fifth inning. McVey came through again, pitching Chicago to a 6–2 victory.[25]

After two losses to St. Louis, Hartford traveled to Chicago for another pair of games. This time, Spalding took no chances and deployed Cal McVey immediately. Hartford led 2–1 after five innings, but Chicago scored six times in the sixth, led by Adrian Anson, who tripled and doubled in the inning. With five base hits and four runs in the ninth, Hartford nearly made another miraculous comeback, but Remsen popped out to first base, extinguishing Hartford's hopes. McVey had proven his captain right again, as Chicago's 7–6 victory clinched the National League pennant.[26]

A nine-game winning streak to close the season allowed Hartford to take second place from St. Louis. The final standings, which until 1882 were based on total wins, not winning percentage, were as follows:

Team	W	L
Chicago	52	14
Hartford	47	21
St. Louis	45	19
Boston	39	31
Louisville	30	36
New York	21	35
Philadelphia	14	45
Cincinnati	9	56

Once again, several Hartford players produced excellent individual statistics. In his abbreviated season, Tommy Bond completed 45 games, winning 31, with a 1.68 ERA. Candy Cummings posted 16 victories, a 1.67 ERA, and 5 shutouts. The much-maligned Dick Higham assembled a 24-game hitting streak, batting .327 and tying for the league lead with 21 doubles.[27] He led the Dark Blues in batting and slugging by wide margins and had none of the problems of which he had so often been accused in the past.

Despite these excellent personal performances, Hartford's lack of team harmony was a major impediment to capturing the first National League pennant. Between Ferguson's constant badgering, the strife between the manager and star pitcher, and what the *New York Clipper* called "not only a lack of unanimity in support of the pitching, but a sort of jealousy as to which pitcher was to be known as the regular man," Hartford's record suffered.[28] Still, if the Dark Blues could have just managed to beat a part-time pitcher named Cal McVey, the National League pennant would have landed in Hartford. Give credit to Al Spalding, who had been criticized earlier in the year for not having an effective substitute pitcher, for pushing the right button with McVey. The strong Iowan, who started only six games all year, won all four of his starts against Hartford, providing the winning margin for the White Stockings, who finished five victories in front of the Hartfords.[29]

The discord within the Dark Blues' ranks didn't end with the completion of the final game. Not satisfied with Tommy Bond's dismissal from the Hartford club, Bob Ferguson continued to press his grievance at the National League's annual meeting in December. He presented a written complaint asking for Bond's permanent expulsion from the league for "defamatory charges made, but not sustained, by him." After considering the evidence, which included a letter from Bond in which he made "an unqualified retraction of the charges," the league ruled that Bond's dismissal from the Hartford club was sufficient punishment. To Harry Wright's delight, Bond was free to honor the contract he had signed with Boston for 1877.[30]

Chapter 25

Bulkeley's Deal

With the depressed economy weakening attendance, most National League teams finished the 1876 season in the red. In Brooklyn, the poor economy only compounded problems for the Mutuals, whose gate receipts had been shrinking for years due to persistent suspicions of player corruption. As the *Chicago Tribune* reported, the Mutuals had become an "infirmary for the refuge of players whose lack of reputation or ability — nearly always the former — have shut them out from other clubs." Things were so bad in 1875 that the Mutuals nearly failed to field a team, but William Cammeyer, who managed the Union Grounds and became the Mutuals' president in 1875, hastily assembled a ragged group of players. A few of them received regular salaries; the remainder were paid from gate receipts, if there were any. At the end of 1875, the team's balance sheet was such that Cammeyer decided to forego the club's final western trip.[1]

At the end of the 1876 season, Cammeyer again decided that his Mutuals, now in the National League, couldn't afford to make their final road trip. He informed the western clubs that his club would be staying home to play amateur teams instead. This decision, as Cammeyer was fully aware, directly defied the league rule mandating each club complete their schedule or face expulsion. In 1875, as president of the White Stockings, William Hulbert had counseled others to be understanding of Cammeyer's decision. Now, with the credibility of his new league at stake, he could no longer be so forgiving. If the Mutuals did not make their final road trip, Hulbert would be forced to expel them.[2]

Cammeyer's position put Hulbert, who was already anticipating the expulsion of the bankrupt Athletics for not completing their schedule, in a bind. Losing the Athletics, for whom he had a personal dislike, didn't bother him much, but banishing two teams from his eight-team league would be problematic. Hoping to avoid this, Hulbert teamed with Charles Fowle of the St. Louis club, to entice the Mutuals to complete their schedule by offering financial incentives. The two men agreed to guarantee Cammeyer $400 for two games in Chicago and $400 more for three games in St. Louis. Furthermore, they would ensure that the Mutuals played all these games in one week in order to limit travel expenses. The $800 guarantee would fully cover all costs of the trip, and it didn't include any additional money the Mutuals might earn in Cincinnati and Louisville. In response to this incredibly generous offer, and with full knowledge that he was risking expulsion from the league, Cammeyer replied, "It is impossible."[3]

Why would Cammeyer, confronted with the huge carrot of Hulbert's unprecedented offer, and the equally large stick of expulsion from the National League, refuse to go west? Cammeyer had offered some clues in a July newspaper interview. He described his players coming to him with better offers from other teams and being forced to tell them that he couldn't match the salaries. Even Joe Start, who had played his entire career in New York, was preparing to leave. Cammeyer said, "If I was to say to him, 'Joe stay,' he would do it. But that would not be doing him justice, so I let him go as I do the others. In fact, I am thinking about letting them all go, and getting an entire new set of men for next season."[4]

So, in midseason, Cammeyer admitted he was thinking of simply scrapping his existing nine and starting over again with a new team. If this was his plan, expulsion of the Mutuals would not be so frightful, presuming Cammeyer could re-enter the league with a new club. But where would this new team come from? Some thought it would be the best collection of honest, local amateur players Cammeyer could find. Others thought it would be the amateur Chelsea club of Brooklyn. The *Brooklyn Eagle* provided a clue to this team's true identity as early as August, when it noted that all of the Hartfords except for two were from Brooklyn, and curiously stated, "This would be a splendid Brooklyn Atlantic team for 1877...."[5]

In Hartford, the league's smallest city, the Dark Blues' coffers had been ravaged by the recession. Attendance had plummeted from 41,000 in 1875 to just 18,000 in 1876, and the club reportedly lost $5,000. The *Chicago Tribune* said, "Hartford is not and never was a large enough town to support a club without some wealthy man to run his hand into his pocket at the close of the season. Mr. Bulkeley has enjoyed that pleasure several years, and seems to like it."[6]

In Bulkeley's predicament, Cammeyer saw an opportunity. What better way to start over in Brooklyn than to bring in the well-respected, pennant-contending Hartford club? Besides, the Hartford roster included many former Brooklyn players, whose presence Cammeyer believed would revive the city's interest in baseball. There were even rumors circulating that Cammeyer saw a side benefit to his Mutuals being expelled from the league. If expelled, the Mutuals' games would be expunged from the league record. Such a move would disproportionately benefit Hartford over Chicago, since the Dark Blues had not fared as well against the Mutuals as the White Stockings had. This might allow Cammeyer to bring in not only a reputable team, but a championship one as well.[7]

When rumors of an impending deal hit the streets, Bulkeley quickly denied their veracity. A Middletown newspaper reported, "Manager Bulkeley announces positively that there is no truth in the rumor that has been extensively circulated that the Hartford club will go to Brooklyn next season and make that city its headquarters." The *Courant* said, "There is no reason for the proposed removal, as Hartford from a financial point of view is much better than Brooklyn. When times are good and money is plenty, Hartford people turn out quite numerously to witness the ball games."[8]

Cammeyer also denied the rumors. The *Brooklyn Eagle* reported, "Manager Cammeyer says that the report of the Hartford team coming to Brooklyn in 1877 is 'all bosh.' If it is, it's bad for Brooklyn, that's all that can be said. But people here don't believe it is 'bosh.'"[9]

The *Chicago Tribune* acknowledged the ongoing talks, but didn't believe Cammeyer could coax Bulkeley to Brooklyn. "The fact of the matter is, the Union Grounds have become a stench in the nostrils of New Yorkers, and the great majority of honest people propose to let it severely alone in the future. Mr. Bulkeley knows this, and therefore it is more than probable that he will prefer to stay in Hartford with his men; for what man can touch filth and remain undefiled?"[10]

Despite warnings like these, there were several clues that a move was in the works. In August, New York fixture Joe "Old Reliable" Start, who had vowed to finish his career in New York, appeared to know something, signing with Hartford for 1877. Meanwhile, Cammeyer hadn't signed any players, yet he was telling everyone he planned to have a nine on his grounds. In perhaps the most telling move, Bulkeley signed his players to personal contracts made to him, not the Hartford Base Ball Club.[11]

The *Brooklyn Eagle* completely supported the rumored move. "It's the only thing that can be done to bring about a return to the old time paying attendance at the Union Grounds, and the sooner the arrangement is consummated, the better," the newspaper opined in November.[12]

Three months later, the *Eagle* lectured the Hartfords on the wisdom of making the move. "Hartford has ceased to be a good locality for a professional club to reap profit in which does not stand at the head of the class.... If this was the case in 1876 when the club had the powerful team it then possessed, things are not going to improve this season with a weakened team.... It will be readily seen therefore, how vitally important it is to the general interest of League club teams that Brooklyn in 1877 should be represented by just such a strong and reliable team as the Hartford club could bring them. In fact in every respect it is to the interests of that Club to come to Brooklyn, and it is to be hoped that they will soon see that it is so."[13]

Although close to cutting a deal for several months, Bulkeley and Cammeyer could never quite consummate the agreement. The stumbling block was, of course, money. Cammeyer offered to pay all expenses in exchange for 25 percent of the receipts. Hartford held out, offering Cammeyer 20 percent. Complicating the deal was the National League's new rule stipulating that visiting teams receive 15 cents for each person entering the grounds. The only exceptions would be the players themselves, policemen in uniform, and ten other individuals. This meant stockholders and season ticket holders would no longer be excluded from the attendance count that determined the visiting team's share of the gate. Hartford had a large number of such patrons who purchased season tickets that allowed entrance to games, exhibitions, and even practices at substantial savings over buying individual tickets. If the Dark Blues remained in Hartford, the new rule would result in a significant loss of revenue. A move to Brooklyn, where every spectator who entered the grounds was required to pay cash on the spot, would prevent this.[14]

Believing that he and Bulkeley would soon reach agreement, Cammeyer proceeded with his premeditated plan to let the Mutuals die, and the club did not make its final road trip. The *Chicago Tribune* acknowledged Cammeyer's calculated move, saying, "The Mutual Club's failure was fairly to be attributed to a bargain made by Bulkeley to lease the Union Grounds for the new club...."[15]

Hulbert was now forced to carry out the promised expulsions or risk losing credibility as a reformer. At the National League meeting that December, the Athletics tried to stave off banishment with written petitions and questionable arguments for being allowed to remain in the league. A.G. Mills of the Chicago club replied at considerable length, completely annihilating the Athletics' defense.[16]

While the Athletics were fighting for their lives, the Mutuals didn't bother to appear and defend themselves. Their only representation was a letter from Cammeyer. Sounding very much like a man who already had a certain team from Connecticut primed to move to Brooklyn, Cammeyer "acknowledged the corn," saying it was "no use for the League to have rules if it did not enforce them." By unanimous vote, both the Athletics and Mutuals were barred from the National League.

With the Mutuals' demise, the only thing remaining for Cammeyer to do was wrap things up with Bulkeley. Despite the apparent inevitability of the move, Hartford newspapers continued to be in denial. The *Hartford Post* condemned those who spread the story of the Dark Blues' imminent relocation. "The Brooklyn Eagle and other papers which publish the slops compiled by one Henry Chadwick still insist upon publishing the statement that the Hartford Club is to play games in Brooklyn next season. This statement is a lie, as Chadwick well knows...."[17]

If an agreement had been left to Cammeyer and Bulkeley alone, the *Post* might have been correct. As it was, Hulbert, now president of the National League after Bulkeley resigned following a one-year term, was keenly interested in seeing the transfer take place. He viewed it as a way to improve the financial stability of the entire league, since it would pay every member club "to play a strong and honest team in Brooklyn over the same team in Hartford." As a result, Hulbert brokered an agreement in which the other league clubs would allow Bulkeley to keep more home revenue, if he moved his club to Brooklyn. In Brooklyn, the Hartfords would only have to pay visiting league clubs 12.5 cents per ticket sold, instead of the 15 cents other home clubs had to pay. The other clubs felt this concession would benefit them in the long run, since the Dark Blues' move to Brooklyn would relieve them of having to be "interested spectators of close races between gate receipts [in Hartford] and hotel bills, with the hotel bills a hot favorite to win."[18]

So, on March 5, with the support of William Hulbert, and after "enough negotiations to have concluded a treaty with England," William Cammeyer, Morgan Bulkeley, and Bob Ferguson finally signed the contract that moved the Dark Blues to Brooklyn. The historic agreement made the Dark Blues the first club to change cities without a change of ownership, predating the infamous move of the Dodgers from Brooklyn to Los Angeles by more than eighty years.

The name of the transferred club was now open for debate. Consideration was given to simply retaining the Mutuals' name, but the *Chicago Tribune* advised otherwise: "There is no reason why Bob Ferguson should make himself a missionary to reclaim the latter name from the depths into which it had fallen." Henry Chadwick advocated calling the club the Atlantics. Management chose another route, morphing names into the oxymoronic "Hartford Club of Brooklyn." The intention was to draw on the reputation of the Hartford nine for its skill and honesty, while also adhering to the National League rule requiring clubs to bear the name of the city in which they were located.[19]

In the end, all parties, except Hartford baseball fans, got what they wanted. The National League was able to flex its muscles and uphold its authority over individual clubs by expelling the Mutuals and Athletics, while simultaneously strengthening the financial health of the league. William Cammeyer got a new, presumably more profitable, tenant for his grounds, and

Morgan Bulkeley was relieved of having to pull money from his own pocket to aid his club's bottom line.[20]

Despite their disappointment at losing a major league team, the *Hartford Courant* took the high road, saying, "The Hartford Club, retaining the old name and most of the old members, who are so well known, will continue to draw the interest of Hartford people, and will be glad to rejoice at its successes."[21]

Chapter 26

A New Home

Upon arriving in Brooklyn, Bob Ferguson, with Morgan Bulkeley's blessing, began to assume full control of the team off the field, as well as on the diamond. William Cammeyer initially believed that he would act as the Hartfords' corresponding secretary, but after a week of dealing with the autocratic Ferguson, Cammeyer decided to let him take care of this task, "as I feel assured that I would draw myself into trouble."[1]

In addition to garnering nearly complete authority over the Hartfords, Ferguson was trying to influence the newly-released National League schedule. To avoid a repeat of the previous season's debacle with the Mutuals and Athletics, Hulbert commissioned Harry Wright to develop a pre-determined schedule so that teams would no longer be left to establish game dates themselves. Ferguson complained bitterly that the results of Wright's efforts unduly favored the White and Red Stockings, especially on holidays such as Bunker Hill Day, which was a local holiday in Boston, Decoration Day, now called Memorial Day, and the Fourth of July. "Chicago and Boston want all the cream, the rest of the clubs take water," complained Ferguson.[2]

Ferguson's griping deeply disturbed Harry Wright. "I did nothing but dream about it when I did sleep and think of it when awake, all night," Wright told Hulbert. He did not want to acquiesce to Ferguson's demands, since the previous year Hartford had gotten the plum assignment of playing in Chicago on Independence Day. "If he [Ferguson] was one of the kind to appreciate a favor of such a nature it would be different. If he insists on having his own way I believe on ignoring him entirely, and seeing to it that things are different there next year. With Cammy this whole matter would have been settled long ago." Wright knew that the hard-headed Ferguson liked to "paddle his canoe in his own way," but if he continued on, especially in regard to the schedule, then "breakers are *dead ahead*, and should he not alter his course, he will be swamped."[3]

When not busy intimidating people, Ferguson focused on finding a replacement for his erstwhile pair of pitching aces, Tommy Bond and Candy Cummings, who were now in Boston and Cincinnati, respectively. Cummings left the Hartfords after his request for a salary increase was refused. Fergy eventually signed untested right-hander Terry Larkin, who had pitched previously with the Brooklyn Alaskas and Ilion, New York, clubs. Although he possessed a swift curveball and an excellent change of pace, many critics downgraded Hartford's prospects since Larkin, who less than a decade later would be arrested and institutionalized for a binge of violent crimes, was small and inexperienced. As he had proven in the past, though, Ferguson was an astute judge of talent. In Larkin, Captain Bob saw remarkable potential, and he was practicing with him four days a week in hopes of transforming him into another Bond.[4]

Ferguson also needed to replace the potent bat of Dick Higham, who had signed with the independent Syracuse Stars, after Harry Wright had shown some interest in signing him for 1877. Wright told Higham, "If not with us or the Hartfords, I would like to see you with the Cincinnati team, provided you balanced yourself as well as you did when with the Hartfords — to the best of any knowledge. Dick, I would like to see you do well, and would be glad to assist you, if at all certain that you would do well by yourself. You know what I mean, so will say no more."[5] John Cassidy, who signed with Hartford after the New Haven went bankrupt late in the 1876 season, would take Higham's place in right field. According to the *Louisville Courier-Journal*, Cassidy was "the best-looking man on the nine. A handsome set of teeth and a good-natured face [were] also agreeable accompaniments."[6]

The Hartfords did upgrade their first base position with the signing of Joe Start, who was at the peak of a long career that began in 1860. Start was so well respected that he was chosen by a Brooklyn author as the main character in a novel entitled *Thirty Years on the Ball-Field*.[7]

The Hartfords also exchanged one weak-hitting, slick-fielding center fielder for another, replacing Jack Remsen with Jim Holdsworth. Like Remsen, Holdsworth also went through an elaborate wind-up as he prepared to strike the ball, so much so that reporters dubbed him "the dancing batter."[8]

The National League's second season featured several changes from its first. The league now consisted of only six teams, as Hulbert made no effort to replace the expelled Mutuals and Athletics. Each team would play the others twelve times, according to Harry Wright's fixed schedule. The fair-foul rule was eliminated, thus requiring the ball to pass third or first base in fair territory, just as in today's game. Hartford and Boston had experimented with this proposed rule change in an exhibition game played at the end of 1876. Six balls were ruled foul that would have been fair under the old rules.[9]

In light of the weak economy, the league also enacted several measures aimed at tightening controls on expenses. Each player would be required to pay $30 per year for his uniform and pay for the upkeep himself. While on road trips, players would be assessed 50 cents per day to cover the cost of food and lodging.[10] Subsequent years saw additional regulations, including the incorporation of the "reserve clause" in 1880. This rule permitted each team to "reserve" five players who could not be signed by any other league club. This suppressed salaries by eliminating competition for the services of the best players. The reserve clause was eventually applied to entire rosters and remained in effect until 1975.

Between the lines, the champion White Stockings would have a different look, as Al Spalding announced his retirement from pitching. During the season he would play first and second base, pitching in only four games. Although there had been whispers that his effectiveness was waning, the move was surprising, since he led the league in 1876 with 47 wins. Of his decision, Spalding later explained, "I knew that I was slipping before anybody else did, and that it was my time to retire."[11] Chicago signed an able replacement in George Bradley, who had amassed 45 wins in 1876, including an amazing 16 shutouts.

Boston appeared to have regained their championship form with two strategic acquisitions. First, Deacon White returned to the fold after spending one year in Chicago. In addition, Tommy Bond would handle the pitching duties. After Bond's release from Hartford, Boston president N. T. Apollonio immediately traveled to Hartford and signed the young fireballer. Harry Wright excused Bond's unfounded accusations against Ferguson, saying that the "quiet, unassuming, and reserved" lad had silently endured Ferguson's abuse as long as he could. Finally, when he couldn't take it any longer, he "lost control of himself and, boy like, for he is not much more in years or experience, talked wildly and made assertions that he could not prove, and was sorry enough for it afterwards, no doubt." Uncle Harry dismissed any concerns about Bond being a troublemaker. "I have no fear but he will prove a different person. It shall be our endeavor to develop all the good there is in him, and restrain the bad. In fact to make a man of him, if it is in him.... A pitcher we know he is."[12]

Despite the earlier rumors that they would join the National League, New Haven had no organized baseball club of note in 1877. Talk of organizing a semi-pro team had surfaced in late winter, but nothing materialized. Charlie Pabor, who had committed to managing a New Haven nine in 1877, should there be one, saw the reality of the situation and left to sign with the Columbus (Ohio) Buckeye club. New Haven residents did get to see the Brooklyn Hartfords play an exhibition game against a New Haven club at Hamilton Park. Several hundred fans watched the six-inning affair in very cold weather.

A few members of the old New Haven nines played, including Fred Goldsmith, Ed Somerville, and Jim Keenan.[13]

As the new season approached, Hartford residents were more interested in an upcoming scientific exhibition than their old team's opening game in Brooklyn. On April 27, Alexander Graham Bell and his aides were in Connecticut to demonstrate the viability of the modern telephone. Bell appeared at Skiff's Opera House in New Haven, while an associate faced another audience at Roberts' Opera House in Hartford. Thomas Watson, Bell's chief assistant, was in Middletown, talking with each city alternately and jointly over wires borrowed from the Atlantic and Pacific Telegraph Company. Several songs were performed in Middletown, and when the Hartford and New Haven audiences simultaneously heard the lyrics, they burst forth in applause. Bell predicted that in the future, "telephony would be in use generally in dwellings, just as gas and water are supplied — not luxuries but necessaries ... communication could be established with the butcher, the baker, and ... conversation could be carried on with distant cities for purposes of trade, business, etc."[14] The telephone would become a practical tool in 1878 when the nation's first telephone exchange was established in New Haven.

The season opened on April 30 with Boston visiting the Hartfords in their new Brooklyn home. A large crowd was expected for Tommy Bond's return to the National League. Interest was heightened by the fact that he would face his old nemesis Bob Ferguson. Despite the rosy predictions, only 500 spectators paid the 50-cent admission fee to the Union Grounds. This count included members of the press, who, according to the league's new rules, were required to pay to enter the grounds. Upon learning of the need to pay, the annoyed journalists threatened to stop announcing upcoming Brooklyn games unless they were admitted free of charge. Afraid of losing the free advertising, Cammeyer relented and paid their way. While uncertain weather limited the crowd somewhat, the National League's standard 50-cent admission charge was the real issue. For years, there had been an ongoing debate about whether the proper admission fee to a ballgame was 25 or 50 cents. The National League had always maintained a 50-cent charge, as Hulbert believed the higher price bolstered the league's image as exclusive entertainment. It was now being said that Brooklyn residents wouldn't pay such a steep price, resulting in a loss of patronage.[15] This was not exactly the scenario Morgan Bulkeley had envisioned when uprooting his club from Hartford.

The game was a tight one. Boston led 1–0 in the fifth when their defense committed two errors, putting Jack Burdock on third and Tom Carey on first. Bob Ferguson then stepped to the plate, eager for revenge against his former accuser. After watching a few of Bond's pitches go by, he exacted his pound of flesh with a long double to center field. Burdock scored easily, and Carey should have scored to give Brooklyn the lead, but he inexplicably stopped at third. Moments later, Carey compounded his blunder when he was caught off the bag on Tom York's grounder to third base. Another Boston error loaded the bases with only one out, and it looked like Hartford would surely take the lead. However, Bond reached back and increased the velocity of his pitches, and the game remained tied at one until it was called after eleven innings.[16]

The two rivals didn't meet again until the Hartfords traveled to Boston for two games in early June. Upon arriving, Ferguson boasted openly that the Hartfords would pound Tommy Bond all over the field. After hearing this, the Boston crowd was even more partial than usual, and when Bond retired Ferguson three consecutive times, howls of derision rained down on the Brooklyn captain.[17] The Hartfords dropped both games, 8–2 and 18–6, leaving their record at a disappointing two wins and five losses.

Between the two Boston games, Brooklyn played three games at their old ball grounds in Hartford. Two games against the expelled Athletics and one against the Hartford Amateurs were expected to draw large crowds, but the city of Hartford had apparently lost interest in its vagabond team. The largest crowd for any of the three games was just 500 spectators.[18] These were the club's only appearances in Hartford. A game against the Chicago White Stockings, scheduled for later in the year, was rained out.

After the two losses in Boston, the Hartfords began playing better. Led by the pitching of rookie Terry Larkin, they took a pair of games from the Red Stockings in Brooklyn, winning each 7–0. Larkin was the undeniable star of these victories, completely out-pitching Bond. In the two games, Larkin allowed a total of seven hits, no walks, and no wild pitches. Bond, on the other hand, took both losses, yielded 21 hits, threw several wild pitches, and committed several fielding errors.[19]

Full of confidence after these victories, the Hartfords reeled off six wins in their next seven games. Once again, Bob Ferguson received the lion's share of the credit for the team's success. The nine, especially young members like Larkin and Bill Harbidge, relied heavily on his guidance. When one of his pitches was called a ball, Larkin would turn around and explain or apologize to Ferguson. Upon swinging and missing, or letting a called strike go by, Hartford batters would immediately turn to face Ferguson for instruction. The *Chicago Tribune* found the situation amusing, saying, "It is at times almost comical to see the men try to play with one eye on the ball and the other on the Captain."[20]

Prodded by Ferguson's constant badgering, the Hartfords fashioned a surprising 10–6 record and a second-place standing. The Louisville nine, led by ace pitcher Jim Devlin and hard-hitting outfielder George Hall, held first place, while the reigning champion White Stockings were struggling. George Bradley, who would finish the season with a losing record and an ERA two runs higher than in his exceptional 1875 season, was not filling Spalding's shoes as anticipated. Ross Barnes's production also fell dramatically, due mostly to illness but also to the elimination of the fair-foul hit which he had perfected.[21] Limited to just 22 games, Barnes never approached his typical offensive numbers.

At the end of June, Hartford departed on a long road trip, hoping to advance on first-place Louisville. Unfortunately, the team finished the grueling five-week tour with a 5–11 record, a performance that toppled them into fourth place. The reported reason for their drop-off was that many players had signed with other clubs for the following year, making them less interested in obeying their current captain and working hard for the Hartfords. While this may have been a factor, especially on a team ruled by Ferguson, probably more important was that Terry Larkin was ill for most of the trip and unable to pitch with his usual effectiveness.[22] On more than one occasion, John Cassidy and Ferguson were forced to handle the pitching duties while Larkin was sick in bed.

On August 13, the Louisville Grays were still in first place with a 27–13 record, five victories in front of Boston. They made a long eastern swing with important series in Boston and Brooklyn. The Grays dropped the first game of the trip, 6–1, to the Red Stockings, as pitcher Jim Devlin, normally a good hitter, struck out four times. They then arrived in Brooklyn for the final three games of their season series with the Hartfords. Many of the Grays professed confidence in returning to their winning ways. The Boston game was an aberration, they said. "You won't see our nine whipped like that again this season, you bet, no sir!" They had good reason to be confident, having beaten Brooklyn six times in nine previous matches. When the Grays saw that Brooklyn was missing Tom York, their confidence grew even more. "We've got 'em dead," they proclaimed.[23]

Surprisingly, the Hartfords took the first game, 5–1, prompting the *Louisville Courier-Journal* to note that the Grays seemed "too anxious for success to be sufficiently nerved for such a contest." But the next day was worse, as Hartford held the Grays scoreless for just the second time all year, winning 7–0. After the third game with the Hartfords ended in a 1–1 tie, the Grays returned to Boston for three games. Louisville dropped the first game, 3–2, leaving the two teams tied for first place with identical 27–17 records. Suspicions about the Grays' play spread around the league. The Grays then lost the final two games in Boston, 6–0 and 4–3. They were now winless in seven straight games; the best they could manage was the 1–1 tie with the Hartfords.[24]

26. A New Home

The Grays returned to Brooklyn to replay the drawn game and extended their losing streak to seven with a 6–3 loss to the Hartfords. The next day, the same clubs met in New Haven. Initial indications were that it would be a regular National League game, but New Haven residents were disappointed to learn that it would only be an exhibition game. Still, 700 spectators came out for the game. Despite using back-up outfielder Frank Lafferty to pitch, Louisville beat Hartford 6–4 in 10 innings.[25] Prior to this eastern trip, Louisville had won six of nine matches against Brooklyn, scoring an average of seven runs per game. In their next four meetings, Louisville lost three and tied one, while managing a grand total of just five runs. Then, in a meaningless exhibition in which they didn't even play their best nine, the Grays scored more runs against Brooklyn than they had in the previous four games combined. Something certainly seemed strange.

Upon their return to Louisville, the local club was taunted by the *Louisville Evening News,* whose writer appeared prophetic: "The Louisville Grays, alleged base-ball players, have returned from their triumphal tour ... and will play the Amateurs on the Louisville grounds this afternoon. It will scarcely be profitable to throw the game to the Amateurs, as the pennant does not depend on it...."[26] Meanwhile, Boston continued winning and clinched the pennant at the end of September. Tommy Bond was the main reason for Boston's return to glory, leading the league in virtually every important pitching category, including wins, shutouts, earned run average, and strikeouts. Louisville, which had started the season 27–13, went 8–12 the rest of the way.

Shortly after the season concluded, the *Louisville Courier-Journal* reported that it had learned some interesting things about the Grays. Suspicions arose during midseason when some players started appearing in "royal style," wearing diamond pins and rings. When the club fell apart during their eastern trip, these suspicions were finally investigated.[27]

The club directors pieced together a story from the players' telegraph correspondence which confirmed the illicit gambling associations of Jim Devlin, George Hall, and Al Nichols. Nichols knew a gambler named James McCloud who paid both Devlin and Hall $100 to throw a game at Cincinnati. They then threw a couple of non-league games for which they claimed never to have received payment. Despite the highly suspicious results, none of the players ever admitted throwing any of the crucial losses in Boston and Brooklyn. Shortstop Bill Craver, who had earned a tainted reputation over the course of his career, was the only player who refused to allow the club to examine his telegraph records.[28]

On October 30, 1877, the Louisville Grays formally expelled Hall, Devlin, Nichols, and the uncooperative Craver. Hulbert felt that the Louisville scandal presented an opportunity for the National League to prove its integrity to the paying public, telling Bob Ferguson, "Certainly nothing can be lost to the legitimate game by the conviction and punishment of the thieves and scoundrels who infest it and (who) by their presence as players bring disgrace and contempt upon it ... the exposure and conviction upon their own confession of the four men named, makes our forthcoming League meeting an excellent time and place to strike an effective blow." At the December meeting, officials permanently banned the four Louisville players. Despite repeated personal pleas by some of the players, most notably Jim Devlin, Hulbert remained true to his word and never let any of them return to his National League. In 1878, Bob Ferguson, who became field manager of Chicago that season, appealed to Hulbert for Hall's reinstatement. But Hulbert remained adamant, saying Hall had "stab[bed] his employer, the clubs of the league, and his fellow players. For a paltry sum, which he did not need, he sold not only himself, but you and me."[29]

The Hartfords finished the season in third place behind Boston and Louisville with a 31–27 record. This was a surprisingly strong finish, given that the team had lost their two star pitchers and their best batter. Larkin proved his critics wrong, finishing third in the league in wins and second in ERA at 2.14, just a shade behind Bond's 2.11. Cassidy led the team in batting with a .378 average, good for second in the league behind Boston's Deacon White. Joe Start batted over .300, and Tom York had an excellent power year, leading the team in doubles and triples.

On another note, Connecticut hosted its final major league game in 1877. Three weeks after the Louisville-Brooklyn exhibition, the White Stockings and Hartfords met in New Haven. Unlike the earlier exhibition game, this one counted in the standings, and despite sparse attendance, the Hartfords beat Chicago, 11–9.[30]

Chapter 27

Connecticut Revival?

Attendance in Brooklyn had been only marginally better than in Hartford, and despite the National League's monetary concessions, the Hartfords still finished the season an estimated $2,500 in the red. Realizing in midseason that the move to Brooklyn was failing, Morgan Bulkeley informed Hulbert that he was ready to leave baseball. There was also speculation that not only the Hartfords' president, but the entire club, would be out of the league after the season. This rumor was fueled by the revelation that Bob Ferguson apparently planned to forsake the Hartfords and take several members of the nine with him, having signed them to personal contracts to himself, not to the Brooklyn club.[1]

The likely departure of Bulkeley and the possible disbanding of the Hartfords set Ben Douglas, who had left the Blues after the 1875 season, into action. Still refusing to believe that professional baseball couldn't work in Connecticut, Douglas put up $300 of his own money and criss-crossed Hartford garnering support for returning National League baseball to the city. By late summer, he had raised over $4,000 toward his cause. Douglas then frequented Brooklyn ball fields, scouting players for his Hartford nine. The *Brooklyn Eagle* praised Douglas, saying, "He is a good judge of character, beside which he has a winning way with him, which of course, has its influence in assisting him to control a professional team." The *Eagle* thought that the players he was reportedly assembling appeared to be strong, but perhaps hard to handle, since several had "peculiar dispositions and tempers, but no doubt Mr. Douglass [sic] possesses some happy gift or other which will produce a happy family feeling."[2]

Hartford newspapers ran with the story of a resurrected Hartford club as if it was a certainty. Readers were told that Tom Carey would captain the nine while Doug Allison would also return, moving his family back to Hartford over the winter. In mid–November, Fred "Tricky" Nichols and former Hartford Dark Blues player Steve Brady practiced on the Dark Blues' old

Wyllys Street grounds, reportedly as a warm-up for their 1878 season in Hartford.[3]

Despite the optimism of the Hartford press, there were still significant obstacles to Douglas' plan. The *Chicago Tribune* predicted that the high salaries Douglas was offering would bankrupt the team before the end of the season. The newspaper cautioned prospective players to "remember that there is no Bulkeley with a bank account back of this venture." More problematic was the National League's rule barring a team from a city with a population under 75,000. Although Hartford had not been required to meet this standard in 1876 when they were selected as one of original National League clubs, the League could now hold them to it.[4]

Douglas countered the latter concern with the dubious reasoning that his club would simply be a re-organization of the existing Hartfords, for which the minimum population rule had already been waived. While it was true that the Brooklyn club still officially controlled the territory of Hartford, Douglas, who had personally been out of baseball for nearly two years, was going to have a hard time showing that his club was a continuation of the Brooklyn club.[5]

For consideration at the National League meeting in December, Douglas sent a letter that was "half application and half claim," presumptuously stating that his club desired "to remain in the league." For Douglas to receive a favorable ruling, it was essential for him to demonstrate that his new team was the legitimate successor to Ferguson's club. The league decided to hold any action until the following day when Bob Ferguson was scheduled to speak on behalf of Douglas. When Ferguson failed to appear, it was resolved that Douglas's club was not a justifiable extension of the Brooklyn Hartfords. Furthermore, should Douglas still want to join the league, he would need to submit a new application which would require unanimous approval, since Hartford lacked the required population. This ruling, combined with the fact that Ferguson had "abandoned" the Brooklyn club by signing with Chicago and taking Joe Start, Terry Larkin, John Cassidy, and Bill Harbidge with him, left the National League directors to conclude that the Hartford baseball club had "vacated its membership" in the league.[6]

After being denied his bid to return major league baseball to Hartford, Douglas hatched a new strategy. Instead of re-applying for a team in Hartford, Douglas would take his club to Providence. Putting a National League team in Rhode Island's capital city was not a new idea. During their struggles in 1876, rumors had Bulkeley moving the Dark Blues to Providence, which, the *Chicago Tribune* said, was "about three times as large as Hartford, and twenty times as enterprising." The main benefit of Providence was that its 100,000 residents eliminated any concerns about the National League's population requirements. Harry Wright liked the idea so much that he invited Douglas to meet with him and representatives of the Lowell, Massachusetts, club, who Wright was also pushing to enter the league. After the talks, Wright encouraged Douglas to send Providence's paperwork to the league office. "Don't *procrastinate*, Ben, send them on. We want to vote on it."[7] Douglas's application was approved, and the Providence Grays remained a capable team in the National League for eight years, winning two championships during that time.

The denial of Douglas's application sealed Connecticut's fate. Never again would the state be home to a major league baseball team. In 1884, an opportunity arose to join the Union Association, a weak major league that lasted but one season. Union Association founder Henry Lucas was searching for a fourth eastern team to balance against his western teams and thought Hartford was the answer. However, when the winter of 1883–1884 passed without any response from Connecticut, Lucas was forced to admit Altoona, Pennsylvania, as the final team.[8]

Since the nineteenth century, Connecticut's closest association with major league baseball probably came in 1962 when the Houston Colt .45's were admitted to the National League. The nickname was selected as the winning entry in a public contest to name the team. It honored Samuel Colt's gun, which, as "the gun that won the west," played a large role in Texas history. The Colt Firearms Company in Hartford gave permission for the team to use its name and emblem of crossed guns. The temporary stadium where the Houston team initially played was named Colt Stadium. At a groundbreaking ceremony for what would later become the Astrodome, Paul Richards, general manager of the Houston team and former minor league player in Hartford, helped city officials use Colt revolvers to blast holes in the ground.[9]

The Houston club played as the Colt .45's for three seasons, but at the end of the 1964 season, a dispute arose between the Colt Company and the team. The Colt Company was unhappy about the club sublicensing the Colt name to manufacturers of baseball souvenirs. Rather than sacrifice the revenue or share it with Colt, Houston president Roy Hofheinz chose to change the team's name. In 1965, the Colt .45's became the Houston Astros in honor of the Texas city's role in the nation's space program.[10]

Although major league baseball hasn't been seen in Connecticut in well over 100 years, minor league baseball has thrived in the state. The first minor league team arrived almost immediately after the demise of the National League Hartfords, when in 1878 Ben Douglas, Jr., brought an International League team to New Haven. After being forced out of the Providence club early in the 1878 season, Douglas learned that the New Bedford team had dropped out of the International Association. Since the New Haven baseball scene appeared dead for 1878, Douglas hastily assembled a team that was admitted into the International Association. The nine was short on talent, and attendance at the Howard Avenue Grounds was sparse. As a result, Douglas lost $400 in his first month in New Haven.[11]

In a desperate attempt to keep his dream alive, Douglas moved the club to Hartford in hope of drawing larger crowds. In a May 17 letter to the *Hartford Courant*, Douglas explained, "I have received permission to change the name and residence of the club to Hartford.... I propose giving the people of Hartford some seventy odd first-class international and league games. All I ask of the advocates of base ball in Hartford is to purchase season tickets.... Hartford will not be ashamed of her new club." Attendance wasn't much better in Hartford, and two months later Douglas' club was expelled from the International Association for failing to pay a visiting club.[12]

In the final two decades of the nineteenth century, Connecticut cities fielded teams in three different minor league organizations: the Atlantic Association, the Atlantic League, and the Eastern League. In 1899, the Connecticut State League was formed with teams in eight Connecticut cities. In 1913, the league was renamed the Eastern Association, in honor of Massachusetts entries from Pittsfield, Springfield, and Holyoke.

As for the three Connecticut cities that once hosted major league teams, Hartford and New Haven have since been represented by many minor league teams, but Middletown has had professional baseball in only one season since. In 1910, the Middletown Jewels and three other Connecticut clubs played in the Trolley League, a new Class D minor league, which was four steps below the major league level. The Jewels played on Asylum Street in the general vicinity of the Mansfields' old grounds. For their Opening Day ceremonies, the Jewels invited former Mansfield players Jim O'Rourke and Tim Murnane to attend. O'Rourke responded enthusiastically, saying, "It is with pleasure that I acknowledge receipt of your very cordial invitation to be with you at the opening game of the season. I wish to thank you for your very kind invitation and assure you that if it is possible for me to arrange my affairs I will be most happy to be present. I wish your league and your club the best of success. I am thinking, though, they will have to go some to equal the good record of the Mansfield's of 1872."[13] Unfortunately, neither O'Rourke nor Murnane were able to attend the festivities.

New Haven hosted a minor league team every year from 1899 through 1932. New Haven native George Weiss was instrumental in running many of these teams. His first came in 1919, when he purchased the New Haven team in the Class A Eastern League. The team was immediately dubbed the "Weissmen" by the local press. They later became known as the "Profs" in honor of Yale. Weiss later became general manager of the New York Yankees, helping to build the Yankees' dynasty of the 1950s. George Weiss was elected to the Hall of Fame in 1971.

Two of Hartford's many minor league teams, the Senators and the Chiefs, achieved prominence throughout the state. The Senators played from 1902 to 1935, finishing first in their league five times. Lou Gehrig, Jim Thorpe, Leo Durocher, and Hank Greenberg all wore the Senators' uniform early in their careers. As part of its 100th anniversary celebration in 2001, Minor League Baseball compiled a list of the "100 Best Minor League Baseball Teams." The 1931 Hartford Senators, featuring future major league pitcher Van Lingle Mungo and the previously mentioned Paul Richards, came in at #26.

The Chiefs, also known as the Laurels and Bees at various times during their existence, were the Eastern League affiliate of the National League Boston Braves from 1938 to 1952. Several future major leaguers graced the Chiefs' roster, including Hall of Fame pitcher Warren Spahn. The 1944 team was ranked #99 on Minor League Baseball's list.[14] The Chiefs were the last professional team to play in Hartford. When the Boston Braves moved to Milwaukee prior to the 1953 season, they offered to sell the Chiefs franchise for $1. There were no takers. Despite recent attempts, no professional baseball team, not even a minor league one, has played in Hartford since the Chiefs' last game on September 7, 1952.

Today, Connecticut is home to a Double A minor league team: the New Britain Rock Cats (affiliate of the Minnesota Twins). A second minor league team, the Bluefish, have played in Bridgeport since 1998 as a member of the independent Atlantic League.

Although only an active imagination can rekindle Connecticut's major league days, reminders of that wonderful era can still be seen today, if one looks hard enough. The grave sites of Morgan Bulkeley (Cedar Hill Cemetery in Hartford), Ben Douglas, Jr. (Indian Hill Cemetery in Middletown), and Jim O'Rourke (St. Michael's Cemetery in Bridgeport) can all be visited. The Benjamin Douglas family home still stands on South Main Street in Middletown. Jim O'Rourke's house stood until 2009 on Pembroke Street, just south of Interstate 95, in Bridgeport. The Orator's home had been the subject of much publicity recently, as historians attempted to prevent its destruction in Bridgeport's latest round of urban development. A statue of O'Rourke is being planned for the city. Vintage base ball, played by the rules and customs of the nineteenth-century game, has become popular in Connecticut. The Middletown Mansfields, Hartford Dark Blues, and New Haven Elm City clubs have all been represented by these vintage clubs.

What remains of the actual major league field sites? A visit today to Howard Avenue in New Haven gives no indication that a major league ballpark once stood there. The grounds were still being used for baseball as late as 1882, but by 1888, Rosette Street had been extended further east, dividing the site of the ballgrounds. Today, the parcel of land is tightly packed with multi-family homes.[15]

In Middletown, the site of the old Mansfield Grounds sits in a neglected part of the city. The land is now partially bisected by Connecticut highway Route 9, Omo Street, and Maplewood Terrace. It is unclear when baseball stopped being played there. Again, there is no indication that major league baseball was once played on the site.

The Hartford Base Ball Grounds no longer exist. In fact, even the corner of Wyllys Street and Hendricxsen Avenue has disappeared. Wyllys Street was reconfigured so that it no longer runs directly in front of the Church of the Good Shepherd, which is still a functioning parish. Hendricxsen Avenue, now dead-ended three blocks short of Wyllys Street, has been replaced by the church driveway.

Following the Dark Blues' departure, the ball grounds hosted various sporting matches, such as Trinity College track and field meets, amateur baseball and the games of Ben Douglas's International Association team. Non-sporting events, like the Dr. Carver Shooting Exhibition and the Van Amburgh Great Golden Menagerie, were also held there. Without a major league tenant, though, the park was worth more for its lumber, and on May 8, 1879, the *Hartford Courant* reported the sad demise of the once state-of-the-art ballpark. "The base ball grounds, for ball purposes, have been abandoned. All the portable property has been sold. The grand-stand, which cost a considerable sum of money, was disposed of for about a song."

Unlike visits to the former sites of the Mansfield and Elm City club fields, a visit to the site of the old Hartford Base Ball Grounds provides an inspiring journey back in time. It is one of only two original National League ballpark sites to remain at least partially undeveloped. The other is a section of Grand Avenue Park in St. Louis. A visitor can actually stand on the original location of home plate and look out upon a green lawn that stretches back several hundred feet from Wyllys Street until it meets an imposing brownstone structure. The Caldwell Colt Memorial House, which now stands where Jack Remsen once patrolled center field, was constructed in 1895 by Elizabeth Colt.

From the center of this lawn, the dark blue onion dome above the Colt factory is clearly visible. Several trees border the open greenery, some probably old enough to have held the rowdy boys who often climbed them to get a free look at the game. Despite the decades since Connecticut was home to major league baseball, one can picture opposing batters vainly flailing at a Candy Cummings curveball, the "hurrahing" of Mark Twain and his Hart-

27. Connecticut Revival?

ford compatriots, the church bells ringing out a hymn, and captain Bob Ferguson booming out, "Have a care, boys!" and threatening to exact physical punishment if they did not.

In the summer of 2007, Ron Bolin, a resident of neighboring Wethersfield and a baseball historian, spearheaded a drive to honor the Dark Blues with an appropriate historical marker at the site of the Hartford Base Ball Grounds. Money was raised and a marker was placed at the site in the summer of 2008. The commemorative text reads:

The view from home plate at the former Hartford Base Ball Grounds, looking directly out to center field. An expanse of green lawn still stretches back several hundred feet from Wyllys Street until it meets the imposing brownstone structure of the Caldwell Colt Memorial House, which now stands where Jack Remsen once patrolled center field. This grand companion building to the adjacent Good Shepherd Church was built in 1895 by Elizabeth Colt in memory of her last surviving child, who drowned in 1894 (Library of Congress).

> Site of the
> Hartford Base Ball Grounds
> 1874—1876
>
> Home of the Hartford Dark Blues
> Professional Base Ball Club
> National Association 1874–1875
> National League 1876.
>
> One of the original eight National League ball fields,
> it was once considered the finest in the country.
> It featured a covered wooden grandstand, fence, press box,
> clubhouses for both teams and a seating capacity of 4300.
>
> Dedicated to the City of Hartford and the men who played
> here and shaped the early history of our national pastime.

May this monument forever serve as a reminder of the glorious days when Connecticut, the Nutmeg State, made critical contributions to the development of major league baseball as we know it today.

Postscript: In February 2009, just seven months after being dedicated, the marker was stolen, and has not been recovered.

Appendix A:
The Players, by Team

Middletown Mansfields

Frank Allen—Frank "Ham" Allen was the Mansfield back-up shortstop. His true date and place of birth have not been determined. This much we do know: Ham Allen, who played with the Marlboro, Massachusetts, Fairmounts in 1869 and 1870, joined the Mansfields in 1871. He played for two seasons with Middletown and then apparently moved on to play in the International Association, possibly with the Lynn and Taunton clubs.[1]

Willis Arnold—After resigning his post as business manager for the 1875 New Haven club, Arnold returned to Middletown and played with an amateur team there for the remainder of the season. In 1876, the Providence team of the New England Association gave Arnold a second chance at managing. He continued his managerial career with Auburn, New York, Springfield, and the Albany club of the International Association. In Albany, Arnold found the most success. In 1878, he guided his club to an impressive eighteen game winning streak. The unbeaten string included a victory over the National League Boston Red Stockings and Arnold's old teammate Jim O'Rourke. He resigned after the 1879 season, returning to Middletown, where he and his wife, Mary Dorrigan of New Haven, had their first child in September 1880. Arnold died in Albany, New York, in 1899.[2]

Clytus "Cy" Bentley—Cy Bentley, a carpenter by trade, was the team's number-one pitcher, starting 17 of the club's 24 games. After starring for the amateur Mansfields since 1869, the professional competition proved to be a little too tough for Bentley. He finished the season with 2 wins and 14 losses and an ERA of 6.10. Besides his struggles on the diamond, Bentley's personal life was filled with tragedy. He missed the Mansfields' first victory of the season due to the death of his mother. Then there was the mid-season death of his infant son. Finally, just six months after the Mansfields' season abruptly ended, Bentley himself died of tuberculosis. He was only 22. His former Mansfield teammates attended the funeral en masse.[3]

Edward Booth—Edward H. Booth played second base and the outfield for the Mansfields. Eddie was the only Mansfield to continue playing professionally for the remainder of the 1872 season, signing with the Brooklyn Atlantics, who undoubtedly recalled his five hits against them a week before the Mansfields collapsed. A true journeyman, Booth played for six different teams in his five year career, including the

New York Mutuals in the National League in 1876. In 1877, he played right field with the Buckeye club of Columbus, Ohio, of the International Association.[4] His date and place of death are unknown.

Asa Brainard — Asa Brainard didn't have much of a career left after his stint with the Mansfields. He played only a few more years, showing none of his previous skill. Brainard had his share of struggles after retiring from baseball. He lived with his mother in Staten Island and didn't have many things to keep him busy. He contacted his old manager Harry Wright, looking for help in getting back into baseball as an umpire. "I am in want of something to do and think it little enough for the B.B. (Base Ball) community to give to one who has done so to elevate the game." Despite his plea, Brainard never did become an umpire. He later moved to Denver, where he operated the Markham Hotel billiard room. He died there of pneumonia in 1888, the first of the famous 1869 Red Stockings to pass away.[5]

Frank Buttery — Frank Buttery played third base and outfield during the season, but he did his best work as the change pitcher for the Mansfields. After his baseball career, Buttery ran a general store in the Silver Mine section of New Canaan, Connecticut. He wed Mary Guthrie at the age of 38. He died in 1902 of complications of an injury he suffered while on a hunting trip a few years before. On the trip, he accidentally shot himself, resulting in the amputation of the toes on one foot.[6]

John Clapp — Clapp signed with the Philadelphia Athletics in 1873, remaining there through the 1875 season, at which point he resigned from the club in a dispute over money. The disagreement started when Clapp, who was born in Ithaca, went home in mid-season to catch for the Ithaca nine, who were playing a big game against their rival, Binghamton. As a penalty for leaving the team, the A's fined him $200. At the end of the season, when the A's denied Clapp's request to refund the money, he resigned. This precipitated a bidding war for his services, which ended when he signed a $3,000 contract with St. Louis.[7]

Clapp bounced around with various National League teams for seven seasons, batting a respectable .283 for his career. During that stretch, he established the ironman record for playing 212 consecutive games.[8] This was an amazing feat, considering Clapp was a catcher at a time when men of that position wore little or no protection.

One other highlight of Clapp's career came in 1881, when he earned the nickname "Honest John" for refusing to accept a bribe. After a couple of shady characters offered him $5,000 to throw a game by allowing passed balls when men were on base, Clapp contacted the authorities. A plan was hatched to expose the gamblers by having Clapp speak with them on the phone while police listened on another line. During the phone conversation, Clapp pretended to go along with the scheme. As the gamblers spoke with Clapp, their guilt became obvious to the police.[9]

Starting in 1883, Clapp ran a saloon in partnership with Mets pitcher Jack Lynch. The beer house didn't make much money, so Clapp returned to Ithaca as a policeman in 1890. He served on the force for fourteen years until he died of a heart attack while on duty. He was helping carry a drunken man back to the police station when his heart gave out. John was survived by his widow and four children.[10]

George Fields — George Fields was the Mansfields' utility player, playing mostly third base but also some outfield and shortstop. He was born in Waterbury, Connecticut, and returned there to live after his stint with the Mansfields. He worked as a brass turner at the Waterbury Clock Company for many years. In his spare time, he helped run the Monitor Baseball club of Waterbury, which was the first team of future Hall of Famer Roger Connor. Fields was the longest surviving Mansfield, dying in 1933 at the age of 82.[11]

Frank McCarton— Frank McCarton remained in Middletown for several years after the Mansfields disbanded. He became captain of the O.V. Coffin Hook and Ladder Company and married Ann Powers, a local girl who provided Frank with four children while in Middletown.[25] During the years after his lone professional season, McCarton played many games with Middletown amateur teams. In 1872, McCarton finished second in both batting average and slugging percentage on the Mansfields. He hit .329 for the year, outhitting men such as O'Rourke and Clapp, both of whom would later become big stars in the league. It's a mystery why his career didn't extend past this one abbreviated season. It seems that some team would have taken a chance on him. Amazingly, this potential star was reduced to playing in pick-up games, like the one he played with the O.V. Coffin Hook & Ladder team against a team of Hartford firemen.[26] He later moved to the Bronx where he became a policeman. McCarton died in 1907 at the age of 53, suffering from gangrene of the stomach.[12]

Tim Murnane—Colorful Tim Murnane initially remained in Middletown after the Mansfields disbanded and became quite interested in the city's volunteer fire department. When the O.V. Coffin Hook and Ladder Fire Company was incorporated in November 1872, Murnane was elected to office. He didn't see much action with the fire company because shortly thereafter he accepted secretary Hicks Hayhurst's offer to join the Philadelphia Athletics. Hayhurst had been impressed with Murnane's leaping catch earlier in the year. Murnane also received an offer from Harry Wright to join Boston, but Tim chose Philadelphia. Murnane suggested that Boston take Jim O'Rourke instead, but Wright felt that, although O'Rourke was a good player, the Irishman would never be accepted in Boston unless he removed the leading "O" from his name.[13]

Murnane played with Philadelphia for two seasons and then joined the Red Stockings for the 1876 campaign. In that year, Tim recorded the first stolen base in the new National League. He continued with Boston in 1877, and in 1878 he became the first player engaged by Ben Douglas for Providence's new professional club. Murnane played the following year with the Capitol City Club of Albany and then retired. After several years of commercial pursuit, Murnane organized the Boston club of the Union Association in 1884, playing and captaining the team. When the Union Association disbanded, Murnane joined the Jersey City club in the Eastern League for a couple of months and then retired permanently. He tried his hand at umpiring for the National League in 1886. At the same time, he founded a weekly newspaper, the *Boston Referee*, which covered the odd combination of baseball and polo. After this publication folded, Murnane wrote freelance articles for the *Boston Globe* and *New York Clipper*.[14]

In 1887, Murnane was employed by the *Boston Globe* and quickly became the baseball editor. In a few short years, he was nationally known as a powerful, opinionated editor, highly respected by all. Tim was a staunch supporter of the old-time game. He wrote in 1897, "There will never be any better players than George Wright, Ross Barnes, Mike Kelly, Fred Dunlap, Ed Williamson and quite a few others almost equally prominent in their day." Remembering Middletown and its old ballplaying days, Murnane wrote, "I have promised myself a visit to that city on the occasion of the next reunion of that old guard who flourished like mountain flowers before baseball was taken into the law courts, at a time when the game was full of sentiment and the attitude of the player toward the fan was absolute friendship, long before there was any big financial return. How different professional baseball is at the present time! And more's the pity."[15]

On February 7, 1917, Murnane and his wife went to take in a show at Boston's Schubert Theater. The next morning, he was planning to go south to cover the Red Sox' spring training camp. As he entered the theater, Murnane suddenly dropped to the floor, dead of a heart attack. This was a complete shock to everyone, since he appeared to be in good health and spirits when he dropped off his daily copy at the office that day. Murnane's death was front-page news in Boston. The *Boston Globe* remembered Tim as "a man of the utmost simplicity of character and of wonderful ideals, which survived all the experiences of a life that make most men cynics. He saw men truly, but he idealized the game with which most of his career was bound up. He believed in baseball sincerely as a former of character and as a great factor in making Americans better men."[16] Many retired and active ballplayers, including Babe Ruth, attended Murnane's funeral.

At his death, Murnane left only a small estate for his widow and six children, two from a previous marriage. To help the grieving family, a benefit game was held which matched the Boston Red Sox against an All-Star team. On a crisp September afternoon, 17,000 fans came to Fenway Park to see a collection of the game's best players on one field. Grover Cleveland Alexander, Walter Johnson, Johnny Evers, Wally Schang, Shoeless Joe Jackson, Eddie Collins, Ty Cobb, and Tris Speaker, all played without pay. Former heavyweight boxing champ John L. Sullivan was also present, coaching first base during the game.[17]

Prior to the game, the star players faced-off in several baseball skill competitions. Shoeless Joe won the long throw contest, Mike McNally of Boston the "bunt and run" contest, and Babe Ruth the fungo-hitting contest. Ray Chapman circled the bases in 14 seconds, earning himself a silver cup. During these contests, Will Rogers rode onto the field on his horse, lassoing members of both teams to the fans' wild delight. About $14,000 was raised, and the American League paid for a large monument to be placed on Tim's grave.[18]

At the game, a leather-bound memorial book, signed by American League president Ban Johnson and all eight American League team owners, was presented to Tim's widow. The text read, in part, "Timothy Hayes Murnane was gathered to his fathers on February 7, 1917, after about 45 years of active service to baseball, first as a player of prominence and then as an able organizer, a wise executive and an authoritative writer. The American League of professional baseball clubs expresses its deep sense of the loss the national game has sustained by his death, recognizing that in his devotion to baseball, which he put above all interests of clubs or players, he best served the welfare and ideals of the League."

For many years, the Boston Base Ball writers handed out the Tim Murnane award. At the 1978 Hall of Fame induction ceremony, Murnane was honored with the J.G. Taylor Spink award, given by the Baseball Writers Association "for meritorious contributions to baseball writing."

Jim O'Rourke—The most successful Mansfield alumnus was James Henry O'Rourke. Virtually every book on the early history of baseball features his name prominently. During his prolific 45-year career, O'Rourke participated in the game as a player, manager, umpire, and league president. Whether it was a big game in the pennant race or the latest controversy involving players' rights, O'Rourke was always in the middle of things.

After his year with the Mansfields, O'Rourke joined the Boston Red Stockings for the 1873 season. When O'Rourke first arrived in Boston, Wright encouraged him to hide his Irish ancestry by changing his surname to "Rourke." This was unthinkable to Jim, who replied, "Mr. Wright, I would rather die than give up my father's name. A million dollars would not tempt me." Jim's wife later recalled, "I don't think they fully appreciated royal blood in Boston 30 years ago. Why, Jim is a lineal descendent of King Tiernan O'Rourke of Ireland." As a result of his convictions, O'Rourke became a hero to Boston's Irish community, and the Irish children loved to follow him through the streets. Jim recalled that while in Boston "They called me 'Harry Wright's boy.' He took me to live with his family, and, had I been spoilable, I would have been spoiled in a short time. But the things my mother taught me kept me straight."[19]

O'Rourke played in Boston for six years, and in five of those seasons the Red Stockings took the championship. From 1873 to 1875, the Boston club dominated the National Association. In 1876, however, Boston finished fourth in the new National League. At the start of that year, it was O'Rourke who stroked the first hit in the fledgling league, singling in the top of the first inning on Opening Day. After their disappointing fourth-place finish in 1876, the Red Stockings rebounded nicely and took the pennant the next two years. During those years, O'Rourke was always among the league leaders in many offensive categories. Perhaps his best year was 1877, when he led the league in runs scored and on-base percentage, and batted .362.

Although an excellent batter, O'Rourke's mediocre fielding, especially at first base, often exasperated his manager. Wright criticized his play there, saying, "A first baseman should not stand with his arms folded, thinking of 'the girl I left behind me,' when the ball is being delivered to the bat, as he does frequently thereby letting many a ball get by him that he should have fielded." Wright continued, "He [O'Rourke] does not know what it is to get off his base a yard or two for a wild throw and stop it, or handle it and get back as Start or Mills or Dehlman would. He has a stubborn disposition and two or three times last season refused to catch when I sent him behind the bat. Of course he had to go, but I have had to threaten him more than once to send him off the field. Our games in England I was very near doing it, for his general bad play. You can imagine how bad it was when Spalding said unless I made O'Rourke do better it would be better to stop the game...."[20]

O'Rourke's stubborn nature was also evident in his dealings with the Red Stockings' notoriously cheap owner Arthur Soden. One such run-in was reportedly responsible for the "reserve clause" being added to players' contracts. In 1879, O'Rourke decided to jump to the Providence Grays, where George Wright, who left Boston the previous year, was the manager. O'Rourke's move was precipitated by the Red Stockings' rule that players pay for their uniforms and ante-up 50 cents a day for meal money. Grief-stricken at the possible loss of O'Rourke, Boston fans attempted to convince him to stay by taking a collection to pay the twenty dollars for the uniform. O'Rourke declined his loyal fans' offer and transferred to Providence, a move which helped bring the championship to that city.[21] Stung by the loss of his star player, Soden introduced the reserve clause into player contracts, which essentially bound a player to one team for the duration of his career. The reserve clause remained an integral part of baseball's labor agreement until it was struck down in 1977, paving the way for free agency.

In 1880, Jim returned to Boston, joining his brother John as the first siblings to play together in a major league outfield. After one year, O'Rourke went to Buffalo as player-manager, leading the team to four-straight winning seasons. In 1885, he joined the New York Giants and played on their first pennant winning teams in 1888 and 1889.

O'Rourke was extraordinarily well educated at a time when most ballplayers weren't. He attended Yale law school in the off-season and graduated with a law degree in 1887. O'Rourke's nickname, "Orator," reflected his law school background and flowery language. The suitability of the nickname is illustrated by O'Rourke's incredible response to John Peters, a Buffalo player, who had simply asked for a raise. Orator Jim said, "I'm sorry but the exigencies of the occasion and the condition of our exchequer will not permit anything of the sort at this period of our existence. Subsequent developments in the field of finance may remove the present gloom and we may emerge into a condition where we may see fit to reply in the affirmative to your exceedingly modest request."[22]

With his Ivy League background, O'Rourke was a verbose advocate of player's rights, especially during the Players League movement in 1890. The Players League was formed as a result of tension between players and owners dating back to the National League power-grab in 1876. Since the inception of the National League, player salaries had dropped, freedom of movement had been lost due to the reserve clause, and players were subject to all manner of harsh discipline, including expulsion and blacklisting. When owners refused to lift salary limits, the players moved to form a rival league. Most star players were on board, and financial backers were found to create an eight-team league. O'Rourke was one of many New York Giants who jumped to the renegade league. When peace terms were agreed to after one year, the Players League disbanded, and O'Rourke went back to the Giants.

O'Rourke remained with the Giants until he was released after the 1892 season. Pat Powers remembered the day he handed O'Rourke his release this way: "I was designated by Pres. Day to hand Mr. O'Rourke his written release in '92. Jim tore up the paper and, throwing it on the ground, remarked, 'That is what I think of you.' This brought on a heated argument and Jim and I remained in the clubhouse during the entire game working out warm compliments. The next day it was all over and I have always considered Mr. O'Rourke one of my best friends ever since."[23]

O'Rourke was appointed manager of Washington in 1893. After one year at the helm, he was released. He became a regular umpire for the National League in 1894. After one season as an arbiter, Jim returned to Bridgeport and organized the Connecticut Baseball League. In addition to being the founder and president of the league, O'Rourke also found time to manage and play for the Bridgeport club. Although the club was originally dubbed the "Victors," O'Rourke's gift for gab, and his willingness to argue with umpires, caused the team's name to be changed to the "Orators."[24]

In 1904, at the age of 52, O'Rourke got the itch to play in the Big Leagues once more. He convinced John McGraw, the manager of his old New York Giant club, to allow him to play in a game at the tail-end of the season. The Giants were in the process of wrapping up the pennant, and McGraw gave his consent. On September 22, O'Rourke suited up for his return to the major leagues. Before the game, he was given a standing ovation and was presented with a three-foot floral arrangement. During the contest, O'Rourke showed himself to be "very nimble," and he had no trouble catching the pitches of Hall of Famer Joe McGinnity. O'Rourke also recorded the final base hit and final run of his major league career. He caught the full nine innings in the Giants' pennant-clinching game, making him the oldest player in major league history to play a full game. Two weeks later, McGraw allowed another old Giant, 46-year-old Dan Brouthers, to play in two games for the Giants on October 3 and 4.[25]

At the age of 58, "Uncle Jeems" was featured in a *New York Herald* article entitled "Keeping One Foot Out of the Grave," which profiled older athletes who were still active. Even at his advanced age, O'Rourke still caught every other day for the Bridgeport club. He even retained the look of an old-time ballplayer, sporting a full handlebar mustache. When asked for the secret to his longevity, O'Rourke replied, "Secret? Well, if you call it a secret, the secret's just this: Baseball — it is the real elixir of life. It keeps the mind young by association with young minds; it keeps the body young by the best exercise man ever invented. It uses every faculty — every good faculty — a man's got, and amuses him when he's using it. That's what keeps a man young, that's what's kept me young; that's what's kept me feeling twenty." O'Rourke added, "Baseball has kept me so happy and healthy that there is not a minute of my past life I would not willingly live over."[26]

Besides ballplaying, O'Rourke's later years were spent practicing law, tending to his real estate investments, and dabbling in politics. He was a devoted family man with a wife, six daughters, and a son. His son James also went to Yale and played briefly with the Yankees. On a very cold New Years Day in 1919 O'Rourke went to visit one of his law clients. Despite his daughters' urgings to take a streetcar, O'Rourke chose to walk since he was in a hurry. O'Rourke's impatience, coupled with the cold weather, left him with a severe cold which quickly turned into pneumonia. A week later, O'Rourke was dead. Baseball dignitaries, politicians, and fans packed the church for Jim's funeral.[27]

During his prolific 22-year career, James Henry O'Rourke batted .310 and amassed over 2,300 hits. His on-field accomplishments and devotion to the game were acknowledged in 1945 when the Veteran's Committee bestowed upon him the ultimate baseball honor by electing him to the Hall of Fame.

Jim Tipper— Jim Tipper was a fixture with the Mansfields, playing the outfield for them from 1867 through 1872. He missed only the Mansfields' first year of existence. In 1873, he played on various amateur teams in Middletown. The next year, he returned to the National Association, joining the new Hartford entry. The following year, he moved to the New Haven club. After his stint in the National Association, Tipper bounced around with several International Association clubs, including Providence, Lynn, and Rochester. In 1895, while staying at a New Haven lodging house, Tipper died of tuberculosis. The previous night, he hadn't felt well and went to bed early. Although other men were sleeping in the same room, none were aware that Tipper was dying during the night. Tipper was married at one time but had not been in contact with his wife for several years.[28]

Hartford Dark Blues

Bob Addy, 1874 —Addy played three more seasons before being dismissed by Cincinnati, reportedly for drinking. Afterwards, he opened a skating rink in an attempt to popularize baseball on ice. After the rink failed, he moved west, settling in Idaho where he operated a hardware store.[29] Addy died April 9, 1910, in Pocatello, Idaho.

Art Allison, 1875 —The brother of Doug Allison, Art was signed in midseason to play first base after Ev Mills was injured. His major league career ended after playing with Louisville in 1876. He died on February 25, 1916, in Washington, D.C.

Doug Allison, 1875–77—Allison played sparingly for Providence in 1878 and 1879. After retirement, he returned to his old job of marble cutting in Philadelphia. He later worked for the Post Office Department in Washington, D.C. He died at age 71 on his way to work there, on December 19, 1916.[30]

Tom Barlow, 1874 — See "Appendix B: The Curious Case of Tommy Barlow."

Billy Barnie, 1874 — Barnie played 45 games for Hartford, mostly at catcher. After his playing career, he managed several clubs, including Baltimore for nine years, before returning to Hartford. Barnie owned the 1896 Hartford entry in the Atlantic League, but sold the team the following year. He came back to Hartford in 1899 as manager of the Eastern League entry. While managing the Hartford club, Barnie died on July 15, 1900, of pneumonia. His team wore mourning badges on their uniform for the next 30 days.[31]

John Bass, 1877 — Bass played one game for Hartford in 1877, most likely as an emergency replacement player. He had earlier played in the National Association in 1871 and 1872. Born in 1850, John was the last of six children of the well-known Rev. Job Bass family of Brooklyn. He served in the Civil War and later became the regular shortstop for the Forest City Club of Cleveland in 1871. While living in Brooklyn in 1888, Bass contracted tuberculosis, and as many people at the time did, he moved to Denver where it was thought the clean air would help him recover. The Denver YMCA ministered to him while sick, but he died eight weeks later "and was buried among strangers."

Jay Sanford, a member of the Society for American Baseball Research (SABR), learned that Bass was buried in an unmarked grave in Riverside Cemetery in Denver. Due to Jay's efforts and the help of others, a marker with a brass plaque listing Bass' Civil War service and baseball exploits was placed on the grave site. On September 18, 2004, a memorial service was held at the cemetery, and a gravestone was dedicated at the previously unmarked site.[32]

Tommy Bond, 1875–76 — After joining Boston for the 1877 season, Bond rung-up 40, 40, and 43 victories for the Red Stockings, making him the only pitcher in National League history to win 40 games three years in a row. In 1877, Bond became the first "triple crown" pitcher when he led the National League with 40 wins, 170 strikeouts, and a 2.11 ERA for Boston. According to Charley Snyder, who was Bond's catcher in 1878, Bond was an early practitioner of the spit ball. "Tommy Bond used to wet his fingers and produce a peculiar shoot on his ball, yet he was never given much credit for it, nor was he advertised all over the country as a spitball pitcher."[33] Bond amassed an amazing 221 wins before turning 25 years old, but he managed only 13 wins after that due to a sore arm. Upon retiring from the game, Bond coached at Harvard and helped develop two future Hall of Famers, John Clarkson and Tim Keefe.

Late in his life, Bond enjoyed being recognized as an early ballplayer, and he made frequent appearances at both Boston ballparks. In 1907, Bond and Candy Cummings teamed up once again in an old-timers game played on Paddock's Island, near Boston. Cummings started the game, "holding his opponents down like a regular Cy Young." Bond then came in, and "his curves seemed as deceptive as they were in the good old days." In 1936, Bond, George Wright, and Deacon White received life-time passes to all American and National League parks. In 1925, he attended a ceremony at the Grand Central Hotel in New York which kicked off the celebration of the National League's 50th season. Five of the seven surviving players from the 1876 season were in attendance. In addition to Bond, Tom York, George Bradley, Jack Manning, and Alonzo Knight were in attendance. Ultimately, Bond was the final survivor of the National League's first season. He died at the home of his daughter in Boston on January 24, 1941, at the age of 84.[34]

Bill Boyd, 1874 — Boyd played with the Atlantics in 1875, his last year in the majors. He died on September 30, 1912, in Jamaica, New York.

Stephen Brady, 1874–75—Brady played 25 games for Hartford in 1874 and one in 1875 before going to the Washington club. From 1883 to 1886, he played for the New York Metropolitans in the American Association. After his ballplaying days, he was part of the Brady Brothers firm in Hartford, which made mineral water and soft drinks. Brady died in Hartford on November 1, 1917.[35]

Morgan Bulkeley, 1875–77—On the one year anniversary of the founding of the National League, William Hulbert presented Bulkeley with a fancy desk set, which was engraved with the words, "Presented To The Hon. Morgan G. Bulkeley, President of The Nat'l Baseball League, Many Thanks For A Great Year, From William A. Hulbert, 2nd Feb. 1877."

After leaving baseball, Bulkeley embarked on a stellar business and political career. He became president of Aetna in 1879, mayor of Hartford in 1880, governor of Connecticut in 1888, and United States Senator in 1905, serving until 1911. In 1885, Bulkeley married Frances Briggs Haughton, with whom he had three children. He remained a life-long baseball fan, often attending games in Washington while he served as a United States Senator.

In 1907, he served on the commission headed by Abraham Mills, whose task was to determine the origin of baseball. Bulkeley appended the following statement to the commission's final report: "I personally remember as a boy in East Haddam, Conn., before 1846, playing the game of One and Two Old Cat, and remember with great distinctness the early struggles in Brooklyn, N.Y., between the two rival clubs, the Atlantics and Excelsiors, and later the Stars, with Creighton as pitcher. This was some ten to fifteen years before the National organization. I was present, representing the Hartford club, at the formation of what is now the National League at the Central Hotel, Broadway, New York City, about 1875 or 1876, and was its first President, with Nick Young, Secretary."

No long before his death in 1922, Bulkeley recalled, "Baseball isn't the game that it was when I was a boy, or when I was President of the National League. I know that it is a better game in many ways because it has developed from the good start we gave it. What I like about it is that it has not departed so much from the old way of playing that I cannot enjoy it."

Bulkeley died at the age of 85 on November 6, 1922, at his home in Hartford. Upon his death, National League club owners, on the motion of Charles Ebbets of Brooklyn, approved a resolution calling for the league to "inscribe on its records its appreciation of the invaluable aid rendered by him as a founder of the national game...." Based on his one-year stint as the first president of the National League, Bulkeley was elected to the Hall of Fame in 1937. Hulbert, the real force behind the league, wasn't elected until 1995.[36]

Josh Bunce, 1877—Bunce played left field for the Hartfords on August 27, 1877, when several of Brooklyn's players were out sick. This was the extent of his major league career. He had been playing with the Nameless club. There is some question about this player's identity, with some researchers raising the possibility that he actually could have been one of the Bunce twins, Frederick or Henry, who had played with the Hartford Charter Oaks in the 1860s.

Jack Burdock, 1875–77—Burdock was an excellent fielder who led all second basemen in putouts from 1876 to 1880. Later in his career, Burdock suffered injuries and began drinking, earning himself the nickname "Black Jack." Despite his difficulties with alcohol, Burdock had a long, productive career. Only three players from the first National League season—Cap Anson, Jim O'Rourke, and Paul Hines—had longer careers. Later in life, Burdock lived in Brooklyn, where he worked as an attendant at Prospect Park until 1924 when he retired. The next year, Burdock was invited to appear at Ebbets Field when Dazzy Vance was presented $1,000 and a medal for being the MVP in the National League in 1924.[37] Burdock died on November 28, 1931, in Brooklyn.

Tom Carey, 1875–77—Carey played with Providence in 1878 and then finished his major league career with Cleveland in 1879. Carey, who had served in the Civil War, died August 16, 1906, at a Veterans' Home in San Francisco, California. For some time, he was listed in baseball encyclopedias as having been born with the name "J. J. Norton." The SABR Biographical Committee has since shown that to be untrue.

John Cassidy, 1876–77—Cassidy played eight more seasons. His best year was 1877, when he finished second in the league in batting with a .378 average. Cassidy died in Brooklyn after a year-long illness on July 2, 1891.[38]

William Arthur (Candy) Cummings, 1875–76—After his request for a salary increase was denied by Bulkeley, Cummings signed with Cincinnati for the 1877 season, but he finished the year with just 5 wins against 14 losses. He applied for, but didn't receive, the manager's job in Buffalo in 1878. He played semi-pro ball in Albany and then went home to Ware, Massachusetts. He learned the painting and wallpapering business and played amateur ball through 1884. He moved to Athol, Massachusetts, and ran his own decorating business for the next 32 years. He spent much of his last years defending his claim to be inventor of the curveball. Mostly due to this claim, Cummings was elected to the Hall of Fame in 1939. He made several return trips to Hartford to visit Morgan Bulkeley around 1913 and 1914. He died in Toledo, Ohio, on May 16, 1924.[39]

Ben Douglas, 1874–75—Douglas is a virtually unknown pioneer of baseball in New England. Of the six New England cities to have major league clubs, Ben Douglas started the original club in three of them, Middletown, Hartford, and Providence. Upon his resignation from the Hartford club prior to the 1876 season, it was said that "Mr. Douglas has worked hard for the interest of the Hartford club, and had it not been for him the Hartfords would not have attained the celebrity they have. It might be said that he laid the foundation stone of the club...."[40]

His career in major league baseball came to an end in Providence. Arriving in Providence early in 1878, Douglas tended to a wide variety of duties, both large and small. He chose the site for the club's ball field and oversaw the subsequent construction of Messer Park. He also had the duty of engaging players for the club. The first player Douglas signed was his old friend, Tim Murnane. He also pulled together the finer details of running a club, including ordering scorecards and the league-mandated turnstiles from Harry Wright. Because it was so new, the Providence club didn't even have its own stationery, so Douglas was forced to correspond on old Hartford stationery with the name of that club and its officers crossed out.[41]

Despite all his preparation, Douglas still didn't know when his club would be playing. Normally, Douglas would have been engrossed in scheduling games, since he was accustomed to the old ways where clubs could play anyone, anytime. Now, though, the National League had instituted a pre-set schedule to eliminate the confusion that frequently occurred when teams arranged games themselves. Unfortunately, by mid–March the league office still hadn't sent out the schedule, and Douglas was getting impatient. While he cooled his heels, Douglas practiced his new club for two hours a day in a local gymnasium.[42]

Douglas was so anxious to know his league schedule because he wanted to begin arranging other games in between the National League games. There were still plenty of talented nines that weren't in the National League, and good money could be made playing them. In fact, in 1877, about 50 professional, non-league clubs existed, many of whom played and beat National League clubs. Some of these banded together in 1877 and formed the International Association. Although it had many excellent players, this new league couldn't compete with the National League because it made many of the same organizational mistakes that destroyed the old National Association.[43]

When it came to scheduling these outside clubs, Douglas was in for a surprise, since the National League had recently prohibited this practice. Prior to 1877, games between League clubs and outside clubs were not restricted in any way. However, the National League soon realized that while these outside matches were profitable in the short term, they cut profits in the long run. So many games were being played that the market was becoming saturated. So, to ensure that when fans paid money to see a game it was for one between National League teams, the League limited games with outside clubs. All preseason games were banned, and during the season no games with outside clubs were allowed on League grounds. As the *Chicago Tribune* so bluntly put it, "The truth is, gentlemen of the smaller cities, the League ... finds that it doesn't want you on their grounds ... The League can make more money off thirty first-class games than they can off sixty ... and they are going to play the thirty with the clubs they think most likely to interest their patrons."[44]

While understandably infuriating outside clubs, the new restrictions also upset some League clubs who were still interested in earning extra money on off days. Douglas felt that these games could provide yearly revenues of $4,000 for his club. As he explained, "It's a long jump from Providence to Chicago without getting one cent." Douglas was also puzzled about why League clubs couldn't play outside clubs before the season officially started on May 1. He told Harry Wright, "I see no harm in playing say Yales in Hartford in April. They want to meet us this Apr 14."[45]

As Douglas awaited his team's schedule, he was aware of some animosity brewing against him. He advised Harry Wright to ignore any of the "mean stories" being circulated around Providence about him. "If ever a man worked for an Association I have for Providence both by night and by day. You know Harry that my whole soul is in base ball. If any one writes you about me give them my past record...." Douglas had suspicions that somebody on the Providence team wanted to run him out of the manager's position. "There is a man here who wants my position."[46]

His worst fears came true before the season even began. While on the field practicing his men, Douglas received a message instructing him to meet with the club's board of directors at 5 P.M. Thinking it was just normal club business, Douglas arrived at the meeting unconcerned, but he was shocked to learn that the directors had voted to relieve him of his duties as manager because he was "not competent to fill the bill."[47]

Incredulous with the club's actions, Douglas refused to sign his release. The directors responded by threatening to withhold the $1,000 he had invested in the club unless he resigned. After all his accomplishments in baseball, Douglas couldn't understand why he was being dismissed. In a sad letter to Harry Wright, he pled his case.

> You know me Harry for many seasons. You know I have spent a large sum of money from [18]66 to [18]78 trying my level best to build up the Dear Old Game and now after my hard hard work here to be disgraced.... It is not on account of drink for I do not drink. It is not on account of dishonesty for God knows I am honest. It is not on account of bad women for I care nothing for them. I have always tried to act the part of a gentleman and square man by all.

Did I not run the Champions of Conn 6 seasons, the Dear Old Mansfields of Middletown. Did I not break into the World of Manager 2 seasons the celebrated Hartfords, 2nd only to the Champion Bostons season of 75 and yet these greenhorns say my past record is good for nothing ... I have lost 6 month's time from business at home where I had steady salary of $1500/yr. I have spent money like water. First for Hartford where I raised $4000 this last season and only for action of League would have been there ... Drew good clean money out of bk (bank) at home. My hard earnings paid Mesr Carey, York, Hines, Higham, Hague, Allison, Nichols, $700 — advance money last winter or I would lost them. Providence would have had no League team only for me, and this is my reward ... Can you do anything for me *Friend Harry*. I don't ask money Oh know for that I have enough only I do ask my friends in the game to protect against this outrage."[48]

Wright was a little slow to respond to this cry for help, so a nervous Douglas sent off another note two days later. "I am in trouble here will you please write Horace Bloodgood chairman of Board of Directors of Providence Club in my behalf. My players have all protested against my removal from Management and want me with them. It's the Town talk and all in my favor.... Your influence would be of great assistance to me now, and I shall never forget it of you if you will.... God knows I have done my duty and it's hard to be thrown out without a fair trial. My *whole money, heart*, and *soul* is in this Club."[49]

Shortly thereafter, Douglas received a highly complimentary letter from Wright, but it was too late to save his position in Providence. "Your kind communication of the 10th came duly to hand & I can assure you it gave me great comfort. These people know more about base ball then I do, in their minds. After making a dupe of me they threw me one side. To the honor & credit of my players (God bless them) they done all in their power to have me retained. Murnane talked over 1 hour before board for me also Higham and Carey who were spokesmen for the balance but it was no go Harry. I had to resign my place or be kicked out. I had my whole heart in it sure, but I won't bother you further.... I retire with the consciousness of having done my whole duty and in return have been snubbed. No more Rhode Island for me."[50]

Douglas's $1,400 annual salary and $500 worth of club stock were bought out. It was later reported that Providence forced Douglas out because the directors were concerned about his "indiscretion" in communicating and making dates with International Association clubs.[51] Douglas was caught in the middle of the battle between the National League and outside clubs, and it apparently cost him his career in baseball. The Providence team that Douglas had assembled finished third in the six-team National League.

After leaving Providence, Douglas still held the support of many in the city who were "greatly in favor of Mr. Douglas, and, to speak the truth, he has been shamelessly used. No manager has been chosen in his place ... so things promise to be hot this season in the management of the decidedly wild men we have here." Douglas returned to the city to watch the opening game of the Grays in 1878. In 1885 after the Grays disbanded, Douglas attended a meeting in Providence to decide what to do after the Providence club left the NL. Douglas was greeted warmly by those who ran the club in 1878. Douglas offered the opinion, from his own sad experience, that an amateur or semi-pro team wouldn't be profitable in a city that once had a National League team.[52]

After his aborted 1878 attempt in the International Association, Douglas returned to Middletown and rejoined the family pump factory. In 1890, he was assigned a patent

(#434790) for a new, easier to use, stove polish. Two years later, Douglas started the "Iron-clad Stove Polish" factory at the foot of Center Street in Middletown.[53]

In 1893, the 44-year-old Douglas married 20-year-old Nellie Sault, daughter of a Brooklyn foundry owner. This came as a surprise to Douglas's friends, who apparently were unaware of the 44-year-old Douglas's relationship with the 20-year-old girl. In 1905, Ben Douglas Junior died in Connecticut Valley Hospital where he had lived for five years.[54]

Jack Farrell, 1874 — Born in Hartford, "Hartford Jack" played in three games at the end of 1874, batting .385. This was the extent of his major league career, although he did play with the 1884 Hartford club in the Connecticut State League. After his career, Farrell ran a café at 340 Park Street and was active in Hartford politics.[55] He died in Hartford on November 15, 1916.

Bob Ferguson, 1875–77 — Ferguson signed to manage and play third base for Chicago in 1878. Under his guidance, the White Stockings finished a disappointing fourth in a six-team league. He played five more years in the National League, four as the Troy, New York, second baseman and manager. He finished his career in 1884 with Pittsburgh of the American Association. As baseball evolved, Ferguson's tyrannical leadership style became less tolerable. In 1883, his Philadelphia team refused to play for him. After retiring from playing, Ferguson served as an umpire in the major leagues until 1891, when infirmities prompted his retirement. Ferguson's temperament served him well as the prototype no-nonsense umpire. His philosophy was "Never change a decision, never stop to talk to a player — make 'em play ball and keep their mouths shut and never fear but the people will be on your side and you'll be King of the Umpires." Upon his sudden death in 1894, it was reported that "the funeral parlors were not large enough to accommodate the crowd of people who came."[56]

William (Cherokee) Fisher, 1874 — Fisher had a strong penchant for alcohol and was bounced from several clubs for drinking and insubordination. After being expelled from Cincinnati in 1876, the *Hartford Courant* said of Fisher, "He was too much of a beer pitcher." Throughout his career, he never played consecutive years with the same team, making it seven different clubs in seven years. He later became a fireman in Chicago.[57] Fisher died September 26, 1912, in New York City.

Bill Harbidge, 1875–77 — "Yaller Bill" Harbidge was signed as a backup catcher. Although Anson said, "Harbidge was not even a fair catcher; in fact, according to my estimate, he was a poor one," he lasted nine years in the major leagues.[58] He died in Philadelphia on March 17, 1924.

Scott Hastings, 1874 — Hastings played three more seasons with three different teams. Anson said he was "a fair all-around player, but by no means a wonder." He was later employed in a wholesale clothing house. He moved to San Francisco, where he became quite wealthy. Hastings died on August 14, 1907, in Sawtelle, California.[59]

Richard Higham, 1876 — After his stint with the Syracuse Stars in 1877, Higham returned to the National League with the Providence Grays in 1878, leading the league in doubles and runs scored. In 1879, he played in the International Association. He became a National League umpire in 1881 and was recognized as the first umpire to wear a face mask. In 1882, under dubious circumstances, he became the only umpire expelled from the major leagues for "selling" or "offering to sell" games. He lived in Chicago for the last ten years of his life, dying there on March 18, 1905.[60]

Jim Holdsworth, 1877 — Holdsworth played only one more game in the National League, in 1882 with Troy. He played center field on Douglas's 1878 International Association team. Holdsworth died on March 22, 1918, in New York City.

Charley Jones, 1875 — Jones signed with Hartford after the National Association Keokuk club disbanded. He played in one game for Hartford. He went on to have a solid twelve-year major league career.

Terry Larkin, 1877 — In his three full seasons, the last two with Chicago, Larkin won 29, 29, and 31 games. Anson called him "a rattling good man and a really first-class pitcher, who would have won more games than he did had he met with the support that he should have had." During a practice near the end of the 1879 season, Anson lined a ball off Larkin's head, sending the pitcher to an asylum for some time. Larkin recovered but was unable to pitch effectively again. He closed his major league career the following year with an 0–5 record for Bob Ferguson's Troy club. After his baseball career, Larkin was known to over-indulge in liquor, and in 1883, while drunk, he shot his wife, injuring her. Two years later, he arrived at his bartending job with two pistols and challenged his employer to a duel.[61] Larkin died September 16, 1894, in Brooklyn, New York.

John Maloney, 1877 — Maloney played one game with the Hartfords, making three errors in center field. This marked the end of his major league career.

Jack Manning, 1874 — Manning played 42 games for Baltimore in 1874, before playing one game for Hartford. He became an effective change pitcher for Boston in 1875 and 1876, going a combined 33–7 in those years.

Everett Mills, 1874–76 — 1876 was the end of Mills' major league career. He played on Douglas's International Association team in 1878 and worked for Morgan Bulkeley at Aetna in the late 1870s.[62] Mills lived in Hartford for several years after he quit the game but later moved to Newark, New Jersey, where he was a Court Officer in Essex County. He died in Newark on June 22, 1908. Mills's nephew, Rupert Frank Mills, was a four-letter man at Notre Dame from 1912 to 15, playing football with Knute Rockne. He also played in the major leagues, playing one year as a first baseman with the Newark Peppers of the short-lived Federal League.

Fancy O'Neil, 1874 — In his only major league appearance, O'Neil played right field for the Dark Blues against Boston on October 23, 1874. He was a long-time member of the Hartford Amateur team. Until recently, his given first name was unknown. It appears to have been Michael, and he seems to have had difficulties later in life. The October 30, 1895, *Hartford Courant* reported a story under the headline "Crazy 'Fancy' O'Neil" which describes O'Neil's attempted knife attack on his employer. "Michael O'Neil, known as 'Fancy' O'Neil, an old-time boxer and ball player, was taken to the Connecticut Hospital for the Insane at Middletown yesterday.... O'Neil has been crazy for some time and has been in five different asylums." The date and place of his death are currently unknown.

Jay Pike, 1877 — Lip Pike's brother, Jacob, played his only major league game on August 27, 1877, filling in for one of several sick Brooklyn players. He had been playing with the Concord club. Society for American Baseball Research (SABR) biographical researchers have raised the possibility that this Pike is listed incorrectly in the baseball encyclopedias. They believe it is possible that Lipman Pike's other brother, Israel, may have been the one who played one game for the Hartfords in 1877.

Lipman Pike, 1874 — Pike played his last game at age 42 in 1887 for the New York Metropolitans of the American Association. After retiring from baseball, he became a successful haberdasher in Brooklyn. On October 10, 1893, Pike died in Brooklyn at the age of 48.

Paddy J. Quinn, 1875 — Signed as a catcher for Bond after the Keokuk Westerns disbanded, Quinn played five games for Hartford. This was the end of his major league career.

Jack Remsen, 1875–76—Remsen played major league ball for five more seasons. He returned to Hartford in 1886 to manage and play center field for Hartford's Eastern League entry. Jack and his wife Emma lived in New York as late as 1921. His place and date of death are unknown.

George "Orator" Shaffer, 1874—Shaffer, "a promising young Philadelphia amateur," was added to the 1874 team to bolster the offense. He played nine games for the Dark Blues, batting only .229, but stroking one of Hartford's two home runs that year. He went on to a thirteen-year career, including a great year for Indianapolis in 1878.

Joe Start, 1877—Start followed Ferguson to Chicago in 1878, then joined Providence for seven years, including their 1879 and 1884 championship seasons. He had an excellent season in 1884, at the age of 42, finishing third on the team in batting and runs scored. He finished his career in 1886 with Washington. Adrian Anson said, "His reputation was in every way above reproach, both on and off the field."[63] After his career, he ran the Lakewood Inn in Warwick, Rhode Island, before retiring to Providence, where he died at the age of 84 on March 27, 1927.

Bill Stearns, 1874—Stearn's final year of major league ball was 1875, when he produced a 1–14 record for Washington. This left him with a career won-lost record of 12–64. His .158 winning percentage is one of the worst in history. Stearns died in Washington, D.C., on December 30, 1898.

Ed "Live Oak" Taylor, 1877—A late-season addition to replace sick players, Taylor played two games for Brooklyn, the first on August 21, 1877. He didn't play major league ball again until 1884 when he joined Pittsburgh in the American Association.

Jim Tipper, 1874—See entry under Middletown Mansfields.

Tom York, 1875–77—York played eight more seasons, including five with Providence. He tried umpiring in the National League in 1886 but quit in midseason, saying, "I would rather live on a dollar a day than stand the blackguarding which every umpire is subject to." York was also instrumental in forming the Connecticut State League, and he managed the Norwich team in that league. For several seasons, York served as a guard at the press box at the Polo Grounds. In 1925, he attended a celebration of the National League's 50th season at the Grand Central Hotel in New York. Five of the seven surviving players from the 1876 season were in attendance. By that time, he had "developed quite a paunch, but his shoulders are as straight and his chin lifted as high as when he was an active star." At his death in 1936, plans were underway to honor him along with George Wright, Deacon White, and Tommy Bond at that season's All Star game in Boston as the last surviving players of the National League's first season.[64]

New Haven Elm City Club

John "Stud" Bancker—This Philadelphia native played 19 games for New Haven, the last on June 5. He finished the season with the Providence nine.[65] His date and place of death are unknown.

Tommy Barlow—See "Appendix B: The Curious Case of Tommy Barlow."

Booth—Played one game at shortstop for New Haven on May 1, 1875, against the Philadelphia Centennials in New Haven. He went 0 for 2 at the bat and committed one error.

John Cassidy—Joined New Haven for the final six games of the 1875 season. He played with New Haven in 1876, before going to Hartford at the end of the season. See his entry under the Hartford Dark Blues.

Lester Dole—After his one game with New Haven in 1875, Dole became a teacher at St. Paul's school in Concord, New Hampshire. In 1878, he became one of the first secondary school teachers to coach as well, when he was hired as director of the school's new gym and also acted as rowing coach. He coached the boys in cricket and football, gave boxing and fencing lessons, and supervised the swimming at the swimming hole. He was a great favorite with all the boys because of his enthusiasm for athletics. Dole continued to teach gymnastics and coach at St. Paul's for many years. He died in Concord, New Hampshire, on December 10, 1918.[66]

Evans—Played outfield in one game for New Haven on June 1, 1875, against Washington. Evans singled twice in four at-bats, drove in one run, and scored one himself. This was the only game of his career.

Billy Geer—Although it seems unlikely, baseball encyclopedias list Geer as 15 years old when he played with New Haven in 1875. Dismissed from New Haven after being arrested for stealing goods while on a road trip, Geer resurfaced in the National League in 1878 with Cincinnati. He bounced around for a few more seasons before undertaking a criminal career in more earnest, often involving passing bad checks. Researcher Peter Morris has found this description of Geer's criminality in the *Detroit Free Press* in 1897: "The police has information that the man who did the smooth act of cashing checks at Heyn's bazaar and Golding Bros. for $27 each is a noted check swindler named William H. Geer. He was once a ball player, but in 1892 began making his police record by forging a check in Minnesota. He served a term for this in the Stillwater penitentiary. The board of pardons of that state released him on parole in 1896. Then he turned up in Salt Lake City, where he represented himself as an agent of the National Cash Register Company, of Dayton, O., and thereby cashed a number of worthless checks. He operated in Boston later, under the names of R. H. Dwight, George M. Miles, J. B. Rowan, R. A. Myers, J. R. Mott and Edward Lyon. Again he appeared in Providence, R. I., and again in New York. In all these places he played the same game. He usually represents himself as a traveling man for some well-known business house and carries bogus letters from the firms." In 1907, Geer was arrested for passing bad checks in Richmond, Virginia. Newspaper coverage of the arrest stated that Geer was also wanted in Freeport, Illinois, and Boston.[67] The date and place of his death are unknown.

Fred Goldsmith—A New Haven native, Goldsmith played one game with New Haven as an emergency substitute on October 23 versus Hartford. He played second base and went 2 for 4, earning praise from the *Hartford Courant*, which said, "Goldsmith, the new man, bids fair to become a good man for some club if he can be induced to enter the professional arena." He pitched one game for New Haven in 1876 before joining the London (Ontario) Tecumseh club of the International Association. He played with them through 1878. He returned to the major leagues in 1879. He won more than 20 games for four straight seasons while pitching for the Chicago White Stockings, including their three consecutive championship seasons of 1880–1882. Goldsmith tended bar in several places before settling down to the business of market gardening near Detroit. In his later years, Goldsmith claimed to have been the originator of the curveball. Although in 1939 *The Sporting News* concluded that both Goldsmith and Candy Cummings should be considered co-inventors, Goldsmith's claims are dubious. Goldsmith died March 28, 1939, at the age of 86, just a few weeks before Cummings was enshrined in the Baseball Hall of Fame. Goldsmith died a bitter man for the lack of recognition he received for the curveball.[68]

Charlie Gould— Gould played and managed in Cincinnati in 1876. He retired after the 1877 season, but remained with the Cincinnati club as assistant secretary and groundskeeper for three years. He died on April 10, 1917, at his son's home in Flushing, New York. Gould was buried in the family plot in Cincinnati, but no marker was placed at the site. In 1951, Cincinnati Reds president Warren Giles launched a drive to erect an impressive monument on Gould's previously unmarked grave.[69]

Washington Ritter "Rit" Harrison—Harrison was born in Waterbury, Connecticut, and was most likely playing with the Bridgeport TBs when called to serve as a replacement player for New Haven on May 20, 1875. He managed two hits, including a double, in four trips to the plate. Harrison died in Bridgeport on November 7, 1888.

Jim Keenan— Keenan was a 17-year-old New Haven native who played five games for the Elm City club in 1875. He batted a measly .077. He later played several seasons in the American Association. He died September 21, 1926, in Cincinnati, Ohio.

George Knight—After scoring a complete-game victory in the only game he ever pitched, Knight went to New York to study medicine. He became a doctor and rose to the position of the head of the "State School for Imbeciles" in Lakeville, Connecticut. Knight died suddenly at a political meeting in Lakeville on October 4, 1912.[70]

George Latham— After playing one season in Canada, Latham returned to major league ball in 1877, playing for the tainted Louisville club in 1877. In 1878, Latham returned home and played for the Utica club in the International Association. He played one more year in the International Association before taking a two-year hiatus from baseball to work for the Treasury Department in Washington, D.C. He returned to major league baseball in 1882, playing three seasons in the American Association. Latham played for his hometown Utica team in 1886 and 1887, then retired from playing to manage. Latham died on May 26, 1914, in Utica.[71]

Henry Luff— From 1876 to 1881, Luff did not play major league baseball. From 1882 to 1884, he bounced around in the American and Union Associations. He died October 11, 1916, in Philadelphia.

Tim McGinley—McGinley played nine games for the Boston Red Stockings in 1876, batting a paltry .150, and never played major league ball again. He died November 2, 1899, in Oakland, California.

John McKelvey— John McKelvey led New Haven in many offensive categories, but never played in the major leagues again. In 1876, he returned to his native Rochester where he played with the local amateur team and took a job as a clerk in the post office. He retired from the post office in 1920 at the age of 72. McKelvey died in Rochester on May 31, 1944, at the ripe old age of 96. He had been born prior to the Civil War and died just before D-day of World War II. He was the last survivor from the National Association. He was believed to have introduced the curveball in Rochester after learning it from Candy Cummings. "I was playing for New Haven when Cummings and his team came over," said McKelvey. "I was a third baseman as well as an outfielder. My best asset was that I could hit. But I will admit Mr. Cummings and his curveball had us fooled. I taught Aleck Burke [star pitcher in Rochester] about 1876 how to throw a curve. We would go onto the street in front of my home and I would show him the trick and have him pitch to me."[72]

Fred "Tricky" Nichols — Nichols pitched for the Boston Red Stockings in 1876 after the New Haven team disbanded. He joined St. Louis in 1877, winning 18 games, while losing 23. He pitched three more seasons, his last being in 1882 with Baltimore of the American Association for whom he went 1–12. He died August 22, 1897, in Bridgeport, Connecticut.

Charlie Pabor — Pabor managed the independent New Haven team in 1876, but he never played major league ball after the 1875 season. He retired from the diamond and became a policeman in New Haven. In his later years, Pabor lost interest in baseball and did not attend a game in his last 25 years. He steadfastly stated that no modern player could compare to the pioneers of the game such as George Wright, Joe Start, and Al Spalding. He died of pneumonia on April 23, 1913, in New Haven.[73]

Johnny Ryan — Ryan played two more years of major league ball, including being a starting outfielder for Louisville in the 1876 National League. He later returned to his native Philadelphia, where he became a police officer in 1891. Ryan died on March 22, 1902, while on duty. He was called to a saloon to break up a fight, and while arresting one Joseph Hemple, a struggle ensued. Hemple, who was said to very strong as he was a professional contortionist and acrobat, kicked Ryan in the stomach and fled the scene. Hemple was later arrested and charged with murder, as Ryan had died from the blow.[74]

John Smith — Smith's only major league appearance came on May 21, 1875, against the Athletics in New Haven. He went hitless in three trips to the plate and made three errors at shortstop. The date and place of his death are unknown.

Ed Somerville — Somerville signed with Louisville for the 1876 season, where he was the starting second baseman. He batted only .188 and never played major league ball again. He died the following year, at the age of 24, on October 1, 1877, while in London (Ontario), Canada.

Sullivan — Played outfield in two games, May 15 and May 17, both losses to Washington in New Haven. This was the extent of his major league career. He fared well in his pair of games, getting three hits in eight at-bats.

Jim Tipper — See entry under Middletown Mansfields.

George Trenwith — After playing in New Haven's final six games of 1875, Trenwith never played major league ball again. He died February 1, 1890, in Philadelphia.

Sam Wright — Played two games with Boston in 1876 after the independent New Haven club disbanded. Wright didn't play in the major leagues again until 1880, when he played nine games at shortstop for Cincinnati, batting a miserable .088. He was released by Cincinnati and played one final game with Boston at the end of the 1881 season, possibly serving as an emergency substitute for an injured player. Sammy never married, but brother Harry's three children by his first wife often lived with him. Sammy later settled in the Dorchester section of Boston, where he headed the cricket department at the Wright & Ditson Sporting Goods store. He opened his own sporting goods store in Jersey City, New Jersey, in 1885. Sammy died at the old Wright homestead in Boston of a cerebral hemorrhage on May 6, 1928.[75]

Appendix B:
The Curious Case of Tommy Barlow

Born in 1852, Thomas H. Barlow grew up in Brooklyn, New York, playing ball every afternoon as most young lads in the baseball-crazed city did. Tommy, as he was affectionately called, became so skilled at the game that by the age of twenty he was a promising young catcher for the Brooklyn Atlantics in the National Association. He handled the deliveries of teenage hurler Jim Britt, who, at the tender age of 16, had also begun his professional career with the Atlantics in 1872. After two seasons as battery-mates, both Barlow and Britt departed the pathetic Atlantics, who had won barely a quarter of their games during that time. Britt never played major league ball again, while Barlow signed with the Hartford Dark Blues.

In young Barlow, the Dark Blues knew they were getting a hitter noted more for his short hits than long ones. Tommy was one of the first practitioners of the bunt, executing his strategic hit with a bat turned from no more than 24 inches of wood. He had so thoroughly mastered the maneuver that critics, who thought the innovation unworthy of a professional player, dubbed it "Barlow's dodo." Dark Blues' president Morgan Bulkeley told one newspaper reporter, "I don't know whether it's right or not according to baseball rules, but he does it.... Some baseball players think that is all right. Some insist that it isn't fair. It is an entirely new freak in baseball...."[1]

But it is not for his clever handling of the bat for which Barlow is remembered, if he is remembered at all. Instead, he is remembered for the sad manner in which his career, and his life, came to an end. Countless ballplayers have been forced from the game they loved due to the evils of the bottle, but Barlow may have been the first to lose his career to drugs.

Tommy Barlow's tragic story of morphine addiction is so compelling that Ken Burns's highly acclaimed documentary, *Baseball*, included a dramatic reading of the following letter from Barlow, which appeared in the September 16, 1877, edition of the *Boston Times*.

It was on the 10th of August, 1874, that there was a match game of baseball in Chicago between the White Stockings of that city and the Hartfords of Hartford, now of Brooklyn. I was catcher for the Hartfords, and Fisher was pitching. He is a lightning pitcher, and very few could catch for him. On that occasion he delivered as wicked a ball as ever left his hands, and it went through my grasp like an express train, striking me with full force in the side. I fell insensible to the ground, but was quickly picked up, placed in a carriage, and driven to my hotel. The doctor who attended me gave a hypodermic injection of morphine, but I had rather died behind the bat then have had that first dose. My injury was only temporary, but from taking prescriptions of morphine during my illness, the habit grew on me, and I am now powerless in its grasp. My morphine pleasure has cost me eight dollars a day, at least. I was once catcher for the Mutuals, also for the Atlantics, but no one would think it to look at me now.[2]

Addiction to morphine, first isolated from opium in 1803 by a German pharmacist, who named it after *Morpheus*, the Greek god of dreams, was not uncommon in the latter half of the nineteenth century. It's been estimated that the addiction level in the United States at that time was a startling two to five percent of the adult population. By the mid–1850s, morphine had gained popularity with doctors, who considered its pain-relieving benefits nothing short of remarkable. The Civil War provided ample opportunity to put morphine's anesthetizing qualities to use. Unfortunately, the addictive characteristics of the drug went largely unnoticed until after the war when an estimated 300,000 soldiers returned home from the front lines with the "army disease," morphine addiction.[3]

Apart from Civil War veterans, most addicts, surprisingly, were ladies of the middle and upper classes. These women were frequent customers of what is now called the "patent medicine" industry. Spurred by itinerant salesmen criss-crossing the countryside hawking colorfully named elixirs, such as Hunt's Lightning Oil, Wintersmith's Chill Tonic, Gooch's Mexican Syrup and Mrs. Winslow's Soothing Syrup, the industry marketed cures for virtually any ailment, including children's teething pains, coughing fits, dysentery, and "women's trouble." What the hucksters failed to divulge to their naive customers was that many of these concoctions contained huge quantities of morphine. It was largely the sale of these patent medicines that led to the creation of the Food and Drug Administration, whose charter was to approve all foods and drugs meant for human consumption. Once tested, patent medicines were quickly banned.[4]

It would appear from his story that Tommy Barlow was another victim of accidental morphine addiction, resulting from treatment for a baseball injury. As a detailed, first-person account from an eyewitness to the events, Barlow's testimony would presumably be highly reliable. I envisioned a poignant story being woven from Barlow's moving account of his addiction, bolstered with details from the pages of Hartford's three daily newspapers. Surely, the hometown press would have provided extensive coverage of such a dramatic tragedy as Barlow described.

Much to my chagrin, however, further research failed to corroborate any of the particulars that Barlow described, quickly transforming his tale from a fundamental element of Hartford's baseball past to a troubling historical mystery. What really ended Barlow's career? Was it the supposed injury and resulting morphine addiction, or was it Barlow's "indiscretions," as the *Hartford Post* reported at the end of the season?[5] Let's scrutinize Barlow's statement, point by point.

The Date and Opponent. Barlow stated unequivocally that the injury occurred on August 10, 1874, against the Chicago White Stockings. The Dark Blues did indeed play that day, but their opponent was the Philadelphia Whites, not Chicago.

The Location. Barlow declared that his injury occurred in Chicago. The Dark Blues played only two games in Chicago all year, yet both were in May. In both those contests, newspaper reports indicate that Barlow played complete games at shortstop with no mention of any injury.

The Positions. Barlow said he was injured while catching the lightning deliveries of Cherokee Fisher, one of the fastest pitchers in the country. Records indicate, however, that Barlow never caught a single game for the Dark Blues during the 1874 season, playing 32 games at shortstop. Furthermore, Bill Stearns, not Cherokee Fisher, pitched the August 10 game.

The Injury. No mention of this injury, or any other injury to Barlow, was reported in any of the three Hartford daily newspapers. Starting in August, Barlow missed most of the last two months of the 1874 season, but the press usually omitted a reason for Barlow's absence or said it was due to illness, never injury.

So no contemporary newspaper report confirms Tommy Barlow's tale. Perhaps his mind, clouded by the haze of morphine, misremembered some details, as the reference to the Mutuals, for whom it appears he never played, seems to attest. Let's give Tommy

Tommy Barlow (1873), shortstop for the Hartford Dark Blues. His absence from the club over the last two months of the 1874 season remains a mystery. Barlow claimed that an on-field injury and subsequent morphine prescription resulted in an addiction which effectively ending his promising career (courtesy *The Daily Graphic: An Illustrated Evening Newspaper*).

the benefit of the doubt and assume the basic elements of his story, a baseball-related injury leading to morphine addiction, are true and try to determine the most likely time of the injury's occurrence.

A detailed review of the final months of the 1874 season shows that in early July Barlow was playing well, so well, in fact, that the *Hartford Times*, in a bit of hometown hyperbole, labeled him the best shortstop in the league. Barlow was indeed playing well, sparking the Dark Blues' offense and excelling in the field, although not up to the standards of premier shortstops George Wright and Davy Force. Shortly thereafter, two strange incidents occurred which may have hinted at impending trouble. In mid–July, Barlow was late for a game against the Philadelphia Athletics, delaying the start for fifteen minutes while the Dark Blues awaited his arrival. Two weeks later, Barlow missed a non-league game against an amateur club from Bristol. His unexpected absence forced Hartford to use team president Gershom Hubbell, the former Charter Oak player, in right field.[6]

On August 10, the supposed day of his injury in Chicago, Barlow and the Dark Blues met the Philadelphia Whites in Hartford. Due to third baseman Bill Boyd's sudden departure for the Brooklyn Fire Department, Hartford was forced to rework its lineup. Fisher was moved from his usual spot in the pitcher's box to third base in place of Boyd. Bill Stearns pitched to backup receiver Bill Barnie, and Barlow played the full nine innings at shortstop.[7]

The following day, the same two teams met again in Hartford. On this day, "Barlow came on to the field sick ... when he should have been in bed." His performance sustained this claim, as he failed to stop even one ball while at shortstop and his weakened condition forced him to the bench in the seventh inning.[8] This is the first mention of Barlow being ill, and it corresponds with his August 10 date.

The next day, the Dark Blues traveled to Boston for another game with the Philadelphia Whites. Barlow was "sick and didn't go," forcing regular second baseman Bob "The Magnet" Addy to play shortstop. A few days later, Barlow's health had improved enough for him to meet the team at Martha's Vineyard, although he was still not in the lineup. At the end of August, Barlow returned to his shortstop position and played regularly for two weeks, although his health was still quite poor and his play was not up to its usual standards.[9]

On September 10, the Dark Blues beat the Chicago White Stockings in Hartford. Barlow played the entire game at shortstop and even managed to fool Chicago's star center fielder Paul Hines with the hidden ball trick, a stratagem that some say Barlow originated. The next day, he was again "quite sick" and did not appear on the diamond for the rematch against Chicago, nor for any other games for the remainder of the season.[10]

September 14 found Barlow still "too ill to come to the grounds." Three days later, suffering from a vague "complication of disorders," Barlow was admitted to Hartford Hospital under the care of Dr. Horace Fuller, a respected Hartford physician and visiting doctor at Hartford Hospital. Despite the compassionate doctor's care, his condition worsened, and for a time it was believed he would not survive. A rumor that Tommy had actually succumbed quickly swept through the city. Scrambling to confirm the report, newspaper reporters learned that Barlow was still "alive and kicking." Appreciating how Mark Twain felt when he declared, "The reports of my death have been greatly exaggerated," Barlow promised to throttle the man who was responsible for starting the gossip.[11]

Tommy remained in the hospital for several weeks. The *Hartford Times* offered an attempt at humor, saying, "Barlow has not made a short-stop at the hospital." In October, Barlow got some relief from his long convalescence, managing to get out to the ball grounds to watch his teammates take on the Boston Red Stockings.[12] During his recuperation, reports of his condition varied. Some said that he would soon be well enough to rejoin the nine, while others alleged his condition was so serious that he would never play ball again.

Acting on the *Hartford Times*' suggestion that "a little substantial sympathy would not come amiss," the Dark Blues organized a benefit game for their fallen teammate. Hartford residents supported their stricken shortstop, purchasing 600 tickets at 25 cents each to raise a tidy $150. In another show of kindness, club directors voted to pay Barlow his full salary, even though he had hardly played for the last two months. Although these compassionate gestures might indicate Barlow's troubles were not self-inflicted, the *Hartford Post's* season recap claimed that Barlow's absence occurred after he "became used up and went to the hospital as the result of his indiscretions." The last news on Barlow in 1874 came in December, when the *Hartford Times* reported that Barlow was "down sick again, and it is doubtful if he ever plays ball again."[13]

After reviewing the record, two games appear to be prime candidates for the possible injury. The first is August 10, when Barlow and the Dark Blues met the Philadelphia Whites in Hartford. This corresponds with the date when Barlow claimed he was injured and is supported by the fact that the following day, August 11, he showed up at the field impaired. Despite the apparent agreement on the date, all other details conflict with Barlow's version of events. That day, Barlow played shortstop, and Bill Stearns, not Cherokee Fisher, pitched. Furthermore, all newspaper accounts said Barlow arrived at the field the next day sick, not injured. Nineteenth-century newspapers were prone to oblique references when discussing the personal behavior of ballplayers. A heavy drinker might be "unsanitary" or have "loose personal habits." However, if Barlow was injured as stated, there would be no reason to sugarcoat his absence. There is nothing embarrassing about a serious injury on the ball field, and newspapers routinely reported on them.

The other potential date for the mysterious injury is the September 10 game against the White Stockings. This date is, perhaps just coincidentally, similar to August 10. On that day, the Dark Blues played the correct opponent, the Chicago White Stockings, although they met in Hartford, not Chicago. This contest marked Barlow's last appearance of the season, so it is conceivable that an injury could have occurred during the game. However, the same two problems arise. Barlow doesn't appear to have caught in this game, and no newspaper mentioned him suffering an injury of any kind.

Perhaps the remainder of Barlow's career can offer some clues. The next season, he attempted a return to baseball, claiming he was in excellent health and never in better condition. He received advance money to return to his hometown Atlantics, but then proceeded to sign a contract with the New Haven club. Upon learning that Barlow had first signed with the Atlantics, Willis Arnold, New Haven's business manager, visited Brooklyn to question him. Barlow's defense of his actions were flimsy and inconsistent, so Arnold cancelled his contract and stopped payment on the $200 advance check he had given Barlow. Believing the matter could be settled amicably, Arnold did not bring up the case with the National Association's Judiciary Committee.[14]

Tommy's season was no less bizarre than his off-season. He began the year expecting to be the Atlantics' starting catcher. However, by May he hadn't appeared in any games and was reduced to umpiring their games while weak-hitting Jake Knowdell caught. The catching-poor Atlantics used six different receivers during the year, none of them Barlow. This, coupled with the *Brooklyn Eagle's* mid-season report that his "physique had been materially weakened by his Winter's illness," indicates continued health problems.[15]

In the late spring, Barlow left or was released from the Atlantics and joined New Haven. He played just one game at shortstop before returning to the Atlantics, where he played a single game at the end of July against Chicago. In that game, he played second base and committed two errors. Sadly, this was Tommy's last major league appearance.[16]

For the next two years, Barlow bounced around with several amateur clubs in New York, including a reunion with Jim Britt on the Ilion nine in 1876. Prior to the 1877 season, it was reported that Barlow was "himself again after a protracted illness, and will be able to wield the bat again this season." But Barlow did not play major league ball that year, and by the end of the season Tommy found himself locked up in a Brooklyn jail.

The trouble began in New York while Barlow was walking down Broadway. He came upon a sidewalk display of goods in front of a clothing store. He stopped to examine the merchandise. While holding either a pair of stockings or a necktie, Barlow couldn't remember, one of the clerks accused him of attempting to steal the goods. Barlow said the clerk hit him, and Barlow returned the favor. He was then arrested. On September 7, Barlow appeared in Brooklyn court, charged with petty larceny. Barlow defended his actions, saying that he was under the influence of morphine at the time and wasn't even sure if he had committed the crime. Despite this defense, he was sentenced to ten days in the city prison.[17]

Tommy was held in a small third-story jail above the Court of Special Sessions, a holding pen for men sentenced to short prison terms. A reporter from the *New York Telegram* met Barlow there and found him to have the "livid, haggard expression" of an addict. Prior to his arrest, Barlow had been swallowing twelve grains of morphine a day. Now under a doctor's care in jail, he was being weaned off of the drug with progressively smaller doses and was showing the ill effects of withdrawal.[18]

During the interview, Barlow provided a few additional details to the account of his injury. He said it happened in the first inning of the game in Chicago. The first batter for the White Stockings reached base. As catcher, Barlow moved up closer behind the plate in order to prevent a stolen base. Then, according to Barlow, came Fisher's fateful pitch.

The writer asked if Barlow was capable of playing ball while under the influence. Barlow responded, "I could, but I do not want to. All that I care to do is lie down somewhere and read novels without the books."

The reporter asked Barlow if he could reform, and Barlow stated emphatically that he could not. Although he knew he should, Barlow said he lacked the will and moral courage to resist. "There is no hope for me," he said. "I shall go along until it is time to commit suicide, and then I suppose I shall commit it. When I do not have the morphine I can hardly walk; as soon as I get it I am as strong as a lion."[19]

So what do we make of this mystery? We are left with three possibilities regarding the demise of Barlow's career: (1) he was injured on the ball field and became addicted to morphine just as he described, (2) he became addicted to morphine for some other reason, or (3) Barlow was never addicted to morphine and simply fabricated the story to help get him off the hook for his theft.

It is somewhat plausible that Barlow's absence at the end of the 1874 season could be viewed as consistent with an injury and subsequent addiction. One can imagine an injury causing him to miss a two-week stretch. Upon returning to the field, the effects of the addiction might have become too severe, sidelining him for the remainder of the season. Despite this possibility, this author believes scenario 1 is not true. The details of Barlow's story are undeniably wrong, and it is difficult to believe that he ever suffered a catastrophic injury on the field. The most telling evidence is that illness or sickness were nearly always given as the reasons for Barlow's absence. Only two sources gave any more specifics for Barlow's hospital stay, and neither mention injury. There was the *Hartford Times'* report that Barlow was admitted for "complications of disorders," and the *Hartford Post* said he went in "as the result of his own indiscretions." Nowhere, other than his own letter to the newspaper after his arrest, was an injury ever discussed. The only evidence that bolsters Barlow's story is that the start of his troubles do appear to coincide with the date he cited in his letter.

While it's suspicious that talk of an injury never surfaced until Barlow himself brought it up three years after it supposedly occurred, and only after being arrested for theft, the idea that Barlow simply made up the morphine addiction story in 1877 seems unlikely. It is possible that Barlow was attempting to generate sympathy by recalling his days as a popular player of the national pastime, but the trouble with this theory is that it fails to explain why Barlow's career came to a crashing halt back in 1874. Besides, the *New York Telegram* reporter's eyewitness account of Barlow's condition in jail would seem to confirm the addiction.

Scenario 2 seems most likely. Something certainly brought his career to an abrupt end, and it very well could have been morphine addiction unrelated to a baseball injury. At the time, morphine was used as a panacea for almost everything. The chronic conditions that were most likely to be treated with morphine were venereal disease, alcoholism, and opium addiction. While purely speculative, any one of these conditions certainly fit the definition of the "indiscretions" mentioned in the *Hartford Post*.

After his appearance in Brooklyn court, Barlow's trail grows disappointingly cold. His name last appeared in the 1880 Brooklyn city directory, and he appeared in the 1880 census as a 28-year-old ballplayer born in New York. The *Sporting News* reported that he was dead by 1888. In 1894, the *Clipper*'s William Rankin contacted several old Atlantics players in an attempt to determine the first practitioner of the bunt, for which Barlow was a possible candidate. All of Barlow's former teammates agreed that his life had come to some sort of tragic end, but none knew the date or location of his death. [20]

Probably the only way to conclusively solve this mystery is to obtain Barlow's medical records from Hartford Hospital. The still-existing hospital, which celebrated its 150th anniversary in 2004, has said confidentiality rules dictate that private medical records, even ancient ones, can't be released without a court order or permission from the family. Whatever the esteemed Dr. Fuller wrote in those ancient medical charts, a promising young ballplayer's career, and his life, began a sad, precipitous decline while playing for the Hartford Dark Blues.

Appendix C:
Game Logs: 1874–1877

Following are the results of all National Association and National League games played by the Middletown Mansfields, the Hartford Dark Blues and the New Haven Elm City club. Non-league games for the Mansfields and Dark Blues are also included. National Association and National League games are shown in bold type. The Connecticut team's score is listed first. Length of games that were other than 9 innings is shown in parentheses.

Middletown Mansfields —1874

Date	Opponent and Location	Score
Apr 20	Junior Mansfields at Middletown	26–2
Apr 26	**Troy Haymakers at Troy**	**0–10**
Apr 27	**Troy Haymakers at Troy**	**10–27**
Apr 29	**New York Mutuals at Brooklyn**	**0–12**
May 2	**Brooklyn Atlantics at Middletown**	**8–2**
May 4	Wesleyan Freshman class	32–2 (5)
May 16	**Troy Haymakers at Middletown**	**10–18**
May 18	Yale University at New Haven	16–9
May 22	**Cleveland Forest City Club at Middletown**	**10–5**
May 24	**Lord Baltimores at Baltimore**	**6–13**
May 25	**Washington Nationals at Washington**	**28–23**
May 28	Baltimore Olympics at Baltimore	13–15
May 29	**Philadelphia Athletics at Philadelphia**	**11–27**
May 31	Elizabeth (New Jersey) Resolutes at Elizabeth	8–5
Jun 3	**New York Mutuals at Brooklyn**	**4–6**
Jun 8	Trinity College at Middletown	48–6
Jun 15	**Boston Red Stockings at Boston**	**3–24**
Jun 17	Waterbury Rose Hills at Waterbury	22–1
Jun 18	Bridgeport Club at Bridgeport	31–4
Jun 19	**Lord Baltimores at Baltimore**	**5–11**
Jun 20	Waterbury Mutuals at Waterbury	22–12

Date	Opponent and Location	Score
Jun 21	Brooklyn Eckfords at Hartford	26–6
Jun 22	Brooklyn Eckfords at Middletown	36–6
Jul 3	Boston Red Stockings at Hartford	6–16
Jul 4	Boston Red Stockings at Middletown	12–25 (8)
Jul 6	Waterbury Mutuals at Middletown	30–3
Jul 10	Junior Mansfields at Middletown	24–0
Jul 13	Junior Mansfields at Middletown	23–3
Jul 17	Wallingford Quinnipiacs	17–0
Jul 23	Troy Haymakers at Springfield, MA	0–7
Jul 27	New York Mutuals at Middletown	9–26
Aug 1	Lord Baltimores at Baltimore	4–8 (5)
Aug 2	Lord Baltimores at Baltimore	9–19
Aug 3	Philadelphia Athletics at Philadelphia	4–17
Aug 5	New York Mutuals at Brooklyn	3–14
Aug 6	Brooklyn Atlantics at Brooklyn	8–15
Aug 7	Norwalk Mutuals at Norwalk	28–0 (7)
Aug 9	Brooklyn Atlantics at Hartford	8–11

New Haven Elm City Club — 1875

Date	Opponent and Location	Score
Apr 19	Boston Red Stockings at Boston	0–6
Apr 21	Boston Red Stockings at New Haven	3–14
Apr 26	Brooklyn Atlantics at New Haven	2–3
May 1	Philadelphia Centennials at New Haven	5–12
May 5	Hartford Dark Blues at Hartford	3–6
May 8	Philadelphia White Stockings at New Haven	2–3
May 10	Philadelphia White Stockings at New Haven	0–13
May 11	New York Mutuals at New Haven	1–2 (11)
May 15	Washington Nationals at New Haven	4–8
May 17	Washington Nationals at New Haven	7–10
May 20	Philadelphia Athletics at New Haven	5–12
May 21	Philadelphia Athletics at New Haven	2–15
May 26	Brooklyn Atlantics at Brooklyn	4–14
May 27	New York Mutuals at Brooklyn	5–8
May 29	Washington Nationals at Washington	10–11
May 31	Washington Nationals at Washington	9–2
Jun 1	Washington Nationals at Washington	7–8
Jun 3	Phila. White Stockings at Philadelphia	2–18
Jun 4	Philadelphia Athletics at Philadelphia	5–13
Jun 5	Philadelphia Athletics at Philadelphia	2–14
Jun 11	Hartford Dark Blues at New Haven	0–12
Jun 12	Hartford Dark Blues at Hartford	3–2
Jun 14	Hartford Dark Blues at Hartford	0–10
Jun 17	Philadelphia Athletics at New Haven	4–6
Jun 23	Philadelphia Athletics at Philadelphia	2–18

Date	Opponent and Location	Score
Jun 24	Philadelphia Athletics at Philadelphia	1–12
Jul 2	Boston Red Stockings at New Haven	10–5
Jul 19	Chicago White Stocking at New Haven	1–4
Jul 20	Chicago White Stocking at New Haven	6–1
Jul 22	Chicago White Stocking at New Haven	3–4
Jul 23	St. Louis Brown Stockings at New Haven	0–6
Jul 24	Hartford Dark Blues at New Haven	3–4
Jul 28	St. Louis Brown Stockings at New Haven	7–3
Jul 30	St. Louis Brown Stockings at New Haven	7–9
Jul 31	Boston Red Stockings at Boston	2–8
Aug 9	New York Mutuals at New Haven	2–4
Aug 13	New York Mutuals at New Haven	0–4
Aug 14	Hartford Dark Blues at Hartford	3–17
Aug 16	Hartford Dark Blues at New Haven	2–5
Aug 18	Phila. White Stockings at Philadelphia	2–3
Sep 11	Brooklyn Atlantics at Brooklyn	13–6
Sep 24	Boston Red Stockings at New Haven	1–16
Sep 27	New York Mutuals at Brooklyn	2–4
Sep 28	New York Mutuals at Brooklyn	8–6
Oct 4	Hartford Dark Blues at New Haven	0–18
Oct 23	Hartford Dark Blues at New Haven	3–8
Oct 28	Boston Red Stockings at New Haven	7–10

Hartford Dark Blues —1874

Date	Opponent and Location	Score
Apr 8	Picked Nine at Hartford	28–6
Apr 11	Trinity College at Hartford	unknown
Apr 15	Trinity College at Hartford	38–4
Apr 18	Yale University at Hartford	12–2
Apr 21	Bridgeport TBFUS at Hartford	66–3 (5)
Apr 27	Philadelphia Whites at Hartford	snowed out
Apr 30	Boston Red Stockings at Boston	snowed out
May 1	New York Mutuals at Hartford	10–7
May 5	Philadelphia Athletics at Hartford	10–9
May 6	Yale University at New Haven	6–4
May 7	Lord Baltimores at Hartford	22–2
May 9	Trinity College at Hartford	27–2
May 11	Lord Baltimores at Hartford	16–6
May 12	Boston Red Stockings at Hartford	3–25
May 13	Boston Red Stockings at Hartford	1–8
May 21	Philadelphia Whites at Philadelphia	4–6 (10)
May 22	Lord Baltimores at Hartford	7–9
May 23	Philadelphia Athletics at Philadelphia	4–12
May 25	Philadelphia Whites at Philadelphia	rained out
May 27	Chicago White Stockings at Chicago	3–9

Date	Opponent and Location	Score
May 30	Chicago White Stockings at Chicago	8–14
Jun 3	Philadelphia Athletics at Cincinnati	rained out
Jun 4	Princeton University at New Jersey	14–6
Jun 5	Brooklyn Atlantics at Brooklyn	8–1
Jun 6	New York Mutuals at Brooklyn	2–5
Jun 9	Brooklyn Atlantics at Hartford	15–4
Jun 12	Yale University at Hartford	17–8
Jun 16	Philadelphia Athletics at Hartford	4–11
Jun 19	Philadelphia Athletics at Hartford	6–11
Jun 21	Boston Red Stockings at Boston	1–15
Jun 22	Chicago White Stockings at Hartford	10–14
Jun 24	Hartford Amateurs at Hartford	22–8
Jun 25	Boston Red Stockings at Hartford	13–14
Jun 26	New York Mutuals at Brooklyn	rained out
Jun 27	New York Mutuals at Brooklyn	3–7
Jun 30	Yale University at Hartford	7–0
Jul 1	Yale University at Hartford	9–8
Jul 3	Princeton University at Hartford	18–14
Jul 4	Harvard University at Hartford	18–1
Jul 7	Philadelphia Whites at Hartford	15–2
Jul 10	New York Mutuals at Hartford	13–4
Jul 12	Brooklyn Atlantics at Hartford	rained out
Jul 13	Brooklyn Atlantics at Hartford	2–6
Jul 14	Hartford Amateurs at Hartford	15–1
Jul 16	TBFUS club of Bridgeport at Bridgeport	15–2
Jul 22	Bristol Clippers at Hartford	36–0
Jul 23	New York Mutuals at Brooklyn	5–13
Jul 24	Philadelphia Whites at Philadelphia	8–4
Jul 25	New York Mutuals at Brooklyn	3–7
Aug 1	Hartford Amateurs at Hartford	10–3 (6)
Aug 10	Philadelphia Whites at Hartford	6–3
Aug 11	Philadelphia Whites at Hartford	5–6 (12)
Aug 12	Philadelphia Whites at Boston	10–23
Aug 13	Philadelphia Whites at Boston	rained out
Aug 15	Acushnets at Martha's Vineyard	unknown
Aug 24	Stamford Amateurs at Stamford, CT	35–0
Aug 30	Springfield Amateurs at Springfield, MA	44–0
Sep 1	New York Mutuals at Hartford	0–14
Sep 3	New York Mutuals at Hartford	3–7
Sep 5	Brooklyn Atlantics at Hartford	21–15
Sep 7	Brooklyn Atlantics at Hartford	3–7
Sep 8	Josh Hart's Theatre Comique	30–9
Sep 10	Chicago White Stockings at Hartford	7–5
Sep 12	Chicago White Stockings at Hartford	1–14
Sep 17	Chicago White Stockings at Hartford	rained out
Sep 18	Chicago White Stockings at Hartford	rained out
Sep 19	Picked Nine at Wolcottville, CT	25–2

Date	Opponent and Location	Score
Sep 22	Philadelphia Whites at Hartford	2–6
Sep 23	Yale University at New Haven	16–7
Sep 24	Brooklyn Atlantics at Brooklyn	8–9
Sep 25	Philadelphia Athletics at Philadelphia	13–14
Sep 28	Stamford Amateurs at Hartford	30–5
Sep 29	Lord Baltimores at Hartford	rained out
Sep 30	Lord Baltimores at Hartford	4–9
Oct 1	Lord Baltimores at Hartford	14–4
Oct 3	Boston Red Stockings at Boston	6–15
Oct 5	Boston Red Stockings at Hartford	4–7
Oct 6	Boston Red Stockings at Hartford	6–7
Oct 9	TBFUS of Bridgeport at Bridgeport	19–2
Oct 11	Yale University at Hartford	rained out
Oct 13	New York Mutuals at Brooklyn	4–18
Oct 14	Brooklyn Atlantics at Brooklyn	6–9
Oct 16	Brooklyn Atlantics at Brooklyn	2–3
Oct 23	Boston Red Stockings at Hartford	1–13
Oct 24	Boston Red Stockings at Boston	8–11
Oct 26	Philadelphia Athletics at Hartford	2–5
Oct 27	Philadelphia Athletics at Hartford	10–3
Oct 28	Philadelphia Whites at Hartford	9–4
Oct 29	Barlow's Benefit	unknown
Oct 30	Boston Red Stockings at Worcester	17–11
Oct 31	Boston Red Stockings at Boston (exhibition)	5–13

Hartford Dark Blues — 1875

Date	Opponent and Location	Score
Apr 20	Picked Nine at Hartford	24–1
Apr 21	Picked Nine at Hartford	13–3
Apr 22	Picked Nine at Hartford	26–1
Apr 23	Hartford Amateurs at Hartford	30–0
Apr 24	Brooklyn Atlantics at Hartford	6–5
Apr 26	Picked Nine at Hartford	16–2 (10)
Apr 27	Brooklyn Atlantics at Hartford	10–1
Apr 29	Hartford Amateurs at Hartford	14–0
Apr 30	Yale University at Hartford	9–0
May 3	Philadelphia Centennials at Hartford	13–4
May 5	New Haven Elm Citys at Hartford	6–3
May 6	Philadelphia Centennials at Hartford	rained out
May 7	New York Mutuals at Hartford	8–3
May 8	Washington Nationals at Hartford	16–0 (8)
May 10	Washington Nationals at Hartford	9–1
May 12	Philadelphia Whites at Hartford	4–1
May 13	Philadelphia Athletics at Hartford	6–2
May 14	Philadelphia Athletics at Hartford	10–2
May 15	Brooklyn Atlantics at Brooklyn	8–1
May 17	Brooklyn Atlantics at Brooklyn	5–0

Date	Opponent and Location	Score
May 18	Boston Red Stockings at Hartford	5–10
May 19	Boston Red Stockings at Boston	2–13
May 20	Brooklyn Atlantics at Brooklyn	10–1
May 21	New York Mutuals at Brooklyn	1–0
May 22	Philadelphia Athletics at Philadelphia	4–10
May 24	Philadelphia Whites at Philadelphia	5–6
May 25	Washington Nationals at Washington	8–5
May 26	Washington Nationals at Washington	6–2
May 28	Philadelphia Athletics at Philadelphia	postponed
May 29	Brooklyn Atlantics at Brooklyn	9–5
May 31	New York Mutuals at Brooklyn	3–1
Jun 2	Philadelphia Whites at Philadelphia	2–11
Jun 3	Brooklyn Atlantics at Hartford	9–4
Jun 5	Yale University at New Haven	3–1
Jun 8	Yale University at New Haven	10–3
Jun 9	New Haven Elm Citys at New Haven	rained out
Jun 11	New Haven Elm Citys at New Haven	12–0
Jun 12	New Haven Elm Citys at Providence	2–3
Jun 14	New Haven Elm Citys at Hartford	10–0
Jun 15	Yale University at Hartford	12–2
Jun 17	Boston Red Stockings at Boston	0–4
Jun 19	Chicago White Stockings at Chicago	0–1 (11)
Jun 22	St. Louis Red Stockings at St. Louis	1–8
Jun 23	St. Louis Brown Stockings at St. Louis	1–7
Jun 24	St. Louis Red Stockings at St. Louis	11–6
Jun 25	St. Louis Brown Stockings at St. Louis	rained out
Jun 26	St. Louis Red Stockings at St. Louis	9–0
Jun 28	St. Louis Brown Stockings at St. Louis	rained out
Jun 29	Chicago White Stockings at Chicago	4–1
Jul 1	Geulph Maple Leafs at Geulph, Canada	17–2
Jul 3	Boston Red Stockings at Boston	1–3
Jul 5	Boston Red Stockings at Hartford	0–7
Jul 7	New York Mutuals at Hartford	1–9 (6 – rain)
Jul 8	New York Mutuals at Hartford	2–6
Jul 10	TBFUS of Bridgeport at Bridgeport	6–0
Jul 14	Philadelphia Whites at Hartford	8–0
Jul 15	Chicago White Stockings at Hartford	3–4
Jul 16	Philadelphia Whites at Hartford	rained out
Jul 17	Philadelphia Whites at Hartford	14–5
Jul 21	Chicago White Stockings at Hartford	4–1
Jul 24	New Haven Elm Citys at New Haven	4–3
Jul 26	St. Louis Brown Stockings at Hartford	rained out
Jul 27	St. Louis Brown Stockings at Hartford	4–2
Jul 29	St. Louis Brown Stockings at Hartford	rained out
Jul 31	St. Louis Brown Stockings at Hartford	1–7
Aug 4	Brooklyn Atlantics at Brooklyn	rained out
Aug 5	New York Mutuals at Brooklyn	1–1 (9 – rain)

Appendix C

Date	Opponent and Location	Score
Aug 6	Brooklyn Atlantics at Brooklyn	13–0
Aug 7	New York Mutuals at Brooklyn	3–1 (11)
Aug 10	New York Mutuals at Hartford	7–0
Aug 12	New York Mutuals at Hartford	1–1 (9 — rain)
Aug 14	New Haven Elm Citys at Hartford	17–3
Aug 16	New Haven Elm Citys at New Haven	5–2
Aug 19	Philadelphia Whites at Philadelphia	1–5
Aug 20	Brooklyn Atlantics at Brooklyn	2–0
Aug 21	New York Mutuals at Brooklyn	7–3
Aug 23	New York Mutuals at Brooklyn	postponed
Aug 24	New York Mutuals at Brooklyn	3–2
Aug 26	New York Mutuals at Hartford	8–2
Aug 27	New York Mutuals at Hartford (exhibition)	15–3
Aug 30	Philadelphia Whites at Philadelphia	11–3
Aug 31	Experts at Harrisburg, PA	3–1
Sep 2	Cincinnati Blue Stockings at Cincinnati	13–1
Sep 3	Cincinnati Ludlows at Cincinnati	4–6
Sep 4	Louisville Eagles at Louisville	15–10
Sep 6	Louisville Olympics at Louisville	20–6
Sep 7	St. Louis Brown Stockings at St. Louis	8–2
Sept 9	St. Louis Brown Stockings at St. Louis	12–4
Sep 11	St. Louis Brown Stockings at St. Louis	0–9
Sep 13	St. Louis Brown Stockings at St. Louis	3–0
Sep 14	Chicago White Stockings at Chicago	1–1 (9 — dark)
Sep 15	Chicago White Stockings at Chicago	3–10
Sep 16	Chicago White Stockings at Chicago	13–4
Sep 18	Chicago White Stockings at Chicago	3–14
Sep 19	Stars at Cincinnati	8–3
Sep 20	Covington (Kentucky) at Covington	unknown
Sep 21	Philadelphia Whites at Cincinnati	9–13
Sep 22	Harrisburg Experts at Harrisburg, PA	9–1
Sep 23	New York Mutuals at Brooklyn	8–6
Sep 25	Boston Red Stockings at Hartford	0–6
Sep 29	Boston Red Stockings at Boston (exhibition)	4–1
Sep 30	Stars of New London at New London	20–0
Oct 1	Brown University at Providence	11–4
Oct 2	Boston Red Stockings at Boston	2–3 (7)
Oct 4	New Haven Elm Citys at New Haven	18–0
Oct 5	Philadelphia Athletics at Philadelphia	4–7
Oct 6	Philadelphia Athletics at Philadelphia	7–7 (4 — dark)
Oct 8	Philadelphia Athletics at Philadelphia	8–1
Oct 9	Brooklyn Atlantics at Brooklyn	20–7
Oct 12	Philadelphia Athletics at Hartford	18–2
Oct 13	Philadelphia Athletics at Hartford	7–8 (10)
Oct 14	Philadelphia Athletics at Hartford	10–10 (9)
Oct 15	New Haven Elm Citys at Hartford	rained out
Oct 16	New Haven Elm Citys at Hartford	rained out

Date	Opponent and Location	Score
Oct 18	St. Louis Brown Stockings at Hartford	5–0
Oct 19	Boston Red Stockings at Hartford	3–7
Oct 20	St. Louis Brown Stockings at Hartford	4–10
Oct 21	St. Louis Brown Stockings at Hartford	18–7 (8 — dark)
Oct 22	Yale University at Hartford	9–4 (7)
Oct 23	New Haven Elm Citys at New Haven	8–3 (8 — dark)
Oct 25	Chicago White Stockings at Hartford	5–3
Oct 26	Chicago White Stockings at Hartford	9–2
Oct 27	Chicago White Stockings at Hartford	17–6
Oct 28	Trinity College at Hartford	20–0
Oct 29	Boston Red Stockings Hartford	9–8 (7 — dark)
Oct 30	Boston Red Stockings at Boston	4–7

Hartford Dark Blues —1876

Date	Opponent and Location	Score
Apr 12	Trinity College at Hartford	16–2
Apr 15	Trinity College at Hartford	18–0
Apr 19	Hartford Charter Oaks at Hartford	20–1
Apr 27	New York Mutuals at Brooklyn	3–8
Apr 28	New York Mutuals at Hartford	rained out
Apr 29	Boston Red Stockings at Boston	3–2
May 1	Boston Red Stockings at Hartford	15–3
May 3	New Haven Elm Citys at Hartford	4–6
May 4	New Haven Elm Citys at New Haven	6–7
May 5	New York Mutuals at Brooklyn	4–3
May 6	Philadelphia Athletics at Philadelphia	6–3
May 8	Philadelphia Athletics at Philadelphia	7–5
May 10	New Haven at New Haven	6–2
May 13	New York Mutuals at Hartford	28–3
May 15	New Haven Elm Citys at Hartford	7–1
May 16	Philadelphia Athletics at Hartford	8–2
May 17	Boston Red Stockings at Boston	8–3
May 19	Boston Red Stockings at Hartford	12–2
May 20	New Haven Elm Citys at New Haven	6–5
May 23	Chicago White Stockings at Hartford	4–6
May 25	Chicago White Stockings at Hartford	4–1
May 27	Chicago White Stockings at Hartford	1–8
May 30	Cincinnati Red Stockings at Hartford	6–0
Jun 1	Cincinnati Red Stockings at Hartford	2–8
Jun 3	Cincinnati Red Stockings at Hartford	7–2
Jun 6	St. Louis Brown Stockings at Hartford	8–4
Jun 8	St. Louis Brown Stockings at Hartford	6–3
Jun 10	St. Louis Brown Stockings at Hartford	6–0 (6 — rain)
Jun 13	Louisville Grays at Hartford	4–0
Jun 15	Louisville Grays at Hartford	6–1
Jun 17	Louisville Grays at Hartford	1–0
Jun 21	Louisville Grays at Louisville	5–5 (13)

Appendix C

Date	Opponent and Location	Score
Jun 22	Louisville Grays at Louisville	3–0
Jun 24	Louisville Grays at Louisville	2–7
Jun 26	Louisville Grays at Louisville	3–0
Jun 27	Cincinnati Red Stockings at Cincinnati	4–2
Jun 29	Cincinnati Red Stockings at Cincinnati	13–6
Jul 1	Cincinnati Red Stockings at Cincinnati	rained out
Jul 2	Columbus Buckeyes in Columbus	2–5
Jul 4	Chicago White Stockings at Chicago	3–0
Jul 6	Chicago White Stockings at Chicago	6–2
Jul 8	Chicago White Stockings at Chicago	3–9
Jul 11	St. Louis Brown Stockings at St. Louis	0–2
Jul 13	St. Louis Brown Stockings at St. Louis	0–3
Jul 15	St. Louis Brown Stockings at St. Louis	0–2
Jul 17	Indianapolis at Indianapolis	unknown
Jul 18	Alleghenies at Allegheny	unknown
Jul 20	Newcastle club at Newcastle, PA	unknown
Jul 21	Philadelphia Athletics at Philadelphia	6–4
Jul 22	New York Mutuals at Brooklyn	3–7
Jul 30	New Haven Elm Citys at Hartford	7–4
Aug 1	Philadelphia Athletics at Hartford	8–4
Aug 2	Philadelphia Athletics at Hartford	15–5
Aug 5	New York Mutuals at Hartford	1–4
Aug 7	New York Mutuals at Hartford	1–2
Aug 9	Philadelphia Athletics at Hartford	9–1
Aug 10	Bridgeport at Bridgeport	8–9
Aug 11	New York Mutuals at Brooklyn	14–4
Aug 12	Philadelphia Athletics at Philadelphia	11–15
Aug 14	Philadelphia Athletics at Philadelphia	5–4
Aug 16	New Haven Elm Citys at New Haven	5–5 (13)
Aug 18	Boston Red Stockings at Boston	5–4
Aug 19	Boston Red Stockings at Boston	4–13
Aug 21	Boston Red Stockings at Hartford	10–4
Aug 22	Boston Red Stockings at Hartford	5–6
Aug 31	Providence at Providence, RI	4–0
Sep 1	Fall River at Fall River, MA	4–2
Sep 2	Providence at Providence, RI	12–2
Sep 5	Louisville Grays at Hartford	6–1
Sep 6	Louisville Grays at Hartford	6–3
Sep 8	Cincinnati Red Stockings at Hartford	rained out
Sep 9 9 AM	Cincinnati Red Stockings at Hartford	14–4
Sep 9 3 PM	Cincinnati Red Stockings at Hartford	8–4
Sep 12	Chicago White Stockings at Hartford	8–7
Sep 13	Chicago White Stockings at Hartford	2–6
Sep 15	St. Louis Brown Stockings at Hartford	2–6
Sep 16	St. Louis Brown Stockings at Hartford	4–6
Sep 20	Ithaca at Ithaca	5–4 (11)
Sep 22	Syracuse Stars at Syracuse	1–0

Date	Opponent and Location	Score
Sep 23	Syracuse Stars at Syracuse	5–5 (7)
Sep 26	**Chicago White Stockings at Chicago**	6–7
Sep 27	**Chicago White Stockings at Chicago**	10–16
Sep 29	**St. Louis Brown Stockings at St. Louis**	2–5
Sep 30	**St. Louis Brown Stockings at St. Louis**	4–1
Oct 2	Indianapolis at Indianapolis	5–3
Oct 4	**Louisville Grays at Louisville**	6–0
Oct 5	**Louisville Grays at Louisville**	11–2
Oct 6	**Cincinnati Red Stockings at Cincinnati**	7–4
Oct 7	**Cincinnati Red Stockings at Cincinnati**	11–6
Oct 9	**Cincinnati Red Stockings at Cincinnati**	11–0
Oct 16	Binghamton Cricket Club at Binghamton	0–6 (5 — dark)
Oct 17	**New York Mutuals at Brooklyn**	3–0
Oct 20	**Boston Red Stockings at Boston**	5–0
Oct 21	**Boston Red Stockings at Boston**	11–1
Oct 24	Boston Red Stockings at Hartford (exhibition)	7–8
Oct 26	Boston Red Stockings at Providence (exhib.)	5–10
Oct 27	Boston Red Stockings at Boston (exhibition)	4–12
Oct 29	Boston Red Stockings at Boston (exhibition)	9–13

Hartford Dark Blues —1877

Date	Opponent and Location	Score
Apr 30	**Boston Red Stockings at Brooklyn**	1–1
May 2	Rochester at Rochester	4–0
May 3	Rochester at Rochester	6–1
May 8	**Chicago White Stockings at Chicago**	5–6
May 10	**Chicago White Stockings at Chicago**	14–10
May 15	**St. Louis Brown Stockings at St. Louis**	2–6
May 17	Indianapolis at Indianapolis	2–1
May 18	**Louisville Grays at Louisville**	12–2
May 19	**Louisville Grays at Louisville**	5–9
May 24	Columbus Buckeyes in Columbus, OH	2–1 (12)
May 25	Columbus Buckeyes in Columbus, OH	11–2
May 28	Pittsburgh Alleghenys at Pittsburgh	9–1
May 31	Philadelphia Athletics at Hartford	5–1
June 1	Philadelphia Athletics at Hartford	8–5
Jun 2	**Boston Red Stockings at Boston**	2–8
Jun 4	**Boston Red Stockings at Boston**	6–18
Jun 5	Hartford Amateurs at Hartford	4–3 (10)
Jun 8	Syracuse Stars at Brooklyn	0–2
Jun 9	**Boston Red Stockings at Brooklyn**	7–0
Jun 11	Brooklyn Chelseas at Brooklyn	4–3
Jun 12	**Boston Red Stockings at Brooklyn**	7–0
June 14	Yale University at New Haven	3–0
Jun 16	**St. Louis Brown Stockings at Brooklyn**	5–3
Jun 18	**St. Louis Brown Stockings at Brooklyn**	3–2
Jun 19	**Chicago White Stockings at Brooklyn**	13–1

Appendix C

Date	Opponent and Location	Score
Jun 21	Chicago White Stockings at Brooklyn	6–0
Jun 23	Louisville Grays at Brooklyn	3–5
Jun 25	Louisville Grays at Brooklyn	5–4
Jun 26	Boston Red Stockings at Boston	4–2
Jun 27	Louisville Grays at Brooklyn	1–4
Jun 28	Harvard University at Brooklyn	6–1
Jul 2	Tecumseh at London, Ontario	13–3
Jul 4	St. Louis Brown Stockings at St. Louis	6–7 (11)
Jul 5	St. Louis Brown Stockings at St. Louis	1–6
Jul 7	Louisville Grays at Louisville	4–14
Jul 11	Cincinnati Red Stockings at Cincinnati	6–2
Jul 12	Cincinnati Red Stockings at Cincinnati	15–9
Jul 13	Chicago White Stockings at Chicago	3–6
Jul 14	Chicago White Stockings at Chicago	9–4
Jul 16	St. Louis Brown Stockings at St. Louis	2–3 (12)
Jul 17	St. Louis Brown Stockings at St. Louis	13–3
Jul 18	St. Louis Brown Stockings at St. Louis	2–10
Jul 19	Louisville Grays at Louisville	7–10
Jul 20	Louisville Grays at Louisville	8–3
Jul 21	Louisville Grays at Louisville	6–11
Jul 23	Springfield at Springfield, IL	10–0
Jul 24	Cincinnati Red Stockings at Cincinnati	8–9 (10)
Jul 25	Cincinnati Red Stockings at Cincinnati	1–5
Jul 26	Chicago White Stockings at Chicago	1–7
Jul 30	Allegheny at Allegheny	0–2
Jul 31	Allegheny at Allegheny	6–0
Aug 1	Allegheny at Allegheny	4–3
Aug 2	Philadelphia Athletics at Philadelphia	11–1
Aug 3	Philadelphia Athletics at Philadelphia	7–5
Aug 6	Brooklyn Chelseas at Brooklyn	14–2
Aug 7	Boston Red Stockings at Brooklyn	1–4
Aug 8	Boston Red Stockings at Brooklyn	3–5
Aug 9	Hartford Amateurs at Hartford	rained out
Aug 10	Boston Red Stockings at Boston	4–2
Aug 11	Boston Red Stockings at Boston	7–4
Aug 20	Louisville Grays at Brooklyn	5–1
Aug 21	Louisville Grays at Brooklyn	7–0
Aug 23	Louisville Grays at Brooklyn	1–1
Aug 25	Cincinnati Red Stockings at Brooklyn	rained out
Aug 27	Cincinnati Red Stockings at Brooklyn	5–1
Aug 28	Cincinnati Red Stockings at Brooklyn	7–13
Aug 29	Indianapolis at Brooklyn	rained out
Aug 31	Louisville Grays at Brooklyn	6–3
Sep 1	Louisville Grays at New Haven (exhibition)	6–4 (10)
Sep 4	Chicago White Stockings at Brooklyn	7–1
Sep 8	St. Louis Brown Stockings at Brooklyn	15–6
Sep 11	St. Louis Brown Stockings at Brooklyn	0–3

Date	Opponent and Location	Score
Sep 12	St. Louis Brown Stockings at Brooklyn	2–3
Sep 14	Chicago White Stockings at Brooklyn	5–2
Sep 15	Chicago White Stockings at Brooklyn	3–4
Sep 17	Orange at Orange, NJ	8–3
Sep 18	St. Louis Brown Stockings at Brooklyn	7–4
Sep 21	Chicago White Stockings at Brooklyn	11–3
Sep 22	Chicago White Stockings at New Haven	11–9
Sep 26	Boston Red Stockings at Boston	4–14
Sep 27	Boston Red Stockings at Boston	2–13
Sep 29	Boston Red Stockings at Boston	4–8
Oct 3	Boston Red Stockings at New Haven (exhib.)	4–6

Notes

For the period 1872–1877, primary sources have been utilized to the greatest extent possible. These include contemporary newspapers, sporting periodicals, and personal correspondence. The three Hartford daily newspapers, the *Post, Times,* and *Courant,* provided a wealth of information. The *New Haven Evening Register* provided the best coverage of baseball in New Haven. The *Middletown Constitution* and *Middletown Sentinel and Witness* were weekly newspapers which provided often skimpy coverage of the Mansfields' endeavors. The *Hartford Post,* whose Middletown correspondent was the Mansfield's president, Augustus Putnam, provided the most complete coverage of the Mansfields' development from an amateur club to a major league team. The *Chicago Tribune,* especially its Sunday edition, was filled with priceless news, notes and gossip of the day concerning all major league teams. Secondary sources were also used to place baseball developments in the larger context of American society.

The Harry Wright correspondence provides great insight into the thoughts and feelings of baseball pioneer Harry Wright. The Henry Chadwick Scrapbooks were valuable, as were what I have termed the "Notre Dame Scrapbooks," possibly compiled by long-time *New York Clipper* writer William Rankin. Part of the Joyce Sports Research Collection housed in the Hesburgh Library, the Notre Dame Scrapbooks include newspaper clipping of the early game, with much of the material relating to the 1870s (Parts 1–3 and 7 of the scrapbook collection proved especially useful to my research, focusing as they did on 1870–1877). Regrettably, the clippings in both the Chadwick and Notre Dame scrapbooks are trimmed such that it is impossible to identify the original sources. In these cases, I have identified the source simply as "Chadwick Scrapbooks" or "Notre Dame Scrapbooks." If the origin could be determined, it is named in the reference note.

Introduction

1. Some may quibble with my description of these Connecticut clubs as major league teams. Hartford was in the National League — yes, the same National League of today's Mets, Dodgers and Braves — so there is no question there. The question is about the National Association (NA), in which both the Middletown Mansfields and New Haven Elm City clubs played. The NA was most certainly the first *professional* league, preceding the Na-

tional League from 1871 to 1875, but some say it was not a *major* league, a term with a somewhat nebulous definition. In 1968, the Special Baseball Record Committee decided that the NA was not a major league due to its "erratic schedule and procedures." The NA certainly had its share of problems, most notably a large number of teams dropping out during the 1872 and 1875 seasons, but with the added knowledge that the last 40 years of baseball research has provided, I think that if the committee were meeting today, the decision would be different. For the period 1871–1875, the National Association had the best players in baseball competing among a predefined set of competitors for a championship. There was no league more organized or that played a better caliber of baseball than the National Association. For these reasons, many baseball historians, including myself, consider teams that played in the National Association as major league teams.

Chapter 2

1. John Husman, *Nineteenth Century News*, Spring 1995, pp. 1–2.
2. *Ibid.*
3. Jack Selzer, *Baseball in the Nineteenth Century: An Overview* (Cooperstown, NY: Society for American Baseball Research, 1986), p. 4.
4. Harold Seymour, *Baseball: The Early Years* (New York: Oxford University Press, 1960), pp. 24–25.
5. Seymour, *Baseball: The Early Years*, pp. 25–50.
6. Seymour, *Baseball: The Early Years*, p. 51.
7. William J. Ryczek, *Blackguards and Red Stockings: A History of Baseball's National Association, 1871–1875* (Jefferson, NC: McFarland, 1992), pp. 5–6.
8. Seymour, *Baseball: The Early Years*, p. 26.
9. Seymour, *Baseball: The Early Years*, pp. 28–29, 31.
10. Seymour, *Baseball: The Early Years*, pp. 36–37.
11. Seymour, *Baseball: The Early Years*, p. 42.

Chapter 3

1. George Earlie Shankle, *State Names, Flags, Seals, Songs, Birds, Flowers, and Other Symbols* (New York: H.W. Wilson, 1941), p. 41.
2. "The Charter Oak City," *Scribner's Monthly* 13, no. 1 (Nov. 1876), p. 8.
3. *San Francisco Alta* (California) newspaper, March 3, 1868.
4. Dean Nelson, "A Century of Connecticut Inventions," *Hog River Journal*, http://www.hogriver.org/issues/v03n02/connecticut_inventions.htm.
5. In his book, *Yale Yesterdays*, Clarence Deming recalled the appearance of the "spring bat" at a Yale baseball practice one day, saying, "The New York firm of Peck & Snyder was the forerunner of the Spalding of today as a baseball emporium. About the year 1868 they sent up to the nine a curio in bats for a try out. It was a novelty as a hard wood — ash — stick; and for several inches, beginning two or three inches from its bigger end, it was cut lengthwise by a saw into quadrants. Its theory was an elastic hit and it had the humorous quality of a weird staccato when it took the ball. But nobody on the nine before or since could make the bat work except one day, when in a game with the champion professionals at the Union Grounds, Brooklyn, 'Tom' Hooker, Yale pitcher, took the odd bat, caught the ball just right and hit to far right field a ball which for distance was said to be the record hit of those grounds."
6. *Hartford Courant*, September 24, 1858.
7. Quinnipiack Base Ball Club Constitution and By-laws, 1860.
8. Pine Grove Base Ball Club Constitution and By-laws, 1859.
9. David Block, *Baseball Before We Knew It* (Lincoln: University of Nebraska Press, 2005), p. 224; *Hartford Courant*, December 2, 1858.
10. *Hartford Courant*, May 19, 1860, September 17, 1860, and October 27, 1860.
11. *Hartford Courant*, June 23, 1862, June 30, 1862, and May 19, 1862.
12. Phyllis Kihn, "The Charter Oak Nine," *Connecticut Historical Society Bulletin*, April 1961, p.56; *Hartford Courant*, July 2, 1862.
13. *Hartford Courant*, September 11, 1862, and May 13, 1863.

Chapter 4

1. Seymour, *Baseball: The Early Years* (New York: Oxford University Press, 1960), p. 42.
2. Marshall D. Wright, *The National Association of Base Ball Players, 1857–1870* (Jefferson, NC: McFarland, 2000), p. 140; William J. Ryczek, *Blackguards and Red Stockings: A History of Baseball's National Association, 1871–1875* (Jefferson, NC: McFarland, 1992), p. 6.
3. Seymour, *Baseball: The Early Years*, p. 42; John Freyer and Mark Rucker, *Peverelly's National Game* (Charleston, SC: Arcadia, 2005), p. 9.
4. *Hartford Courant*, July 25, 1867, and October 17, 1864; Phyllis Kihn, "The Charter Oak Nine," *Connecticut Historical Society Bulletin*, April 1961, p. 60.
5. *Hartford Courant*, October 9, 1866, and August 15, 1867.
6. *Hartford Courant*, July 24, 1868, and September 9, 1868; *Hartford Post*, July 27, 1868, and July 28, 1868; *Middletown Constitution*, August 5, 1868.
7. Harold Seymour, *Baseball: The People's Game* (New York: Oxford University Press, 1990), p. 467.
8. Clarence Deming, *Yale Yesterdays* (New Haven, CT: Yale University Press, 1915), pp. 194–196.
9. Deming, *Yale Yesterdays*, pp. 194–196.
10. *Hartford Courant*, April 13, 1866, and August 13, 1866; *Middletown Constitution*, May 8, 1867.
11. *Middletown Constitution*, November 7, 1866.
12. *Middletown Constitution*, October 13, 1869.
13. *Hartford Courant*, August 15, 1866.
14. *Hartford Courant*, September 26, 1866.
15. *Bat and Ball*, reprinted in *Hartford Courant*, October 16, 1866.
16. David B. Potts, *Wesleyan University, 1831–1910: Collegiate Enterprise in New England* (Middletown, CT: Wesleyan University Press, 1999), p. 46.
17. *Yale Courant* quoted in *Yale Alumni Magazine*, May 2002; Judith Schiff; *Time Magazine*, June 25, 1923.
18. *Hartford Post*, November 3, 1866, and November 7, 1866. After the victory over the Charter Oaks' second nine, the giddy Forest City club boasted that they would like to "harness" the Charter Oaks' first nine. The *Hartford Post* found this challenge laughable and warned Middletown that if they played the first nine of the Charter Oaks they would find that "they had the biggest elephant they ever undertook to harness." The matter was put to rest when the Charter Oaks declared they would not demean themselves by playing the Forest Citys.
19. *Chicago Inter Ocean*, May 24, 1874.
20. *Middletown Press*, September 17, 1887.
21. *Hartford Courant*, September 25, 1866; *Middletown Constitution*, September 26, 1866.
22. *Middletown Constitution*, April 17, 1867.
23. *Hartford Post*, February 20, 1867.
24. *Hartford Post*, February 20, 1867.
25. Kihn, "The Charter Oak Nine," p. 57.
26. Kihn, "The Charter Oak Nine," pp. 56, 60.
27. "The Charter Oak City," *Scribner's Monthly* 13, no. 1 (Nov. 1876), p. 11; Mark Twain, as special correspondent to *San Francisco Alta* (California) newspaper, March 3, 1868.
28. Kihn, "The Charter Oak Nine," p. 63.
29. Seymour, *Baseball: The Early Years*, p. 45–46.
30. Marshall D. Wright, *The National Association of Base Ball Players, 1857–1870*, pp. 137–138, 180–186.
31. *Hartford Courant*, March 14, 1867.

Chapter 5

1. Harold Seymour, *Baseball: The Early Years* (New York: Oxford University Press, 1960), pp. 48–49.
2. Seymour, *Baseball: The Early Years*, pp. 45–54.
3. Seymour, *Baseball: The Early Years*, pp. 49, 55.
4. Seymour, *Baseball: The Early Years*, p. 55.
5. Seymour, *Baseball: The Early Years*, p. 56.
6. William J. Ryczek, *When Johnny Came Sliding Home: The Post–Civil War Baseball Boom, 1865–1870* (Jefferson, NC: McFarland, 1998), pp. 175–177.
7. Phyllis Kihn, "The Charter Oak Nine," *Connecticut Historical Society Bulletin*, April 1961, p. 64.
8. Kihn, "The Charter Oak Nine," p. 64; *Hartford Courant*, May 15, 1868, June 16, 1868, and June 13, 1868.

9. Elizabeth A. Warner, *A Pictorial History of Middletown* (Norfolk, VA: Donning Company Publishers, 1990), p. 65; William J. Ryczek, *Blackguards and Red Stockings: A History of Baseball's National Association, 1871–1875* (Jefferson, NC: McFarland, 1992), p. 12; *Middletown Press*, September 29, 1959.

10. *Middletown Sentinel and Witness*, May 6, 1870; *Hartford Post*, April 28, 1870.

11. *Hartford Post*, May 18, 1870; *Hartford Post*, July 9, 1870; *Middletown Sentinel and Witness*, June 24, 1870; George Arbuckle Craig, "My First Recollections of Middletown," speech to Middletown Conversational Club, Middlesex Historical Society.

12. *New York Clipper*, July 16, 1870.

13. *Middletown Sentinel and Witness*, June 24, 1870; *Wesleyan Argus*, June 15, 1870.

14. *New York Clipper*, June 11, 1870.

15. *Hartford Post*, August 11, 1870; *Middletown Constitution*, April 17, 1872.

16. *Hartford Post*, August 29, 1870.

17. *Hartford Post*, September 2, 1870; *Meriden Daily Republican*, September 5, 1870.

18. *Hartford Post*, September 3, 1870; *Middletown Sentinel and Witness*, February 11, 1870, and May 27, 1870.

19. *Meriden Daily Republican*, September 5, 1870; *New York Clipper*, December 10, 1870; Ryczek, *Blackguards and Red Stockings*, p. 28; *Hartford Post*, September 3, 1870.

20. Ryczek, *Blackguards and Red Stockings*, pp. 7–8, 119.

21. *Wesleyan Argus*, October 12, 1870; Ryczek, *Blackguards and Red Stockings*, pp. 83-84.

22. *Hartford Post*, September 30, 1870.

23. *Hartford Post*, October 31, 1870.

24. *Hartford Post*, October 31, 1870; Henry Dana Artemas Ward Diary, 1870.

25. *Hartford Post*, September 13, 1870.

26. *Hartford Post*, September 13, 1870. When word of Putnam's version of events reached the Meriden club, they were outraged and accused Putnam of trumping up the charges because of his association with the Mansfields. Meriden insisted that the crowd at the ballgame consisted of all classes of people, including Meriden's finest gentlemen. If anyone threw rocks, it was just a few small children who were immediately stopped. After the game, the Mansfields made no complaints about unfair treatment and even shot pool with the Meriden team at the local billiards room. Given the state of local news coverage at the time, the truth of the matter undoubtedly lay somewhere between these two accounts.

27. *Hartford Post*, November 3, 1870.

Chapter 6

1. Jack Selzer, *Baseball in the Nineteenth Century: An Overview* (Cooperstown, NY; Society for American Baseball Research, 1986), p. 7; William J. Ryczek, *When Johnny Came Sliding Home: The Post-Civil War Baseball Boom, 1865–1870* (Jefferson, NC: McFarland, 1998), p. 248.

2. William J. Ryczek, *Blackguards and Red Stockings: A History of Baseball's National Association, 1871–1875* (Jefferson, NC: McFarland, 1992), p. 12; *New York Clipper*, March 11, 1871.

3. Ryczek, *Blackguards and Red Stockings*, pp. 12–13.

4. *New York Clipper*, February 17, 1872. For the 1872 season, the wrist snap and bent elbow deliveries were officially sanctioned; a move the *New York Clipper* felt was a mere formality since it was obvious that pitchers were already using them. If they weren't, the *Clipper* reasoned, pitchers like Dick McBride and George Zettlein couldn't achieve their speed nor Candy Cummings his curve.

5. Ryczek, *Blackguards and Red Stockings*, pp. 33–34.

6. John Thorn, email to 19th century baseball Yahoo group.

7. Stephen Hanks, et al., *150 Years of Baseball* (Lincolnwood, IL: Publications International, 1989), p. 34.

8. Ryczek, *Blackguards and Red Stockings*, pp. 60–61.

9. Seymour, *Baseball: The Early Years* (New York: Oxford University Press, 1960), pp. 61-65.

Chapter 7

1. *Hartford Post*, March 25, 1871, and May 16, 1871.

2. *Hartford Post*, March 14, 1867; *Middletown Constitution*, April 17, 1872.

3. *Hartford Post*, March 25, 1871, April 5, 1871, and April 24, 1871.

4. *Hartford Post*, May 13, 1871.

5. *Hartford Post*, May 22, 1871.

6. *Middletown Sentinel and Witness*, June 2, 1871; *Hartford Post*, May 22, 1871, May 29, 1871, and May 30, 1871.
7. *Hartford Post*, June 2, 1871, June 7, 1871, and September 14, 1871.
8. *Hartford Post*, May 22, 1871, and June 10, 1871; *Boston Globe*, January 24, 1915.
9. *Hartford Post*, June 10, 1871.
10. William J. Ryczek, *Blackguards and Red Stockings: A History of Baseball's National Association, 1871–1875* (Jefferson, NC: McFarland, 1992), pp. 31, 65–66; *Hartford Post*, June 16, 1871; Harold Seymour, *Baseball: The Early Years* (New York: Oxford University Press, 1960), pp. 53–54.
11. *Middletown Constitution*, July 6, 1870; *New York Times*, July 6, 1870; *Hartford Post*, July 6, 1871.
12. *Hartford Post*, August 4, 1871, August 6, 1871, and August 8, 1871; *New York World*, August 8, 1871.
13. Robert Schaefer, "The Lost Art of Fair-Foul Hitting," *The National Pastime* 20 (2000), pp. 3, 4.
14. William E. McMahon, "Albert Goodwill Spalding," *Baseball's First Stars*, ed. Frederick Ivor-Campbell, Robert Tiemann, and Mark Rucker (Cleveland: Society for American Baseball Research, 1996), pp. 154, 155; David Voigt, *American Baseball* (Norman: University of Oklahoma Press, 1966), pp. 44–45.
15. Harry Wright to Ben Douglas Junior, July 22, 1871.
16. *Hartford Post*, August 11, 1871.
17. *Hartford Post*, August 14, 1871.
18. *New York Clipper*, April 20, 1872.
19. *Boston Globe*, January 17, 1915.
20. *Middletown Constitution*, July 12, 1871.
21. *New Haven Daily Palladium*, September 11, 1871.
22. *Bridgeport Standard*, September 11, 1871.
23. *New Haven Weekly Palladium*, September 21, 1871.
24. *Bridgeport Standard*, September 18, 1871.
25. *Hartford Post*, September 18, 1871; *Bridgeport Standard*, September 18, 1871; *Middletown Sentinel and Witness*, September 22, 1871.
26. *Middletown Sentinel and Witness*, September 22, 1871.
27. *New Haven Weekly Palladium*, September 21, 1871.
28. *New Haven Weekly Palladium*, September 21, 1871.
29. *Bridgeport Standard*, September 18, 1871, and September 19, 1871.
30. *Hartford Post*, September 18, 1871; *New Haven Weekly Palladium*, September 21, 1871.
31. *New Haven Weekly Palladium*, September 21, 1871; *Middletown Sentinel and Witness*, September 22, 1871.
32. *New Haven Weekly Palladium*, September 21, 1871.
33. *Wesleyan Argus*, November 15, 1871; *Hartford Post*, October 26, 1871.

Chapter 8

1. *Hartford Post*, March 8, 1872; *New Haven Daily Palladium*, September 29, 1870.
2. *Middletown Constitution*, February 28, 1872.
3. *1872 Dewitt Baseball Guide*, p. 99.
4. *New York Clipper*, March 2, 1872.
5. *New Haven Daily Palladium*, March 23, 1872; *Hartford Post*, March 23, 1872.
6. Harry Wright to Ben Douglas Junior, March 25, 1872.
7. Harry Wright to Ben Douglas Junior, April 8, 1872.
8. *Ibid.*
9. Compendium of the 10th United States Census, 1870; William J. Ryczek, *Blackguards and Red Stockings: A History of Baseball's National Association, 1871–1875* (Jefferson, NC: McFarland, 1992), p. 95.
10. *Hartford Post*, April 9, 1872.
11. Harry Wright to Ben Douglas Junior, April 19, 1872.
12. *New York Clipper*, April 20, 1872.
13. *Hartford Post*, April 24, 1872.
14. Harry Wright to John Clapp, January 18, 1872.
15. Frank V. Phelps, "John Edgar Clapp," *Nineteenth Century Stars*, ed. Robert L. Tiemann and Mark Rucker (Kansas City, MO: Society for American Baseball Research, 1989), p. 29.
16. Conversation with Wesleyan University professor Jon Barlow, 1993.
17. *Middletown Press*, April 26, 1910.
18. *Middletown Press*, April 26, 1910; *Boston Globe*, February 27, 1910.
19. *Wesleyan Argus*, March 13, 1872.

Chapter 9

1. Preston Orem, *Baseball 1845–1881 from the Newspaper Accounts* (Altadena, CA: Self-published, 1961), p. 145.

2. *Boston Globe*, January 24, 1915.
3. *Ibid.*
4. *Ibid.*
5. *Waterbury Daily American*, April 9, 1872.
6. *Hartford Post*, April 23, 1872.
7. William J. Ryczek, *Blackguards and Red Stockings: A History of Baseball's National Association, 1871–1875* (Jefferson, NC: McFarland, 1992), p. 41.
8. *Troy Daily Times*, April 27, 1872.
9. *Middletown Constitution*, May 1, 1872.
10. *Troy Daily Times*, April 27, 1872.
11. *Middletown Constitution*, May 1, 1872.
12. *Meriden Daily Republican*, July 6, 1872.
13. *New York Clipper*, May 4, 1872.
14. *Bridgeport Post*, April 27, 1872.
15. *New York Clipper*, May 4, 1872.
16. Ryczek, *Blackguards and Red Stockings*, pp. 184–185.
17. *New York World*, April 30, 1872.
18. *New York Herald*, April 30, 1872.
19. *New York Herald*, April 30, 1872; *New York World*, April 30, 1872.
20. *New York Times*, April 30, 1872.
21. *Hartford Post*, May 1, 1872.
22. *Hartford Post*, May 3, 1872; *New York Clipper*, May 11, 1872.
23. *Hartford Times*, June 22, 1872.
24. *Hartford Post*, May 3, 1872.
25. *New York Clipper*, May 11, 1872; *Meriden Daily Republican*, May 3, 1872.
26. *Wesleyan Argus*, May 15, 1872; *New Haven Register*, May 7, 1872; *Boston Globe*, January 24, 1915.
27. *Middletown Sentinel and Witness*, May 10, 1872; *Hartford Post*, May 9, 1872.
28. *Hartford Post*, May 9, 1872; *New Haven Register*, May 9, 1872; *Hartford Courant*, May 13, 1872.
29. *Middletown Sentinel and Witness*, May 10, 1872.
30. *Hartford Post*, May 17, 1872; *New Haven Weekly Palladium*, May 23, 1872.
31. *Middletown Constitution*, May 22, 1872; *Boston Globe*, January 24, 1915.
32. *New Haven Weekly Palladium*, May 23, 1872; *Boston Globe*, January 24, 1915.
33. Harold Seymour, *Baseball: The Early Years* (New York: Oxford University Press, 1960), p. 75.
34. *New Haven Register*, May 23, 1872; *Hartford Times*, May 23, 1872.
35. *Cleveland Morning Daily Herald*, May 24, 1872.
36. *New York Times*, May 26, 1872 and May 31, 1872.

Chapter 10

1. William J. Ryczek, *Blackguards and Red Stockings: A History of Baseball's National Association, 1871–1875* (Jefferson, NC: McFarland, 1992), p. 76.
2. James D. Smith III, "Robert T. (Bobby) Mathews," *Nineteenth Century Stars*, ed. Robert Tiemann and Mark Rucker (Kansas City, MO: Society for American Baseball Research, 1989), p. 83; Peter Morris, *A Game of Inches: The Story Behind the Innovations That Shaped Baseball*, vol. 1 (Chicago: Ivan R. Dee, 2006), p. 151, quoted from John Thorn and John Holway, *The Pitcher* (New York: Prentice Hall, 1987), p. 164.
3. Ryczek, *Blackguards and Red Stockings*, p. 211.
4. *Baltimore News American*, May 25, 1872; *Baltimore Sun*, May 25, 1872.
5. Ryczek, *Blackguards and Red Stockings*, p. 43; *Hartford Post*, May 27, 1872.
6. *Hartford Post*, May 30, 1872; *Baltimore News American*, May 29, 1872.
7. Ryczek, *Blackguards and Red Stockings*, p. 29.
8. *New York Clipper*, June 8, 1872; *Philadelphia Inquirer*, May 30, 1872; *Philadelphia Press*, May 30, 1872.
9. *Elizabeth Daily Journal*, August 8, 1872.
10. *Elizabeth Daily Journal*, April 16, 1872, and May 31, 1872.
11. *Elizabeth Daily Journal*, June 1, 1872.
12. *Hartford Post*, June 3, 1872.
13. Chadwick Scrapbooks; *New York World*, June 4, 1872.
14. *Hartford Post*, June 5, 1872.
15. Ryczek, *Blackguards and Red Stockings*, pp. 86–87.
16. *Hartford Post*, June 5, 1872, and June 6, 1872.
17. *Boston Herald*, June 7, 1872; *Boston Daily Journal*, July 10, 1872.
18. *Hartford Post*, June 10, 1872.
19. *Meriden Daily Republican*, June 14, 1872.
20. *Boston Globe*, January 24, 1915; *New Haven Daily Palladium*, June 15, 1872; *Hartford Post*, June 15, 1872.
21. *Boston Globe*, January 24, 1915.
22. *New Haven Weekly Palladium*, June 20, 1872; *Hartford Post*, June 15, 1872.

23. Harry Wright to Ben Douglas Junior, May 31, 1872.
24. *Boston Evening Traveler*, June 17, 1872.
25. Chadwick Scrapbooks.
26. Chadwick Scrapbooks.
27. Chadwick Scrapbooks; *Boston Globe*, June 17, 1872; *Boston Herald*, June 17, 1872.
28. *Boston Globe*, January 24, 1915.
29. *Hartford Post*, June 20, 1872; *New Haven Daily Palladium*, June 20, 1872.
30. *Hartford Post*, May 16, 1872; *Hartford Times*, June 22, 1872.
31. *Hartford Times*, June 20, 1872, and June 22, 1872.
32. *Hartford Times*, June 22, 1872.
33. *Hartford Times*, June 22, 1872; *Hartford Post*, June 22, 1872.

Chapter 11

1. Harry Wright to Ben Douglas Junior, June 4, 1872.
2. Harry Wright to Worcester Park Association, June 14, 1872.
3. *Elizabeth Daily Journal*, June 29, 1872, and July 1, 1872.
4. Harry Wright to Ben Douglas Junior, June 29, 1872.
5. *Elizabeth Daily Journal*, July 3, 1872.
6. *Hartford Times*, July 5, 1872.
7. *Ibid.*
8. *Ibid.*
9. *Ibid.*
10. *Ibid.*
11. *Meriden Daily Republican*, July 6, 1872.
12. *Middletown Sentinel and Witness*, June 28, 1872.
13. *Meriden Daily Republican*, July 6, 1872.
14. *Hartford Times*, July 5, 1872; *Hartford Post*, July 2, 1872.
15. *Elizabeth Daily Journal*, July 5, 1872.
16. *Elizabeth Daily Journal*, July 5, 1872.
17. *Middletown Constitution*, July 10, 1872.
18. *Elizabeth Daily Journal*, July 5, 1872.
19. *New Haven Weekly Palladium*, July 11, 1872; *Boston Globe*, January 24, 1915.
20. *New Haven Weekly Palladium*, July 11, 1872.
21. *Hartford Times*, July 5, 1872.
22. *New Haven Weekly Palladium*, July 11, 1872.
23. *Hartford Times*, July 5, 1872.
24. *Hartford Times*, July 5, 1872; *Middletown Constitution*, July 10, 1872; *Meriden Daily Republican*, July 6, 1872.
25. George Wright, *Record of Boston Base Ball Club, Since Its Organization* (Boston: Rockwell & Churchill, 1874), p. 26.

Chapter 12

1. *Boston Globe*, January 24, 1915; *Middletown Penny Press*, February 8, 1917.
2. *Hartford Post*, July 8, 1872; *Middletown Daily Constitution*, July 11, 1872; *Hartford Post*, July 15, 1872; *New Haven Register*, July 18, 1872.
3. *Meriden Daily Republican*, July 20, 1872.
4. *Hartford Times*, July 24, 1872; *Springfield Daily Republican*, July 24, 1872.
5. *Hartford Times*, July 24, 1872; *Hartford Post*, July 24, 1872.
6. *Hartford Post*, July 29, 1872; *Middletown Sentinel and Witness*, June 28, 1872, and July 26, 1872.
7. Harry Wright to Ben Douglas Junior, June 29, 1872; *The New York Genealogical and Biographical Record*, January 2007, pp. 5–13.
8. *Hartford Post*, July 29, 1872; William J. Ryczek, *Blackguards and Red Stockings: A History of Baseball's National Association, 1871–1875* (Jefferson, NC: McFarland, 1992), p. 99.
9. *Hartford Post*, July 29, 1872.
10. *Middletown Sentinel and Witness*, August 2, 1872.
11. *Middletown Sentinel and Witness*, August 2, 1872; *Hartford Post*, July 29, 1872.
12. *Hartford Post*, July 29, 1872; John Thorn and Pete Palmer, *Total Baseball*, 2nd ed. (New York: Warner Books, 1991), p. 414.
13. *Baltimore News American*, August 2, 1872.
14. *Baltimore News American*, August 2, 1872; *Hartford Post*, August 2, 1872.
15. *Baltimore News American*, August 3, 1872.
16. Chadwick Scrapbooks; *Philadelphia Inquirer*, August 5, 1872.
17. *Philadelphia Public Record*, August 5, 1872; *Philadelphia Inquirer*, August 5, 1872.
18. *Philadelphia Public Record*, August 5, 1872; *Philadelphia Inquirer*, August 5, 1872.
19. *Philadelphia Inquirer*, August 5, 1872.
20. *Hartford Post*, August 5, 1872; *New Haven Register*, August 6, 1872.
21. *New Haven Register*, August 6, 1872.

22. *New Haven Register*, August 6, 1872; Chadwick Scrapbooks.
23. *New York World*, August 7, 1872; Chadwick Scrapbooks.
24. Chadwick Scrapbooks; *Hartford Post*, August 6, 1872.
25. *Hartford Post*, August 8, 1872, and August 10, 1872.
26. *Hartford Post*, August 10, 1872.
27. *Ibid*.
28. *Middletown Daily Constitution*, August 12, 1872; *Hartford Post*, August 11, 1872.
29. *Middletown Daily Constitution*, August 14, 1872; *Hartford Post*, August 14, 1872, and August 15, 1872.
30. *Middletown Sentinel and Witness*, August 16, 1872, *Wesleyan Argus*, September 26, 1872.
31. *Middletown Sentinel and Witness*, August 16, 1872; *Hartford Post*, September 16, 1872, and September 26, 1872.

Chapter 13

1. *Hartford Courant*, January 7, 1873.
2. Mark Twain as special correspondent to *San Francisco Alta* (California) newspaper, March 3, 1868; Justin Kaplan, *Mr. Clemens and Mark Twain* (New York: Touchstone, 1966), p. 140; Bill Hosley, "Hartford: Silicon Valley of the 19th Century," 2001 presentation.
3. *Hartford Times*, March 23, 1874.
4. *Scribner's Monthly*, November 1876, p. 3.
5. Insurance Men's Banquet for Cornelius Walford, Allyn House, Hartford, October 12, 1874; Paul Fatout, ed., *Mark Twain Speaking* (Iowa City: University of Iowa Press, 1976), pp. 89, 90.
6. *Hartford Post*, March 5, 1874, and February 25, 1874; *Hartford Courant*, January 27, 1874. Ben Douglas subsequently learned that George Hall had actually skipped the meeting intentionally because he had already signed with Boston. Douglas wrote a letter to the *Courant* under the title "Baseness of a Base Ballist." In it, Douglas lambasted Hall for saying he would play for Hartford even though he had an offer from Boston. "I supposed I was dealing with a gentleman of his word. I am now glad we found him out, for it is our intention to have none but square, gentlemanly professionals in our eleven players." (*Hartford Courant*, January 27, 1874, January 30, 1874, February 2, 1874, and February 3, 1874.)
7. *New York Clipper*, January 31, 1874.
8. *Middletown Daily Constitution*, February 26, 1874; *Hartford Courant*, March 2, 1874.
9. *Middletown Daily Constitution*, March 9, 1874. Several contemporary sources have reported that the Hartford Base Ball Grounds featured three trees in the outfield, *in front of the fence and in play*. Some even going so far as to identify the trees as apple trees. A review of the historical evidence does not support this. It appears that the *only* primary source supporting the treed outfield is Oakley H. Bailey's 1877 bird's eye view drawing of Hartford. In this drawing, Bailey included three trees in the outfield, one each in center, left, and right, with the center fielder standing under the branches of the middle tree. If these trees truly existed, it would seem logical that, on occasion, they would have interfered with the play on the field. Yet none of Hartford's three daily newspapers ever mentioned trees impacting a game. There are several descriptions of batted balls rolling to the outfield fence, but not once was it reported that a tree limited a long hit or impeded an outfielder. It seems likely that the trees Bailey depicted on the baseball field actually represented the trees that bordered the enclosure.
10. *Hartford Post*, March 27, 1874, and April 9, 1874.
11. *Hartford Post*, November 2, 1874.
12. *Boston Globe*, January 24, 1915.
13. *New York Clipper*, December 21, 1872; William J. Ryczek, *Blackguards and Red Stockings: A History of Baseball's National Association, 1871–1875* (Jefferson, NC: McFarland, 1992), p. 46.
14. Adrian Anson, *A Ball Player's Career* (Chicago: Era Publishing, 1900; reprinted Mattituck, NY: Amereon House, 2001), p. 51.
15. Robert H. Schaefer, "The Lost Art of Fair-Foul Hitting," *The National Pastime* 20 (2000), p. 9.
16. *Chicago Daily Herald*, August 19, 1910; Schaefer, "The Lost Art of Fair-Foul Hitting," pp. 8–9.
17. *Middletown Daily Constitution*, March 18, 1874; *New York Clipper*, July 28, 1866, December 15, 1866, and July 9, 1881.
18. *Hartford Courant*, March 14, 1874; *New York Times*, March 7, 1874.

Chapter 14

1. *Hartford Courant*, April 6, 1874, April 7, 1874, and April 20, 1874; *Hartford Times*, April 20, 1874; *Hartford Post*, April 8, 1875.
2. *Hartford Courant*, April 20, 1874, and May 12, 1874.
3. *New York Clipper*, April 18, 1874.
4. *Hartford Courant*, April 27, 1874; *New York Clipper*, May 2, 1874, and May 9, 1874.
5. *Hartford Courant*, April 30, 1874, and May 1, 1874; Harry Wright to Gershom Hubbell, May 1, 1874.
6. *Hartford Courant*, May 2, 1874.
7. *Hartford Courant*, May 6, 1874.
8. *Hartford Courant*, April 20, 1874, and May 12, 1874.
9. *Chicago Inter Ocean*, May 24, 1874.
10. *Hartford Post*, May 13, 1874.
11. *New York Clipper*, May 23, 1874; *Hartford Courant*, May 14, 1874, and June 5, 1907.
12. *Hartford Post*, May 27, 1874.
13. *Hartford Post*, June 22, 1874, July 23, 1874, September 3, 1874, and November 2, 1874; *New York Clipper*, July 4, 1874; *Hartford Courant*, July 22, 1874.
14. William J. Ryczek, *Blackguards and Red Stockings: A History of Baseball's National Association, 1871–1875* (Jefferson, NC: McFarland, 1992), pp. 158–166.
15. Chadwick Scrapbooks.
16. Al Kermisch, "From a Researcher's Notebook: Ball Player Pike Beat Race Horse at 100 Yards," *Baseball Research Journal* 8 (1979), p. 14; *Hartford Courant*, July 22, 1874, August 25, 1874, and September 8, 1874; *Hartford Times*, September 23, 1874.
17. *Hartford Courant*, August 11, 1874; *Brooklyn Eagle*, February 23, 1875.
18. See Appendix B for a complete discussion of Barlow's absence.
19. *Hartford Post*, October 29, 1874.
20. *Hartford Post*, November 2, 1874.

Chapter 15

1. *Middletown Daily Constitution*, February 3, 1875; Frank V. Phelps, "Robert V. Ferguson," *Nineteenth Century Stars*, ed. Robert L. Tiemann and Mark Rucker (Kansas City, MO: Society for American Baseball Research, 1989), p. 43.
2. *Hartford Courant*, October 30, 1875.
3. Albert G. Spalding, *America's National Game* (Lincoln: University of Nebraska Press, 1992), pp. 195, 196; William J. Ryczek, *When Johnny Came Sliding Home: The Post-Civil War Baseball Boom, 1865–1870* (Jefferson, NC: McFarland, 1998), pp. 208, 209.
4. William J. Ryczek, *Blackguards and Red Stockings: A History of Baseball's National Association, 1871–1875* (Jefferson, NC: McFarland, 1992), pp. 109–111.
5. Chadwick Scrapbooks; *Hartford Post*, January 27, 1875; Spalding, *America's National Game*, pp. 195, 196.
6. Spalding, *America's National Game*, pp. 201–203.
7. Chadwick Scrapbooks.
8. *New York Clipper*, June 5, 1875.
9. Spalding, *America's National Game*, p. 484.
10. John Thorn, ed., *The Armchair Book of Baseball* (New York: Scribner's, 1987), pp. 70–72.
11. *New York Herald*, quoted in *Middletown Daily Constitution*, April 21, 1875; *Hartford Times*, March 17, 1875.
12. *Hartford Courant*, July 16, 1907.
13. *The Sporting News*, December 18, 1886.
14. *Boston Globe*, March 24, 1876.
15. *New York Clipper*, quoted in Richard A. Puff, "Thomas J. York," *Nineteenth Century Stars*, ed. Robert L. Tiemann and Mark Rucker (Kansas City, MO: Society for American Baseball Research, 1989), p. 142.
16. *Hartford Post*, April 2, 1875.
17. *Hartford Courant*, April 3, 1875; *Hartford Post*, February 26, 1875.
18. *Hartford Courant*, January 14, 1923.
19. *Hartford Courant*, January 14, 1923.
20. *Hartford Post*, February 3, 1875; *New York Clipper*, February 6, 1875, and November 14, 1874.

Chapter 16

1. New Haven Preservation Trust website. http://www.nhpt.org/History%20Pages/1820–1890.htm.
2. *New Haven Evening Register*, January 8, 1875, and January 13, 1875.
3. *New Haven Evening Register*, February 17, 1875; *Middletown Constitution*, February 17, 1875.
4. *New Haven Evening Register*, February 17, 1875, February 23, 1875, March 5, 1875; *Middletown Constitution*, February 17, 1875

5. *New Haven Evening Register*, January 8, 1875.
6. Christopher Devine, *Harry Wright: The Father of Professional Baseball* (Jefferson, NC: McFarland, 2003), pp. 175–176.
7. *New Haven Evening Register*, February 23, 1875, and March 4, 1875; Harry Wright to Charlie Gould, March 15, 1875.
8. *New Haven Evening Register,* February 17, 1875; *Middletown Constitution*, February 17, 1875.
9. *New Haven Register*, March 2, 1875; *New York Clipper*, February 27, 1875; *Hartford Post*, February 22, 1875.
10. *New Haven Evening Register*, January 31, 1875, and July 22, 1876; *Brooklyn Eagle*, July 18, 1876.
11. *New Haven Evening Register*, March 4, 1875; McKelvey clippings in vertical file at Rochester Central Library — circa 1940.
12. Harry Wright correspondence, quoted in Devine, *Harry Wright*, p. 135; *New York Clipper*, May 1, 1875.
13. William J. Ryczek, *Blackguards and Red Stockings: A History of Baseball's National Association, 1871–1875* (Jefferson, NC: McFarland, 1992), p. 182.
14. *New Haven Evening Register*, March 17, 1875, and March 29, 1875; *New York Sunday Mercury*, reprinted in Peter Morris, *A Game of Inches: The Stories Behind the Innovations That Shaped Baseball*, vol. 2, (Chicago: Ivan R. Dee, 2006), p. 324.
15. *New Haven Evening Register*, February 17, 1875, March 4, 1875, March 5, 1875, March 19, 1875, and March 29, 1875; *Middletown Constitution*, February 17, 1875.
16. *New Haven Evening Register*, March 19, 1875, March 29, 1875, and April 9, 1875; *Middletown Constitution*, April 21, 1875.
17. Harry Wright to Charlie Gould, March 15, 1875.
18. *New Haven Evening Register*, March 17, 1875; *Middletown Constitution*, April 21, 1875; *Brooklyn Eagle*, February 23, 1875, and April 13, 1875.
19. *New Haven Evening Register*, April 17, 1875.
20. Harry Wright to Charlie Gould, April 9, 1875.
21. *New Haven Evening Register*, April 9, 1875: *Hartford Post*, February 3, 1875.

Chapter 17

1. *New Haven Evening Register*, April 12, 1875.
2. *New Haven Evening Register*, April 17, 1875.
3. *New Haven Evening Register*, April 26, 1875, and April 12, 1875.
4. *New Haven Evening Register*, April 20, 1875.
5. Harry Wright to Charlie Gould, April 9, 1875
6. *New Haven Evening Register* April 17, 1875, April 21, 1875, and April 22, 1875.
7. *New Haven Evening Register*, April 26, 1875; *New Haven Journal & Courier*, April 26, 1875.
8. *New Haven Evening Register*, April 27, 1875.
9. *Hartford Courant*, April 26, 1875; *New York Clipper*, May 1, 1875; *Hartford Times*, April 26, 1875.
10. *Brooklyn Eagle*, May 8, 1875.
11. *New Haven Evening Register*, May 3, 1875.
12. *Hartford Courant*, May 6, 1875; *New Haven Evening Register*, May 6, 1875.

Chapter 18

1. *New Haven Evening Register*, May 12, 1875; *Hartford Courant*, May 18, 1875.
2. *New Haven Evening Register*, May 17, 1875; *Hartford Courant*, May 18, 1875.
3. *Hartford Times*, May 21, 1875.
4. *Brooklyn Eagle*, April 13, 1875, May 19, 1875, and July 28, 1875; *Hartford Times,* March 13, 1875, and May 24, 1875; *New Haven Register*, March 2, 1875, and May 21, 1875; *Hartford Courant*, May 21, 1875.
5. *Hartford Courant*, May 11, 1875, May 15, 1875, and April 21, 1875; *New York Clipper*, May 8, 1875.
6. *Hartford Courant*, May 18, 1875.
7. Harry Wright to Ben Douglas Jr., April 20, 1875.
8. *Hartford Courant*, May 19, 1875; *Meriden Daily Republican*, May 18, 1875.
9. *Hartford Courant*, May 19, 1875; *Hartford Times*, May 19, 1875; *Chicago Tribune*, May 19, 1875.
10. Arthur Bartlett, *Baseball and Mr. Spalding: The History and Romance of Baseball* (New York: Farrar, Straus, and Young, 1951), p. 48.

11. *Hartford Courant*, May 19, 1875; *Clipper*, May 29, 1875.
12. *Hartford Times*, May 19, 1875; *Hartford Post*, May 19, 1875.
13. William J. Ryczek, *Blackguards and Red Stockings: A History of Baseball's National Association, 1871–1875* (Jefferson, NC: McFarland, 1992), pp. 205–207; *New York Clipper*, May 29, 1875.
14. *Hartford Courant*, May 19, 1875; *Boston Herald*, May 19, 1875.
15. *Hartford Courant*, May 19, 1875.
16. *New York Clipper*, November 4, 1871; *Hartford Courant*, May 19, 1875.
17. *Hartford Courant*, May 20, 1875.
18. Paul Fatout, ed., *Mark Twain Speaking* (Iowa City: University of Iowa Press, 1976), pp. 246, 247.
19. Twain speech to New England Society of New York, December 1876, in Charles Neider, ed., *Mark Twain: Plymouth Rock and the Pilgrims and Other Speeches* (New York: Harper & Row, 1984).
20. *Brooklyn Eagle*, August 18, 1875; *Seaside Gazette* (Mass.), August 17, 1875.
21. *Boston Herald*, quoted in *Hartford Times*, May 19, 1875.
22. *Boston Advertiser*, quoted in *Hartford Courant*, May 21, 1875; *Boston Herald*, May 20, 1875.

Chapter 19

1. *New Haven Evening Register*, May 26, 1875.
2. *New Haven Evening Register*, May 29, 1875.
3. Harry Wright to George Latham, January 18, 1875, January 30, 1875, February 6, 1875, and February 17, 1875.
4. *Literary Digest*, May 23, 1914,
5. *Hartford Courant*, May 31, 1875.
6. *Brooklyn Eagle*, June 9, 1875
7. *Chicago Tribune*, May 30, 1875.
8. *Ibid.*
9. *Ibid.*
10. *Ibid.*
11. *Hartford Times*, May 22, 1875.
12. *New Haven Evening Register*, June 12, 1875; *Hartford Courant*, June 12, 1875.
13. *New Haven Evening Register*, June 8, 1875, and June 12, 1875; *Hartford Courant*, June 12, 1875; *New Haven Journal*, quoted in *Hartford Courant*, June 14, 1875.
14. *New Haven Register*, quoted in *Hartford Courant*, June 15, 1875; *New Haven Evening Register*, June 14, 1875.
15. *Hartford Courant*, June 15, 1875, and June 16, 1875.
16. *Hartford Courant*, June 16, 1875.
17. *New Haven Evening Register*, June 21, 1875.
18. *New Haven Evening Register*, June 22, 1875.

Chapter 20

1. *New York Clipper*, June 19, 1875; *New Haven Register*, August 21, 1875; *Hartford Courant*, July 27, 1875; *Hartford Times*, August 11, 1875.
2. *Sporting Life*, December 3, 1884, quoted in Peter Morris, *A Game of Inches: The Stories Behind the Innovations That Shaped Baseball*, vol. 1. (Chicago: Ivan R. Dee, 2006), p. 134.
3. *New York Clipper*, July 10, 1875; *Hartford Post*, June 18, 1875.
4. *Chicago Tribune*, June 20, 1875; *Hartford Courant*, October 31, 1913.
5. Chadwick Scrapbooks; William J. Ryczek, *Blackguards and Red Stockings: A History of Baseball's National Association, 1871–1875* (Jefferson, NC: McFarland, 1992), p. 197.
6. *Boston Globe*, February 27, 1910.
7. *New Haven Evening Register*, July 3, 1875.
8. *Hartford Post*, July 6, 1875; *Hartford Courant*, July 5, 1875; *Hartford Times*, July 6, 1875.
9. *Hartford Times*, July 2, 1875; *Hartford Post*, July 2, 1875, and July 7, 1875; *Hartford Courant*, July 7, 1875.
10. *Hartford Post*, July 8, 1875, and July 9, 1875.
11. *Hartford Courant*, July 15, 1875.
12. *New Haven Evening Register*, July 19, 1875.
13. *Hartford Courant*, July 20, 1875.
14. Albert G. Spalding, *America's National Game* (Lincoln: University of Nebraska Press, 1992), pp. 204–206.
15. *Chicago Tribune*, July 24, 1875.
16. *Boston Advertise*, quoted in *Chicago Tribune*, July 26, 1875; Arthur Bartlett, *Baseball and Mr. Spalding: The History and Romance of Baseball* (New York: Farrar, Straus, and Young, 1951), pp. 76, 77.
17. *Boston Herald*, July 30, 1875; Spalding, *America's National Game*, pp. 204–206.

18. *Hartford Times*, August 3, 1875, reprinted from *Boston Globe*.
19. *Boston Herald*, July 30, 1875; Spalding, *America's National Game*, pp. 204–206.

Chapter 21

1. *New Haven Evening Register*, April 13, 1876.
2. *Syracuse Courier*, reprinted in *Brooklyn Eagle*, August 31, 1875.
3. *New Haven Register*, September 14, 1875 and September 15, 1875.
4. *New York Clipper*, October 2, 1875, quoted in William J. Ryczek, *Blackguards and Red Stockings: A History of Baseball's National Association, 1871–1875* (Jefferson, NC: McFarland, 1992), p. 196; *Brooklyn Eagle*, September 24, 1875; *New Haven Evening Register*, September 25, 1875.
5. *Chicago Tribune*, September 19, 1875; *New Haven Register*, September 27, 1875.
6. *New Haven Evening Register*, September 15, 1875, and September 25, 1875.
7. *New Haven Evening Register*, September 29, 1875.
8. *Hartford Courant*, August 11, 1875.
9. *Hartford Courant*, August 13, 1875; *Hartford Times*, August 13, 1875; *New Haven Register*, August 23, 1875.
10. *Hartford Times*, October 25, 1875.

Chapter 22

1. David Voigt, *American Baseball: From the Gentlemen's Sport to the Commissioner System*, vol. 1 (Norman: University of Oklahoma Press, 1966), p. 62.
2. Tom Melville, *Early Baseball and the Rise of the National League* (Jefferson, NC: McFarland, 2001), pp. 76, 82.
3. *Hartford Times*, February 5, 1876.
4. *Ibid*.
5. *Spalding's Official Baseball Guide*, 1877.
6. *New York Clipper*, quoted in *Hartford Times*, February 11, 1876.
7. *Hartford Times*, February 4, 1876.
8. *New Haven Evening Register*, October 11, 1875, and October 25, 1875.
9. *New Haven Union* and *New Haven Register*, quoted in *Hartford Courant*, February 5, 1876; *New Haven Evening Register*, February 4, 1876, and February 5, 1876.
10. *Philadelphia City Item*, quoted in *Hartford Times*, February 11, 1876.
11. *Hartford Courant*, February 9, 1876; *Boston Globe*, quoted in *Hartford Times*, February 11, 1876; *New Haven Evening Register*, February 4, 1876, and February 6, 1876; Neil MacDonald, *The League That Lasted: 1876 and the Founding of the National League of Professional Baseball Clubs* (Jefferson, NC: McFarland, 2004), p. 37.
12. *Philadelphia City Item*, quoted in *Hartford Times*, February 11, 1876; *New Haven Evening Register*, February 11, 1876.
13. *Brooklyn Eagle*, September 24, 1875, and April 15, 1876; *New Haven Evening Register*, April 6, 1876, and February 24, 1876.
14. *New Haven Evening Register*, February 19, 1876, and February 28, 1876.
15. *Hartford Times*, February 10, 1876, February 26, 1876, and February 28, 1876; *Hartford Post*, February 28, 1876; *Brooklyn Eagle*, March 4, 1876.
16. *New Haven Evening Register*, March 8, 1876.
17. *Hartford Times*, February 10, 1876, and February 28, 1876; *Hartford Post*, March 2, 1875; William J. Ryczek, *Blackguards and Red Stockings: A History of Baseball's National Association, 1871–1875* (Jefferson, NC: McFarland, 1992), p. 227.

Chapter 23

1. *New York Clipper*, February 21, 1874.
2. *Chicago Tribune*, June 29, 1875, and June 30, 1875.
3. *Chicago Tribune*, August 20, 1875.
4. *Hartford Times*, February 25, 1876.
5. Stephen Freedman, "The Baseball Fad in Chicago, 1865–1870: An Exploration of the Role of Sport in the Nineteenth-Century City, *Journal of Sport History* 5, no. 2 (Summer 1978), pp. 58, 59; *Hartford Times*, April 3, 1876.
6. Chadwick Scrapbooks.
7. *Ibid*.
8. Arthur Bartlett, *Baseball and Mr. Spalding: The History and Romance of Baseball* (New York: Farrar, Straus, and Young, 1951), pp. 90–92.
9. *Hartford Times*, April 28, 1876.
10. David Nemec, *The Great Encyclopedia of 19th Century Major League Baseball* (New York: Donald I. Fine Books, 1997), p. 69.

11. *Hartford Times*, May 1, 1876; *Hartford Courant*, May 1, 1876.
12. *Hartford Post*, September 20, 1876; *Hartford Times*, May 2, 1876; Christopher Devine, *Harry Wright: The Father of Professional Baseball* (Jefferson, NC: McFarland, 2003), p. 125.
13. *New Haven Evening Register*, April 15, 1876, April 22, 1876, April 27, 1876, and April 29, 1876.
14. *Hartford Courant*, May 4, 1876.
15. *Hartford Courant*, May 5, 1876.
16. *Ibid.*
17. *Hartford Times*, quoted in *Chicago Tribune*, May 28, 1876; *Chicago Tribune*, April 23, 1876.
18. *Chicago Tribune*, May 24, 1876.
19. *Hartford Post*, May 26, 1876; *Hartford Courant*, May 26, 1876; *Hartford Times*, May 26, 1876.
20. *Hartford Post*, May 24, 1876.
21. William J. Ryczek, *Blackguards and Red Stockings: A History of Baseball's National Association, 1871–1875* (Jefferson, NC: McFarland, 1992), pp. 149, 150; "People and Events: The Panic of 1873," PBS, http://www.pbs.org/wgbh/amex/grant/peopleevents/e_panic.html.
22. *Hartford Courant*, May 30, 1876.
23. *Chicago Tribune*, June 8, 1876.
24. *Hartford Courant*, June 13, 1876, and June 14, 1876; 1875 Hartford City Directory; *Hartford Times*, June 10, 1876.
25. *Hartford Courant*, May 31, 1876; Joseph M. Overfield, "William Arthur Cummings," *Baseball's First Stars*, ed. Frederick Ivor-Campbell, Robert Tiemann, and Mark Rucker (Cleveland: Society for American Baseball Research, 1996), p. 43.
26. *New York Clipper*, July 3, 1875; *St. Louis Times*, quoted in *Hartford Times*, July 18, 1876; *Louisville Courier-Journal*, May 19, 1877.
27. Mark Alvarez, *The Old Ball Game* (Alexandria, VA: Redefinition, 1995), p. 145.
28. Harry Wright to Henry Chadwick, September 14, 1876.
29. *Hartford Times*, May 9, 1876; *Hartford Courant*, June 2, 1876; *Hartford Post*, June 2, 1876.
30. *Hartford Times*, June 2, 1876.
31. *Hartford Courant*, June 7, 1876, June 9, 1876, and June 12, 1876.
32. *Louisville Courier-Journal*, June 14, 1876, June 16, 1876, and June 18, 1876; *Chicago Tribune*, June 25, 1876, and July 2, 1876.
33. *Chicago Tribune*, June 18, 1876; *Brooklyn Eagle*, July 7, 1876.

Chapter 24

1. *Chicago Tribune*, July 5, 1876.
2. *Hartford Courant*, July 6, 1876; *Hartford Times*, July 5, 1876; *Hartford Courant*, January 14, 1923.
3. *Hartford Times*, July 7, 1876, and April 24, 1876; *Chicago Tribune*, July 7, 1876.
4. *Hartford Post*, July 7, 1876.
5. *Chicago Tribune*, July 9, 1876.
6. *Chicago Tribune*, July 2, 1876.
7. *St. Louis Globe-Democrat*, July 12, 1876.
8. Chadwick Scrapbooks; *Hartford Post*, July 17, 1876.
9. Chadwick Scrapbooks; *St. Louis Globe-Democrat*, July 16, 1876.
10. *Philadelphia Inquirer*, February 26, 1922.
11. Neil MacDonald, *The League That Lasted: 1876 and the Founding of the National League of Professional Baseball Clubs* (Jefferson, NC: McFarland, 2004), p.149; *The Sporting News*, March 10, 1888, quoted in Peter Morris, *A Game of Inches: The Stories Behind the Innovations That Shaped Baseball*, vol. 1 (Chicago: Ivan R. Dee, 2006), p. 478.
12. *Chicago Tribune*, July 16, 1876; *Hartford Courant*, July 31, 1876.
13. *Chicago Tribune*, June 18, 1876.
14. *New York Sunday Mercury*, reprinted in *New Haven Evening Register*, July 3, 1876; MacDonald, *The League That Lasted*, pp. 173, 182.
15. *New Haven Evening Register*, August 5, 1876, September 25, 1876, and August 21, 1876; *Hartford Courant*, August 24, 1876.
16. *New Haven Evening Register*, August 24, 1876.
17. *Hartford Courant*, August 24, 1876; *New Haven Evening Register*, September 26, 1876, and September 30, 1876.
18. *Hartford Courant*, August 21, 1876.
19. Albert G. Spalding, *America's National Game* (Lincoln: University of Nebraska Press, 1992), pp. 195, 196.
20. *Wilkes Spirit of the Times*, reprinted in *Brooklyn Eagle*, July 26, 1873.
21. *Hartford Times*, August 24, 1876.
22. *Hartford Times*, August 26, 1876.
23. *Chicago Tribune*, September 9, 1876; *Brooklyn Eagle*, September 5, 1876; *New Haven Evening Register*, September 7, 1876.

24. *Hartford Courant*, August 2, 1876; *Hartford Times*, September 9, 1876, and September 11, 1876; MacDonald, *The League That Lasted*, p. 188.
25. Chadwick Scrapbooks; *Chicago Tribune*, September 14, 1876.
26. *Chicago Tribune*, September 27, 1876.
27. Larry R. Gerlach and Harold V. Higham, "Dick Higham, Star of Baseball's Early Years," *The National Pastime* 21 (2001), p. 77.
28. *New York Clipper*, November 4, 1876.
29. *Hartford Times*, April 8, 1876.
30. Chadwick Scrapbooks.

Chapter 25

1. *Chicago Tribune*, July 23, 1876, and October 18, 1876; Tom Melville, *Early Baseball and the Rise of the National League* (Jefferson, NC: McFarland, 2001), p. 85.
2. Melville, *Early Baseball and the Rise of the National League*, p. 85.
3. Melville, *Early Baseball and the Rise of the National League*, p. 86; *Chicago Tribune*, September 24, 1876.
4. *Hartford Times*, July 22, 1876.
5. *Chicago Tribune*, July 23, 1876; *Brooklyn Eagle*, August 17, 1876.
6. John Thorn, David Pietrusza, Michael Gershman, Pete Palmer, and Mathew Silverman, eds., *Total Baseball*, 6th ed. (Kingston, NY: Total Sports Publishing, 1999); *Chicago Tribune*, August 6, 1876.
7. *Chicago Tribune*, September 24, 1876.
8. *Middletown Daily Constitution*, July 31, 1876; *Hartford Courant*, July 28, 1876.
9. *Brooklyn Eagle*, August 1, 1876.
10. *Chicago Tribune*, October 18, 1876.
11. *Chicago Tribune*, July 23, 1876.
12. *Brooklyn Eagle*, November 16, 1876.
13. *Brooklyn Eagle*, February 9, 1877.
14. *Hartford Post*, March 26, 1874, and January 27, 1875; *New York Clipper*, February 10, 1877.
15. *Chicago Tribune*, October 1, 1876.
16. Chadwick Scrapbooks.
17. *Hartford Post*, January 16, 1877.
18. *Chicago Tribune*, March 4, 1877; Melville, *Early Baseball and the Rise of the National League*, p. 100; *Louisville Courier-Journal*, quoted in *Chicago Tribune*, August 6, 1876.
19. *Chicago Tribune*, March 11, 1877, and March 18, 1877.
20. Melville, *Early Baseball and the Rise of the National League*, p. 86.
21. *Hartford Courant*, March 9, 1877.

Chapter 26

1. Harry Wright to William Hulbert, March 23, 1877, and March 28, 1877.
2. Harry Wright to William Hulbert, April 16, 1877.
3. Harry Wright to William Hulbert, March 28, 1877, and April 16, 1877; Harry Wright to William Cammeyer, March 29, 1877.
4. *Hartford Post*, February 6, 1877; *Chicago Tribune*, April 1, 1877; *Hartford Courant*, October 31, 1913.
5. Harry Wright to Richard Higham, February 10, 1877.
6. *Louisville Courier-Journal*, May 20, 1877.
7. *Chicago Tribune*, June 24, 1877.
8. *Louisville Courier-Journal*, May 19, 1877 and May 20, 1877.
9. *Boston Herald* quoted in *Hartford Times*, October 30, 1876.
10. *Spalding's Official Baseball Guide*, 1877.
11. Arthur Bartlett, *Baseball and Mr. Spalding: The History and Romance of Baseball* (New York: Farrar, Straus, and Young, 1951), pp. 118, 119.
12. Harry Wright to Henry Chadwick, September 14, 1876.
13. *New Haven Evening Register*, March 3, 1877, and May 28, 1877; *Brooklyn Eagle*, April 5, 1877, and March 7, 1877.
14. *New Haven Morning Journal and Courier*, April 28, 1877.
15. Melville, *Early Baseball and the Rise of the National League*, pp. 112, 113; Chadwick Scrapbooks.
16. *Hartford Times*, May 1, 1877; Chadwick Scrapbooks.
17. Chadwick Scrapbooks; *Hartford Times*, June 4, 1877.
18. *Hartford Courant*, June 1, June 2 and June 6, 1877.
19. Notre Dame Scrapbooks.
20. *Chicago Tribune*, July 14, 1877, Notre Dame Scrapbooks.
21. Chadwick Scrapbooks.
22. Chadwick Scrapbooks; *Hartford Times*, July 24, 1877.
23. Chadwick Scrapbooks.

24. J. E. Findling, "The Louisville Grays' Scandal of 1877," *Journal of Sport History* 3, no. 2 (1976), p. 182.
25. *New Haven Evening Register*, August 21, 1877, and September 3, 1877.
26. *Louisville Courier-Journal*, September 12, 1877.
27. Findling, "The Louisville Grays' Scandal of 1877," p. 182.
28. Findling, "The Louisville Grays' Scandal of 1877," pp. 182–185.
29. William Hulbert to Bob Ferguson, November 8, 1877; Findling, "The Louisville Grays' Scandal of 1877," p. 185.
30. *New Haven Evening Register*, September 17, 1877, and September 24, 1877.

Chapter 27

1. Notre Dame Scrapbooks, November 17, 1877; Tom Melville, *Early Baseball and the Rise of the National League* (Jefferson, NC: McFarland, 2001), p. 100; Harold Seymour, *Baseball: The Early Years* (New York: Oxford University Press, 1960), p. 86.
2. *Chicago Tribune*, September 8, 1877; *Hartford Times*, November 19, 1877; Chadwick Scrapbooks; *Brooklyn Eagle*, October 28, 1877.
3. *Hartford Courant*, October 4, 1877, and October 5, 1877; *Hartford Times*, November 19, 1877.
4. *Chicago Tribune*, September 8, 1877; Chadwick Scrapbooks.
5. Chadwick Scrapbooks; *Hartford Post*, August 18, 1877; Harry Wright to Benjamin Van Delft, February 9, 1877, and March 22, 1877.
6. *Chicago Tribune*, December 9, 1877; *Hartford Times*, December 6, 1877; *Hartford Post*, December 6, 1877; *Spalding's Official Baseball Guide*, 1878.
7. *Chicago Tribune*, July 23, 1876; Harry Wright to Ben Douglas, Jr., January 8, 1878, and January 28, 1878.
8. David Nemec, *The Beer and Whiskey League: The Illustrated History of the American Association — Baseball's Renegade Major League* (New York: Lyons Press, 2004), p. 80.
9. *Hartford Courant*, January 4, 1962.
10. *Hartford Courant*, October 21, 1964.
11. *Hartford Times*, April 23, 1878, May 4, 1878, and May 20, 1878; *Hartford Post*, July 20, 1878; *New Haven Evening Register*, March 4, 1877.
12. *Hartford Times*, May 20, 1878; *Hartford Courant*, May 17, 1878.
13. *Middletown Sun*, May 7, 1910.
14. "Historians Weiss, Wright Rank 100 Best Minor League Baseball Teams," *The Official Site of Minor League Baseball*, http://web.minorleaguebaseball.com/milb/history/top100.jsp.
15. *Hartford Courant*, June 5, 1882.

Appendix A

1. *Total Baseball* lists Allen as "Homer, (Ham)." His true name was probably Frank E. Allen, nickname "Ham." The Middletown City Directory listed him as Frank E. Allen, although the *Hartford Post* (May 16, 1871) called him Edward A. Allen. As a catcher for the Marlboro Fairmounts in 1869 and 1870, he was listed as "F. (Ham) Allen."
2. *Hartford Post*, April 24, 1876; *Albany Evening Journal*, September 25, 1878, October 11, 1878, and April 12, 1880; Connecticut Vital Records.
3. *Hartford Post*, February 27, 1873.
4. Preston Orem, *Baseball 1845–1881 from the Newspaper Accounts* (Altadena, CA: Self-published, 1961), p. 281; unnamed newspaper clipping in Hall of Fame Library player folder.
5. Asa Brainard to Harry Wright, October 12, 1882, and December 10, 1882; Joseph M. Overfield, "Asa Brainard," *Nineteenth Century Stars*, ed. Robert L. Tiemann and Mark Rucker (Kansas City, MO: Society for American Baseball Research, 1989), p. 17.
6. Connecticut Vital Records; *Norwalk Hour*, December 16, 1902.
7. *Ithaca Daily Journal*, December 19, 1904.
8. William J. Ryczek, *Blackguards and Red Stockings: A History of Baseball's National Association, 1871–1875* (Jefferson, NC: McFarland, 1992), p. 71
9. *Ithaca Daily Journal*, December 19, 1904.
10. Frank V. Phelps, "John Edgar Clapp," *Nineteenth Century Stars*, ed. Robert L. Tiemann and Mark Rucker (Kansas City, MO: Society for American Baseball Research, 1989), p. 29; *Ithaca Daily Journal*, December 19, 1904.
11. *Waterbury Republican*, September 23, 1933.
12. *Hartford Post*, September 7, 1875;

Connecticut Vital Records; *Hartford Post*, May 1, 1876; *New York Times*, June 18, 1907. McCarton's age is somewhat questionable. The encyclopedias list him as 17 years old in 1872, but four references in the Middletown Vital Records show different ages. All indicate he was born no later than 1851, and one shows him being born as early as 1848, which would have made him 24 years old in 1872. His New York death certificate, however, indicates McCarton was indeed 17 during the 1872 season.

13. *Hartford Post*, November 9, 1872; *Middletown Penny Press*, February 8, 1917; *Boston Globe*, January 15, 1915.

14. Rich Eldred, "Timothy Hayes Murnane," *Baseball's First Stars*, ed. Frederick Ivor-Campbell, Robert L. Tiemann, and Mark Rucker (Cleveland: Society for American Baseball Research, 1996), p. 115.

15. Rich Eldred, "Timothy Hayes Murnane," p. 115; *Boston Globe*, January 24, 1915.

16. Horace Murnane to Lee Allen, September 10, 1962; *Boston Globe*, February 8, 1917; *Boston Globe*, February 11, 1917.

17. Jack Kavanagh, "The Silver King Remembered," *Sports Heritage*, January/February 1987.

18. *New York Times*, September 28, 1917.

19. Bernard J. Crowly, "James Henry O'Rourke," *Baseball's First Stars*, ed. Frederick Ivor-Campbell, Robert L. Tiemann, and Mark Rucker (Cleveland: Society for American Baseball Research, 1996), p. 124; Robert Smith, *Baseball in America* (New York: Holt, Rinehart, and Winston, 1961), pp. 41, 44; *Middletown Press*, April 26, 1910; *Boston Globe*, February 27, 1910.

20. Harry Wright to Henry Chadwick, January 2, 1875.

21. Robert Smith, *Baseball in the Afternoon* (New York: Simon & Schuster, 1993), p. 74.

22. Lee Allen, "Cooperstown Corner," *The Sporting News*, February 10, 1968.

23. *Boston Globe*, February 27, 1910.

24. George Tuohey, *A History of the Boston Base Ball Club* (Boston: M. F. Quinn & Co., 1897), p. 218; *Bridgeport Post*, April 26, 1945.

25. Overfield, "Asa Brainard," p. 12; Crowley, "James Henry O'Rourke," p. 125; Jordan Deutsch and Richard Cohen, et al., *The Scrapbook History of Baseball* (New York: Bobbs-Merrill, 1975), p. 57.

26. *New York Herald Magazine*, January 16, 1910.

27. Crowley, "James Henry O'Rourke," p. 125; *Bridgeport Post*, January 9, 1919.

28. *Hartford Post*, March 11, 1876, and April 19, 1876; *New Haven Journal & Courier*, April 22, 1895.

29. Joseph M. Overfield, "Robert Edward Addy," *Nineteenth Century Stars*, ed. Robert L. Tiemann and Mark Rucker (Kansas City, MO: Society for American Baseball Research, 1989), p. 7.

30. Richard Puff, "Douglas L. Allison," *Baseball's First Stars*, ed. Frederick Ivor-Campbell, Robert L. Tiemann, and Mark Rucker (Cleveland: Society for American Baseball Research, 1996), p. 2.

31. *Hartford Courant*, July 16, 1900.

32. *Brooklyn Eagle*, September 28, 1888; *Denver Post*, May 6, 2004.

33. *Washington Post*, December 15, 1907.

34. *New York Times*, February 3, 1925; *Hartford Courant*, February 3, 1925; *San Francisco Call*, August 11, 1907; *The Sporting News*, April 30, 1936; *Washington Post*, January 25, 1941.

35. *Hartford Courant*, November 2, 1917.

36. Spalding, *America's National Game* (Lincoln: University of Nebraska Press, 1992), p. 23; Joe Hoppel, ed., *Baseball's Hall of Fame* (New York: Arlington House, 1988), p. 34; David Pietrusza, "Morgan Gardner Bulkeley," *Baseball's First Stars*, ed. Frederick Ivor-Campbell, Robert L. Tiemann, and Mark Rucker (Cleveland: Society for American Baseball Research, 1996), p. 15.

37. Mark S. Sternman, "John Joseph Burdock," *Baseball's First Stars*, ed. Frederick Ivor-Campbell, Robert L. Tiemann, and Mark Rucker (Cleveland: Society for American Baseball Research, 1996), p. 16; *Charleston (West Virginia) Gazette*, May 20, 1925.

38. *Sporting News*, July 4, 1891.

39. Joseph M. Overfield, "William Arthur Cummings," *Baseball's First Stars*, ed. Frederick Ivor-Campbell, Robert L. Tiemann, and Mark Rucker (Cleveland: Society for American Baseball Research, 1996), p. 43.

40. *Hartford Times*, June 15, 1878; *Bristol Press*, quoted in *Hartford Times*, April 4, 1876.

41. Nicholas Acocella and Donald Dewey, *Encyclopedia of Major League Baseball Teams* (New York: HarperCollins, 1993), p. 471; Ben Douglas Junior to Harry Wright, March 5, 1878.

42. Ben Douglas Junior to Harry Wright, March 18, 1878.

43. Harold Seymour, *Baseball: The Early Years* (New York: Oxford University Press, 1960), p. 94.

44. Seymour, *Baseball: The Early Years*, p. 101.
45. Ben Douglas Junior to Harry Wright, March 22, 1878, and March 24, 1878.
46. Ben Douglas Junior to Harry Wright, March 18, 1878, and April 9, 1878.
47. Ben Douglas Junior to Harry Wright, April 9, 1878.
48. *Ibid.*
49. Ben Douglas Junior to Harry Wright, April 11, 1878.
50. Ben Douglas Junior to Harry Wright, April 13, 1878.
51. *Hartford Courant*, April 11, 1878.
52. *Rochester Daily Union*, April 29, 1878, reprinted from *Providence Dispatch*; *Providence Journal*, May 2, 1878, and December 19, 1885.
53. *Hartford Courant*, December 10, 1892.
54. *Middletown Tribune*, October 18, 1893; *Middletown Penny Press*, March 4, 1905.
55. *Hartford Courant*, November 16, 1916.
56. Jonathan Fraser Light, *The Cultural Encyclopedia of Baseball* (Jefferson, NC: McFarland, 1997), p. 761; James L. Terry, *Long Before the Dodgers: Baseball in Brooklyn, 1855–1884* (Jefferson, NC: McFarland, 2002), p. 143.
57. *Hartford Courant*, July 28, 1876; Adrain Anson, *A Ball Player's Career* (Chicago: Era Publishing, reprinted Mattituck, NY: Amereon House, 2001), p. 51.
58. Anson, *A Ball Player's Career*, p. 101.
59. Anson, *A Ball Player's Career*, p. 51.
60. Larry R. Gerlach and Harold V. Higham, "Dick Higham, Star of Baseball's Early Years," *The National Pastime* 21 (2001), p. 78.
61. Anson, *A Ball Player's Career*, pp. 101, 104; John Thorn and Pete Palmer, *Total Baseball*, 2nd ed. (New York: Warner Books, 1991), p. 437.
62. *New York Clipper*, April 17, 1880.
63. Anson, *A Ball Player's Career*, p. 101.
64. *New York Times*, February 3, 1925; *Hartford Courant*, February 3, 1925; Richard A. Puff, "Thomas J. York," *Nineteenth Century Stars*, ed. Robert L. Tiemann and Mark Rucker (Kansas City, MO: Society for American Baseball Research, 1989), p. 142; *Hartford Courant*, February 24, 1894, March 8, 1894, and March 12, 1894; *New York Times*, February 4, 1926.
65. *Hartford Courant*, July 15, 1875.
66. Arthur Pier's history of St. Pauls, quoted in Axel Bundgaard, *Muscle and Manliness: The Rise of Sport in American Boarding Schools* (Syracuse: Syracuse University Press, 2005), p. 93.
67. *Detroit Free Press*, December 3, 1897; *Richmond Times Dispatch*, May 3, 1907.
68. *Hartford Courant*, October 25, 1875; Anson, *A Ball Player's Career*, pp. 110–111; *The Sporting News*, April 6, 1939.
69. Steven D. Guschov, *The Red Stockings of Cincinnati: Base Ball's First All-Professional Team* (Jefferson, NC: McFarland, 1998), p. 142.
70. *Hartford Courant*, April 11, 1910, and October 5, 1912.
71. "Juice Latham, Veteran, Steps to Bat," *Literary Digest*, May 23, 1914.
72. *Rochester Times Union*, May 31, 1944: *Rochester Democrat and Chronicle*, June 1, 1944; *New Haven Evening Register*, January 31, 1876; McKelvey clippings in vertical file at Rochester Central Library — circa 1940.
73. *New York Times*, April 28, 1913.
74. *Philadelphia Inquirer*, March 23, 1902.
75. Christopher Devine, *Harry Wright: The Father of Professional Baseball* (Jefferson, NC: McFarland, 2003), p.111.

Appendix B

1. Robert H. Schaefer, "The Lost Art of Fair-Foul Hitting," *The National Pastime* 20 (2000), p. 9; *Chicago Daily Herald*, August 19, 1910.
2. *Boston Times*, September 16, 1877.
3. Sandra Stencel, ed., "War on Drugs," *CQ Researcher* March 19, 1993.
4. Edward Bok, *The Americanization of Edward Bok* (New York: Scribner's, 1921); on-line edition published by Bartleby.com, May 2000.
5. *Hartford Post*, November 2, 1874.
6. *Hartford Times*, July 8, 1874, and July 14, 1874; *Hartford Post*, July 23, 1874.
7. *Hartford Times*, August 11, 1874; *Hartford Courant*, August 11, 1874.
8. *Hartford Times*, August 12, 1874; *Hartford Post*, August 12, 1874; *Hartford Courant*, August 12, 1874.
9. *Hartford Times*, August 13, 1874, and August 15, 1874; *Hartford Post*, September 8, 1874.
10. *Hartford Post*, September 11, 1874, and September 12, 1874.

11. *Hartford Times,* September 14, 1874, September 19, 1874, September 21, 1874, September 22, 1874, and September 29, 1874; *Hartford Courant,* September 21, 1874.

12. *Hartford Times,* September 29, 1874, and October 12, 1874; *Hartford Courant,* October 5, 1874; *Hartford Post,* October 24, 1874.

13. *Hartford Times,* October 21, October 23, 1874, October 30, 1874, and December 12, 1874; *Hartford Post,* October 30, 1874, and November 2, 1874.

14. *New Haven Register,* March 2, 1875; *New York Clipper,* February 27, 1875; *Hartford Post,* February 22, 1875.

15. *Brooklyn Eagle,* April 13, 1875, May 19, 1875, and July 28, 1875.

16. *Hartford Times,* March 13, 1875, and May 24, 1875; *New Haven Register,* March 2, 1875.

17. *Chicago Tribune,* February 18, 1877, and September 16, 1877; *New York Times,* September 9, 1877.

18. *New York Telegram,* reprinted in *St. Louis Globe-Democrat,* September 13, 1877.

19. *Ibid.*

20. *Sporting News,* March 10, 1888; Schaefer, "The Lost Art of Fair-Foul Hitting," p. 9.

Bibliography

Books

Acocella, Nicholas, and Donald Dewey. *Encyclopedia of Major League Baseball Teams.* New York: HarperCollins, 1993.

Alvarez, Mark. *The Old Ball Game.* Alexandria, VA: Redefinition, 1995.

Anson, Adrian. *A Ball Player's Career.* Chicago: Era Publishing, 1900. Reprint. Mattituck, NY: Amereon House, 2001.

Arcidiacono, David. *Middletown's Season in the Sun: The Story of Connecticut's First Professional Baseball Team.* East Hampton, CT: Self-published, 1999.

_____. *Grace, Grit and Growling: The Hartford Dark Blues Base Ball Club, 1874–1877.* East Hampton, CT: Self-published, 2003.

Astor, Gerald. *The Baseball Hall of Fame 50th Anniversary Book.* New York: Prentice Hall, 1988.

Bartlett, Arthur. *Baseball and Mr. Spalding: The History and Romance of Baseball.* New York: Farrar, Straus and Young, 1951.

Benson, Michael. *Ballparks of North America.* Jefferson, NC: McFarland, 1989.

Block, David. *Baseball Before We Knew It.* Lincoln: University of Nebraska Press, 2005.

Bundgaard, Axel. *Muscle and Manliness: The Rise of Sport in American Boarding Schools.* Syracuse: Syracuse University Press, 2005.

Chadwick, Henry. *Base Ball Manual.* London: Routledge, 1874.

Cruse, Katherine. *The Changing Face of Main Street in Middletown, Connecticut.* Wesleyan University Thesis, 1981.

Deming, Clarence. *Yale Yesterdays.* New Haven, CT: Yale University Press, 1915.

Deutsch, Jordan, and Richard Cohen, et al. *The Scrapbook History of Baseball.* New York: Bobbs-Merrill, 1975.

Devine, Christopher. *Harry Wright: The Father of Professional Base Ball.* Jefferson, NC: McFarland, 2003.

Evans, Mary Bunce. *Child's Recollections of the Seventies.* 1931.

Fatout, Paul, ed. *Mark Twain Speaking.* Iowa City: University of Iowa Press, 1976.

Freyer, John, and Mark Rucker. *Peverelly's National Game.* Charleston, SC: Arcadia, 2005.

Goldstein, Warren. *Playing For Keeps. A History of Early Baseball.* Ithaca, NY: Cornell University Press, 1989.

Guschov, Steven D. *The Red Stockings of Cincinnati: Base Ball's First All-Professional Team.* Jefferson, NC: McFarland, 1998.

Hanks, Stephen, et al. *150 Years of Baseball.* Lincolnwood, IL: Publications International, 1989.

Hoppel, Joe, ed. *Baseball's Hall of Fame.* New York: Arlington House, 1988.

Ivor-Campbell, Frederick, Robert Tiemann, and Mark Rucker, eds. *Baseball's First Stars.* Cleveland: Society for American Baseball Research, 1996.

James, Bill. *Bill James Historical Baseball Abstract.* New York: Villard Books, 1986.

Jones, Donald D. *Former Major League Teams.* Jefferson, NC: McFarland, 1995.

Jones, Mary Glover. *Our Old Town — Particularly Washington Street.* Middletown, CT: 1930.

Kaplan, Justin. *Mr. Clemens and Mark Twain.* New York: Touchstone, 1966.

Lanigan, Ernest J. *The Baseball Cyclopedia.* New York: The Baseball Magazine Company, 1922. Reprint. Jefferson, NC: McFarland, 2005.

Lansche, Jerry. *Glory Fades Away: The 19th*

Century World Series Rediscovered. Dallas: Taylor, 1991.

Levine, Peter. *A.G. Spalding and the Rise of Baseball.* New York: Oxford University Press, 1985.

Light, Jonathan Fraser. *The Cultural Encyclopedia of Baseball.* Jefferson, NC: McFarland, 1997.

Lowenfish, Lee. *The Imperfect Diamond: Baseball's Labor Wars.* New York: Da Capo Press, 1991.

MacDonald, Neil. *The League that Lasted: 1876 and the Founding of the National League of Professional Baseball Clubs.* Jefferson, NC: McFarland, 2004.

Melville, Tom. *Early Baseball and the Rise of the National League.* Jefferson, NC: McFarland, 2001.

Middletown and Its Leading Businessmen. Boston: Mercantile Publishing, 1890.

Moreland, George. *Balldom.* New York: Balldom Publishing, 1914.

Morris, Peter. *A Game of Inches: The Stories Behind the Innovations That Shaped Baseball.* 2 vols. Chicago: Ivan R. Dee, 2006.

The National Pastime, Special Pictorial Issue: The Nineteenth Century. Cooperstown, NY: Society for American Baseball Research, 1984.

Neider, Charles, ed. *Mark Twain: Plymouth Rock and the Pilgrims and Other Speeches.* New York: Harper & Row, 1984.

Nemec, David. *The Great Encyclopedia of 19th Century Major League Baseball.* New York: Donald I. Fine Books, 1997.

_____. *The Beer and Whiskey League: The Illustrated History of the American Association—Baseball's Renegade Major League.* New York: Lyons Press, 2004.

Orem, Preston. *Baseball 1845–1881 from the Newspaper Accounts.* Altadena, CA: Self-published, 1961.

Palmer, Harry, and J.A. Fynes, Frank Richter, W.I. Harris. *Athletic Sports in America, England, and Australia.* Philadelphia: Hubbard Brothers, 1889.

Peverelly, Charles. *American Pastimes.* Self-published, 1868.

Porter, David, ed. *Biographical Dictionary of American Sports: Baseball.* New York: Greenwood, 1987.

Potts, David B. *Wesleyan University, 1831–1910: Collegiate Enterprise in New England.* Middletown, CT: Wesleyan University Press, 1999.

Richter, Francis. *Richter's History and Records of Baseball.* Philadelphia: 1914. Reprint. Jefferson, NC: McFarland, 2005.

Roer, Mike. *Orator O'Rourke: The Life of a Baseball Radical.* Jefferson, NC: McFarland, 2006.

Ryczek, William J. *Blackguards and Red Stockings: A History of Baseball's National Association, 1871–1875.* Jefferson, NC: McFarland, 1992.

_____. *When Johnny Came Sliding Home: The Post–Civil War Baseball Boom, 1865–1870.* Jefferson, NC: McFarland, 1998.

Selzer, Jack. *Baseball in the Nineteenth Century: An Overview.* Cooperstown, NY: Society for American Baseball Research, 1986.

Seymour, Harold. *Baseball: The Early Years.* New York: Oxford University Press, 1960.

_____. *Baseball: The People's Game.* New York: Oxford University Press, 1990.

Shatzkin, Mike, ed. *The Ballplayers: Baseball's Ultimate Biographical Reference.* New York: Arbor House William Morrow, 1990.

Shankle, George Earlie. *State Names, Flags, Seals, Songs, Birds, Flowers, and Other Symbols.* New York: H.W. Wilson, 1941.

Soos, Troy. *Before the Curse: The Glory Days of New England Baseball, 1858–1918.* Hyannis, MA: Parnassus Imprints, 1997.

Spalding, Albert G. *America's National Game.* New York: American Sports Publishing Co., 1911. Reprint, with introduction by Benjamin Rader. Lincoln: University of Nebraska Press, 1992.

Smith, Robert. *Baseball in America.* New York: Holt, Rinehart and Winston, 1961.

_____. *Baseball in the Afternoon.* New York: Simon & Schuster, 1993.

Stark, Benton. *The Year They Called Off The World Series.* Garden City Park, NY: Avery, 1991.

Terry, James L. *Long Before The Dodgers: Baseball in Brooklyn, 1855–1884.* Jefferson, NC: McFarland, 2002.

Thorn, John, David Pietrusza, Michael Gershman and Pete Palmer, eds. *Total Baseball VI.* New York: Total Sports Publishing, 1999.

Thorn, John, ed. *The Armchair Book of Baseball.* New York: Scribner's, 1987.

Tiemann, Robert, and Mark Rucker, eds. *Nineteenth Century Stars.* Kansas City, MO: Society for American Baseball Research, 1989.

Tuohey, George. *A History of the Boston Base Ball Club.* Boston: M.F. Quinn, 1897.

Turner, Gregg, and Melancthon Jacobus. *Connecticut Railroads: An Illustrated History.* Hartford: Connecticut Historical Society, 1986.

Voigt, David. *American Baseball: From the Gentlemen's Sport to the Commissioner System.* Vol. 1. Norman: University of Oklahoma Press, 1966.

Warner, Elizabeth. *A Pictorial History of Middletown.* Norfolk, VA: Donning Company Publishers, 1990.

Wright, George. *Record of Boston Base Ball Club, Since its Organization.* Boston: Rockwell & Churchill, 1874.

Wright, Marshall D. *The National Association of Base Ball Players, 1857–1870.* Jefferson, NC: McFarland, 2000.

Zoss, Joel, and John Bowman. *Diamonds in the Rough: The Untold History of Baseball.* New York: Macmillan, 1989.

Articles

Camp, Walter. "Base-Ball for the Spectator." *The Century: A Popular Quarterly* 38, no. 6 (1889): 831–838.

"The Charter Oak City." *Scribner's Monthly: An Illustrated Magazine For The People* 13, no. 1 (Nov. 1876): 1–21.

Devine, Christopher. "Harry Wright: The Most Important Baseball Figure of the 19th Century?" *Baseball Research Journal* 31 (2001): 35–38.

Eves, Jamie H. "The Hartford Dark Blues, 1876–1877." *The Connecticut League of History Bulletin* 54, no. 2 (2001):7, 9.

_____. "The Hartford Dark Blues, 1876–1877." *The Connecticut League of History Bulletin* 54, no. 3 (2001): 11–14.

Faulkner, D.W. "The Hartford Blues." *Greater Hartford Business*, April 1982: 20–33.

Findling, J.E. "The Louisville Grays' Scandal of 1877." *Journal of Sport History* 3, no. 2 (1976): 176–187.

Freedman, Stephen. "The Baseball Fad in Chicago, 1865–1870: An Exploration of the Role of Sport in the Nineteenth-Century City." *Journal of Sport History* 5, no. 2 (Summer 1978): 42–64.

Geduld, Herb. "Lipman at the Bat." *Jewish World Review*, Oct. 22, 1998.

Gerlach, Larry R., and Harold V. Higham. "Dick Higham." *The National Pastime* 20 (2000): 20–32.

_____, and _____. "Dick Higham, Star of Baseball's Early Years." *The National Pastime* 21 (2001): 72–80.

"Juice Latham, Veteran, Steps To Bat." *Literary Digest* May 23, 1914: 1–21.

Kermisch, Al. "From a Researcher's Notebook: Ball Player Pike Beat Race Horse at 100 Yards." *Baseball Research Journal* 8 (1979): 13–14.

Kihn, Phyllis. "The Charter Oak Nine." *Connecticut Historical Society Bulletin* April 1961: 56–64.

Moore, Glenn. "Ideology on the Sportspage: Newspapers, Baseball, and Ideological Conflict in the Gilded Age." *Journal of Sports History* 23, no. 3 (1996): 228–255.

Nelson, Dean. "A Century of Connecticut Inventions." *Hog River Journal.* http://www.hogriver.org/issues/v03n02/connecticut_inventions.htm.

Schaefer, Robert H. "The Lost Art of Fair-Foul Hitting." *The National Pastime* 20 (2000): 3–9.

Newspapers

Albany Evening Journal
Baltimore News American
Baltimore Sun
Boston Globe
Boston Herald
Boston Journal
Boston Post
Boston Traveler
Bridgeport Post
Brooklyn Eagle
Chicago Tribune
Elizabeth (NJ) *Daily Journal*
Hartford Courant
Hartford Post
Hartford Times
Louisville Courier-Journal
Lowell (MA) *Daily Courier*
Meriden (CT) *Daily Republican*
Middletown (CT) *Constitution* (weekly)
Middletown Daily Constitution
Middletown Press (previously known as *Penny Press*)
Middletown Press, Centennial Edition — September 28, 1984
Middletown Sentinel and Witness
Middletown Sun
Middletown Tribune
Middletown Tribune Souvenir Edition — 1896
New Britain Record
New Haven Daily Palladium

New Haven Journal & Courier
New Haven Register
New Haven Weekly Palladium
New York Clipper
New York Herald
New York Times
New York World
Norwalk (CT) *Hour*
Philadelphia Inquirer
Philadelphia Press
Philadelphia Public Record
Providence (RI) *Evening Bulletin*
Rochester (NY) *Daily Union*
San Francisco Alta
Sporting Life
Springfield (MA) *Daily Republican*
Trinity College Tablet
Troy (NY) *Daily Times*
Washington (DC) *Evening Star*
Waterbury Daily American
Wesleyan Argus
Yale Alumni Magazine
Yale Alumni Weekly

Other

Barlow, Jon. Research on the Middletown Mansfields (available at Middlesex Historical Society in Middletown, CT).

Beadle's Dime Base Ball Player.
Compendium of the 10th U.S. Census, 1870.
Craig, George Arbuckle. "My First Recollections of Middletown." Speech to Middletown Conversational Club, Middlesex Historical Society.
Dewitt's Base Ball Guide.
Harry Wright Correspondence (available on microfilm from the Society for American Baseball Research Lending Library).
Henry Chadwick Scrapbooks (available on microfilm from the Society for American Baseball Research Lending Library).
Henry Dana Artemas Ward Diary, 1870, Middlesex Historical Society.
Middletown and Hartford City Directories.
Player Folders (available at the Giamatti Research Center at the National Baseball Hall of Fame in Cooperstown, NY).
Notre Dame Scrapbooks (available at the Joyce Sports Research Collection at the University of Notre Dame's Hesburgh Library).
Spalding's Official Baseball Guide, 1877 and 1878.

Index

Numbers in *bold italics* indicate pages with photographs.

Active Baseball Club of Wappinger Falls (NY) 139
Addy, Bob 98–99, 104, 201
Aetna Baseball Club of New Britain (CT) 39
Aetna Insurance Company 96, 107, 203
African American baseball clubs 23
Agalles 25
Agallian Baseball Club of Wesleyan University (Middletown) 25, 29
Air Line Railroad 35–36, 68
Alaska Baseball Club of Brooklyn 180
Alert Baseball Club of Hartford 29
Alert Baseball Club of Norwalk (CT) 29
Alert Baseball Club of Rochester (NY) 116
Alexander, Grover Cleveland 198
Allen, Frank (Ham) 46, 51, 58, 64, 81, 89, 195
Alligator Baseball Club of Hartford 19
Allison, Art 201
Allison, Doug 7–8, 86, 111, 127–128, 187, 201, 206
Allyn House (Hartford) 29
Altoona, Pennsylvania 189
American Telegraph (Hartford) 19
Amy Stone Dramatic Troupe 48
Anson, Adrian (Cap) 44, 47, 70, 140, 155–156, *159*, 171, 203, 207–209
Antietam, Battle of 26
Apollonio, N.T. 181
Arnold, Willis 46, 58, 62, 64, 93, 114, 116, 118, 195
Arnold's Store (Middletown) 24
Association of Connecticut Base Ball Players 30
Astrodome (Houston, Texas) 189
Atlantic Association 190
Atlantic Baseball Club of Brooklyn 10, 22, 28–29, 32–33, 35, 47–49, 54, 61, 65–66, 71–72, 90–91, 94, 99, 101, 106, 108–109, 115–116, 120–122, 125–126, 131, 133, 136, 143–146, 169, 174, 177
Atlantic League 190

Baltimore Baseball Club (Lord Baltimores or Canaries) 69, 72, 76–77, 88–89, 94, 98, 101, 103–106, 108, 117
Baltimore Olympics Baseball Club 70, 79
Bancker, John (Stud) 116, 119, 131, 209
Barlow, Tommy 99, 101, 105–106, 116, 125, 131, 213–214, *215*, 216–219
Barlow's dodo (bunt) 99
Barnes, Ross 7–8, 49, 127–128, 140, 146, 156, 184, 197
Barnie, Bill 99, 202
Barrows, Frank 85
Bass, John 202
Batterson, James 96
Belden, John 28, 134, 162–163
Bell, Alexander Graham 182
Bellan, Esteban, (Steve) 44, 48
Bentley, Cy 37, 39–40, 46, 58, 62–66, 69, 71, 76–77, 85–86, 89, 91–93, 195
The Big Four 140–141, 147–148, 154–155, 208
Birdsall, Dave 76
Blackwell, Josiah 35
Bolin, Ron 193
Bond, Tommy 109–110, *112*, 122, 128, 134, 136–137, 139, 144–146, 156, 158–159, 161, 163, 165–167, 169–172, 180–183, 185–186, 202
Booth, ____ 124, 209
Booth, Eddie 50, 53, 62, 66, 77, 81, 89, 91, 158, 195
Booth, John Wilkes 21
Borden, Joseph (aka Joe Josephs) 156–157

255

Boss Tweed 38, *39*, 141
Boston Braves 191
Boston Red Sox 3, 7, 119, 198
Boston Red Stockings 7–8, 42, 44, 49–50, 56, 61, 72, 74–76, 78, 80–84, 94, 101–106, 113, 118–120, 126–132, 136–142, 144–146, 148, 154–159, 165, 167–172, 181–186, 195
Boyd, Bill 90, 98, 104–105, 122, 145, 202
Bradley, George 136, 163, 166–167, 181, 184, 202
Bradley, H.L. 115
Brady, Stephen 105, 187, 203
Brainard, Asa *34*, 48, 86–89, 92, 196
Brainard, Leonard 87
Bridgeport (CT) Baseball Club 29
Bridgeport Bluefish 191
The Bridgeport Friendly United Social Base Ball Baseball Club 116, 124, 138, 211
Bridgeport (CT) Orators Baseball Club 200
Britt, Jim 66, 213, 217
Brooklyn Hartfords Baseball Club 173–188
Brouthers, Dan 200
Brown, Lew 156
Buckeye Baseball Club of Columbus (OH) 181, 196
Buffalo (NY) Baseball Club 12
Bulkeley, Eliphalet 107
Bulkeley, Morgan *107*, 111–113, 139, 149–151, 153–154, 157, 160–161, 164, 170, 173–179, 182, 187–188, 191, 203
Bunce, Joshua 203
Bunker Hill Day 179
Burdock, Jack 110, 123, 127–128, *133*, 134, 137, 139, 145–146, 154–155, 157–158, 166–167, 182, 203–204
Bushnell Park (Hartford) 19, 23
Bushong, Al (Doc) *102*
Buttery, Frank 51, 58, 60, 62, 66, 77, 81, 83, 85, 92, 196

Cameron Trotting Park (Bridgeport) 52
Cammeyer, William 32, 173–177, 179, 182
Capitol City Baseball Club of Albany (NY) 197
Carey, Tom 8, 110, 122, 127–128, 134, 159, 182–183, 187, 204
Carnegie, Andrew 147
Cartwright, Alexander 9
Cassidy, John 144, 151, 180, 184, 186, 188, 204
Centennial Day 119
Chadwick, Henry 41, 55, 57, 90, 110, 137–138, 153, 177, 233
Champion, Aaron 33
Chapman, John (Jack) 108, 115
Chapman, Ray 198
Charter Oak Tree 19, *20*, 28–29

Charter Oak Trotting Park (Hartford) 77, 80, 91, 97
Chester Baseball Club of Norwich (CT) 29
Chicago White Stockings 44–45, 62, 101, 106, 137, 139–142, 145–149, 152–159, 164–166, 171–172, 179, 181, 183, 186
Church of the Good Shepherd (Hartford) 97, 158–159, 192
Cincinnati Red Stockings 33, *34*, 48–50, 87, 115, 139, 148, 161–163, 165, 168, 170–171
Civil War 9, 15, 19, 21, 26, 29, 111, 202, 204
Clapp, John 58, 60–62, 66–67, 69, 71, 76–78, 81, 83, 85–86, 88–90, 92, 166–167, 196
Clemens, Samuel *see* Twain, Mark
Clinton, Jimmy 136
Clipper Baseball Club of Ilion (NY) 58
Cobb, Ty 198
Coffin, O.V. 36, 47, 197
Collier's Rooms (New York) 41
Collins, Eddie 198
Colt, Caldwell 192
Colt, Elizabeth 97, 192
Colt, Samuel 14, *15*
Colt's Arm Manufacturing Company 15, *16*, 96, 127, 189, 192
Connecticut River 35, 47, 61, 77, 86, 95
Connecticut State League 190, 207, 209
Connor, Roger 197
Cooperstown, NY 9
Corbin, ___ 113
Craver, Bill 69, 158, 185
Creighton, Jim 11, 203
cricket 18, 105, 210, 212
Cummings, Arthur (Candy) 8, 44, 48, 64–65, 71, 110, 122–123, 127–128, 130, 134, 136–137, 139, 146, 158, 161–162, 170–171, 180, 192, 204
curveball 43, 69, 110, 127, 134, 136–138, 210–211
Cuthbert, Ned 73, 166

Daniels, Charlie 113, 120–122
Davidson, Alex 42, 57
Davis, James Whyte 32
Decoration Day 179
Deep River, CT 18
Dehlman, Harmon 199
Deming, Clarence 24, 28, 67, 234
Devlin, Jim 137, 161, 184–186
Dole, Lester 119, 125, 131, 210
Dorgan, Mike 62, *63*
Doubleday, Abner 9
Douglas, Benjamin, Jr. 26, *27*, 39–40, 46, 50–51, 55–58, 60, 65–67, 72, 74, 77, 79–80, 82, 87, 92, 95–97, 103, 126, 187–190, 204–207

Index

Douglas, Benjamin, Sr. 26, *27*
Douglas Park (Middletown) 23
Douglas Pump Company 26, 206
Dunlap, Fred 197
Durocher, Leo 191

Eagle Baseball Club of New York 10
Eastern Association 190
Eastern League 190
Ebbets, Charles 203
Ebbets Field 204
Eckford Baseball Club of Brooklyn 10, 28, 51, 54, 61, 68, 71–72, 77–78, 86, 94
Ecliptic Baseball Club of Middletown 29
Elm City Baseball Club of New Haven: 157–158, 168–170, 181–182, formation 114–118; National Association season 119–126, 131–135, 138–140, 142–144; National League application 150–152
Elysian Field 10
Empire Baseball Club of New York 10
Evans, _____ 125, 210
Evers, Johnny 198
Excelsior Baseball Club of Brooklyn 10–11, 110, 203

fair-foul hit 43, 49, 180, 184
Fairmount Baseball Club of Marlboro (MA) 46, 195
Faneuil Hall (Boston) 141
Farrell, Jack 207
Fenway Park 3, 198
Ferguson, Bob 90, 108–109, 111–113, 118, 122–123, 126–128, 131, 133–134, 136–137, 139, 145, 154, 156, 159, 161–162, 164, 166, 169–170, 172, 177, 179–184, 186–188, 193, 207
Fields, George 46, 58, 66, 85, 89, 196
Fire, Great Chicago 45, 96
Fisher, William (Cherokee) 76–77, 98–100, 103–104, 156, 207
Fisler, Wes 38
Force, Davy 44
Forest City Baseball Club of Cleveland (OH) 42, 61, 68, 72, 86, 92, 94
Forest City Baseball Club of Middletown 26–29
Forest City Baseball Club of Rockford (IL) 22, 42, 44, 47, 49–51, 54, 70, 98
Fowle, Charles 148, 173
Frale's Excelsior Band 48
Frontier Baseball Club of New York 108
Fuller, Dr. Horace 216, 219
Furniss, Tom 39, 51, 96

gambling 11, 32, 48, 63–64, 103, 108, 147–148, 169–170, 185–186
Gedney, Al 86

Geer, Billy 116, 119, 123, 143–144, 210
Geer and Pond Store (Hartford) 24
Gehrig, Lou 191
gloves, fielding 43, *101–102*, 124
Goldsmith, Fred 182, 210–211
Goodyear, Charles 14
Gotham Baseball Club of New York 10
Gould, Charlie *34*, 49, 76, 81, 115–116, 118–119, 131–132, 135, 139, 161, 211
Grand Avenue Park (St. Louis) 166, 192
Grand Central Hotel (New York) 149, 202, 209
Grant Baseball Club of Collinsville (CT) 91
Greenberg, Hank 191

Hague, Bill 206
Hall, George 96, 184–186, 240
Hamilton Park (New Haven) 35, 52, 67, 120, 181
Hampden Park (Springfield, MA) 86
Harbidge, Bill 183, 188, 207
Harrison, Washington Ritter "Rit" 125, 211
Hartford Amateur Baseball Club 105, 183, 208
Hartford Base Ball Grounds 97, 100, 103, 112–113, 127, 139, 154, 160–161, 188, 192, *193*
Hartford Bees 191
Hartford Charter Oak Baseball Club 19, *20*, 21, 26, 28–30, 35–36, 97, 203
Hartford Chiefs 191
Hartford Dark Blues: formation 95–99; "Grand Base Ball Match" with Boston; 126–130; move to Brooklyn 173–178; National Association seasons 100–111, *112*, 113–146, National League season 153–154, *155*, 156–172
Hartford Fire Insurance Group 96
Hartford Hospital 216, 219
Hartford Laurels 191
Hartford Senators 191
Harvard University Baseball Club 28, 110, 202
Hastings, Scott 44, 68, 98–100, 103–104, 137, 207
Hayhurst, Hicks 73, 197
Hero Baseball Club of Middletown (African American) 23
hidden ball trick 159, 216
Higham, Richard 69, 87–91, 153–154, 156, 158, 167, 171, 190, 206–207
Hill, George 18
Hines, Paul 137, 171, 203, 206, 216
Hippodroming 32
Hockanum Baseball Club of North Manchester (CT) 29
Hofheinz, Roy 189
Holdsworth, James 145, 180, 207
Hotchkiss, Julius 27, 28

Houston Astros 189
Houston Colt .45's 189
Howard Avenue Grounds (New Haven) 115, 117–118, 120, **121**, 192
Howard Baseball Club of Hartford 29
Hubbell, Gershom 19, **20**, 35, 41, 95–98, 100, 102, 104, 107, 160, 215
Hulbert, William 140, 142, 147, **148**, 149–152, 154–155, 173–174, 176–177, 179–180, 182, 185–187, 203

Independent Baseball Club of Hartford 19
International Association 189–190, 192, 195–196, 201, 205–208, 210
Ithaca (NY) Baseball Club 196

Jackson, Joe 198
Jay Cooke & Company 160
Jewel Baseball Club of Middletown 190
Johnson, Ban 198
Johnson, Walter 198
Jones, Charlie 208
Josephs, Joe *see* Borden, Joe Borden
Josh Hart Comedy Troupe 105

Keenan, Jim **125**, 131, 182, 211
Kekionga Baseball Club of Fort Wayne (IN) 42
Kelly, Mike 197
Kelly, William 46
Kenney, John 48
Kerns, James 41
King Charles II 19
King James II 19
Knickerbocker Baseball Club of Albany (NY) 32
Knickerbocker Baseball Club of New York 9–10, 32
Knight, Alonzo 202
Knight, George 144, 211
Knowdell, Jake 125, 217
Kraft, Robert 4
KuKlux Baseball Club of Oneida (NY) 139

Larkin, Terry 180, 183–184, 186, 188, 208
Latham, George (Juice and Jumbo) 131–132, 135, 144, 211
Lee, Robert E. 21
Lenz, David 52
Leonard, Andy 128
Liberty Baseball Club of Norwalk (CT) 29, 51
Lincoln, Abraham 15, 21
Lincoln Baseball Club of New Britain (CT) 26
Lone Star Baseball Club of New Orleans 98
Los Angeles Dodgers 177
Louisville Grays Baseball Club 148–149, 151, 163, 165, 171, 183–186

Lucas, Henry 189
Luff, Henry 117, 119–120, 131, 134, 143–144, 211
Lynch, Jack 196
Lynn (MA) Baseball Club 195, 201

Maloney, John 208
Manhattan Baseball Club (NY) 10
Manning, Jack 202, 208
Mansfield, Gen. Joseph 26
Mansfield Baseball Club of Middletown: amateur seasons 26, 36–40, 46–54; National Association application 55–58; National Association season 61–95
Mansfield Grounds (Middletown) 47–48, 192
Mansfield Junior Baseball Club 40, 62, 85, 93
Marks, Benson 46, 48
Martin, Alphonse 8, 128
Marvin Baseball Club of Norwichtown (CT) 29
Mason, William 15
Massachusetts game 12
Mathews, Bobby 69, 110, 125, 144–145, 158, 163
Mazeppa Baseball Club of Stamford (CT) 19
McBride, Dick 69–70, 89
McCarton, Frank 46, 58, 60, 62, 93, 197
McDonald, Jack 66
McDonough House (Middletown) 38, 47, 88
McGeary, Michael 89–90, 166
McGinley, Tim 131, 138, 144, 211
McGinnity, Joe 200
McGraw, John 200
McKelvey, John 116, 119, 122–123, 211
McLoud, James 185
McNally, Mike 198
McVey, Cal 8, **34**, 44, 49, 58, 76, 128, 138, 140–141, 146, 156, 159, 165, 171–172
Mechanics Baseball Club of Hartford 19
Meyerle, Levi 70
Mills, A.G. 176, 203
Mills, Charlie 38, 91
Mills, Everett 8, 98–99, 111, 122, 128–129, 157–158, 167, 208
Mills Commission 203
Milwaukee Braves 191
Minnesota Twins 191
Miss Porter's School for Girls (Farmington, CT) 23
Monitor Baseball Club of Waterbury (CT) 29, 196
Monitor Baseball Club of Westport (CT) 30
morphine addiction 106, 213–219
Morrill, John **156**
Morris, Peter 111, 210
Morrissey, "Big" John 48

Index

Mungo, Van Lingle 191
Murnane, Tim *51*, 53, 58, 60–62, 67–68, 73, 76, 78, 81, 85, 89, 92–93, 124, 156, 190, 197–198, 204
Mutual Baseball Club of Waterbury (CT) 85

National Association of Base Ball Players 12–13, 21, 29–30, 32, 41–42
National Association of Professional Base Ball Players: demise 147–152; formation 41–45
National League, formation of 147–150
New Britain Baseball Club 30
New Britain Rock Cats Baseball Club 191
New Haven Hospital 24
New Haven Profs Baseball Club 190
New York Baseball Club 10
New York Giants 200
New York Mutual Baseball Club 10, 38–39, 42, 44, 61, 64–65, 71–72, 87–88, 90–91, 94, 101, 103, 106, 108–110, 116, 124, 131, 139, 144–145, 148, 156, 158, 165, 168, 173–176, 179
New York Yankees 3, 7, 190–191
Newington Grounds (Baltimore) 69
Nichols, Al 185
Nichols, Fred (Tricky) 116, 119–120, 122–124, 131, 134–135, 140, 144, 151, 187, 212
Noble, Tom 40
Nook Farm (Hartford) 96
nutmeg 14

Oceanic Baseball Club of Mystic (CT) 30
Oceanus Baseball Club of Hartford 23
Ohio (steamship) 105
Old Elm Baseball Club of Pittsfield (MA) 49
Olin, Stephen 25
O'Neil, Fancy 208
O'Rourke, Jim 8, 58, *59*, 60, 62, 65, 76–77, 81, 89, 91, 103, 128, 138, 191, 198–201
Osceola Baseball Club of Stratford (CT) 51–54, 58, 60, 64

Pabor, Charlie 144, 151, 169, 181, 212
Paige Compositor 16
Panic of 1873 160
Parks, Bill 132
Patriot's Day 119
Pearce, Dickey 44, 136
Pequot Baseball Club of New London (CT) 29, 35
Perroy, ____ 131
Peverelly, Charles 22
Philadelphia Athletic Baseball Club 22, 37–38, 41–45, 61, 64, 70, 72–73, 84, 89–90, 94, 98–99, 101, 103, 105–106, 135, 145, 148, 165, 171, 173–174, 176, 179–183
Philadelphia Centennial Baseball Club 119, 124, 131–133, 146

Philadelphia White Stocking Baseball Club 101–102, 105–106, 110, 124, 145, 150, 156
Phoenix Insurance Company 96
Pike, Jay 208
Pike, Lipman 44, 77, 89, 99, 103–106, 208
Pine Grove Baseball Club of New Haven 18, 29
Pocahontas Baseball Club of New York 10
Porter, Sarah 23
Portland Baseball Club (ME) 12
Providence Grays Baseball Club 189, 199, 204–207
Public Garden (Boston) 141
Putnam, Augustus 40, 50, 54–55, 57, 65, 72, 233
Putnam Baseball Club of Brooklyn 10
Putnam Baseball Club of Troy (NY) 49

Quinn, Paddy J. 208
Quinnipiac Baseball Club of Wallingford (CT) 85
Quinnipiack Baseball Club of New Haven 18

Rackliff, William 40, 55, 76–77, 98
railroads, growth of 35–36
Red Cloud Baseball Club of Southington (CT) 91
Remsen, Jack 111, 123, 128–129, 134, 158, 165–167, 171, 180, 192, 209
Resolute Baseball Club of Elizabeth City (NJ) 70–71, 79–80, 82–84
Richards, Paul 189, 191
Rockefeller, John D. 147
Rogers, Will 198
Root, Elisha 15
Rose Hill Baseball Club of Waterbury (CT) 62
Rough and Ready Baseball Club of Hartford 19
Russell Manufacturing Company (Middletown) 26
Ruth, George Herman (Babe) 198
Ryan, Johnny 117, 119, 131, 134–135, 142, 212

St. Louis Brown Stockings 119, 136, 139, 145, 148–149, 159, 162, 165–168, 171
St. Louis Red Stockings 119, 145
San Francisco Giants 191
Sanford, Jay 202
Schang, Wally 198
Schofield, J.W. 42
scorecard (1872) *74–75*
Shaffer, George 209
Smith, Carlos 114
Smith, Gus 40
Smith, John 125, 212

Soden, Arthur 199
Somerville, Ed 131, 134, 138, 144, 182, 212
Spahn, Warren 191
Spalding, Al 7–8, 22, 49–50, 58, 69, 76, 81, 83, 103, 108, 110, 120, 127–130, 132, 138–142, 154, 156, 158–159, 164–165, 169, 171–172, 181, 199, 212
Speaker, Tris 198
spring base 73
spring bat 18, 234
Star Baseball Club of Brooklyn 36, 48–50, 64, 110
Star Baseball Club of Syracuse (NY) 63, 180, 207
Start, Joe 158, 174–175, 180. 186, 188, 209
State Hospital for the Insane (Middletown) 26
Stearns, Bill 98–99, 104, 209
Stevens, Kate 23
Stowe, Harriet Beecher 96
Sullivan, ____ 124, 212
Sullivan, John L. 198
Sunday baseball 25
Sutton, Ezra 140, *141*, 155

Taunton Baseball Club (MA) 195
Taylor, Ed (Live Oak) 209
Tecumseh Baseball Club of London, Ontario 144, 210
Tecumseh House (London, Ontario) 143
Thatcher, J.M. 41
Thorpe, Jim 191
Tipper, Jim 46, 58, 60, 62, 73, 76, 81, 89–90, 92–93, 99, 117, 119–120, 143, 201
Tontine Hotel (New Haven) 114, 120
Travelers Insurance Company 29, 96
Trenwith, George 144, 212
Tri-Mountain Baseball Club of Boston 12
Trinity College Baseball Club 23, 37, 73
Triple Crown 137
triple play 158
Tunxis Baseball Club (Miss Porter's School) 23
Twain, Mark 15–16, *17*, 29, 95–96, 129–130, 192
Twichell, Rev. Joseph 129
Tyler, Julius 115
Tyler, Philos 168

Uncas Baseball Club of Norwich (CT) 29
Union Association 189, 197, 211
Union Baseball Club of Bridgeport (CT) 60
Union Baseball Club of Brooklyn 51
Union Baseball Club of Morrisania (Brooklyn) 29

Union Grounds (Brooklyn) 32, 173, 175–176, 182
United States Hotel (Hartford) 29

Vance, Dazzy 204
Vintage Base Ball Clubs 191

Ward, William 115
Washington, George 14
Washington Baseball Club of New York 10
Washington (D.C.) National Baseball Club 22, 35, 50, 61, 70, 72, 94, 119, 124, 132–133, 146
Washington (D.C.) Olympic Baseball Club 41–42, 61, 70, 72, 86, 94, 98
Waterbury Baseball Club (CT) 29
Watson, Thomas 182
Weiss, George 190–191
Wesleyan University Baseball Club 25, 36, 46, 66–67
West Haven Horse Rail Road 115
West Rock (New Haven) 120
Western Baseball Club of Keokuk (IA) 119, 146, 208
Western Union Telegraph 117, 160–161
White, Jim (Deacon) 138, *140*, 141, 146, 156, 181, 186, 202
Whitney, Eli 14
wicket (bat and ball game) 18
Williamson, Ed 197
Wolters, Rynie 38, 68
Wood, Jimmy 161
Worcester, Massachusetts Park Association 79
Wright, George 33, *34*, 50, 76, 83, 103, 117, 127–128, 197, 199, 202, 209, 212
Wright, Harry 33, *34*, 42, 49–50, 56–58, 74, 76, 79–80, 84, 87, 95, 102, 105, 108, *109*, 111, 113, 115, 117–118, 120, 126, 128, 131–132, 141, 155–157, 162, 172, 179–181, 189, 196–197, 199, 204–106
Wright, Sam, Sr. 33
Wright, Sammy, Jr. 116–117, 119, 124, 131, 151, 212

Yale University Baseball Club (New Haven) 24–25, 29, 40, 66–68, 100, 120, 135, 138, 205
Yankee Stadium 3
York, Tom 111, 128, 137, 145–146, 157, 167, 183–184, 186, 202, 206, 209
Young, Cy 202
Young, Nick 41, 203
Young Pacifics Baseball Club of Hartford 23

Zettlein, George 62–63, 67, 86

www.ingramcontent.com/pod-product-compliance
Ingram Content Group UK Ltd.
Pitfield, Milton Keynes, MK11 3LW, UK
UKHW041933140426
5217IPUK00014B/453